US-MEXICO TRADE:
PULLING TOGETHER OR
PULLING APART?

CONGRESS OF THE UNITED STATES   OFFICE OF TECHNOLOGY ASSESSMENT

Recommended Citation:

U.S. Congress, Office of Technology Assessment, *U.S.-Mexico Trade: Pulling Together or Pulling Apart?*, ITE-545 (Washington, DC: U.S. Government Printing Office, October 1992).

For sale by the U.S. Government Printing Office
Superintendent of Documents, Mail Stop: SSOP, Washington, DC 20402-9328
ISBN 0-16-038096-0

Foreword

In a matter of months, Congress will be asked to ratify or reject what is likely to be the final round of debate over the proposed North American Free Trade Agreement (NAFTA). One side in this debate argues that a NAFTA will mean increased prosperity for the United States and Mexico. Others hold that it would lead to ruthless economic competition based on low wages, and hence to stagnant productivity on both sides of the border. The most dismal predictions see a wholesale movement of U.S. manufacturing to Mexico.

In this report, requested by the House Committee on Education and Labor and the Senate Committee on Labor and Human Resources, OTA finds little likelihood that a NAFTA, by itself, will lead to the most dismal scenarios. But OTA's analysis also indicates that market forces alone are not likely to produce the social and economic rewards the heads of both states have promised from a free trade agreement.

For both countries, the key to success in managing the social and economic transformations of the coming decades lies with the institutions that frame public and private choices—decisions made by employers, by workers, by government officials. In the United States, that framework still reflects the mass production era of the first half of the century, when labor and management hammered out an uneasy accommodation and the Federal Government in the New Deal years took on greater responsibilities for managing the macroeconomy and providing a safety net for laid off workers and their families.

More recently, Washington has been backing away from these responsibilities, without replacing them with new institutions and new policies suited to a "postindustrial" U.S. economy that is much more a part of the world economy than even a half-generation ago. The NAFTA debate provides an occasion to reconsider U.S. institutions. Among the reasons for doing so, perhaps the most pressing lies in the social strains that would be created by a future of dead-end jobs for less educated workers in the lower half of the Nation's income distribution.

The subtitle of this report is intended to convey one of its central findings: labor, management, and society at large must pull together in the United States, or the social strains created by "globalization" could pull the Nation apart. The subtitle also conveys a second message: Mexico and the United States, neighbors sharing a 2000-mile border and distinguished by a host of cultural and institutional differences, cannot negotiate a divorce. Their economies are intertwined, and will become more so in the future. A NAFTA could bring out the worst in each nation, or it could put them on the path to mutually supportive high-wage, high-productivity strategies.

JOHN H. GIBBONS
Director

Advisory Panel—U.S.-Mexico Trade

John Stepp, *Chairman*
Restructuring Associates

NOTE: OTA appreciates and is grateful for the valuable assistance and thoughtful critiques provided by the advisory panel members. The panel does not, however, necessarily approve, disapprove, or endorse this report. OTA assumes full responsibility for the report and the accuracy of its contents.

OTA Project Staff—U.S.-Mexico Trade

Lionel S. Johns, *Assistant Director, OTA*
Energy, Materials, and International Security Division

Audrey B. Buyrn, *Program Manager*
Industry, Technology, and Employment Program

John A. Alic, *Project Director*

Margaret L. Hilton, *Deputy Project Director*

Kenneth E. Freeman
Stephen A. Herzenberg
Gretchen S. Kolsrud
Jerry R. Sheehan

Contributors

Robert D. Atkinson
W. Wendell Fletcher
Deanna Hammond, *Congressional Research Service*
Michael J. Phillips
Elizabeth G. Tsehai
Howard Wial

Administrative Staff

Carol A. Guntow, *Office Administrator*
Diane D. White, *Administrative Secretary*

Publishing Staff

Mary Lou Higgs, *Manager, Publishing Services*

Chip Moore

Cheryl Davis   Dorinda Edmondson   Denise Felix
Christine Onrubia   Bonnie Sparks   Susan Hoffmeyer

Contractors

Thomas Bailey
Jack N. Burby
Susan M. Christopherson
Martin Kenney and Richard Florida
Thomas H. Kelly
Sylvia Maxfield
Harley Shaiken
Leslie A. Sklair
Wallace E. Tyner
Gary W. Williams
Particia A. Wilson

Contents

Chapter 1

Summary

Contents

Boxes

Tables

The United States and Mexico are vastly different nations, one rich, the other poor, one with political and legal roots in England, the other a blend of Imperial Spain and ancient native American civilizations. If the countries implement the proposed North American Free Trade Agreement (NAFTA), they would begin an unprecedented experiment in economic integration—the creation of a single market spanning an industrialized country and a developing country with over one-third the population but only one-tenth the per-capita gross domestic product (GDP).

OTA's analysis suggests that market forces alone are not likely to produce significant social and economic rewards following a free trade agreement. To yield substantial rewards, trade liberalization will have to be accompanied by significant changes in other aspects of U.S. and Mexican policies.

- If it is, more open trade could increase prosperity and raise standards of living in both countries.
- If it is not, closer economic links between the two countries could bring out the worst in each, driving down wages and living standards in the United States without accelerating development in Mexico.

To put the United States and Mexico on the right course will require fundamentally changing relations among government, industry, and labor in each country.

In the United States, the necessary changes could begin with Congress serving notice that competing based on low wages is not acceptable and that government and the private sector are committed to creating incentives for high-productivity, high-wage strategies that will yield benefits for communities, workers, and employers throughout the Nation.

In Mexico, a similar commitment may be necessary, in part through a relaxation of the government's hold on labor unions and wage setting. In addition, to complement foreign competition and deregulation in its efforts to strengthen the economy, Mexico's government may need to actively promote human resource development and diffusion of modern technology and organizational practices.

In both the United States and Mexico, negotiations over free trade represent part of a search for new economic strategies that will bring back the prosperity of the 1940s through the 1970s. In this period, with their economies insulated from foreign competition—by protectionism in Mexico and technical superiority in the United States—both countries enjoyed rising investment, consumption, productivity, and output. GDP grew at between 6 and 7 percent a year in Mexico and at roughly half that rate in the United States. By the mid-1970s, workers in the United States and Mexico earned roughly twice in real terms what they had earned 30 years earlier. Since the mid-1970s, stagnant productivity and increasing international competition have brought real wages in both countries back to the level of 1965.

In the United States, the end of the 30-year post-World War II boom has hit less-skilled and less-educated workers particularly hard (ch. 4). From 1973 to 1991, hourly wages of male high school graduates with 1 to 5 years of experience *declined* by 29 percent. From 1980 to 1989, the proportion of full-time workers with annual incomes below the poverty level for a family of four *rose* from 12 to 18 percent. It is in this context that the United States, Mexico, and Canada began negotiating a NAFTA in June of 1991. (This assessment responds to a request from Congress for an evaluation of the effects of an agreement with Mexico on U.S. jobs and economic opportunities; OTA does not deal here with the implications of U.S. trade with Canada.)

OTA's analysis indicates that a NAFTA would not have large aggregate impacts on U.S. jobs and job opportunities for the first 5 years, in part because many NAFTA provisions would be phased in gradually. Over a longer time period, during which the impact of increased investment flows to Mexico would be felt, the impacts could be more substantial. For workers who lose their jobs because of a NAFTA, whether in the short or long run, the consequences can, of course, be devastating.

For the Mexican Government, NAFTA represents the most recent in a series of steps toward a more open- and market-oriented economy and away from a heavily protected, highly regulated one. The first major step took place when Mexico joined the General Agreement on Tariffs and Trade (GATT) in 1986, and began lowering the barriers that had protected its industries for more than 50 years. Now it seeks further industrialization by exposing Mexican firms to the spur of foreign competition and encouraging foreign direct investment (FDI) and transfers of technology that will help create new jobs for a rapidly growing workforce (more than half the population is under 20 years of age—see ch. 6).

Many in the United States worry that more U.S.-based firms will move to Mexico to take advantage of wages and benefits that average roughly one-seventh of U.S. levels and that the shift of investment to Mexico would be at the expense of U.S. workers. After all, when Mexican wages dropped by nearly two and a half times relative to U.S. wages during the economic crisis of the 1980s, production in border *maquiladoras* shot upward. In this view, ''footloose plants'' might also move to Mexico to escape stricter U.S. enforcement of pollution and workplace health and safety standards.

Others in the United States see foreign investment and movement of lower skilled jobs to Mexico as complementing a U.S. economy focused on high-wage, high-skill jobs. In this view, FDI would also generate the wealth Mexico needs to enforce tighter environmental and workplace standards and to provide a growing market for U.S. goods.

OTA's analysis indicates that whether a NAFTA works for or against either country will depend on how integration is managed. Managed well, with adoption of new labor and industrial policies to help the United States adapt to a unified continental market, economic integration could enable U.S. workers to enjoy 1 or 2 percent increases in living standards over the next 15 years. Mexico could grow at the 5 to 10 percent annual pace of developing Asian nations such as Thailand.

Managed poorly, less educated workers in the United States could expect to continue losing about 1 percent of their real wages annually while, after 15 years, Mexican workers would barely recover the ground they lost in the 1980s.

So far, economic integration between the United States and Mexico has not been managed well. NAFTA presents an opportunity to begin managing it better. This report focuses on how to take advantage of that opportunity. In doing so, OTA draws on considerable past analysis of international economic competition and the implications for U.S. workers, including: *Technology and Structural Unemployment: Reemploying Displaced Adults (1986); Making Things Better: Competing in Manufacturing (1990); Worker Training: Competing in the New International Economy (1990); Competing Economies: America, Europe and the Pacific Rim (1991);* and *After the Cold War: Living with Lower Defense Spending* (1992).

PRINCIPAL FINDINGS

The United States and Mexico are negotiating a free trade agreement at a time when workers in the United States, particularly the roughly 50 percent of the labor force that has no more than a high school education, have suffered significant declines in living standards. With or without a NAFTA, further absolute and relative declines in living standards—particularly for those in once high-wage manufacturing industries—are likely over the next 15 years. It will take a concerted national effort, with cooperation among business, labor, and government, to help the less affluent half of the U.S. workforce enjoy even modest improvements in wages and economic security.

Short-Term Impacts

1. Over the next five years, a NAFTA is not likely to have large impacts on job opportunities for U.S. workers, primarily because Mexico, not the United States, has the more protected economy. As a result, **reductions in tariff and non-tariff barriers are more likely to boost U.S. exports to Mexico than Mexican exports to the United States.**

2. Because Mexico has not made a sustained effort to upgrade its technology base and the education and skills of its workforce, products manufactured by Mexico's domestic industry are not likely to compete with sophisticated U.S. manufactured goods. However, **production by U.S. and other foreign investors in Mexico, who have the technology and resources to improve the efficiency of the Mexican workforce, could threaten U.S. workers making more sophisticated products, such as auto engines.**

3. **Although Mexico has a comprehensive set of legal protections for workers that some-**

times exceed those in U.S. law, the exercise of government authority to interpret and enforce those protections seriously compromises workers' rights to form unions, to bargain, and to strike. The Mexican government used these powers to reduce real wages by 40 percent in the 1980s and to keep wage increases modest as the Mexican economy recovered in the early 1990s. Health and safety standards in Mexico are also poorly enforced, especially in smaller enterprises. As a result, while trade with Mexico is not responsible for the current predicament of U.S. workers or the weakness of the U.S. system of labor protection, accelerating economic linkages with Mexico could reinforce downward pressure on U.S. wages and labor standards. Despite this potential, the U.S.-Mexico Memorandum of Understanding on labor issues, a response to congressional pressure, has led only to limited information exchange between the U.S. Department of Labor and its counterpart agency in Mexico. Discussions have skirted core worker rights issues in each country.

4. The impacts of a NAFTA on U.S. workers will vary by and within industry sectors. These impacts will include direct job losses and job creation, as well as downward pressure on wages and benefits for some workers who retain their jobs. Workers in apparel, auto parts, and TV assembly are already suffering job losses due to movement of production to Mexico; NAFTA may reinforce this tendency. Regardless of whether the net effect on U.S. jobs is positive or negative, **the workers most likely to be dislocated (e.g., workers producing standardized commodities such as blue jeans) lack the skills for jobs that may be created (e.g., machinists and technicians in U.S. firms producing capital goods for Mexican factories).** Box 1-A illustrates the difficulties faced by workers already laid off due to trade with Mexico.

Immigration

5. Legal and illegal migration from Mexico to the United States will remain high. **In the short run, a NAFTA promises to reduce employment in Mexico's agricultural and small-firm sectors and thereby increase emigration to the United States.**

Box 1-A—What Happens to U.S. Workers Whose Jobs Move to Mexico?

Since 1983, Pillsbury Green Giant has reduced its workforce in Watsonville, California, by about 1,000 workers. These food processing workers, predominantly Hispanic women, have lost unionized jobs paying $7.50 to $12 per hour. The work has been moved to Gigante Verde in Irapuato, Mexico, where costs for the highly labor-intensive initial processing of broccoli and cauliflower are much lower. In January 1990, the company announced plans to move all cauliflower and broccoli processing (including harvesting, trimming, blanching, and freezing, but excluding final packaging) to Irapuato. Final packaging, a highly automated process, continues to be done in the United States, at Watsonville and at plants in Ohio and Illinois. Watsonville also continues to do some of the initial processing of California-grown vegetables.

Since 1990, the Watsonville workforce has shrunk from 550 workers to 170. A joint union-management-government outplacement and retraining program, established with Federal funds through the EDWAA (Economic Dislocation and Worker Adjustment Assistance) program, provided some help. Santa Cruz County's EDWAA office offered on-site job counseling, retraining, and placement services at the plant. However, the EDWAA grant lasted only 18 months, expiring on July 1, 1992. Retraining focused on English language skills. As funds ran out, many of the workers had been able to improve their English, but not their "marketable skills."

Environment

6. Although Mexico has comprehensive environmental laws not unlike those of the United States, **enforcement has been lax.** Mexico has few inspectors and budgets little for pollution control, cleanup, and inspection. Public pressure for environmental improvement is only now beginning to appear.

7. The jointly prepared *Integrated Environmental Plan for the Mexican-U.S. Border Area* is only a small step toward improving the border environment. Many of the *Plan's* "action items" call for information exchange and more studies, rather than investments in needed cleanup and control. **The *Plan* lacks concrete goals and the financial commitments needed**

for substantial improvements in the border environment.

Longer-Term Social and Economic Impacts

1. **Over a 15-year time frame, a NAFTA could have larger impacts on U.S. workers and economic performance.** Even over these periods, impacts would be limited by the fact that Mexico's economy will remain small compared to that of the United States. Mexico's GDP today is about 4 1/2 percent that of the United States.

2. Notwithstanding conventional economic wisdom (box 1-B), the long-term impact of a NAFTA on U.S. workers and productivity growth could be negative unless government

---

Box 1-B—Free Trade Theory and the Economic Consequences of NAFTA

NAFTA proponents have used neoclassical free trade theory to argue that the United States and Mexico can only benefit from an agreement. OTA's analysis indicates that the neoclassical arguments for free trade are of minor significance. The impact of a NAFTA on productivity growth and unemployment are more important. This is particularly so because NAFTA comes when the United States is in a transition from a national, mass production economy to a continental and global economy—a historical and institutional context ignored by mainstream free trade models.

There are two central components to the neoclassical case for free trade between the United States and Mexico: allocative efficiency and scale economies. The allocative efficiency argument maintains that free trade will benefit the United States and Mexico because the two countries have widely different stocks of capital and labor. As a result, if the United States specializes in the production of capital-intensive goods and Mexico specializes in the production of labor-intensive goods, aggregate output will be higher than if each country produced a full complement of goods internally. The scale economies argument maintains that production for a larger, more integrated market will permit volume-related cost reduction, particularly in Mexico, where there are many small, inefficient plants that historically served only the protected Mexican market.

Economic models suggest that the gains from allocative efficiency improvements will be less than 1 percent of Mexico's GDP. Depending on assumptions, gains from scale economies range between 1 and 9 percent of Mexico's GDP—at most, one-third of 1 percent of U.S. GDP.

More difficult to incorporate into economic models but ultimately of far greater significance will be the influence of closer economic ties on long-run U.S. and Mexican productivity growth (ch. 5, app. 5A). As comparison with Britain, West Germany, and Japan demonstrates, differences in productivity growth stemming from contrasting corporate and national development strategies can, over the course of several decades, generate differences in living standards on the order of 100 percent. In the U.S.-Mexico case, what matters most is whether NAFTA and policies implemented in parallel with it push the United States and Mexico towards high-productivity, human resource intensive paths or low-wage, low-productivity development paths.

A second issue, missing from neoclassical models of NAFTA impacts but potentially very important, is the impact of wage competition on aggregate demand and unemployment. Some analysts worry that competitive erosion of wages in a more integrated global and continental economy could result in wages in the United States and its trading partners that lag behind productivity growth. As some believe happened in the Great Depression, lower wages could cut workers' purchasing power and create unemployment. But rather than worrying that wage reductions might reduce aggregate demand, most economists today take the ''classical'' view that wage reductions reduce unemployment.

While the empirical and theoretical plausibility of a depression due to declining wages remains a subject of controversy, making low wages a central part of full employment policy in North America does run the risk of aggravating unemployment by reducing consumer demand. OTA's analysis suggests that other approaches to achieving full employment in North America be considered, including:

1. direct job creation through investments in improved infrastructure and environmental protection;
2. a North American Development Bank that would help alleviate Mexico's debt burden, thereby enabling Mexico to grow faster, reduce its own unemployment, and reduce U.S. unemployment by slowing emigration and increasing Mexican purchases of U.S. exports;
3. reduced working hours.

and the private sector take steps to prevent that outcome.

a) **NAFTA could precipitate a significant diversion of U.S. investment to Mexico.** Following an agreement, U.S. firms might move existing production to Mexico or build new plants there instead of at home.

   Many firms investing in Mexico will not be responding to specific changes in investment regulations within a NAFTA, but to heightened awareness of Mexico following the NAFTA debate and to the signal that investments in Mexico are "safe." An agreement would make it more difficult for a future Mexican government to reverse policies designed to attract investment.

b) **While massive third-country investment in Mexico is unlikely in the short term, over the longer term a NAFTA could lead to greater Asian and European investment to serve the U.S. market.** To date, Japanese and other third-country firms have not been especially satisfied with investments in Mexico because of its poor infrastructure and lack of local suppliers. By the late 1990s, however, these constraints should begin to fade, making Mexico a more attractive location.

c) **With increased investment in Mexico and a large (over 20 million) and rapidly growing pool of less educated workers there, U.S. employers will gain added leverage in their dealings with less educated U.S. workers.** More such workers in the United States will find themselves competing directly with workers in Mexican plants; increasingly, employers will be able to use the threat of relocation to depress wages here.

   Past experience in the United States indicates that downward pressure on U.S. wages could exist even if the United States enjoys—as it does now—a trade surplus with Mexico. From the 1950s through the 1980s, in most industries, southern U.S. States ran a "trade deficit" with the Midwest; nevertheless, low wages and low levels of unionization in the South contributed to the erosion of industry-wide bargaining, union influence, and manufacturing wages in the Northeast and Midwest.

d) **A NAFTA could reinforce U.S. employers' efforts to compete using low-wage rather than high-wage strategies,** increasing direct competition with Mexico and other developing countries on the basis of wage levels.

POLICY AND THE NAFTA

OTA's analysis suggests that Congress may wish to evaluate NAFTA in light of an agreement's contribution to the effective management of the long-term process of economic integration. The policy options listed in table 1-1 and discussed in detail in chapter 2 are designed to help manage that process. These policy options would encourage U.S. manufacturing and service firms to pursue skill-intensive strategies that generate wage growth for U.S. workers, limit U.S. income inequality, enable positive sum trade with Mexico, and assist dislocated workers.

OTA's analysis indicates the need for major reorientation of U.S. industrial development, training, and labor market policies. The Nation's current economic difficulties—and declining wages—were "made in the USA"; that is where, by and large, they must be solved. OTA's domestic policy options fall into three complementary categories:

1. those that would help provide U.S. firms and workers with the skills and technological know-how to compete on the basis of quality, productivity, and flexibility rather than low wages;
2. policies intended to discourage low-wage, low-skill strategies that can be replicated easily in Mexico and other developing countries; and
3. options that would promote the worker participation and worker commitment necessary to compete on a basis other than wages.

While domestic policy matters most, OTA's analysis indicates that policies and development strategies in Mexico will have an important influence on workers' prospects in the United States. In particular, if Mexico fosters broad-based development, and allows workers to share in its fruits, the resulting wage increases, exchange rate appreciation, reduced emigration, economic growth, and demand for imports will facilitate U.S. adjustment to a high-productivity, high-skill path. OTA's continental policy options suggest ways in which the

Table 1-1—Summary List of Policy Options

I. Domestic Policy Options

Issue Area A: Promoting a Productive Economy (see table 2-2, ch. 2)

1. Approve a modified version of the High Skills, Competitive Workforce Act of 1990
2. Create a comprehensive worker adjustment program
3. Expand Trade Adjustment Assistance
4. Certify basic skills of new labor force entrants
5. Broaden and deepen links between firms
6. Create a Regional and Community Adjustment Corporation, focusing on direct public job creation

Issue Area B: Curtailing Low-Productivity Strategies (table 2-3)

1. Establish national commitment to social welfare through a U.S. Social Charter
2. Discourage low-wage strategies and reduce income inequality through wage and tax policies
3. Discourage State and local economic development based on "bidding wars" to recruit new industry

Issue Area C: Participation in a Productive Economy (table 2-4)

1. Create a Labor Market Productivity Center to foster consensus-building and expand institutional support for work reorganization
2. Create Employee Participation Committees to provide worker "voice" in nonunion as well as unionized companies
3. Extend union representation to more workers and industry sectors
4. Foster institutions for worker voice in the service sector

II. Continental Policy Options (table 2-5)

1. Negotiate a North American Social Charter and establish a North American Commission for Labor and Social Welfare
2. Establish procedures for continental management of trade and investment in autos and other sectors
3. Create a Binational Commission with stable funding to improve the environment and infra-structure in the border region
4. Provide technical assistance to Mexico for improving worker health and safety
5. Provide loans and aid for balanced economic development in Mexico
6. Establish North American works councils to represent employees of companies operating in more than one country
7. Provide trilateral dispute resolution on labor issues
8. Negotiate shorter work time for the continent
9. Establish a Commission on the Future of Democracy in North America

SOURCE: Office of Technology Assessment, 1992.

United States and Mexico could cooperate to foster broad-based development in Mexico that will benefit U.S. workers as well.

OTA's domestic and continental policy options go considerably beyond those so far discussed in the NAFTA debate. The focus of that debate has been on: 1) domestic adjustment policies and funding, which the administration promised as Congress considered "fast track" negotiating authority in the spring of 1991; and 2) a commitment to negotiate labor and environmental issues with Mexico in talks parallel to but not part of NAFTA.

Claiming the administration has not followed through, some labor, environmental, and business interests are likely to urge Congress to vote down NAFTA. Voting no might, however, precipitate the reemergence in Mexico of nationalist hostility to the United States. Particularly if accompanied by a stall in Mexico's recovery, it could threaten the stability of the Mexican political system, reducing the prospects for both democratization and for cooperation with the United States. Political and economic problems, in turn, could worsen Mexico's underemployment problem, keep wages stagnant, and increase emigration. Thus, failure to reach an agreement could increase the immediate pressures on less-skilled U.S. workers and also dim the prospects for improving environmental management along the border.

Moreover, a congressional no vote on NAFTA would be the first refusal to approve a trade agreement in U.S. history. It would signal a further retreat from the Nation's role as defender of open trade within the multilateral system. Erosion of the

Table 1-2—Policy Options for the Near Term

	Domestic Options			
	Promoting a productive economy	Curtailing low-productivity strategies	Participating in productive economy	Continental options
Statements of principles		Approve a U.S. Social Charter recommitting the United States to improving the welfare of U.S. workers		Negotiate a preliminary North American Social Charter
Near-term policies	Approve a modified version of the High Skills Competitive Workforce Act of 1990 Establish a comprehensive worker adjustment system		Approve H.R. 3160, the OSHA reform bill, with its provision for workplace health and safety committees	Provide technical assistance to Mexico to improve health and safety standards Establish a Binational Commission with stable funding to improve environment and infrastructure in border area Negotiate a Japan-North America or Global Auto Pact
Study, reporting, and institution-building options			Fund a private sector, multi-constituency Labor Market Productivity Center and ask it to study how to fill the U.S. representation gap	Establish a North American Commission for Labor and Social Welfare Provide trilateral dispute resolution on labor issues Call for creation of North American works councils

SOURCE: Office of Technology Assessment, 1992.

multilateral system could also diminish prospects for international agreements on environmental and labor issues.

On the other hand, if NAFTA comes before Congress unaccompanied by significant domestic reforms, voting yes might be tantamount to ratifying the mismanagement of economic integration. This could further lock the United States into a low-wage, low-productivity future.

Congress will have 90 days from the time of official notification of an agreement to consult with the administration on NAFTA before turning to implementing legislation. This period offers an opportunity for Congress and the executive to consider the merits of a ''bare'' NAFTA—the narrow trade and investment deal returned by the negotiating teams for the three countries in August 1992—compared with a NAFTA as part of a package that might include complementary domestic and continental social policy measures and parallel understandings with Mexico on environmental and labor issues. Such a package could make it clear to U.S. workers and to U.S. corporations that

North America means to shift away from low-wage, low-productivity development to high-productivity, environmentally and socially sustainable development.

A relatively lengthy period of debate and discussion would necessarily precede adoption of some of the domestic and continental options listed in table 1-1 and discussed in chapter 2. Table 1-2 lists a package of the policy options from table 1-1 that would, taken together, send a positive signal about future development in North America. This package includes options that fall into three categories: 1) statements of principle that could guide domestic and continental development as the United States and Mexico become increasingly interdependent; 2) policy options that could be adopted in the same approximate time frame as NAFTA itself; and 3) study, reporting, and institution-building options. Enacting statements of principle and reporting and institution-building options could help ensure that attention to options that require more extended debate does not flag after the NAFTA spotlight has dimmed.

The first row of table 1-2 suggests that the United States might seek to combine a NAFTA with U.S. and North American social charters. Chapter 2 outlines some of the rights and goals that could be included in a U.S. Social Charter. It would represent a blend of recommitments to familiar social goals, such as full employment, and the definition of new goals—e.g., a right to training for workers throughout their careers, and a reversal of the trend toward greater income inequality—to guide U.S. policy as the Nation adapts to global economic competition. Along with the new Mexican Productivity Accord (ch. 4), a U.S. Charter could help lay groundwork for a North American Social Charter. A skeletal Charter might be negotiated quickly and incorporated in an extended preamble to NAFTA or in a separate accord. It could then be elaborated and implemented through future negotiations over a later period.

The second row of table 1-2 lists a number of concrete policy options that could be implemented in the same time frame as NAFTA approval, including three domestic options:

1. Adopt a modified version of the High Skills, Competitive Workforce Act of 1990. In the domestic arena, the obvious choices for immediate consideration begin with skill development. The administration and Congress have both expressed the view that the United States needs to invest more heavily in human resources, particularly for workers with less education and those with jobs at the base of organizational pyramids. This consensus is reflected in the bipartisan High Skills, Competitive Workforce Act of 1990 (S. 1790 and H.R. 3470).

   This bill would encourage certification of basic and occupational skills, demonstrate new approaches to helping young people move from school to work, foster creation of multiemployer training consortia and diffusion of production practices making better use of workers' knowledge, require all firms with at least 20 employees to spend 1 percent of payroll on training or pay an equivalent sum into a State training trust fund, and encourage the States to create State and local Employment and Training Boards. This act would be the first comprehensive, multifaceted federal effort to move the United States towards a skill-intensive development strategy. A free

trade agreement with Mexico would make it more important than ever for the United States to take a decisive step in this direction.

2. Create a comprehensive U.S. worker adjustment system by enhancing training and income support for unemployed workers. The NAFTA debate on labor market adjustment has focused on whether workers displaced by imports—or the movement of production to Mexico—should be provided with training and income support through Trade Adjustment Assistance (TAA) or a new NAFTA adjustment program. Rather than continue to make assistance for displaced workers depend on why they lose their jobs, OTA's analysis suggests a more comprehensive approach in which increased funding for the Economic Dislocation and Worker Adjustment Assistance (EDWAA) program and the unemployment insurance (UI) system make a full range of services, including long-term training with income support, available to all displaced workers.

3. Pass H.R. 3160, the OSHA reform bill. Workers in the United States are concerned that competition with Mexico will erode health and safety standards here; OTA's analysis indicates that weak U.S. institutions of worker voice—a ''representation gap''—leads to low worker commitment and obstructs pursuit of participative strategies. Congress could respond to worker concerns about health and safety *and* create a modest new institution of worker voice by passing H.R. 3160. The key provisions of this bill include the establishment of health and safety committees in companies with 11 or more full-time employees. Committees and their employee representatives would have specified rights and responsibilities for monitoring and enforcement of health and safety standards. Other provisions, including an employee right to refuse to work in imminently hazardous conditions, would also strengthen health and safety protection.

On the continental front, the second row of table 1-2 lists three concrete policy options that could be implemented in approximately the same time frame as a NAFTA:

1. A program to provide Mexico with technical assistance to improve its workplace health and safety standards.

2. Establishment of a Binational Commission on Border Environment and Infrastructure. This Commission could be provided with a stable funding source outside the annual appropriations processes in the two countries, perhaps based on a binationally negotiated *maquila* investment tax.

3. Negotiation of a Continental (Japan-North America) or Global Auto Pact. Shifting additional auto production to North America would give Mexico the opportunity to build integrated networks of assemblers and suppliers without cutting into U.S. production and jobs.

Finally, the bottom row of table 1-2 lists one domestic and three continental monitoring and institution-building options that would help sustain the debate about the domestic and continental management of economic integration and pave the way for implementation of more comprehensive policies over time:

1. A U.S. Labor Market and Productivity Center, with a board composed of representatives from business, labor, disadvantaged labor market groups, and the training community, to help develop consensus on the labor market and labor law policies necessary to move towards a high-productivity path. As one major task, to be completed within perhaps 2 years of the signing of a NAFTA, the Center could be called on to forward recommendations for filling the U.S. representation gap—the absence of unions or other forms of employee representation in most workplaces.

2. A trinational North American Commission for Labor and Social Welfare, with its own funding and separate from the executive branches of each country, having responsibility for further developing the principles outlined in a North American Social Charter and defining ways of achieving those goals.

3. The creation of a nonbinding trilateral dispute resolution mechanism on labor issues.

4. Provision for North American works councils in companies with significant operations in more than one country of North America.

MEXICO'S INDUSTRIAL DEVELOPMENT PROSPECTS

Analyzing in detail the implications of free trade with Mexico requires understanding the capabilities

Photo credit: Ford Motor Company

Worker training at Ford's Hermosillo, Mexico stamping and assembly plant.

of Mexican industry. Parties to the debate on NAFTA have expressed widely divergent views of Mexico's capabilities and the resulting implications for the United States. At one extreme are those who hold that Mexico has shown itself capable of producing most manufactured goods as well as the United States and that massive flows of investment to Mexico will take place over the next decade to take advantage of cheap labor. At the other extreme are those who believe exposure to competition will decimate historically protected Mexican enterprises to the benefit of U.S. exporters. OTA's analysis indicates that both views mistake one part of the unevenly developed Mexican economy for the whole.

Over the past decade, new plants operated by multinational corporations (MNCs) have demonstrated levels of productivity and quality equal to those in the United States. High-performance "islands of excellence" in Mexico's largely inefficient manufacturing sector span significantly more than simple assembly operations. They include, for example, world-class auto engine and stamping plants. Threatened U.S. workers see these examples— like the recent announcement by Smith-Corona of the transfer of its remaining typewriter production to Mexico—as precursors of wholesale movements of production that could cost their jobs and destroy their communities.

Most of Mexican manufacturing, however, is inefficient and produces low-quality goods using

labor-intensive methods. Compared with, say, South Korea, Mexico has only a few large and technologically sophisticated firms. Unable to compete, many small Mexican manufacturers of apparel, furniture, shoes, and other goods have gone out of business since Mexico began lowering its trade and investments barriers in the mid to late 1980s. More will disappear in the future.

Nonetheless, based on the success of pioneering modern plants and proximity to the U.S. market, Mexico will gain increasing investment. At the same time, Mexico's attractiveness as a location for export-oriented production will be limited by poor infrastructure, shortages of local suppliers, and lack of experienced technicians, engineers, and managers. MNCs can circumvent these bottlenecks—e.g., by paying well enough to attract the most trainable workers from local labor markets—but human resource constraints will limit prospects for smaller Mexican-owned companies.

Mexico did not emphasize vocational training and development of technical professionals and managers during its extended period of import-substitution industrialization (from roughly 1950 until the middle 1980s). Investments in basic education lagged behind those in the successful developing Asian economies. Moreover, Mexico, like the United States, spends its educational resources disproportionately on those at the top of the educational hierarchy.

Given a legacy of protection and human resource bottlenecks, small and medium-sized Mexican firms are only now learning the techniques long since mastered by the better small U.S. firms. As a result, Mexican production for the U.S. market is likely to depend for the next 10 to 15 years on the resources, including technology and managerial expertise, of foreign-based MNCs. Thus, Mexican development may continue to resemble the ''branch plant'' economies of the southern United States from the 1950s to the 1980s. At the same time, the policies of Mexico's government, the rapid expansion of production in parts of northern Mexico, and growing corporate preferences for suppliers willing to locate nearby could foster more rapid and more integrated development than the low-wage, low-tax development strategies in the U.S. South.

THE SECTORS

This part of the summary includes snapshots of four broad sectors analyzed by OTA. Three are manufacturing industries—autos and parts, electronics, and apparel. The fourth consists of agriculture and food processing. Four tables, one for each sector, highlight findings from the body of the report concerning the relative attractiveness of production in the United States as compared with Mexico over the medium-term future of 5 to 15 years. These summaries are based on extensive interviews by OTA staff and contractors, as well as published sources (see chs. 7-10).

To a greater or lesser extent, the four sectors are each part of global industries. Mexican production today depends on imported parts and components. These patterns are not fixed. But Mexico's ability to absorb foreign know-how fast is limited, even with the aid of multinational investment. And while Mexico's competence improves, so will that of Taiwan, Thailand, and Brazil.

Autos and Parts—(table 1-3). U.S.-owned automakers and parts firms are in deep trouble. For two decades they have been pressed by Japanese-owned firms, who now assemble cars and small trucks in U.S. ''transplants.'' The U.S. Big Three have pursued their own international production strategies, which have long included production in Mexico. Since before World War II, the Mexican Government has required automakers to assemble cars in Mexico in order to sell there. More recently, complex export-balancing requirements have led to investments in production for export to the United States (ch. 7).

Assembly and engine plants went into Mexico primarily to satisfy the demands of the Mexican Government; cost advantages with respect to U.S. production, when they exist, have been relatively small. In contrast, production of auto parts having relatively high labor content is substantially cheaper in Mexico. More than 65 Mexican plants already supply wiring harnesses to U.S. (and Mexican) assembly plants. Most *maquiladora* parts plants perform simple operations using unskilled labor, but the world-class assembly and engine plants operated by Ford, Nissan, and other automakers demonstrate that Mexican labor can also compete in quite sophisticated production. Transportation costs eat up most or all of the labor-cost savings for finished

Table 1-3—Autos and Parts

United States	Mexico
Structure of industry and market	
Vehicle Producers. Six major assemblers, several smaller firms, compete through both North American production and imports. Open market but stagnant demand, with limited growth prospects over foreseeable future. Nonetheless, shifts in demand (e.g., for small trucks in place of passenger cars) will create new opportunities to stake out market position.	*Vehicle producers.* Five major firms compete in a historically regulated market, one that remains almost entirely closed to imports. Growth in demand potentially quite rapid, but will depend both on Mexico's overall economic expansion and on shifts in income distribution.
Independent suppliers. Assemblers are streamlining their supply networks, reducing the number of firms they buy from. Many second-and third-tier suppliers will have trouble meeting stringent demands for cost, quality, delivery, and, in some cases, for engineering.	*Independent suppliers.* Mexican-owned supply industry largely uncompetitive. *Maquilas* have focused on labor-intensive items.
Blue- and grey-collar labor force	
Ample supply of skilled and experienced labor, but many transplants prefer nonunion workers over experience. Smaller suppliers, mostly nonunion and paying significantly lower wages than assemblers, have had trouble attracting and retaining skilled employees.	Mexico's blue-collar workforce seems nearly up to world standards in terms of trainability, but high turnover means companies lose much of their human resource investment. Availability of skilled grey-collar workers (technicians, machinists, toolmakers) could restrain expansion.
Technical and managerial labor force	
American managers, in both automakers and suppliers, must adapt more quickly to new competitive conditions.	Capable managers in short supply, particularly at middle levels and for supply firms. Lack of experienced engineers will make it difficult for suppliers to move into technologically demanding niches.
Labor Relations	
Traditionally adversarial. Tentative moves toward more cooperation in U.S. assembly plants but only a few suppliers. Industry shrinkage, nonunion transplants, and movement to Mexico could resurrect adversarial relations.	Much variation. Some local unions co-opted and manipulated by government or by companies. Worker-controlled independent locals could pioneer "negotiated flexibility" but may be repressed.
Availability of Materials, Components, and Other Inputs to Production	
Almost anything is available, but quality sometimes questionable.	Very restricted from local sources.
Infrastructure (transportation, communications, etc.)	
Generally good; deteriorating highway system needs attention.	Ground transport slow, unpredictable, and expensive but improving rapidly, especially near the border. Poor communications promise to be easier to overcome (e.g., through private lines and data links). Water supplies, sewage, waste disposal promise persistent though manageable difficulties.
Government Policies	
Federal. Japanese quotas symbolic in recent years; only major trade restriction is 25 percent tariff on light trucks. Trade friction, especially over sourcing of parts by transplants, will continue.	Heavily regulated, with gradual trade and investment liberalization in recent years. Future human resource and industrial policies could be significant for supplier development.
State. Intense competition to attract major plants through incentive packages. Industrial extension, network building should help improve productivity and adaptability of small- and medium-sized suppliers.	
The Future	
U.S. jobs in parts production (in plants operated both by independent suppliers and the Big Three) will be at greater risk than assembly jobs. Many U.S. parts plants are old and poorly managed. If costs are high and quality low, managers may opt to move to Mexico rather than trying to modernize and improve performance in the United States. A growing supplier base in Mexico might then attract more assembly plants.	Automakers are likely to put new assembly plants into Mexico at rates that depend more on Mexican demand than on U.S. demand.

SOURCE: Office of Technology Assessment, 1992.

vehicles, but engines and other powertrain components can be shipped more cheaply; for engines, Mexican production yields savings of up to 10 percent (e.g., $70 delivered to the United States for an engine with a manufacturing cost of $700).

As many as 150,000 Mexicans now work in export-oriented auto and auto parts plants. It would be too simple to state that all these jobs would otherwise be located in the United States; some would be in other low-wage countries, and some would have been automated if production had remained in the United States (or Canada). It would also be too simple to conclude that U.S. or Japanese automakers will put new plants into Mexico simply because Mexican wages are low. Direct labor accounts for perhaps 10 percent of costs in assembly plants, less for engines—and will decrease with continued improvements in design-for-manufacturability. But the pressure on U.S. parts suppliers suggests continuing movement to Mexico in search of lower costs.

Electronics—(table 1-4). The segments of this industry differ in fundamental ways (ch. 8). Labor costs are a relatively minor concern, with two major exceptions: consumer electronics and some kinds of components. Much of consumer electronics—especially TV production—remains a traditional, mass production business, with low margins and intense cost competition. Only one U.S. firm of any size remains—Zenith—and it produces most of its output in Mexico and other offshore locations. Components and subassemblies for electronic products, such as transformer coils and power supplies, which also have high labor content, have likewise migrated out of the United States, often to Mexico.

Simple personal computers (PCs) are not too dissimilar from TVs in assembly requirements, but product and system designs—and component technologies—change much more rapidly. Except for standardized, low-end PCs, there has been little reason to locate production in low-wage countries. Much the same is true in telecommunications. Labor costs are important for telephones, answering machines, and other types of customer premises equipment. AT&T and other U.S.-based firms now make some of these products in Mexico and others in the Far East. But direct production labor is a minor cost factor for more complex, systems-oriented telecommunications products. These are made in Mexico by multinational firms because the government has

demanded it. Through its controls over market access, Mexico's government has also attracted some production of small computers. Now that IBM, Hewlett-Packard, and other companies have plants there, they are not likely to leave, even though a NAFTA might allow them to ship into Mexico from the United States or elsewhere. But as the government's ability to influence foreign investors wanes, Mexico may have trouble attracting new electronics plants except for the simple assembly operations in which it already specializes—products like TVs, keyboards, and printers.

Mexico's problem in electronics, even more than in autos, is one of organizational competence. Mexican firms, unless they have strong ties to U.S. or third-country firms, have very limited capabilities. Quality standards are low, training poor and turnover high, work organization inflexible, product development and marketing experience minimal. Companies without links to the international economy will have trouble forming them.

Apparel—(table 1-5). Exports from *maquiladora* apparel plants to the United States grew at about 10 percent annually during the late 1980s, and even more rapidly during the last 2 years. These plants assemble basic, commodity-like items (work clothes, underwear) in direct competition with U.S. plants, which sometimes have costs up to twice as great for sewing and manual cutting. Nonetheless, the United States continues to produce large volumes of basic clothing, in part because automation (computerized cutting) and work reorganization (so-called Quick Response strategies, aimed at greater flexibility and responsiveness to market demand) have helped offset higher wage bills (ch. 9). Where quality requirements are higher, or retailers want rapid deliveries of women's clothing and other fashion-sensitive apparel, Quick Response appears especially promising. Here the competition has been from Asia; Mexican apparel firms do not currently compete in this part of the market. But given a NAFTA, some U.S. apparel firms might decide it is easier to move to Mexico than to implement new strategies at home.

The non-*maquila* sector of Mexico's apparel industry includes many small firms that make cheap clothing of poor quality for sale in domestic markets. These firms are in no position to export into the United States. To do so, they would need infusions

Table 1-4—Electronics

United States	Mexico
Structure of industry and market	
Consumer. Most demand filled by imports (VCRs, camcorders, audio, etc.), although final assembly of some large TVs remains. Sales growth a function largely of new product introductions (CD players, Walkmen)—otherwise mostly a replacement market. Few new products developed in the United States.	*Consumer. Maquilas* produce subassemblies and finished products for export to the United States. Domestically-oriented firms have been decimated by import competition since lowering of trade barriers.
Computer equipment. Pioneering industry faced with new challenges as growth slows after many years of expansion and markets fragment into specialized niches. With maturity, production of simpler items has moved abroad, beginning with peripherals and low-end processors.	*Computer equipment.* Little or no independent capability. MNCs and Mexican-owned firms assemble simple machines, produce keyboards, monitors, and other components and subassemblies. Thus far, foreign investment has not led to much growth of Mexican suppliers.
Telecommunications equipment. Still dominated by AT&T, but imports a major factor in simpler customer premises equipment (keysets, PBXs, FAX machines); foreign-based multinationals will continue to seek to expand in the deregulated U.S. market.	*Telecommunications equipment.* Essentially all technology from abroad. With TelMex newly privatized, AT&T has joined Ericsson and Indetel-Alcatel as a third major hardware supplier.
Blue- and grey-collar labor force	
Broad range of skill requirements, from simple assembly to trouble-shooting complex digital systems. Continuing retraining will be needed, particularly in software.	Need for skills will slow movement beyond simply assembly tasks.
Technical and managerial labor force	
Available and adaptable.	Limited.
Labor relations	
Much of electronics has been nonunion. Those sectors that have been organized—e.g., TV production—have been so damaged by foreign competition that labor has little leverage left.	High turnover in *maquilas* in part a symptom of poor underlying relations, as well as ongoing "industrialization of the labor force," but unions in any case docile and ineffectual, with a few exceptions (e.g., TelMex).
Availability of materials, components, and other inputs to production	
Increasing imports even of high-technology components, also production equipment.	Little local production except for simple components.
Infrastructure (transportation, communications, etc.)	
Satisfactory.	Poor (see table 1-3 entry).
Government policies	
Important especially in telecommunications (e.g., the ability of the regional Bell operating companies to enter manufacturing). Highly visible industry will continue to draw trade and technology policy attention.	A privatized TelMex does not necessarily mean an end to government influence. As multinational suppliers continue to compete for future telecommunications sales, their investments and imports of technical know-how will contribute to Mexico's capabilities.
The future	
As electronics becomes more a matter of systems and software, there will be fewer U.S. jobs for less skilled workers. At the same time, a good deal of final assembly will remain in the United States simply because of low direct labor content. Imports of components will continue to increase, but most will come from Asia, not Mexico.	Mexico will continue to produce home entertainment electronics for export, and more complex equipment intended for sale within Mexico. Multinationals and Mexican firms closely linked with multinationals will account for almost all of this production.

SOURCE: Office of Technology Assessment, 1992.

of capital for more modern equipment, better trained workers able to turn out higher quality goods, and managers able to organize production more effi-

ciently and market their goods in an intensely competitive setting; poor distribution channels into the U.S. market have been a particular handicap.

Table 1-5—Apparel

United States	Mexico
Structure of industry and market	
Despite many years of intense import competition, a relatively large number of mostly small apparel firms continue to manufacture in the United States, many in New York, California, and the Southeast. In part, this is because rapid, flexible response to market shifts can compensate for higher direct production costs—especially in fashion-sensitive clothing—in this highly labor-intensive industry.	Although *maquila* plants can produce basic apparel products at costs well under U.S. costs, the Mexican industry is weak overall compared with successful Asian producers. Countries like China can undercut Mexico's costs at the low end, while manufacturers in more advanced Asian countries (e.g., Hong Kong) can supply better cost/quality combinations for fashion-sensitive goods. Domestically oriented Mexican apparel firms have had great difficulty meeting Asian competition since the lowering of import barriers.
Blue- and grey-collar labor force	
Large U.S. cities continue to provide pools of workers, many of them immigrants, willing to work for low wages under sweatshop conditions.	In principle, nearly unlimited; apparel firms often provide the first industrial jobs held by workers from rural areas.
Technical and managerial labor force	
Technical labor (as opposed to design) not particularly important, but management is critical for "Quick Response" strategies.	Poor productivity and quality in much of the industry reflect poor organization and management.
Labor relations	
Industry largely nonunion in the Southeast. Strong unions particularly in New York City have engaged in a lengthy effort to retain jobs and improve working conditions.	Low union coverage became of small size of domestic shops.
Availability of materials, components, and other inputs to production	
Many U.S. textile firms are low-cost producers, but because textiles trade internationally in large volumes, a local textile industry does not confer a great deal of advantage in apparel. Much the same is true for production equipment.	Mexico's textile industry is generally uncompetitive. *Maquila* producers get almost all their cloth from the United States, in part because this has been a condition for favorable tariff treatment.
Infrastructure (transportation, communications, etc.)	
Good transport, communications—including computer links—a requirement for Quick Response.	Problems the greatest for small, independent firms and least for those tightly linked with U.S. apparel manufacturers or retailers.
Government policies	
Extensive structure of import quotas within the framework of the Multi-Fiber Arrangement (MFA), coupled with relatively high tariffs, have provided considerable protection for U.S. production. At the same time, because duties are only levied on foreign value-added, offshore assembly in Mexico and the Caribbean has been encouraged.	While Mexico's exports to the United States are in principle governed by bilateral quotas, in practice almost any apparel items from Mexico can enter in almost any quantity.
The future	
U.S. apparel employment has been declining since the early 1970s, and now stands at something under a million. Many of these jobs have been preserved through business strategies keyed to responsive customer service. To the extent that U.S. firms continue to implement such strategies effectively, they will remain viable against competition from both Mexico and the Far East. But if companies see a NAFTA as meaning easy access to low-wage labor, they may forsake innovative strategies and simply move south of the border. Moreover, continuing U.S. trade restrictions on imports from third countries could lead to greater Asian investment in the Mexican apparel industry.	Whether or not a NAFTA is implemented, Mexico's export-oriented apparel sector will continue to expand. A NAFTA would accelerate this expansion by reducing or eliminating tariffs on Mexican apparel. Most of the export-oriented plants, moreover, currently do sewing on fabric cut in the United States because this qualifies the product for more lenient tariff treatment. With a NAFTA, manual cutting for Mexican assembly would begin moving south of the border, although companies with heavy U.S. investments in automated cutting would probably not relocate these operations.

SOURCE: Office of Technology Assessment, 1992.

None of this is to say that U.S.-based firms, migrating to Mexico in search of low-cost labor, could not prosper in such an environment. A NAFTA that eliminated tariffs on Mexican apparel, which now average 17-18 percent, would accelerate the expansion of sewing in Mexico and lead to the movement of more cutting as well. But so far there has been little transfer of advanced production practices associated with Quick Response. If such practices were to be adopted in Mexico as rapidly and effectively as in the United States, much production that would otherwise remain here would be at risk.

Agriculture and Food Processing—(table 1-6). In Mexico's two-tiered agricultural system, several million small-scale farmers grow subsistence crops (corn, beans) with traditional practices, while a relatively modern agribusiness industry produces fruits and vegetables for export to the United States. The traditional sector has low productivity; indeed, many small farmers cannot feed their own families. The modern sector has been able to capitalize on Mexico's inherent advantages—which stem from climate and growing conditions as well as low wages—to compete effectively with U.S. producers, particularly for labor-intensive fruits and vegetables (e.g., winter tomatoes) (ch. 10).

But Mexico's advantages have their limits. The country has relatively little water and arable land. Agricultural technology remains well behind U.S. practices, for example in use of pesticides, herbicides, and fertilizers. Many farms even in the modern sector get substantially lower crop yields than are common in the United States. Mexico faces constraints in breeding stock; mechanized equipment; know-how concerning what, where, and when to plant; distribution channels; and modern food processing capacity. And even though Mexico appears to have long-term, sustainable advantages for some kinds of fruits and vegetables, the United States has an overwhelming productivity edge in the staple crops of wheat and corn.

For many reasons, then, trade between the two countries' agricultural sectors is more nearly complementary than competitive. For instance, Mexico imports breeding stock and bull semen, sending feeder cattle back to the United States for fattening on cheap U.S. grain. Mexico buys some beef in return. Since U.S. meatpackers have been driving down their labor costs by closing unionized plants

and hiring immigrant workers, for most of them Mexico's still lower wage levels would probably not offset the added costs of transporting grain (or cattle) to feedlots or packing plants south of the border. But here, as in other agricultural sectors, impacts will be shaped by local conditions and transportation costs. Thus, there may be some relocation of cattle feeding and meatpacking from Texas to Mexico after a NAFTA, while the bulk of U.S. production, which takes place farther north, seems unlikely to move. (Because poultry consume less feed per pound of meat, poultry production and processing may prove more mobile.)

Beyond whatever direct job losses result in the United States, the further integration of beef and poultry production and processing—and growing, freezing, and canning of fruits and vegetables—will maintain downward pressure on the wages of U.S. agricultural and food processing workers. At the same time, the ultimate expansion of U.S. agribusiness into Mexico will be limited by that country's modest endowments of fertile land and available

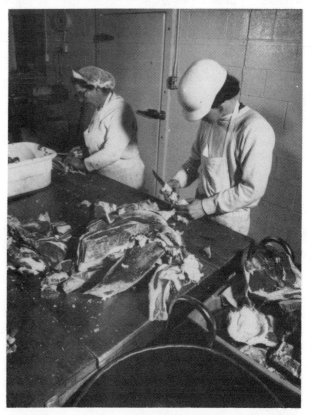

Photo credit: Grant Heilman Photography

Boxing beef.

Table 1-6—Agriculture and Food Processing

United States	Mexico
Structure of industry and market	
Production highly sensitive to local conditions (climate, soil, water supplies). Most sectors and subsectors dominated by relatively large farms, ranches, feeders, and processors. Nonetheless a very large absolute number of small producers (e.g., "family farms") continue to account for substantial shares of output in many sectors. Consumer tastes (e.g., lower consumption of red meat) promise continuing demand shifts.	Many small farmers produce only for local or self-consumption. "Communal" *ejido* sector—in which peasant farmers have had the right to use state-owned land—are now to be privatized. *Ejidos* account for nearly half of Mexican land, but the sector as a whole is inefficient and has been heavily subsidized. Larger farms in export sectors (e.g., winter vegetables) have developed relatively good distribution into U.S. markets.
Blue- and grey-collar labor force	
Low-wage, temporary field labor jobs often hard to fill. Much food processing has been deskilled, with downward pressure on wages.	Large surplus; most of those in the *ejido* sector, or working as day laborers, have little education and limited prospects for mobility.
Technical and managerial labor force	
Many experienced farmers, often generally receptive to new technologies but not necessarily to new business practices.	Severely constrained. Limited capacity to develop hybrid seeds, pesticides, herbicides, fertilizers, or cultivation practices tailored to Mexico's growing conditions, or to adapt technologies from elsewhere.
Labor relations	
Traditionally adversarial in processing (e.g., meatpacking); farmworkers historically unorganized and exploited.	Much self-employment, casual labor in production, particularly in *ejido* sector; rural poverty even worse than urban poverty.
Availability of materials, components, and other inputs to production	
The United States remains a world leader in livestock breeding, development of hybrid crops, agrochemicals, and mechanization. Biotechnology has become the newest source of competitive advantage. However, some current and common practices could prove unsustainable over the next several decades, and serious water supply problems in the West seem likely.	Mexico's modern agricultural sector must import seeds and breeding stock. The traditional sector is more nearly self-sufficient but low in productivity; few small farmers can afford modern agricultural machinery. Limited arable land and water supplies create fundamental restrictions on future production.
Infrastructure (transportation, communications, etc.)	
Advertising strategies frequently used to differentiate products.	Marketing and distribution sometimes still a bottleneck for export products; the added costs can offset Mexico's lower wages. Poor transportation is particularly serious for perishable crops. Little sign of successful marketing strategies based on product differentiation.
Government policies	
Heavily regulated, supported, subsidized, with the farm lobby remaining extraordinarily powerful. Indeed, agribusiness is more directly influenced by government policies than almost any other sector (subsidies, water rights, pesticide regulations, trade restrictions, extension and other technology measures). These very high levels of policy intervention could begin to change with a Uruguay Round GATT agreement.	Policies ranging from price controls on food products to credit allocation for small farmers have served in part as a rural poverty program and a tool to keep people from leaving the land for the cities. Supports and subsidies, including irrigation projects and low-cost fertilizer sales, have been scaled back since the middle 1980s; declining subsidies have cut into the cost advantages of some export crops.
The future	
The impacts of a NAFTA will be localized by product and by region in this sector more than in any other. For example, Florida tomato growers—who have managed to meet Mexican competition for many years through a combination of greater productivity and "strategic" trade protection—might finally begin to lose out. At the same time, California tomato growers, who do not confront Mexican production as directly (because their growing season is later), might be affected little if at all. U.S. agriculture is highly efficient; a NAFTA would have more impact on the choice of crops to be grown in a given location than on absolute levels of production.	A NAFTA, coupled with ongoing domestic policy shifts, promises to lead to greater dislocations in Mexico than in the United States. Declines in subsidies and price supports, and the reform of the *ejido* system, promise to drive even more of Mexico's rural population off the land and into the cities, where there is unlikely to be work for more than a few. Likely consequences include increasing emigration to the United States.

SOURCE: Office of Technology Assessment, 1992.

Table 1-7—Alternative Development Paths for the U.S. Economy

Low-wage, low-productivity growth	High-wage, high-productivity growth
Overall strategy	
• Low cost through scale economies, long production runs, use of contingent workers, outsourcing to low-wage subcontractors, and relocation to low-wage areas. • Sale of limited variety of standardized products and products based on price; product cycles remain fairly long.	• Low cost through economies of scope, use of skilled workers in combination with flexible technology, and cooperation among geographically concentrated vertical and horizontal networks of firms. • Sale of specialized goods and services with short life cycles in markets segmented by quality and attributes tailored to customer needs and tastes.
Organizational structure	
• Decentralized, but control over profit centers maintained centrally. • Significant specialization within management along functional lines, turf boundaries. • Symbolism of the company or plant as a team; hierarchy and top-down control in practice.	• Greater decentralization of authority. • Heavy use of cross-functional management teams, simultaneous product and process engineering. • Flatter hierarchies, authority pushed down in the organization.
Work organization and labor relations	
• Independent worker representation (unions, employee participation committees) weak or nonexistent. • Formal internal flexibility due to lack of work rules, unions; restricted flexibility in practice below team leader level. • Some commitment to employer goals among large-firm, core workers with job security. • External flexibility through hiring/firing of part-time, temporary, contract, less senior workers. • Adversarial, autocratic relations predominate in suppliers, small firms, and among temporary, contract, or part-time workers in large firms.	• Independent worker representation at most workplaces. • Flexibility arrangements negotiated with workers and their representatives on the job. • Worker commitment generally high. • Segmentation of workers into secure and contingent groups limited through internal flexibility and multi-employer labor market intermediaries.
Human resource development and job ladders	
• Minimal training for low level workers, except informally on the job, with short (up to 3-6 months at plant start-up, usually much less) training sessions for team leaders and trusted workers. • Specialized training for grey-collar craft and technical workers. • Little advancement for most workers; some opportunities for team leaders; hiring for most technical positions based on outside credentials.	• Significant development of most employees through on-the-job learning, classroom training. • Increased pay and some upward mobility through experience and mastery of additional skills. • Qualified lower-level employees can take learning sabbaticals to acquire new knowledge, qualify for promotion or switch in occupation.

(Continued on next page)

water. Continued improvements in U.S. agricultural technology, many of them the results of biotechnology, will transfer relatively slowly to Mexico because so many agricultural technologies (e.g., hybrid seeds) must be customized for local growing conditions.

THE UNITED STATES, MEXICO, AND NORTH AMERICA: TWO SCENARIOS

The spectrum of possibilities for future development in the United States, Mexico, and North America can be summarized by describing two alternative futures for each country and for North America as a whole. One alternative would bring back the sustained prosperity of the 1940 to 1970 period. The other would lead to continued decline in the United States, insufficient growth for Mexico to support its rapidly expanding population, and the social and political tensions associated with economic stagnation.

The United States faces a choice between a low-wage, low-productivity path and a human resource intensive, high-productivity path (table 1-7). In the "low-wage" alternative, U.S. firms would use computer technology and limited work reorganization to somewhat expand their product offerings and rate of innovation, but would remain committed to "scientific management" and the routinized production of a limited variety of stand-

Table 1-7—Alternative Development Paths for the U.S. Economy—(Continued)

Low-wage, low-productivity growth	High-wage, high-productivity growth
Wage setting	
• Wages for entry-level employees, technical workers, and upper managers set by the market. • Other wages set at plant or company level by employer. • "Efficiency wage" premia (10-20 percent) for core workers in big firms; some discretionary profit-sharing and merit-based pay.	• Wages for small pool of contingent, secondary workers set by the market. • Most wages set within broad ranges by minimum wage, multi-employer industry-wide or local occupation-specific agreements. • Some flexibility in wages based on negotiated and verifiable criteria—e.g., gain sharing, acquisition of skills.
Interfirm relations	
• Some cooperation between core firms and their suppliers on quality and engineering issues. Greater cooperation impeded by hard bargaining over contract terms, adversarial labor relations within suppliers. • Atomistic competition and little cooperation among small firms on training, technology diffusion, marketing.	• More stable, longer-term links with networked suppliers. In some cases, firm boundaries blur due to extensive cooperation and movement of personnel. • Small firms cluster in industrial districts characterized by cooperation on technology, training, and marketing.
Industrial and labor market policy	
• *Laissez-faire* approach to industrial development punctuated by *ad hoc*, politically motivated protection and subsidies. • Passive (primarily UI) labor market adjustment policies to the extent that budgets permit. • Development of training infrastructure left to the private-sector. • No change in U.S. laws governing union formation, collective representation.	• Federal and regional agencies seed cooperation among linked firms in industrial networks and districts. • Active (i.e., training, job matching) policies to enhance labor market flexibility. • Government catalyzes private-sector cooperation on training, job matching. • Labor law supports creation of worker voice institutions in small as well as large firms and in the service sector.

SOURCE: Office of Technology Assessment, 1992.

ardized goods. As in the past, most workers at the bottom of organizational hierarchies would have jobs that required limited skills. Knowledge and control of production would be embodied in machines and computer programs and monopolized by managers. Subcontracting would increase as part of efforts to find lower wage, more contingent labor.

Under the alternative, high-productivity direction, U.S. firms would employ computer-based technologies and new forms of work organization to design, develop, and produce varied, high-quality and continuously improving goods and services. Employers would foster the innovative capacity and flexibility necessary to compete in this way by training workers and restructuring internally to promote cooperation among workers and managers. Flexible automation would be used to complement and enhance workers' knowledge and skills, not to displace them. Small firms and suppliers would compete by capitalizing on the inherent flexibility of small organizations rather than by paying low wages.

OTA's analysis indicates that Mexico, like the United States, stands at a juncture between two futures. The first alternative would represent a sharp break from Mexican traditions of state guidance of the economy; it would continue and extend 1980s' policies of maintaining low wages and eliminating regulations on investment by foreign multinationals. The second alternative would also be market-oriented compared with the past but would draw more than the first on Mexico's tradition of state-led development and commitment to social justice. The end results would include more even development among regions and across rural and urban areas.

In its development policy under the second scenario, Mexico would look more like many of Asia's developing economies. Rather than trade and industrial policies driven by politics and rent-seeking, Mexico would shift to guided targeting through direct state support, efforts by Mexican firms to collectively improve their technologies, organizational practices, and worker skills, and, to the extent permitted by GATT and NAFTA discipline, strategic protectionism. In the human resource area, too, Mexico would come to resemble countries like Korea, increasing its overall investments, and redirecting them towards a combination of basic education for all, plus technical training for technicians, managers, and engineers. For labor policy, the developmentalist scenario would bring renegotiation of Mexico's social pact so that unions would gain more independence. This is likely to be necessary to inhibit reliance on low-wage strategies, particularly in smaller firms, and to counter autocratic traditions that, unchecked, would probably result in adversarial rather than participative workplace relations.

The greatest danger of NAFTA is that it could bring out the worst in each country. Trade and investment liberalization could reinforce commitment to low-wage business strategies among U.S., Canadian, and Mexican firms; destabilize the attempt to foster less adversarial relations between labor and management; weaken the commitment of U.S. corporations to train less educated U.S. workers; reduce incentives for small and medium-sized U.S. firms to construct and participate in cooperative networks aimed at fostering innovation and technology diffusion; and, in the wake of rising corn imports, reform of the small-scale *ejido* farming sector, and slow wage growth in Mexico, increase the tide of unskilled emigrants from Mexico to the United States. The combined effect would be to encourage growing numbers of U.S. firms to pursue business strategies depending on or compatible with production in Mexico (box 1-C).

Alternatively, the NAFTA debate could lead to a shared commitment to high productivity development in which each country's move in this direction makes it easier for the partner to move in parallel. Broad-based development in Mexico should bring both larger wage increases and more rapid exchange rate appreciation. More rapid and diversified development would reduce emigration to the United States and lead to more rapid expansion of U.S. exports. By contrast, less integrated development and a continuation or worsening of labor surpluses due to *ejido* reform and bankruptcies among smaller Mexican firms would mean slow exchange rate appreciation and a continuation of low wages even in world-class Mexican plants.

The choice of development paths is a stark one. It will have consequences not only for productivity and wages but for social and political stability. In the United States, a low-wage path would widen the gap between workers' aspirations and the jobs available to them. It would likewise widen the gap between rich and poor. Both countries must recognize the stakes before their choices lock them into the wrong path.

Box 1-C—Mass Production, Flexible Production, and Sweatshops in the Garment Industry

The El Paso garment industry provides an example of the dangers for the United States of remaining committed to standardized, high-volume manufacturing in an age when Mexico and other low-wage countries can approach U.S. productivity and quality levels in this kind of production. A center for men's work clothes since the 1920s, El Paso's garment industry expanded rapidly in the 1960s and 1970s due to investment by national mass producers of jeans and men's pants, including Levi Strauss, Farah, Billy the Kid, and Blue Bell. Employment rose from around 3,000 in the 1950s to over 15,000 by the early 1970s. The large plants that employed most El Paso garment workers provided good working conditions, benefits, and paid significantly above the minimum wage. Starting in the 1970s, El Paso began facing increased competition from low-wage countries, including Mexico. Farah, which once employed 8,000 workers in El Paso, shifted most of its sewing to Mexico and Costa Rica. Its El Paso workforce fell below 1,000. Billy the Kid, which once employed 2,000 workers, closed down its El Paso operations. Most of El Paso's losses have been high-volume, low-end jeans and work clothes produced with lead times of as long as a year.

As large plants moved over the border or around the globe, El Paso stemmed its overall loss in apparel employment by expanding production in low-wage "sweatshops." The growth of this segment is reflected in early 1990s employment statistics: large plants, anchored by Levi's seven facilities and over 3,000 employees, account for 60 percent of employment but less than 15 percent of El Paso's garment plants; the remaining 90 establishments, mostly subcontractors, account for 40 percent of employment. Average establishment size is now half what it was in the 1970s. In 1990, in a surprise sweep of 39 small shops by the U.S. Department of Labor, 20 were found to owe workers a total of $85,000 in back wages. Other shops employed underage workers and failed to meet basic health and safety standards. Some immigrant women workers have been willing to tolerate sub-minimum wages, poor working conditions, and sexual harassment because they need employer verification letters to qualify for legal residence in the United States.

(Continued on next page)

Box 1-C—Mass Production, Flexible Production, and Sweatshops in the Garment Industry—(Continued)

As high-volume production moved to developing countries, and to stem the expansion of small, low-wage sweatshops, a local organization of working women, in cooperation with the El Paso business community and local government, has been searching for a third, more economically and socially viable competitive strategy. Worker representatives argue that this industry should not all go to low-wage countries. In their view, restructuring towards flexible production for fashion-oriented markets makes more sense than trying to find jobs for 15,000 less educated workers, many with limited English skills, in other sectors. Their strategy for competing in less price-sensitive markets includes stricter enforcement of fair labor standards to preclude attempts to compete with developing countries based on wages, and cooperative, government-catalyzed efforts by local industry to provide human resource development, technical assistance, credit, and marketing research for small employers. To coordinate this strategy, a 15-member, business-government-labor Fashion Industry Development Commission has been established, along with a pilot Subcontractor Incubator Project intended to demonstrate that subcontractors can operate competitively without resorting to sweatshop conditions.

That it is possible for a high-wage country to retain a presence even in this, the most labor-intensive of all industries, is suggested by the fact that wages and apparel exports in industrialized countries are positively correlated. Higher wage Italian, German, and Japanese garment industries are able to compete by targeting high-quality segments with rapidly changing fashions. El Paso itself has retained some jeans and trouser production in large plants that cater to increasingly fashion-oriented and fragmenting mass production markets (e.g., Levi's Dockers line). The general lesson of the El Paso garment situation is clear. Unless the United States masters more flexible, skill-intensive ways to compete, it will lose out to developing countries in low-end markets and to Europe and Japan in high-end markets. Workers, like those in El Paso who have lost their jobs, will pay the highest price.

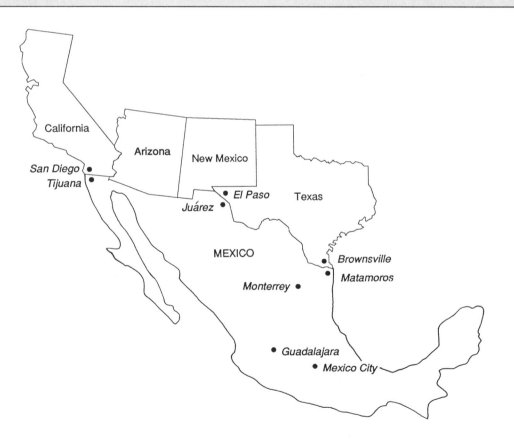

Policy Issues and Options:
Incentives for a High-Productivity Future

Contents

Boxes

Tables

Chapter 2
Policy Issues and Options:
Incentives for a High-Productivity Future

Despite assertions to the contrary, there is no reason to believe that a North American Free Trade Agreement (NAFTA) would automatically benefit the United States (see ch. 1, box 1-B). But OTA's analysis indicates that **a NAFTA, if coupled with other policies designed to strengthen the foundations of each economy, could work to the benefit of both Mexico and the United States.**

This chapter discusses two major groups of policy options designed to stimulate high-productivity development—domestic policies, which would not require bilateral or trilateral negotiations, and continental policies. Table 2-1 summarizes the options in

each group. (The identical table appeared in ch. 1 as table 1-1). Both sets of policy options are based on analysis of what it takes to guide a market economy along a high-productivity path. Studies of dynamic industries and countries suggest that the most important factor is the institutional context in which marketplace competition is embedded (box 2-A). The most productive market economies are not necessarily the least regulated, but those in which institutions—e.g., industry and trade associations, labor unions, corporate structures and policies, legal systems, and informal norms—encourage firms to compete in ways that are economically productive

Table 2-1—Summary List of Policy Options

I. Domestic Policy Options

Issue Area A: Promoting a Productive Economy (for further detail, see table 2-2)

1. Approve a modified version of the High Skills, Competitive Workforce Act of 1990
2. Create a comprehensive worker adjustment program
3. Expand Trade Adjustment Assistance
4. Certify basic skills of new labor force entrants
5. Broaden and deepen links between firms
6. Create a Regional and Community Adjustment Corporation, focusing on direct public job creation

Issue Area B: Curtailing Low-Productivity Strategies (table 2-3)

1. Establish national commitment to social welfare through a U.S. Social Charter
2. Discourage low-wage strategies and reduce income inequality through wage and tax policies
3. Discourage State and local economic development based on "bidding wars" to recruit new industry

Issue Area C: Participation in a Productive Economy (table 2-4)

1. Create a Labor Market Productivity Center to foster consensus-building and expand institutional support for work reorganization
2. Create Employee Participation Committees to provide worker "voice" in nonunion as well as unionized companies
3. Extend union representation to more workers and industry sectors
4. Foster institutions for worker voice in the service sector

II. Continental Policy Options (table 2-5)

1. Negotiate a North American Social Charter and establish a North American Commission for Labor and Social Welfare
2. Establish procedures for continental management of trade and investment in autos and other sectors
3. Create a Binational Commission with stable funding to improve the environment and infrastructure in the border region
4. Provide technical assistance to Mexico for improving worker health and safety
5. Provide loans and aid for balanced economic development in Mexico
6. Establish North American works council to represent employees of companies operating in more than one country
7. Provide trilateral dispute resolution on labor issues
8. Negotiate shorter work time for the continent
9. Establish a Commission on the Future of Democracy in North America

SOURCE: Office of Technology Assessment, 1992.

Box 2-A—Institutions in a Market Economy

The collapse of communism in Central and Eastern Europe and the stagnation of developing country economies with high levels of government intervention underline the virtues of markets in fostering efficiency and decentralizing power. Variations in economic performance among capitalist economies, on the other hand, indicate that deregulated markets do not always translate into the highest performance. German and Japanese institutions differ substantially from each other and from U.S. institutions. These institutions shape corporate decisions and worker behavior.

The right kinds of institutions can help an economy deal with market failure, in particular:

- underinvestments by employers in human resource development and in implementation of new technology (the "software" or "humanware" of work organization as well as the hardware of product and process); and
- the inability of markets alone to ensure cooperation within firms and an appropriate mix of competition and cooperation among firms.

Institutions, Human Resource Development, and Technology Diffusion

Firms in market economies underinvest in human resource development and new technology because they cannot appropriate all the returns from their investments (see Domestic Policy Options, Issue Area A). Companies underinvest in human resource development if workers can be "poached" by "free-riding" competitors. (Human resource development includes not only classroom training but structured on-the-job learning, improvement of interpersonal skills, team-building, and development of the organizational competence and flexibility characteristic of high-performing companies). Companies lose a portion of investments in new technology if the individuals or groups in which technological learning is embodied move to competing firms.

A socially optimal degree of human resource development requires institutions that enable firms to appropriate the full benefits of training and technology investments. Japan and Germany do this quite differently. In Japan, employment security (for some), and the fact that employees cannot easily change jobs in mid-career, mean that firms retain most of their investments in people.[1] In Germany, strong labor unions, a dense network of geographic and sectoral industry associations, and supportive government policies underlie a longstanding system of multifirm apprenticeship and training. Though voluntary, these policies and programs lead most companies to invest heavily in human resources.

A market economy needs other institutions to solve the problem of underinvestment in technological learning. In Japan, employment security and financial linkages among networks of end-product manufacturers and suppliers permit groups of firms to share the benefits of their investments. Industry associations, largely horizontal, perform similar functions in Germany. Both countries rely more than the United States on government to diffuse technical know-how to small- and medium-sized firms.

Institutions, Labor-Management Relations, and Cooperation Among Firms

Two pervasive features of market economies inhibit cooperation between workers and management and between suppliers and their customers. First, the interests of workers and employers often differ, and neither party's separate interests necessarily coincide with the joint interests of both parties or of society as a whole. A similar divergence of interests exists between firms that sell to one another. Second, workers or suppliers may have knowledge that employers or customers cannot readily obtain, but that could benefit both parties—and society—if shared. This may be knowledge about how to improve productivity on the shop floor, how to prevent product failures in the field, or how to design products that will better meet market needs. When interests and information diverge, workers or suppliers may withhold their knowledge—fearing, for example, that divulging it will lead to layoffs or price reductions—and pursue individual goals at the expense of joint and social priorities.

Two kinds of institutions can increase information-sharing and cooperation within market economies (Domestic Options, Issue Areas B and C): voice or participative institutions; and constraints on forms of competition harmful to workers or suppliers. Voice institutions—unions, works councils, regularized consultation between companies and their suppliers—encourage sharing of know-how and a search for "win-win" approaches that produce mutual gain. Constraints on competing at worker or supplier expense—job security, contractual wage

---

[1] *Worker Training: Competing in the New International Economy* (Washington, DC: U.S. Office of Technology Assessment, September 1990).

setting, customs or contracts specifying the distribution of benefits from productivity improvement—help build trust and assure workers and suppliers that sharing knowledge will benefit rather than hurt them.

An Example: Unions and Competition in the Auto Industry

The dynamics of competition in the U.S. auto industry illustrate the synergistic effects of institutions in promoting skill-intensive strategies. By the early 1980s, the Big Three U.S. producers recognized that they needed to fundamentally transform their operations to meet competition from Japanese imports. The United Auto Workers (UAW) accepted the need to moderate wage increases and reorganize production to reduce costs and improve quality (ch. 7). During this ongoing transformation, the presence of a union gave workers a voice in how reorganization would take place and the union contract guaranteed that they would benefit from improvements in competitiveness through greater job security and profit sharing. The automakers and the UAW also negotiated major new human resource development programs to ensure that workers had the problem-solving, technical, and interpersonal skills necessary to implement new production methods. Base wages increased little in real terms, but the union prevented a competitive response based on lower wages. The combination of human resource development, worker voice, and constraints on low-wage strategies contributed to annual increases in labor productivity averaging more than 5 percent in U.S. assembly plants. Real value-added per worker rose at over 10 percent per year from 1984 to 1988.[2]

Among independent parts suppliers, by contrast, unions now represent less than one-third of workers and have little influence on wage setting. As a result, employers were free to try to remain competitive by cutting pay. By 1989, wages in independent parts plants had fallen below the all-manufacturing average and were only 60 percent of Big Three levels—compared to 78 percent in the mid-1970s. Able to lower wages, suppliers had little incentive to invest in skill development and work reorganization. Labor productivity from 1978 to 1988 in independent parts plants rose by only 2.4 percent annually and value-added per worker hour increased less than 1 percent per year.

[2]Productivity figures in this box provided by David Campbell, based on Department of Commerce data.

and socially sustainable. Institutions can do this in three mutually reinforcing ways (corresponding roughly to the three categories of domestic options in table 2-1):

- By creating **incentives for employers and workers to invest in skills and technology**.
- Through **constraints on pursuit of low-wage, low-productivity strategies**. Examples include minimum wages and industry-wide collective bargaining.
- By fostering **worker participation, cooperation among firms, and consultation and consensus-building** between government and the private sector. In the United States, with its tradition of adversarial labor-management relations, promoting worker participation is the greatest challenge, and the one on which OTA's policy options focus.

The three sets of institutional structures reinforce one another. Companies cannot improve their pro-

ductivity and competitiveness without the proper tools. Efforts to promote human resource-intensive strategies will have limited success if firms can easily pursue low-wage strategies. The design and functioning of institutions that enable and encourage firms to pursue dynamic strategies depend on consultation and negotiation among all affected parties. In the United States, the spotlight turned on education and training by Congress, the administration, and the private sector has led to greater awareness of the importance of nonmarket institutions for economic performance. So has the new focus on government as a "catalyst" for private-sector institution building following the deregulatory thrust of recent years.

Business, labor, and government increasingly agree that the United States invests too little in worker training.[1] The reason is the U.S. "institutional deficit"—the absence of mechanisms for multiemployer cooperation, strong unions, and tra-

[1] William B. Johnston and Arnold H. Packer, *Workforce 2000: Work and Workers for the 21st Century* (Indianapolis, IN: The Hudson Institute, June 1987); *Work-Based Learning: Training America's Workers* (Washington, DC: Department of Labor, 1989); *Worker Training: Competing in the New International Economy* (Washington, DC: Office of Technology Assessment, September 1990); *America's Choice: High Skills or Low Wages!* (Rochester, NY: National Center on Education and the Economy, 1990); *Rebuilding America's Workforce: Business Strategies to Close the Competitive Gap* (Homewood, IL: National Alliance of Business, 1992).

ditions of job security that lead to greater investments in skill development and technological competence in countries like Germany and Japan. Both Congress and the Department of Labor (DOL) have been considering measures for reducing the Nation's institutional deficit in skills development. The possible impact of a NAFTA on less-educated U.S. workers underlines the importance of such policies. Rather than government intervening to draw up blueprints for training, or to provide training directly, the institutional perspective suggests that the best role for government is to set conditions under which those who would benefit will take action on their own. OTA's policy options in Issue Area A, table 2-2—and throughout this chapter—focus on ways in which government can stimulate and catalyze change, rather than directly regulate.

Better training by itself would not be enough to push the U.S. economy toward a more dynamic growth path. That would require more fundamental change in government policies and in business strategies and structures. Without effective constraints on wage-based competition and more extensive worker voice institutions (Issue areas B and C, tables 2-3 and 2-4), U.S. firms could respond to competitive pressures by abandoning high-end markets in favor of standardized goods that can be produced by less skilled workers. This would put the United States in direct competition with Mexico and other developing countries in which vast numbers of people are willing to work for a small fraction of U.S. wages. Thus, policies that operate on the demand side of the labor market to change the types of workers that employers seek are a necessary complement to training (the supply side). Without these complementary policies, the United States could find itself moving from a past of jobs without training to a future of training without jobs.

Discussion and debate over competitiveness, jobs, and NAFTA gravitates naturally to manufacturing. Because few service products trade internationally, few service workers compete directly for jobs against workers in other countries. But productivity in the services is just as important for U.S. living standards as productivity in manufacturing—indeed, more so, given that service industries employ over 70 percent of the workforce. Many jobs in the services pay low wages and offer little job security or opportunity for advancement. The only way to create enough high-wage jobs in the United States is to improve productivity in the service sector. Box 2-B suggests some ways in which this might be accomplished.

A word on the scope of OTA's policy alternatives. As table 2-1 suggests, the options analyzed in this chapter range well beyond the usual confines of the NAFTA debate. Some of the policy options discussed in this chapter might be considered in the time frame of a NAFTA vote. Others almost certainly could not. But economic integration between Mexico and the United States will continue regardless of NAFTA. And regardless of the outcomes of the congressional vote, it is possible to pursue a subset of options that lays groundwork for the future. Such a subset might include:

1. principles for guiding domestic and continental policy choices as economic integration proceeds;

2. near-term measures for beginning the construction of a high-wage domestic and continental economy; and

3. study, reporting, and institution-building to sustain debate after the vote, when the spotlight on NAFTA itself has dimmed.

Table 1-2, in chapter 1, included one such subset of policy options.

Regarding the costs of OTA's policy options, there is no avoiding the fact that some would be expensive. At the same time, money for new policies and programs can come from old policies and programs. Many of those old policies and programs have the effect of subsidizing low-wage strategies. They are residues of the mass production era, now past, in which the U.S. economy was more isolated from the rest of the world. Today, Federal funds also go in large amounts to remedial programs for disadvantaged workers that often fail to help them out of the trap of poverty, dead-end jobs, and welfare. Broader and deeper human resource development, coupled with opportunities for good jobs and advancement, should prove less costly over the long run. Finally, many of the ''institution-building'' options would cost very little, because these policies aim to create incentives for private sector action.

Box 2-B—A High-Wage, High-Productivity Service Sector

The service sector includes industries as diverse as retail trade and government, banking and health care, education and temporary help. Large, bureaucratic organizations dominate some service industries. In others, small, specialized firms are the norm. Some service jobs are among the highest paying, most skilled, and most secure in the U.S. economy. Others are classic dead-end jobs.

The examples below suggest two possibilities for improving productivity and quality in service industries. The first resembles the approach common in manufacturing: new technology coupled with human resource development and broader job definitions, so fewer workers can accomplish more and do it better. The second targets workers in unstable jobs in small firms. Such firms have little incentive to invest in human resources because turnover is high. Here, multiemployer institutions could take responsibility for upgrading human resources and for matching workers and job openings as small employers grow, shrink, open, and close.

In both large and small service firms, the transition to high-productivity work organization should be easier than in manufacturing. Although much service work is organized according to "scientific management" principles—low-skill workers in narrowly defined jobs under close supervision (bank tellers, fast food workers)—this approach is not as deeply institutionalized as in manufacturing. More important, many service jobs call on low-level workers to perform varied tasks in direct contact with customers (selecting merchandise, approving credit, offering instruction)—work that is incompatible with scientific management.

Human Resource Development and Broad Job Definitions in Large Organizations

Example 1: Hotel Services—The productivity of German hotel workers is substantially higher than that of their British counterparts.[1] While the difference is partly attributable to the greater use of labor-saving equipment in Germany, it is due mostly to differences in worker training and job definitions. Most German hotel workers have completed an apprenticeship. Apprentices are trained in all major aspects of hotel operation and must pass a uniform nationwide examination. In Britain, hotel workers are less likely to have relevant training. If they have had training, it is less comprehensive than that provided in German apprenticeships. German hotel jobs are also defined more broadly than those in Britain. For example, a hotel receptionist in Germany will make reservations, book guests into rooms, provide advice and information, carry luggage, operate the switchboard, supervise room-cleaning, handle accounts and payments, and in some cases prepare breakfast; in Britain, different employees perform each of these tasks (except in small hotels).

Example 2: Clerical Work—Many U.S. firms have been disappointed with the failure of computer technology to measurably improve the productivity of clerical workers. Careful study in the insurance industry suggests that this is a consequence of traditional forms of work organization that companies have retained even as they invested heavily in computers.[2] Many large insurance companies have created computer software to automate preparation of the standardized policies sold to most of their customers. These software packages require large numbers of low-skilled clerical workers to collect and enter data from customers into the system. The jobs of these clerical workers offer little or no opportunity for skill improvement or on-the-job advancement. These companies have to employ a small number of highly skilled workers to evaluate risk and price specialized insurance policies that cannot be handled by the automated system.

This is not the only way to organize the "production" of insurance. One company employs two kinds of skilled clerical workers—customer service representatives who sell insurance and respond to customer questions and complaints, and claims representatives, who process nonroutine as well as routine claims. Both jobs begin with 5 weeks of classroom training followed by 3 to 6 months of on-the-job training; thereafter, workers may take additional training courses at company expense to qualify for more responsible positions. In 1984, 4 years after instituting this approach, the 2,300 workers in the firm's main office handled a greater volume of business than 5,000 workers at the previous sales peak.

---

[1]A sample of German hotels averaged 4.01 guest-nights per employee, compared to 2.06 in Britain. S.J. Prais, Valerie Jarvis, and Karin Wagner, "Productivity and Vocational Skills in Services in Britain and Germany: Hotels," *National Institute Economic Review*, November 1989, pp. 52-72.

[2]Eileen Appelbaum and Peter Albin, "Computer Rationalization and the Transformation of Work: Lessons from the Insurance Industry," *The Transformation of Work?* Stephen Wood, ed. (London: Unwin Hyman, 1989), pp. 247-265.

(Continued on next page)

Box 2-B—A High-Wage, High-Productivity Service Sector—(Continued)

In the U.S. economy as a whole, many clerical occupations are dead-end jobs. They need not be. Clerical work spans an enormous range of skills, from those of receptionist, to bookkeeping, mastering word processing and spread sheet software, desk-top publishing, and making travel arrangements. The gaps between steps on the office job ladder could be bridged by most employees with a modest amount of structured training and experience. To grasp the potential benefits, imagine what it would be like to routinely call any large organization (a bank, insurance company, department store, or government agency) confident that the person at the other end of the phone would be both competent and courteous.

Unstable Jobs, Small Firms, and Multiemployer Institutions

The contrast between low-wage and high-productivity strategies is unusually stark among small service employers with high turnover. Low-wage employers deskill jobs and use the spot market or temporary help agencies to fill gaps and find replacement workers. The unionized construction industry suggests an alternative. Like many people in the service sector, construction workers have little job security or employer-specific know-how, and move frequently from job to job. Yet this does not prevent unionized construction workers from achieving high productivity, high wages, and a degree of employment security.[3]

Construction trade unions, in cooperation with associations of unionized construction firms, facilitate higher productivity by creating institutions that provide workers with training and promote their mobility across firms. Unionized construction workers must complete multiyear apprenticeships which are administered jointly by unions and employers. While no single employer would be willing to train workers who are so mobile, construction unions negotiate agreements that require all firms that employ workers in a particular trade in a local area to pay for training. In addition, construction trade unions maintain hiring halls that refer workers to available jobs in the local area. Collective bargaining agreements often require employers to contact the union when seeking workers and to give preference to workers referred by the union. Union hiring halls provide workers with a degree of employment security and reduce the cost to employers of locating skilled workers. Finally, construction trade unions negotiate portable employee benefit packages to which all unionized employers in an area contribute.

The apprenticeships, hiring halls, and portable employee benefits found in the unionized construction industry could be models for service industries characterized by small employers and high turnover. Similar arrangements have existed in the past for occupations including waitress.[4] Unions and employer associations, independently or jointly, could also create well-marked pathways for occupational advancement that would encourage workers to improve their capabilities. For example, multiemployer agreements could provide that workers were paid according to their level of knowledge or skill. Among other benefits, this would make it easier for skilled workers to move between small and large service sector firms.

---

[3]Value added per employee has been estimated at 44 to 52 percent higher (undeflated) or 17 to 22 percent higher (deflated) for unionized construction workers compared with their nonunion counterparts. Dale Belman, "Unions, the Quality of Labor Relations, and Firm Performance," *Unions and Economic Competitiveness*, Lawrence Mishel and Paula Voos, eds. (Armonk, NY: M.E. Sharpe, 1992), pp. 41-107.

[4]Dorothy Sue Cobble, "Organizing the Postindustrial Workforce: Lessons from the History of Waitress Unionism," *Industrial and Labor Relations Review*, vol. 44, 1991, p. 419.

DOMESTIC OPTIONS

Issue Area A: Promoting a Productive Economy (table 2-2)

Today, the U.S. labor market adjustment system reflects both a decade of retrenchment and the origins of this system as a way of providing income support for semiskilled workers on temporary layoff. The U.S. Government spends far less than European countries and Canada on adjustment. Most of this money is spent on income maintenance rather than

invested in human resource development (see ch. 5, table 5-3). The United States also has fewer programs than Japan and Europe directed at keeping small firms technologically and organizationally up to date. A productive future for the United States calls for institutions adapted to the 1990s, not the 1930s.

Option 1: Approve a Modified Version of the High Skills, Competitive Workforce Act of 1990

Table 2-2—Issue Area A: Promoting a Productive Economy

Options	Advantages	Disadvantages
1. Approve a modified version of the High Skills, Competitive Workforce Act of 1990 (S. 1790/H.R. 3470).	Encourages training and work reorganization.	Would not immediately compensate workers dislocated by a NAFTA.
1a. Foster certification of occupational skills by establishing uniform standards, as called for in S. 1790/H.R. 3470.	Standardized curricula would improve worker mobility and ensure employers of qualifications.	Standardization could eliminate some currently effective local or firm-specific training programs. Businesses might push for narrow occupational definitions.
1b. Implement a modified version of the levy in S. 1790/H.R. 3470, requiring employers to spend an amount equal to at least 1 percent of payroll on training or else contribute this amount to a trust fund.	Levy generates revenues for workforce development without adding to federal spending. Trained workers need less adjustment assistance if laid off.	May be difficult to identify best uses of training trust funds. Levy-funded training might meet the needs of large and influential employers to the disadvantage of other firms.
1c. Encourage creation of State and local Employment and Training Boards (ETBs) to coordinate training programs and match workers with job vacancies, as called for in S. 1790/H.R. 3470.	ETBs could help employers find qualified workers or train them if necessary. Reduces costs of unemployment insurance and welfare by matching workers to available jobs.	If not carefully managed, might result in cutbacks or elimination of local employment and training programs for the disadvantaged.
2. Establish a comprehensive worker adjustment system by providing quicker response and long-term income support through the Economic Dislocation and Worker Adjustment Assistance program (EDWAA) and enhanced unemployment insurance coverage and benefits.	Provides more displaced workers with services and income cushion during job search. Puts them back to work with better skills.	EDWAA enhancement could cost several billion dollars annually. Job placement could be a bottleneck. Higher UI payroll taxes needed. Some people might take advantage of increased benefits to avoid working.
3. Expand the Trade Adjustment Assistance program (TAA).	Expanded TAA coverage would provide many NAFTA-displaced workers with comprehensive assistance.	Would not cover many workers affected indirectly. Decisions on eligibility would inevitably be somewhat arbitrary.
4. Award nationally recognized "Certificates of Initial Mastery" to encourage young people to improve their basic skills.	Basic skills provide foundation for continuing learning. Certification would encourage employers to provide further training.	Could lead to expensive, bureaucratic testing process without significantly improving school-to-work transition.
5. Broaden and deepen linkages among firms, in both manufacturing and services.	Encourages dynamic industrial networks that can create jobs and help boost productivity and competitiveness.	
5a. Support a national network of business modernization centers, servicing smaller firms.	Would help upgrade basic competence of smaller firms.	Some firms or sectors might "capture" the centers to the disadvantage of others.
5b. Catalyze formation of multi-employer horizontal industrial networks.	Encourages cooperation among firms to their mutual benefit. Helps insulate United States from competition with low-wage countries.	Cooperation may lead to collusion.
6. Create a Regional and Community Adjustment Corporation to respond to temporary dislocations and chronic unemployment through economic redevelopment emphasizing direct job creation.	Provides alternatives to low-skill, low-wage work. Enhances productivity through improvements in infrastructure and public services. Could provide training certification, and stepping stones to good private-sector jobs.	Initial costs high (although partially offset by reduced welfare spending and provision of needed services). Transition to private-sector jobs could be slow.

SOURCE: Office of Technology Assessment, 1992.

Three provisions of this proposed legislation (S. 1790 and H.R. 3470) could raise U.S. human resource investments and productivity growth:

1. certification of occupational skills;
2. requiring all firms with at least 20 employees to spend 1 percent of their payroll on training or pay the equivalent into a State training trust fund; and
3. encouraging creation of State and local Employment and Training Boards (ETBs).

1a: Certify Occupational Skills—Standardized occupational credentials can be an important tool for encouraging industry to define jobs broadly, for providing lower level workers with deeper training, and for making "nonprofessional" occupations more attractive. In Germany, young people who complete a 3- to 4-year apprenticeship and pass a test gain certification in one of some 450 nationally recognized occupations. Curricula and tests are nearly uniform across the country, encouraging small firms to share the costs of training through local business associations. Young people enter apprenticeship programs because they will earn a widely recognized credential. Skill certification helps foster career ladders within and across companies, providing workers with upward mobility and further enhancing commitment. The broad skills and worker motivation that result from its skill certification system give Germany a productive and flexible economy (see the hotel example in box 2-B).[2]

Recognizing the potential benefits of skill certification, the Departments of Education and Labor held a series of regional hearings in April and May of 1992 to explore the establishment of standards. Although an important first step, DOL's Office of Work-Based Learning, which organized these hearings, lacks both statutory authority and a secure funding base. More important, the process begun by the hearings could lead to ad hoc cooperation within particular industries, occupations, or regions rather than a comprehensive national system. This would place limits on geographical and intersectoral mobility and lead to variations in the quality of certifica-

tion. A decentralized process might also leave out workers themselves. Combined with a focus on particular sectors, the result could be definition of narrow, "industry-specific" skills rather than broader occupations that would contribute more to the flexibility of the economy and to worker opportunity. To avoid this danger, S. 1790/H.R. 3470 would create and fund a National Board for Professional and Technical Standards, made up of representatives from business, labor, and government. The board would develop uniform curricula and certification tests.

1b: Training Levy—As written, S. 1790/H.R. 3470, while they call for firms to "train or pay," place no restrictions on the type of training that would qualify. Flying executives to sessions in Hawaii could suffice. Congress may want to modify the bill's language to emphasize training of front-line workers, recognized as a priority in the bill's criteria for distributing funds raised by the levy. Congress could also direct firms that wished to be exempt from the levy to prepare annual "workforce development plans" in conjunction with employee representatives showing, for example, the ways in which training would provide lower level workers, over time, with certifiable skills and internal opportunities for advancement. These plans might be reviewed by State-level Employment and Training Boards, which would distribute funds collected by the levy to qualifying programs.

1c: Employment and Training Boards—Section 601 of S. 1790/H.R. 3470 authorizes $50 million for grants to States to develop coordinated systems for administration of Federal, State, and local employment and training programs. A network of State and local Employment and Training Boards (ETBs) could provide the backbone for such a system. Similar to Canada's recently constituted Labor Force Development Boards, ETBs could be composed of representatives of employers, labor, government, educational institutions, and disadvantaged workers.[3] ETBs could:

---

[2] Studies of matched German and British metalworking, furniture-making, and apparel plants likewise demonstrate that both productivity and product quality are higher because of Germany's training system. *Worker Training*, ibid., p. 88.

[3] This option differs from the administration's "Jobs 2000" proposal, which calls for oversight by currently existing Private Industry Councils (PICs). PICs lack adequate worker representation, reducing pressure to create apprenticeships or other long-term credentialed training that is most important to U.S. productivity growth and worker opportunity. Many PICs lack broad-based business representation as well, leading to domination by a few employers who sometimes use funds as subsidies for "training" carwash attendants or hotel maids. See *Job Training Partnership Act: Inadequate Oversight Leaves Program Vulnerable to Waste, Abuse, and Mismanagement*, GAO/HRD-91-97 (Washington, DC: U.S. General Accounting Office, July 1991).

- Help streamline the array of around 45 Federal education, employment, and training programs that currently spend about $17 billion per year.[4]
- Coordinate the growing number of State training programs aimed at employed workers.
- Help catalyze the creation of training consortia in which firms share the costs and benefits of training.
- With strong linkages to local labor markets, ETBs could—directly and through new industry and occupational training institutions that grew from them—take over the functions of the existing Federal-State Employment Service (ES). At present, the ES is peripheral to the operation of most local labor markets—its offices typically place fewer than 20 percent of job-seekers in permanent jobs, and those jobs pay only half the average wage in the community.
- To complement a role in job placement, ETBs could provide interest and aptitude testing, comprehensive job counseling, and training to unemployed well as to employed workers.

Option 2: Enhance EDWAA and UI—A Comprehensive Displaced Worker System

Option 1 would establish a flexible U.S. training and adjustment system intended to shorten spells of unemployment and increase employer investment in human resource development. It does not directly address the problems of workers who lose their jobs, as a result of trade with Mexico or for other reasons. At present, the United States has three major programs that serve displaced workers. The Economic Dislocation and Worker Adjustment Assistance program (EDWAA), available to all displaced workers, provides occupational counseling, job search assistance, training, and some needs-related income support for workers in training. When possible—for example, upon 60-day advanced notification of plant closing or mass layoff under the 1988 Worker Adjustment and Retraining Notification Act (WARN)—EDWAA provides comprehensive onsite "rapid response" services to workers who are about to be laid off. The second program, Trade Adjustment Assistance (TAA), provides eligible trade-displaced workers with funding for all "reasonable" training expenditures and income support for up to 78 weeks when combined with Unemployment Insurance (UI) benefits. The third program, UI itself, complements TAA and EDWAA by providing some displaced workers with income maintenance. UI only serves about 50 percent of displaced workers (and around 40 percent of all unemployed workers). Many of these people exhaust their benefits before finding a job. For recipients, weekly UI benefits in 1990 averaged $161, 37 percent of previous earnings.[5]

Each of the three major elements of the U.S. worker adjustment system has its limitations. Despite EDWAA's stated goal of "rapid response," administration is highly uneven across States and localities.[6] Some local areas do not enroll workers until 3 to 6 months after layoff.[7] Because EDWAA provides only limited funds for income support, and UI generally runs out at 26 weeks, EDWAA training typically lasts no more than 12 to 16 weeks, often less.[8] While TAA offers longer term training and income support, it covers few workers—only 25,000 in 1991, less than 1 percent of the 2.7 million workers who were unemployed for 6 months or more.[9] A second problem results from the need for certification of eligibility before services can be delivered: while this process has been streamlined

---

[4] This total includes 21 Department of Education programs funded at $11.1 billion (including $4.4 billion in Pell Grants and $3.5 billion in student loans) and 9 DOL programs (primarily under the Job Training Partnership Act) funded at $3.8 billion. *Training Programs: Information on Fiscal Years 1989 and 1990 Appropriations* (Washington, DC: U.S. General Accounting Office, 1989).

[5] William J. Cunningham, AFL-CIO, Statement before the Senate Finance Committee on Unemployment Insurance Problems, Apr. 23, 1991.

[6] *After the Cold War: Living With Lower Defense Spending*, (Washington, DC: Office of Technology Assessment, February 1992), p. 77.

[7] "Study of the Implementation of the Economic Dislocation and Worker Adjustment Assistance Act Phase II Findings," Social Policy Research Associates and Berkeley Planning Associates, May 1992, p. 8. On the importance of rapid service delivery for helping displaced workers find new jobs quickly, see *Technology and Structural Unemployment: Reemploying Displaced Adults (Washington, DC: Office of Technology Assessment, February, 1986)*.

[8] *After the Cold War*, op. cit., footnote 6, p. 85.

[9] Sheldon Friedman, "Terms of Adjustment: It's No Cure for a Bad Trade Pact, But Victimized Workers Need Aid," *Northeast-Midwest Economic Review*, August 1992, p. 8. One reason is that TAA covers only workers who lost their jobs as a direct result of import competition. In the 1988 trade act, Congress extended eligibility to workers in supplier and service firms who were indirectly affected by imports, but no money has been available for benefits. TAA has never covered workers who lose their jobs when plants close and production moves abroad.

somewhat, it still impedes rapid response.[10] The low coverage in the third program, UI, prevents it from compensating for the limits of EDWAA income support.

Initially, the administration took the view that EDWAA was adequate for aiding NAFTA-dislocated workers.[11] In June 1992, however, DOL acknowledged that neither TAA nor EDWAA would be sufficient to deal with NAFTA dislocations, and that a new NAFTA-specific adjustment program might be needed.[12] Then, in August, the president proposed increasing EDWAA funds to provide long-term training and income support for what would be a small fraction of displaced workers (including some of those displaced by NAFTA). A NAFTA-specific adjustment program, in any case, might be ineffective because of slow delivery of services as a result of the time required to certify workers as NAFTA-displaced. On equity grounds, a NAFTA-specific program would be a further example of making services a function of the cause of worker displacement. The many indirect impacts of trade with (and immigration from) Mexico would make defining who was NAFTA-displaced especially tricky. Should suppliers to factories that lose business to imports be covered? What about workers displaced (at least proximately) because investment moves south rather than trade moving north? Or workers who lose jobs because Mexican farmers or manufacturing workers are displaced and then migrate to take jobs in the United States?

Most fundamentally, the impacts of NAFTA displacement will be transmitted quite rapidly through the U.S. labor market as a whole. The U.S. labor market for less educated workers increasingly resembles a spot market in which the impacts of displacement are immediately felt by all similarly skilled workers (because of declining union coverage, the breakdown of internal labor markets, and the falling real minimum wage). As a result, **the basic NAFTA adjustment issue is what an agreement will do to job opportunities for the entire bottom half of the U.S. labor market.** Any improvement in domestic adjustment programs to cope with NAFTA pressures, therefore, should serve all workers. Any such improvement would be more likely to function effectively in combination with other options designed to change the structure of the lower end of the U.S. labor market. Without such complementary changes, even long-term training may yield meager returns.

OTA's review of existing U.S. adjustment programs suggests that a more effective system would combine (and improve on) the rapid response of the EDWAA program while providing long-term income support to workers as in the TAA program. This could be achieved through a combination of the following mechanisms:

- Increase funding for EDWAA (budgeted at $527 million in 1991) so that, in combination with other measures, workers can obtain income support and training funds for longer periods—preferably up to 18 months as in TAA. If EDWAA enrollment tripled and the share of workers receiving long-term training grew to 50 percent as a result of the availability of income support, these changes would cost at most $2.4 billion.[13] This is a small fraction of the over $30 billion cost of displacement to manufacturing workers in the 1983 to 1989 period. (See ch. 4.) It is likely to be a small fraction of the cost of displacement due to NAFTA. Funding for an expanded program could come from general revenues, a payroll tax, or from earmarking tariff revenues. (See Option 3 below.)

- To cushion the impact of displacement and reduce the need for post-UI income maintenance from an expanded EDWAA program, Congress could bolster the UI system in several ways. It could raise average UI benefits to the level recommended by the National Commis-

---

[10] WARN's 60-day plant closing and mass layoff notification provisions have increased the number of workers for whom certification is requested before displacement. In addition, DOL has shortened the time between certification application and determination of eligibility. Still, even workers in large plants that received advanced notice are usually not ruled eligible for TAA until roughly a month after layoff. Personal communication with Walter Corson, Mathematica Inc., August 1992. Training follows still later.

[11] Benét Wilson, "Use Best of TAA, EDWAA to Help Victims of Trade Pact, Officials Say," *Employment and Training Reporter*, Aug. 7, 1991, pp. 983-985.

[12] "Administration Begins Considering Worker Adjustment Program for NAFTA," *Inside U.S. Trade*, June 26, 1992, p. 1.

[13] EDWAA enrolled 187,000 workers in fiscal 1991—roughly 15 percent of all displaced workers. Only about 20 to 30 percent of EDWAA participants enter long-term training. The $2.4 billion estimate assumes that long-term training lasts 18 months on average, with the first 6 months supported by UI and the last 12 months supported by making income maintenance generally available through EDWAA.

sion on Unemployment Insurance—50 percent of lost wages. It could use the total unemployment rate rather than the much lower insured unemployment rate to trigger the extension of benefits beyond the basic 26 weeks. To pay for greater coverage, the Federal Government could raise the wage base used to assess UI taxes—which currently ranges from $7,000 in some States to over $14,000 in a few—and the tax rates themselves. Increasing the money in State unemployment funds would reduce pressure to tighten eligibility and help increase the fraction of workers covered.

- Congress could direct DOL to provide financial incentives for State EDWAA programs that respond rapidly. Disbursement of a portion of available funds, for example, could be made dependent on average time lapse between notice of layoff and provision of key services.

A number of additional changes might further improve a comprehensive displacement system. Since income maintenance at UI levels (even if raised to 50 percent) would often be insufficient to meet workers' needs (e.g., mortgages) and enable them to enter extended training, a loan system could be established that lends workers funds to bring them up to, say, 70 percent of their previous wage (the maximum wage replacement level under the TAA program before 1981). Such loans might also be available for expensive training that is not fully covered by an expanded EDWAA.[14] A well-designed revolving fund might not need new Federal funds if loans were balanced against repayments. TAA could also be amended to provide dislocated workers with health care—the average premium for medical insurance available to workers is $3,200 per year, nearly 40 percent of the average unemployment benefit.[15] As a result, lack of medical insurance often prevents workers from enrolling in long-term training and forces them to take jobs with little opportunity for upward mobility.

The structure of a comprehensive system might differ from the existing EDWAA model by having the ETBs, once set up, replace Private Industry Councils (PICs) in linking EDWAA training and job search programs with local labor market needs and

opportunities. With ETBs helping seed new, multi-employer training programs and serving as labor-market intermediaries, their participation in a comprehensive displacement service would help channel displaced workers in directions that offer real income and career opportunities.

Option 3: Enhance TAA

If Congress does not enact a comprehensive adjustment program, it could, at a minimum, compensate the workers most immediately affected by trade liberalization with Mexico. Unlike the option above, this would not be the kind of systemic change that pushes the United States towards a high-productivity development path. Nor would it protect workers in sectors not directly exposed to trade competition who would be hurt by competition for jobs with those more directly affected.

One way to compensate NAFTA-affected workers would be to bolster the TAA program as a whole. To reduce the time required for certification, to limit the scope for administrative discretion that prevents workers from obtaining benefits, and to increase the number of workers served industrywide and area-wide certification could be considered as a complement to firm- and plant-level certification. Medical insurance could be incorporated within an expanded TAA program (see above). A trust fund financed by existing tariffs would provide one source of funds for expanding TAA. (A new import fee, as called for in the 1988 trade act, could be seen as a trade barrier.) Congress called for the creation of such a trust fund in 1974 as well as 1988, but DOL has not acted on these directives.

Option 4: Certify Basic Skills

To prepare for work in high-productivity firms, new labor market entrants need basic skills in reading, writing, and arithmetic, as well as the ability to work in groups, solve problems, and communicate effectively. The Commission on the Skills of the American Workforce recommended that all 16-year-olds who passed a test on such skills be awarded a "Certificate of Initial Mastery." A nationally recognized credential would help those choosing to enter the labor market after high school and encourage

[14] Early in 1992, President Bush proposed that all workers be provided a credit card providing them training loans. Frank Swoboda, "Bush to Propose Sweeping Changes in Job Training," *Washington Post*, Jan. 17, 1992, p. B1. Loan repayments could be based on future earnings, much like the pilot program in the recently enacted Higher Education Act (S. 1150).

[15] Sheldon Friedman, "Terms of Adjustment," op cit., footnote 9

their employers to provide further training, knowing it would build on a good foundation.

Option 5: Promote Business Modernization Among Small and Medium-Sized Manufacturers and Service Firms

The active labor market policies discussed above focus on workers. To achieve the productivity levels necessary to maintain its living standards, the United States also needs to promote the dynamism of its employers. Such efforts should focus on small and medium-sized enterprises (SMEs), which have fewer resources than large firms and less experience to draw on. Because small companies are less likely to move production abroad, the United States is likely to capture the benefits of support provided to them. Furthermore, SMEs as a class and the service sector as a whole have become a drag on U.S. productivity growth and the competitiveness of large U.S. firms.[16] Because low-wage countries, including Mexico, often have limited technological and human resource endowments—and low productivity beyond the plants of large multinationals—high-performing small firms could pay a pivotal role in slowing the flight of investment and jobs out of the United States. At present, operating as isolated establishments, using outdated technology and organizational practices, they often fail to play this role.

Our foreign competitors foster dynamic small and medium-sized manufacturers in two complementary ways. The first is through industrial extension services that provide firms with assistance on basic organizational and technological matters. Japan, for example, supports a national system of 185 technology extension centers that provide R&D services and technical assistance, testing, training, and advice to manufacturing companies with up to 300 employees.[17] Denmark has established business and government-funded technology service centers in each of its counties. The second approach involves employer-led cooperation to create either of two types of industrial networks. Vertical networks bring suppliers that sell to large companies into associations that facilitate cooperation among their members (e.g., Japanese *keiretsu*). Horizontal networks of mutually dependent small firms pool resources to share overhead costs (e.g., on marketing overseas) and subcontract to each other to fill orders beyond the capacity of individual firms. In northern Italy, for example, networks of cooperating small firms employ advanced technologies and highly skilled workers to produce a wide variety of high quality goods matched to customer needs.[18] In Denmark, the government spent $25 million—equivalent to about $1 billion if scaled to the size of the U.S. economy—to seed the development of industrial networks.[19] By 1991, in a program started 2 years earlier, one in four Danish firms had links to at least one network.

In the context of international competition, declining manufacturing employment, and successful experiences in other countries, the United States has, over the past decade, expanded its efforts to assist small manufacturers. By 1991, 23 States had established industrial extension programs. Five States now share the cost of Manufacturing Technology Centers (MTCs) with the Commerce Department.[20] After installing automated equipment developed in conjunction with the Great Lakes Manufacturing Technology Center (MTC), co-funded by the State of Ohio, an innercity Cleveland plant making connectors for car radio antennas increased its market share and maintained its employment levels. The company had originally planned to relocate this work to Mexico in order to meet demands by General Motors for lower costs.

---

[16] Since the early 1970s, value added per employee in plants with fewer than 500 employees has been growing at only two-thirds the rate in larger plants. Louis G. Tornatzky and Daniel Luria, "Technology Policies and Programmes in Manufacturing: Toward Coherence and Impact," *International Journal of Technology Management*, special issue on strengthening corporate and national competitiveness through technology, vol. 7, 1992, pp. 141-157. Low productivity in producer services, health care, and education also hurts the competitiveness of U.S. manufacturers.

[17] *Competing Economies: America, Europe, and the Pacific Rim* (Washington, DC: Office of Technology Assessment, October 1991), p. 48; Philip Shapira, "Lessons from Japan: Helping Small Manufacturers," *Issues in Science and Technology*, spring 1992, pp. 66-72.

[18] Michael J. Piore and Charles Sabel, *The Second Industrial Divide* (New York, NY: Basic Books, 1984). For more examples and an analytical comparison of horizontal and vertical networks see Michael Best, *The New Competition: Institutions of Industrial Restructuring* (Cambridge, MA: Harvard University Press, 1990).

[19] Stuart A. Rosenfeld, *Technology Innovation and Rural Development: Lessons from Italy and Denmark* (Washington, DC: Aspen Institute for Humanistic Studies, December 1990); personal communication with Niels Nielsen, Danish Technological Institute, Dec. 5, 1991.

[20] See *Competing Economies* op cit., footnote 17, pp. 47-48, where a similar option is discussed in more detail. Centers could, for example, help small companies acquire new technology through leasing of capital equipment. On links between technical assistance and human resource practices, see *Worker Training*, op. cit., footnote 1, pp. 60-64.

Despite these and other positive examples, U.S. industrial extension programs remain small in scale and narrow in scope. In 1990, they helped about 3 percent (11,800) of the 350,000 U.S. manufacturers with fewer than 500 employees.[21] In contrast to programs in other countries, industrial extension in the United States has been narrowly defined. Typically, U.S. programs focus on "hardware" technology and business advice while paying little attention to shopfloor organization and work methods. Not much effort has been focused on stimulating cooperation among firms themselves to create dynamic industrial districts.[22] One danger of a NAFTA is that it might weaken efforts to construct dynamic industrial networks in the United States at a critical, embryonic stage by encouraging SMEs to turn their attention to Mexico. To prevent this, and to encourage modernization, a NAFTA could be complemented by two options that build on existing state and Federal efforts.

5a: A Nationwide Network of Business Modernization Centers—To provide basic assistance to all manufacturing and service employers with less than 500 workers, and to insulate current State efforts from recessionary cutbacks, the Federal Government could work with the States to expand existing industrial extension services into a network of, say, 120 centers. To provide services to perhaps 7 percent of the Nation's SMEs annually might cost about $500 million initially.[23] The program could be cost-shared with the States to encourage the local "ownership" needed for success. If the centers proved effective and gained strong support from their constituents, federal funding could be increased by redirecting funds already spent for business assistance—including, possibly, Small Business Development Centers now supported by the Small Business Administration ($55 million per year) that primarily support low-skill, minimum-wage job creation. Other programs that might be consolidated include the DoD Procurement Assistance Centers, Trade Adjustment Assistance Centers, and Economic Development Administration University Centers.

To overcome the existing emphasis on hardware technologies, the centers should provide services including assistance on work organization, training, management, and product/process design and development. Planning for human resource consulting could be coordinated with Employment and Training Boards (ETBs), should those be established (Option 1c).

5b: Catalyze the Formation of Multiemployer Horizontal Industrial Networks. SMEs, especially in dynamic industry segments (e.g., development of computer software) almost always cooperate informally in ways essential to their collective survival. In the U.S. context, the weakness of industry associations and strength of entrepreneurial individualism tend to make alliances to address cooperative concerns unstable (one reason some countries, including Germany and Mexico, require companies to aggregate into industrial chambers). Building on and learning from the experiences of State Governments and MTCs, the Federal Government might seek to help institutionalize employer-led cooperation to create dynamic, high-wage, industrial networks. One way to start would be a pilot program of perhaps $100 million to support overhead sharing by SMEs on cooperative efforts to develop and diffuse organizational and human resource knowledge. Networks could be cost-shared with States and participating employers. The Federal and State contribution could diminish over time—successful networks, in which firms come to recognize the mutual benefits of their investments, should be self-sustaining. Lessons from a successful pilot program could be used to define ways for business and government to transform existing industry associations from lobbying organizations into institutions that promote continuous industrial upgrading among smaller firms.

Option 6: Create a Regional and Community Adjustment Corporation

To reduce pressures that may lead depressed regions to accept any and all job-creating investments, Congress could create a quasi-public Regional and Community Adjustment Corporation.

---

[21] Shapira, "Lessons from Japan," op. cit., footnote 17.

[22] One exception is in Oregon, where the State Government helped create a consortium of wood products firms. *After the Cold War*, op. cit., footnote 6, pp. 183-184. For more examples, see Gregg A. Lichtenstein, "A Catalogue of U.S. Manufacturing Networks," Gaithersburg, MD, Department of Commerce, National Institute of Standards and Technology, Apr. 20, 1992.

[23] OTA earlier estimated the costs of serving 7 percent of manufacturing SMEs at $120 to $480 million annually. *Competing Economies*, op. cit., footnote 17, p. 48.

The Corporation would direct funds to poorer communities and regions, including those affected by a NAFTA. To limit pork-barrel projects, funding could be allocated based on objective factors such as per-capita income, unemployment, and economic growth rates. With oversight by a board representing business, labor, education, and State and local government, the Corporation could help localities formulate and implement comprehensive economic development programs, including direct job creation where necessary.

Public-sector jobs might be designed to rebuild the Nation's deteriorating infrastructure (which has been linked to the slowdown in U.S. productivity growth) and increase quality and productivity in public services (e.g., educational aides in classrooms, freeing teachers to spend more time with students and less on administrative tasks). Public-sector jobs could have a limited duration (say, 2 years) and be linked with reforms to the U.S. training system, so that workers have greater access to structured training, certification, and greater career mobility. If the United States and Mexico agreed to form a binational Commission on Environment and Infrastructure (as suggested below), the Regional and Community Adjustment Corporation could create jobs in construction and environmental cleanup in the border region.

Even in the short run, most of the costs of public-sector job creation would be offset by savings in welfare expenditures. One set of estimates placed the net cost of providing public jobs to all the unemployed (in 1986) willing and able to work at less than $30 billion, *before* accounting for the value created by their labor.[24] In the longer run, direct public job creation should yield other benefits too. It might reduce the social costs of unemployment, including child and spouse abuse, mental and physical illness, and crime. For example, arrest rates among youths participating in federally funded jobs programs in the late 1970s were 50 percent lower during periods of employment, resulting in savings in criminal justice costs, property losses, and per-

sonal injury estimated at more than $1,000 per participant.

Issue Area B: Curtailing Low-Productivity Strategies (table 2-3)

The options just described would encourage and assist workers, employers, and communities to move toward a high-skill, high-productivity growth trajectory. Congress may also want to make pursuit of the low-productivity alternative more difficult, through policy options such as those discussed below.

Option 1: A U.S. Social Charter

As a first step, Congress could declare its intent to curtail low-productivity, low-wage strategies in a U.S. Social Charter. The Charter might include both a list of social goals and a statement of principles on which to base future policymaking. Examples of provisions that might be considered include:

- a restatement of the longstanding U.S. goal of full employment, perhaps defined as the right to a stable job that pays above-poverty wages;
- a statement of the right to training and education throughout working life;
- reaffirmation of workers' rights to organize and bargain collectively; and
- in light of the social tensions arising from the growing gap between rich and poor, reduction of income inequality (higher incomes at the low end of the distribution also create incentives for employers to increase productivity).[25]

An annual report on progress toward achieving the goals of the U.S. Social Charter would provide an occasion for reviewing progress and updating goals.

Option 2: Discourage Low-Wage Strategies Through Wage and Tax Policies

2a: Increase the Minimum Wage—With its April 1991 increase to $4.25 per hour, the minimum wage in the United States rose to an inflation-adjusted level that was 73 percent of the 1968 peak and 80

---

[24] Philip Harvey, *Securing the Right to Employment: Social Welfare Policy and the Unemployed in the United States* (Princeton, NJ: Princeton University Press, 1989), p. 49. Direct expenses for job creation were estimated as $112 billion (net of taxes generated by now-employed workers), with offsetting welfare savings placed at $83.5 billion.

[25] In 1975, the top 20 percent of U.S. households had 7.4 times the income of the bottom 20 percent; in 1990, the ratio was 9.6 to 1 (based on Census Bureau data from September 1991).

Table 2-3—Issue Area B: Curtailing Low-Productivity Strategies

Options	Advantages	Disadvantages
1. A U.S. Social Charter.	Helps map out a high-skill, high-productivity future.	A statement of principles and goals would have little short-term impact.
2. Discourage low-productivity strategies through wage and tax policies.	Increases worker commitment to the job.	Could raise average U.S. labor costs.
2a. Raise the minimum wage and strengthen enforcement of this and other labor standards.	Encourages firms to reorganize production and upgrade their workforces to cover costs. Reduces welfare costs, helps working poor support families.	Some employers might move production to Mexico or other low-wage countries.
2b. Promote sectoral wage setting through collective bargaining and "extension laws."	Reduces low-wage competition within industry sectors.	Wage increases could be greater than warranted by productivity improvements in some companies or plants.
2c. Narrow the difference between earnings of top executives and hourly workers.	Creates personal incentives for managers to raise the pay of lower-level workers.	Creates incentives for executive compensation packages that would skirt the rules.
3. Discourage State and local "bidding wars" to recruit new industry.	A "gentlemen's agreement" among governors and State economic development officials could stop the drain of revenues better used for other purposes.	If one State broke the agreement, others would feel compelled to follow.
3a. Reduce federal funds for community and regional economic development in proportion to incentives provided by States and localities.	Forces cities and States to make explicit choice between federal funds or incentives to attract new businesses.	
3b. Tax businesses on the value of State and local incentives.	Does not require self-discipline by States.	

SOURCE: Office of Technology Assessment, 1992.

percent of the minimum wage in 1978.[26] The falling real value of the minimum wage contributes to the increasing number of employed people living below the poverty line and decreases the attractiveness of work compared to welfare.

One alternative would be to raise the minimum wage over time (say, 3 years) to perhaps 60 percent of the average hourly nonsupervisory wage—this would have been $6.20 in 1991.[27] As a complementary step, it might be desirable to strengthen DOL enforcement of the minimum wage and other fair

labor standards. The number of inspectors responsible for enforcing labor standards—878 as of June 1991—has fallen to lower levels than that at any time since 1980.[28] Detected child labor violations of the Fair Labor Standards Act have been on the rise since 1985.

Deficiencies in the U.S. health care system also encourage U.S. firms to compete through low-wage, low-skill strategies. As discussed in box 2-C, the United States has lost high-wage, high-benefit auto industry jobs to Canada because Canada's health

[26] Calculated using the personal consumption expenditure component of the gross domestic product deflator from *Economic Report of the President* (Washington DC: U.S. Government Printing Office, 1992), p. 302. Using the Consumer Price Index as the deflator, the 1991 minimum was 68 percent of the 1968 level and 77 percent of the 1978 level.

Some economists have argued that raising the minimum wage causes employers to lay off less skilled workers, but higher wages also stimulate consumption. Recent studies provide no evidence that the 90-cent minimum wage increase between April 1990 and April 1991 led to layoffs. Lawrence F. Katz and Alan B. Krueger, "The Effect of the Minimum Wage on the Fast Food Industry," Working Paper No. 3997, National Bureau of Economic Research, Cambridge, MA, February 1992; David Card, "Using Regional Variation in Wages to Measure the Effects of the Federal Minimum Wage," Working Paper No. 4058, National Bureau of Economic Research, Cambridge, MA, April 1992.

[27] In 1991, the minimum wage stood at 40 percent of average manufacturing wages, excluding overtime, compared with 56 percent in 1968. Based on hourly wages reported in *Employment and Earnings*, January 1992.

[28] "Labor's Child Labor Enforcement Efforts: Developments After Operation Childwatch, Statement of Sarah F. Jagger, Director for Operations, Human Resources Division [U.S. General Accounting Office], Before the Subcommittee on Employment and Housing, Committee on Government Operations, House of Representatives, Redwood City, CA, Aug. 7, 1991," GAO/T-HRD-91-44, pp. 8-9.

Box 2-C—Health Care Costs

Decades of Federal support for biomedical research have given the United States unmatched health care technology, but at prices that have caused growing concern. The Nation now spends 11.2 percent of its gross national product (GNP) on health care, more than any other country. Canada spends 8.6 percent of GNP on health care; Germany, 8.2 percent; Japan, 6.8 percent; and Mexico, 1.7 percent. Spending the most has not given the United States the best health, at least as measured by such indicators as life expectancy at birth (where the United States ties with Israel for fifteenth place), mortality rate (eleventh, tied with Australia), or infant mortality (tied with several nations for thirteenth place).[1]

High health-care costs affect U.S. competitiveness in several ways. First, they increase the cost of U.S. products relative to those made in other countries. As pointed out in chapter 7, health care costs for U.S. automakers exceed those in Germany and Japan by two to three times, adding several hundred dollars to the cost of a car made here. Within the United States, the health care system reduces the cost competitiveness of the Big Three U.S. automakers relative to "transplants" because the latter can hire a young workforce and be assured of substantially lower health insurance costs. Finally, the current system favors low-wage, low-benefit jobs within the United States, and movement of high wage jobs outside the country, as illustrated by shifts in production within the integrated U.S. and Canadian auto industry. Since 1980, Canada has increased its share of high-wage auto assembly jobs to 16 percent of total U.S. and Canadian employment, in part because large unionized employers pay substantially less for health care under Canada's comprehensive national health care system. By contrast, in the restructuring following the U.S.-Canada Free Trade Agreement, it appears the United States will gain primarily low-wage auto parts jobs in companies providing limited health care that therefore have little cost disadvantage compared to Canadian parts producers.

---

[1]*Human Development Report 1991* (New York, NY: Oxford University Press, 1991), tables 1, 17, 32, and 38; and *World Resources 1992-1993* (New York, NY: Oxford University Press, 1992), table 16.3, pp. 250-251. Relative standings on these indicators probably reflect differential access to care—an issue OTA is examining in the assessment *Does Health Insurance Make A Difference?*, scheduled for publication in the fall of 1992. See also *Canadian Health Insurance: Lessons for the United States* (Washington, DC: U.S. General Accounting Office, June 1991), p. 7.

care system puts less of a burden on manufacturers that provide good benefits. More generally, high-wage, high-productivity employers subsidize low-wage U.S. firms because many people holding low-wage jobs rely on health care benefits available to other family members. As it considers proposals for health care reform, Congress may want to consider approaches that would deter employers from competing by providing few or no health benefits.

2b: Promote Sectoral Wage Setting—As discussed in chapter 4, few institutions in the United States limit interfirm wage competition, which can push an entire industry toward low-wage strategies. There are two general approaches to industry wage setting:

1. collective bargaining on a sectoral basis between employer associations and committees of union representatives, as in Germany; and

2. "extension laws" that apply the basic terms of a central agreement negotiated between unions and employers to other firms in a designated industry.

Both approaches leave room for significant flexibility in wage setting. Sectoral agreements, for example, could permit firms to establish pay-for-knowledge ladders, or increase wages if their profits rise.

Congress could encourage sectoral wage-setting by giving the National Labor Relations Board (NLRB) the power to require all unionized firms in an industry to bargain together, either nationally or within a geographical area, perhaps on the basis of a petition from a specified fraction of the relevant employers or unions. Congress could also empower the NLRB to extend the key economic terms of a collective agreement to nonunion employers in the same industry and region, who might otherwise undermine high-wage, high-productivity strategies. As an exploratory option, Congress could begin by directing DOL to identify industry/region combinations in which sectoral wage setting might be tried on a pilot basis (perhaps with Federal funds for industrywide training as an incentive).

2c: Tax Policies to Promote Worker Commitment—Historically, the top marginal tax rate in the United States has been lower than in most other advanced industrial economies. One justification for this has been the ''trickle down'' view—that entrepreneurs create most wealth and that low marginal rates will provide incentives leading to more income for everyone. Industry studies and international comparisons suggest that contemporary wealth creation also has a substantial ''trickle up'' component. That is, efficiency improvements depend on widely diffused skills, worker commitment, and organizational competence. Very high ratios of executive to hourly pay can undermine commitment and cooperation.

Over the past decade, ratios of executive to hourly pay in the United States have risen to unprecedented levels: in 1960, the chief executive officers (CEOs) of the largest 100 U.S. nonfinancial corporations earned 40 times as much before taxes as hourly workers; by 1990, the ratio had risen to 95.[29] Many proposals have been made that would have the effect of narrowing this gap. One approach would build on the precedent of Internal Revenue Service rulings that prevent corporations from deducting ''excessive'' or ''unreasonable'' compensation from taxable revenues. Total compensation above some multiple of the earnings of the lowest paid worker in the corporation would be deemed ''unreasonable,'' and could not be deducted as a business expense. Although companies might find a way around even a carefully crafted law, such measures would nonetheless have a dampening effect, and add the weight of public policy to the negative publicity to which many corporate leaders have already been exposed.

An alternative would be an income tax surcharge on individual earnings that exceed some multiple of the lowest wage in the firm. Such measures would give top executives a personal incentive to raise the wages of their low-level employees. In the context of NAFTA, furthermore, managers would share in any benefits achieved through lower consumer

prices while suffering less risk of displacement than lower level employees. It does not seem unfair to ask them to pay more in taxes. By accompanying an agreement with increases in human resource investments funded through a NAFTA tax surcharge, the United States would lay the basis for trickle-up productivity growth that benefits all citizens.

Option 3: Discourage State and Local ''Bidding Wars'' To Recruit New Industry

During the 1980s, as Federal economic development aid and revenue-sharing dropped, States and cities launched new economic development efforts. Although some—for example, the State industrial extension programs discussed above—provided forward-looking models for Federal policies, the primary focus has been on attracting industry and jobs through tax abatements, subsidies—new roads, industrial parks—and even relaxation of environmental and workplace health and safety standards. Despite periodic flurries of interest in science parks and high-technology development, many State and local programs seem to operate on the premise that any job is a good job.[30]

Often, State and local officials ''bid'' against each other. Companies are more than happy to get what they can from these bidding wars, even though they may have already decided where to put their plant. The bidding drains tax revenues that could be used for productivity-enhancing services such as education. Nor do the expected benefits necessarily arrive. Between 1977 and 1988, for example, when rural southern counties succeeded in attracting new factories based in part on tax incentives, they continued to experience high unemployment and declining real per-capita income. Urban areas in the South, which spent more on education and infrastructure, attracted more and better paying jobs.[31]

As a first step toward ending bidding wars, the Secretary of Commerce could convene a meeting of State economic development directors to try to reach an agreement to stop the practice. If an initial agreement could be reached, it would be in the interests of the States to keep to it, since all would benefit. (Mexico, which sought to make discipline on regional subsidies part of a NAFTA, would

[29] Robert Reich, ''Suite Greed,'' *American Prospect*, winter 1992, pp. 14-16. For more detail, see Graef Crystal, *In Search of Excess* (New York, NY: Norton, 1992). The proposal for excluding ''unreasonable'' compensation from allowable business expenses comes from Reich.

[30] *After the Cold War*, op. cit., footnote 6, pp. 178-184.

[31] Stuart Rosenfeld and Edward Bergman, *Making Connections* (Research Triangle Park, NC: Southern Growth Policies Board, 1989), p. ix.

Table 2-4—Issue Area C: Participation in a Productive Economy

Options	Advantages	Disadvantages
1. Create a private-sector, multi-constituency Labor Market Productivity Center to encourage worker participation, work reorganization, and labor-management cooperation.	Helps build consensus. Could provide technical assistance and trained facilitators for strengthening cooperative labor relations.	Without worker and management commitment, might have little impact.
2. Establish Employee Participation Committees (EPCs) to consult with employers on issues of worker participation and productivity improvement.	Creates voice channels for workers not represented by unions.	Employers might oppose. Workers might not actively participate.
3. Extend union representation.	Expands channels for communication with management and helps assure workers that their interests will be protected if they participate in productivity improvement programs.	Wages and/or job protections won by unions could reduce competitiveness.
3a. Make discharge for union activity subject to damage awards.	Places rights to representation on a par with other employment rights.	Could lead to costly litigation.
3b. "Instant" certification elections.	Reduces scope for confrontational campaign tactics.	Some employers would object.
3c. Permit supervisors to form their own independent unions.	Encourages supervisors to act as middlemen and team builders rather than overseers.	Supervisors might feel cut off from both management and workers.
3d. Foster "network unions" of workers in vertically linked firms.	Discourages suppliers from competing with one another by cutting wages.	Shifting relationships among firms could make it difficult to define network unions.
	Promotes cooperation among workers in companies that do business with one another.	Use of "secondary pressure" could be a blunt instrument for cementing relationships.
4. Encourage worker voice institutions in small firms and the service sector.	Improves job security for workers and creates mobility ladders, while making it easier for firms to locate qualified workers.	

SOURCE: Office of Technology Assessment, 1992.

presumably welcome such an agreement—and might make concessions elsewhere in exchange.) To reduce the temptation to break the agreement, Congress could consider the following two possibilities.

3a: Reduce Federal Funds for Economic Development in Proportion to Industrial Recruitment Incentives—The Federal Government distributed about $6.4 billion to cities and States for community and regional economic development in 1990.[32] Congress could encourage compliance with an agreement to curb bidding wars by directing the administration to reduce funds from these budget categories in proportion to the dollar value of incentives provided by cities and States to attract new businesses.

3b: Make State and Local Tax Incentives Subject to Federal Taxation—Alternatively, Congress could modify Federal tax law so that tax abatements provided by States and localities to businesses would be treated as part of corporate income for Federal tax purposes.

Issue Area C: Participation in a Productive Economy *(table 2-4)*

In recent years, unions, employers, and government officials in Mexico (and Canada) have begun to debate reform of their labor laws. The United States might benefit from a similar debate. The National Labor Relations Act (NLRA, also known as the Wagner Act), passed in 1935, remains the cornerstone of the U.S. system of worker representation. The Act reflects its times—it was written when the U.S. economy was largely self-contained and only tangentially exposed to international competition, and when large companies pursuing mass production strategies with mostly male workforces dominated U.S. manufacturing. The Wagner Act

---

[32] *After the Cold War*, op. cit., footnote 6, p. 173.

also reflects the adversarial labor relations of that era, in which employers and unions battled long and hard. Today, employers and workers in the United States confront foreign firms that in many cases benefit from labor-management cooperation. Moreover, the service sector of the U.S. economy has grown so that it far surpasses manufacturing, while women have entered the workforce in large numbers. The new economy calls for a new approach, with workers enlisted in the effort to improve productivity in all sectors.

Option 1: Create a Labor Market Productivity Center

To encourage participative forms of work organization and help define consensus on institutional innovations for supporting high-productivity strategies, Congress could consider creating a new Labor Market Productivity Center. The Center—governed by a multiconstituency private sector board, including business and organized labor—would support research, education, and information dissemination.

As chapter 4 points out, the United States lacks national institutions for bipartite or tripartite consultation on labor law and other labor policy issues. Canada established a bipartite (labor-management) Labor Market Productivity Center in the mid-1970s that has proved its value in supporting research and dialogue on restructuring labor relations and labor market institutions. If Congress chose to create such an organization here, it could direct the Center to begin by examining methods for increasing worker participation. Specifically, Congress might direct the Center to develop a proposal for filling the U.S. ''representation gap''—the absence of unions or substitute forms of employee representation in most workplaces—within a year after signing of a NAFTA.

In a related step, Congress could put DOL's Bureau of Labor-Management Relations and Cooperative Programs on a statutory footing and restore its funding. Created by the Secretary of Labor in 1980, and funded at about $5.7 million in fiscal 1991, the Bureau has been zeroed out in DOL's budget request for fiscal 1993.[33] The only part of the Federal Government with the specific mission of promoting labor-management cooperation, the Bureau has an experienced staff with a wide range of contacts among unions and employers. This expertise could be lost at a time when a NAFTA promises to create new tensions between labor and management.[34]

Option 2: Create Employee Participation Committees

Despite a great deal of talk, worker participation programs remain relatively rare in U.S. industry. Some nonunion firms have established them, often as part of efforts to remain nonunion. Firms with strong unions facing intense competition have sometimes established programs as part of efforts to improve productivity and quality, as illustrated by the case of Xerox Corp. (box 2-D). But probably no more than 10 to 15 percent of U.S. firms have made serious commitments to worker participation as part of efforts to adopt flexible, high-productivity work organization.[35]

To encourage more firms to move in this direction, Congress could consider calling for Employee Participation Committees (EPCs) at all firms with more than, say, 25 workers.[36] Unlike labor unions, EPCs would not have the right to bargain collectively, but they would have consultation rights and thus provide workers with a voice on the way firms treat and deploy their employees. In some

---

[33] Unpublished memorandum prepared by the Bureau of Labor-Management Relations and Cooperative Programs.

[34] Although Secretary of Labor Lynn Martin announced (in a speech to the National Labor-Management Conference, Washington, DC, May 27, 1992) that DOL will form a new agency to take the Bureau's place, no action has yet been taken and some staff members have already resigned.

Congress might also consider restoring $1 million in funding for grants by the Federal Mediation and Conciliation Service (FMCS), money that was cut from that agency's fiscal 1992 budget. Although the chief mission of the FMCS is to resolve labor disputes, the grants program has helped diffuse cooperative relationships and encourage productivity programs. See, for example, Margaret Hilton and Ronnie Straw, ''Cooperative Training in Telecommunications: Case Studies,'' *Monthly Labor Review*, May 1987, pp. 32-36.

[35] *Worker Training*, op. cit., footnote 1, ch. 4.

Among small firms, worker involvement programs that succeed in raising productivity seem to be more prevalent in union than in nonunion firms. Adrienne E. Eaton and Paula Voos, ''Unions and Contemporary Innovations in Work Organization, Compensation, and Employee Participation,'' *Unions and Economic Competitiveness*, Lawrence Mishel and Paula Voos, eds. (New York, NY: M.E. Sharpe, 1991).

[36] The term is borrowed from Weiler, who also suggests 25 as a reasonable cut-off for requiring an EPC. See Paul C. Weiler, *Governing the Workplace: The Future of Labor and Employment Law* (Cambridge, MA.: Harvard University Press, 1990), p. 285. The rest of this discussion of EPCs draws heavily from pp. 282-295 of Weiler.

Box 2-D—Unions and Productivity

Many economists argue that labor unions, by raising wages above market-clearing levels, interfere with the efficient allocation of resources. Such an analysis neglects the potential productivity-enhancing effects of unions. Unions may be particularly important today, because the ability of U.S. firms to pay high wages and avoid direct wage competition with countries such as Mexico depends on fundamental changes in the way firms develop and use human resources. Unless companies move away from narrow jobs, hierarchy, and centralized authority, they will find it increasingly difficult to keep production in the United States. Nonunion companies may make only cosmetic changes because managers feel threatened by increases in the skills and authority of hourly workers. If union representatives press employers to define competitive strategies that will provide high pay and job security, meaningful change should be more likely to follow.

The history of cooperation and conflict between Xerox and the Amalgamated Clothing and Textile Workers Union (ACTWU) illustrates the positive role a union can play.[1] At the end of the 1970s, Xerox began to lose market share in photocopiers, dropping from 18.5 percent of U.S. sales in 1979 to 10 percent in 1984. By 1988, Xerox had managed to rebuild its market share to 13.8 percent. ACTWU, which represents 4,500 workers at Xerox's main production facility in Webster, New York, played a central role in the turnaround through its involvement in programs of labor-management cooperation that significantly increased the company's labor productivity.

A quality-of-work-life (QWL) program initiated in 1980 marked the beginning of formal cooperative undertakings between Xerox and the ACTWU. The QWL program put production workers together in teams with supervisors, managers, and engineers. Given its slumping business, Xerox laid off workers during 1980 and 1981. In 1982, the company announced it would subcontract some of the Webster plant's production. Union leaders argued that layoffs and subcontracting would erode the trust that had begun to develop between production workers and managers. By threatening to withdraw union support from the QWL program, they persuaded management to establish a joint labor-management team to explore ways of keeping wiring harness production in-house. The study team's recommendations reduced production costs by 28 percent, avoiding the need for subcontracting. During this

---

[1]See the following publications from the Bureau of Labor-Management Relations and Cooperative Programs, Department of Labor, Washington, DC: *Institutionalizing and Diffusing Innovations in Industrial Relations* (1988); *The Changing Role of Union Leaders* (1988); *The Changing Role of First-Line Supervisors and Middle Managers* (1988). Also, Joel Cutcher-Gershenfeld, "The Impact on Economic Performance of a Transformation in Workplace Relations," *Industrial and Labor Relations Review*, vol. 44, January 1991, pp. 241-260; and H. Garrett DeYoung, "Back from the Brink: Xerox Redefines Its Notion of Quality," *Electronic Business*, Oct. 16, 1989, pp. 18-22.

---

respects, EPCs would resemble the works councils found in Germany and other European countries.

EPC representatives at each workplace could be elected by vote of all employees (excluding top managers). In unionized companies, union representatives could serve as EPC representatives. In a multiestablishment firm, a companywide EPC could be established; in such cases, and in large single plants, worker representatives could be elected on a proportional basis from major occupational groups. EPC members would need time off the job and the financial resources to be effective. To ensure a genuine dialogue on the issues most vital to worker interests, employers would have to give EPCs some business information—e.g., on projected employment levels and investment decisions—and access to upper level managers.

EPCs could share responsibility for the annual workforce development plans discussed above (Issue Area A, Option 1). They might also be given a role in the implementation and enforcement of legislated employment standards (e.g., health and safety, the minimum wage). H.R. 3160, the OSHA reform bill, incorporates some aspects of this option. Section 201 of H.R. 3160 would direct firms with 11 or more full-time employees to establish joint workplace health and safety committees, and specifies the committees' rights to information on health and safety matters. If implemented, H.R. 3160 would be a first step toward filling the U.S. representation gap. It could also help counter pressures for downward harmonization of health and safety standards following from a NAFTA.

Although EPCs would extend and help institutionalize worker voice and participative management, they would not substitute for labor unions. Unlike the committees, which would be purely consultative, unions can pressure employers to reorganize work and pursue high-productivity strategies. In addition, through their political activities, same period, the union persuaded management to build a new toner plant in Webster rather than in a low-wage southern State. Working together on plant design and equipment, union and management representatives achieved lower costs and higher projected productivity than the targets for the southern plant.

In their 1983 contract, Xerox and the ACTWU agreed to establish similar study teams before taking decisions on outsourcing in the future. Four of five study teams subsequently formed were able to find ways of retaining work at the Webster plant. The 1983 contract also included a no-layoff guarantee for all Webster production employees. Both provisions were extended in the 1986 contract.

In 1986, union and management greatly increased the scope of their cooperative efforts. They agreed to implement a gainsharing plan and redesigned the company's program for controlling absenteeism. They also established Business Area Work Groups, composed of production workers, engineers, supervisors, and union officials who meet on a biweekly basis to discuss performance, safety, and other workplace issues, along with "organizational effectiveness networks"—joint union-management groups that act as trainers, facilitators, consultants, and change agents. The ACTWU played an integral role in making Xerox a U.S. model of high-productivity, flexible manufacturing. In 1989, the company won the Federal Government's Malcolm Baldrige National Quality Award.

The union—in this case the United Auto Workers (UAW)—also plays a central role in General Motors' Saturn division, an attempt to "reinvent" a giant corporation. Saturn's strategy centers on three elements: advanced technology, including innovations in production methods; highly experienced workers, carefully selected from GM's ranks; and extensive union involvement in shopfloor decisionmaking (and in some cases beyond the shop floor). The Saturn contract, which differs from other GM contracts, puts all production workers on salary, with a portion of their pay linked to productivity, quality, and profits.[2] UAW representatives participate in performance reviews of managers. Production workers can deal directly with suppliers to solve quality problems. Joint union-management teams attack productivity bottlenecks, including product design features. Customer satisfaction has been extraordinarily high, and Saturn's Tennessee plant has been unable to keep up with demand. Perhaps most important, the UAW's involvement at Saturn illustrates potential for plant-level performance improvement that may prove harder to replicate in Mexico than classic lean production.[3]

---

[2]"Saturn," *Business Week*, Aug. 17, 1992, pp. 86-91.

[3]"The Auto and Electronics Sectors in US-Mexico Trade and Investment," report prepared for OTA under contract No. I3-1815 by Harley Shaiken, May 1992, p. 59.

unions can help shape policies for upgrading the skills, jobs, and earnings of large groups of workers and help make a case for investments in training and labor market adjustment programs on a national level.

Option 3: Extend Union Representation

Unions now represent only 12 percent of the private sector U.S. workforce, compared with about 17 percent a decade ago, limiting their ability to work with management for improving productivity. One reason for union decline has been the scope provided under U.S. law for employer opposition during the period between the filing of a petition for a certification election and the time of the election (ch. 4). By contrast, in most provinces in Canada, if 50 or 55 percent of the workers sign union cards, the union is automatically recognized. In the United States, unions often must generate collective anger against the company to win certification, so that the union-management relationship begins as an adver-

sarial one. Congress could reaffirm the Wagner Act's protection of workers' rights to organize and bargain collectively in a variety of ways.

3a: Make Discharge for Union Activity Subject to Damage Awards—At present, the only remedies available to workers fired for pro-union activity during a certification campaign are reinstatement and back pay. Discharged workers have no right to sue for such damages as the loss of a house or car. Nor can they collect punitive damages. Given the steady broadening of legal rights to sue in cases of wrongful dismissal for employment discrimination, violation of an employee's right to privacy, and so on, the very limited remedies in cases of discharge for union activity seem increasingly anomalous. Existing penalties have not prevented the growing use of discharge to deter workers from forming unions.

3b: Instant Elections—Holding certification elections shortly after unions filed petitions—perhaps within 5 days, as in British Columbia and Nova Scotia—would reaffirm the right to organize. Some employers would object to this proposal on the basis that: 1) it restricted their free speech rights to campaign against the union; and 2) it would deprive workers who opposed union formation of resources that employers might provide to counter those provided by the union to its supporters. On the first issue, Congress would have to decide whether employers should have the central role they now enjoy in workers' decisions to form an independent union. On the second, Congress would have to weigh the possibility that workers will make an uninformed decision to join a union against the evidence that extended campaigns allow time for employer intimidation that can undercut employee rights to organize.

3c: Extend the Protections of the NLRA to Supervisors—The Taft-Hartley amendments explicitly deny the protections of the NLRA to first-line supervisors (e.g., foremen). Employers sought the amendments because they did not want supervisors to have divided loyalties in mass production systems that relied on foremen to discipline the workforce and maintain an uninterrupted flow of output. In participative organizations, the supervisor's role undergoes a dramatic shift. Instead of sergeants on the company's side in an adversarial setting, first-line supervisors are supposed to act as team builders, facilitators for problem-solving, and skills developers. They *should* have divided—or rather dual—loyalties and serve not only as management's voice on the shop floor but as the worker's voice off it. As long as supervisors remain subject to top management authority, however, they can be forced to implement policies that cause workers to withdraw their cooperation. Helping supervisors insulate themselves from higher management through formation of their own, separate bargaining units would encourage the transition to more participative organizational practices.

3d: Foster the Creation of "Network Unions"— Large employers pursuing low-wage strategies often provide a small core of workers with job security and relatively high wages, supplementing them with contingent workers (e.g., temporary employees) and purchasing as much as possible from low-wage suppliers. Treating workers outside the core as a cost instead of a resource undermines their commitment to performance improvement. Moreover, the security and high wages of core workers come, to some

extent, at the cost of greater insecurity and lower wages for others, including workers in supplier firms.

To give employees of small supplier firms more representation and more security, Congress could encourage the formation of "network unions" whose members come from vertically related firms; as tighter relations between companies and their suppliers blur the separation between the two, worker representation might do the same. One way of promoting this would be to legalize contracts that foster unionization of suppliers—e.g., clauses barring outsourcing to suppliers that refuse to stay neutral in union certification campaigns. At present, clauses such as these are illegal because of Taft-Hartley amendments restricting "secondary pressure." Section 8(e) of the Taft-Harley Act, however, permits a union and an employer in the construction industry to agree that the employer will "cease doing business with any other person" (including nonunion contractors). This clause could be extended to other sectors.

Option 4: Create Institutions for Worker "Voice" in the Service Sector

The options above would encourage worker participation in large establishments and in small manufacturing companies through network unions anchored in large core firms. Such policies would work less well in firms without stable supplier relationships and in small, high-turnover service establishments—for example, in retailing. This is a significant limitation: small firms and the service sector have been creating most new jobs, exhibit low productivity growth, and generally pay low wages. Multiestablishment labor market structures could reduce the number of low-wage, dead end jobs in small firms and the service sector, and help increase productivity. As discussed in box 2-B, earlier in the chapter, such structures would increase job security and career opportunities for workers in broadly defined occupations (e.g., clerical workers, waitresses).

One option for moving toward a high-skill, flexible service and small-firm sector would be to create multiestablishment EPCs. This could be done administratively through a tripartite National Board for Professional and Technical Standards, currently under consideration by Congress in S. 1790/H.R. 3470 (Issue Area A, Option 1). The Board could define a set of broad occupations, in some cases overlapping industry jurisdictions (e.g., retail food service workers, custodial workers, clerical workers). The NLRB would then supervise elections to multiemployer occupational EPCs from all establishments in a local area. Alternatively, multiemployer EPCs could be worker-initiated: if a certain fraction (say, 10 percent) of employees within a self-defined industry/occupation group requested the formation of an EPC within their geographical area, the NLRB would supervise an election of committee representatives.

Multiemployer EPCs could encourage multiemployer training in the service sector. They could also establish service sector "hiring halls," which would provide a restaurant or women's clothing store with an accredited and experienced employee. Such labor market intermediaries would help reconcile employment volatility in small firms with job security for workers. Multiemployer EPCs could also be stepping stones to geographically based occupational unions.

CONTINENTAL OPTIONS

As the United States becomes more integrated with the world economy, it has less influence over the incentive structures of firms that employ its citizens and sell in its markets. Thus, in addition to reexamining domestic policies, Congress may wish to consider continental policies to accompany the freer flow of goods and capital within North America under a NAFTA.

Following the logic of the domestic policy options, the continental options discussed below and summarized in table 2-5 serve three functions:

Table 2-5—Continental Policy Options

Options	Advantages	Disadvantages
1. Negotiate a North American Social and Environmental Charter including a statement of principles and a plan for implementing them.	Provides a vehicle for promoting upward harmonization and a new social consensus in North America.	Mexico might oppose.
1a. Create a North American Commission for Labor and Social Welfare with a permanent staff drawn from the three countries.	Furthers the goals of a charter, building on the foundation laid by information exchange under the U.S.-Mexico Memorandum of Understanding on labor issues.	Might be opposed by business. Could be seen as a threat to sovereignty, particularly by the Mexican government.
2. Manage continental trade and investment.	Reduces short-term pressures that can undermine labor-management and interfirm cooperation. Stabilizes an open trade regime through pragmatic resolution of key trade tensions, possibly under GATT auspices.	Capture by special interests could lead to mismanaged trade.
2a. Negotiate a Continental Auto Pact with Japan to restore and maintain balanced trade, or a Global Auto Pact also involving the European Community.	Accelerates transfer of high value-added production to North America and purchases from independent U.S. parts suppliers by transplants.	Could become slippery slope to Fortress North America.
2b. Continental investment policy.	Encourages high-value-added production in North America without shielding North American producers from competition.	
2c. Link trade and worker rights in the apparel industry.	Limits low-wage strategies and encourages rising labor standards in the most labor intensive of all manufacturing industries.	Some developing countries would oppose.
3. Establish a Binational Commission on Border Environment and Infrastructure.	Could provide a vehicle for the United States and Mexico to agree upon funding mechanisms independent of annual budget appropriations, such as a "green tax" on U.S. investment in the region or on goods crossing the border.	Might be viewed as a trade barrier. An income tax surcharge on *maquiladora* profits would probably generate opposition from business interests in both countries.
4. Provide technical assistance to Mexico on workplace health and safety issues.	Starting point for actions to promote upward harmonization. Reduces likelihood of "social dumping."	

(Continued on next page)

Table 2-5—Continental Policy Options—Continued

Options	Advantages	Disadvantages
5. Provide financial assistance for Mexican development through a North American Regional Development Bank and/or North American Structural Funds.	Helps Mexico raise living standards, thus reducing competition with U.S. workers and pressures for emigration.	Could be expensive. Could lead to wasteful pork barrel projects in Mexico.
6. Establish North American works councils in firms with more than 1000 employees and more than 100 employees in each of two NAFTA countries.	Provides mechanism for negotiated resolution of labor tensions among the three countries. Should help lessen government influence over Mexican unions.	Likely to be opposed by the Mexican government and some employers.
7. Trilateral dispute resolution on labor issues.	Improves enforcement of existing labor laws in each country. Helps sustain public scrutiny of labor standards and labor rights.	Could be hard to define mutually acceptable principles and procedures, given likely opposition by one or more governments.
8. Shorter work time.	Helps achieve full employment and would probably raise output per hour. Helps manage workforce contraction in industries where total work hours are already declining. Reduces GDP growth rate needed for full employment.	By reducing output levels, could put North America at a competitive disadvantage. Difficult to enforce in small firms. Could lead to increases in moonlighting by those with more time.
9. Create a Commission on the Future of Political Democracy in North America.	Encourages Mexico's transition to pluralist democracy and greater protection of human rights. Helps focus attention on underrepresented groups. Furthers ties among regional-level political bodies in the three countries.	Could generate opposition in all three countries because of fears of loss of national political authority.

SOURCE: Office of Technology Assessment, 1992.

1. to encourage high-productivity strategies within the United States and Mexico;
2. to discourage low-wage strategies; and
3. to promote worker participation and consultation.

The options would create incentives for Mexico to move beyond a policy of attracting investment through low wages, low labor standards, and lax environmental enforcement.

Option 1: A North American Social and Environmental Charter

In Europe, movement toward EC 92 has been accompanied by negotiation of a European Social Charter, followed by an Action Plan and "directives" designed to implement the charter's principles. In Canada, the recently negotiated draft constitution includes a Social Charter that affirms environmental protection and workers' rights. In the U.S. Congress, H.R. 4883, the North American Environmental, Labor, and Agricultural Standards Act of 1992, proposes that a NAFTA be accompanied by negotiation of a trilateral, enforceable set of threshold protections for workers' rights and environmental quality.

Negotiation of a Social and Environmental Charter by the United States, Mexico, and Canada could be an important step toward a high-productivity path for all three countries. In particular, it could provide a checklist of social and environmental principles against which actual practice in North America could be measured as economic integration proceeds. It might also become a vehicle for further definition of national and North American institutions necessary to implement a high-productivity strategy.

Negotiations and implementation could begin with health and safety standards, later perhaps expanding to include a continental minimum wage scaled to the level of development in each country or subnational region, as well as such provisions as continental works councils and trilateral enforcement of worker rights (Options 6 and 7 below). A charter could acknowledge North-South differences and the implications of these differences for migration and each nation's capacity to protect and enhance the environment and natural resources, while stating that action to protect and improve the environment would benefit all citizens of North America, not just those who live near areas of environmental degradation. Recognition of the right of all people to a long and healthy life, to education and training, and to decent living standards could underpin common North American policies towards refugees, asylum-seekers, and other categories of immigrants. By explicitly establishing the linkage between trade, investment, and social issues, the charter would provide an alternative to previous models for trade negotiations, which ignore or distance trade and investment from their broader social impacts.

The definition and implementation of a Social and Environmental Charter might proceed in three stages: a statement of general principles incorporated into a NAFTA preamble or a parallel agreement signed before the NAFTA vote in Congress; negotiation over a specified time period—perhaps 2 years—of an extended Social and Environmental Charter; and subsequent definition of implementation and enforcement mechanisms. The later stages in the process could take place under the auspices of a North American Commission for Labor and Social Welfare.

1a: A North American Commission for Labor and Social Welfare—The initial fast track debate over labor and environmental standards and their relevance to a NAFTA led the U.S. and Mexican Governments to begin a number of information-sharing activities on environmental and labor matters (box 2-E). One approach to sustaining and deepening the dialogue on labor issues would be to create a North American Commission for Labor and Social Welfare. With a staff composed of civil servants from the three countries, the commission could be given administrative responsibility for trilateral labor immigration policies (including, e.g., several of the options listed below). To give the commission autonomy and perspective, it would need its own budget and a mandate to address issues

---

Box 2-E—The DOL-STPS Memorandum of Understanding

In May 1991, the Mexican Ministry of Labor and Social Welfare (STPS) and the U.S. Department of Labor (DOL) signed a Memorandum of Understanding (MOU).[1] The DOL-STPS memorandum calls for information sharing and other forms of cooperation in areas including: child labor; health and safety; employment statistics; and, since the September 1991 meeting of the U.S.-Mexico Binational Commission, under whose auspices the dialogue takes place, worker rights, labor-management relations, and the informal or ''underground'' economies of both countries. The results to date have included jointly drafted papers comparing health and safety and child labor regulation in the two countries, a conference on health and safety in the steel industry, and a series of papers on the informal sector.

MOU activities and the personal contacts established between the two labor bureaus provide a foundation for future activities. But, while it is impossible to interview officials in the Mexican STPS without recognizing their commitment to social welfare and their sophisticated understanding of labor market and industrial relations issues, MOU information exchange has so far skirted the core questions concerning Mexican labor relations. In particular, MOU activities have not led to any change in the positions taken by the administrations of both countries in the face of criticism of the Mexican labor situation: both governments maintain that Mexico has strong labor laws and both avoid any discussion of the relationship between the Mexican Government and Mexican labor unions. As discussed in chapter 4, the reality of basic labor freedoms in Mexico does not necessarily match the rhetoric. This is a complex issue, and the analysis later in OTA's report does not necessarily indicate that fears of U.S. workers are justified or that Mexican worker rights are weaker in general than U.S. rights. But acknowledging the potential weaknesses in Mexico's system of labor protection—and that of the United States—are necessary first steps in adapting these systems to continental interdependence.

---

[1]The text of the MOU appears in the administration's action plan on labor and environmental issues, ''Response of the Administration to Issues Raised in Connection With the Negotiation of a North American Free Trade Agreement,'' May 1, 1991. Canada and Mexico later signed a similar MOU.

from the perspective of the welfare of workers in all three countries. At a minimum, a NAFTA or parallel agreement might charge the commission with producing an annual report that addresses three issues:

1. the current status of labor rights and standards in each country;
2. major labor market trends; and
3. migration.

The U.S. members of the Commission could be charged with writing a short assessment of the joint annual report, noting any sharp disagreements with their Mexican and Canadian counterparts.

Option 2: Manage Continental Trade and Investment

A NAFTA that made it easier for Asian firms to use Mexico as an export platform for shipping into U.S. markets might be good for Mexico but harmful to the United States. Most of the discussion about how to ensure that NAFTA leads to U.S. and Canadian coproduction with Mexico has been framed in terms of rules of origin—i.e., what level of North American content would be required for goods to move tariff-free among the three countries. Rules of origin will vary by sector, with higher required content levels in sensitive cases, including autos and apparel. But given the low level of most U.S. tariffs, some producers might choose to pay duties rather meet required levels of North American content (even though few of those levels promise to exceed 65 percent).

Rules-of-origin for sensitive sectors could be complemented with a negotiated transition to common external trade policies. In cases where imports from outside North America threaten the long-term viability of U.S., Mexican, or Canadian industries, common external policies could include negotiation of continental managed trade. Together with complementary policies designed to foster restructuring within North America, continental managed trade would provide U.S., Mexican, and Canadian firms and their employees with critical breathing space. In considering this option, Congress would have to weigh the benefits of managing continental trade and investment against the drawbacks. All such policies risk outcomes that are ineffectual or counterproductive because ''managed trade'' could be-

come ''politicized trade,'' driven by special interests rather than what makes economic sense. One result, for instance, could be ''capture'' by multinational firms whose interests diverge from those of their workers and the three countries generally.

2a: A Continental (or Global) Auto Pact—In the near term, the United States, Mexico, and Canada might consider negotiations with Japan (and the EC) on trade in autos and parts. Although U.S., Mexican, and Canadian automobile production is now approaching levels of performance achieved in Japan (ch. 7), the collective North American trade deficit in autos and parts seems unlikely to shrink quickly in the absence of trade management because of commitments by Japanese automakers to their workers and suppliers in Japan. Imports from Japan lead to greater excess capacity in North America, contributing to layoffs, downward pressure on wages and labor standards, and intense supplier competition. These work against long-run strengthening of the U.S. and continental industry.

Following the EC's example, the United States might consider combining a NAFTA with negotiation of a Japan-North America Auto Pact.[37] Such a pact could seek Japanese investment in North America in proportion to sales. This might be accomplished in a variety of ways, including 80 percent ''net local content'' or trade balancing provisions (as proposed by the Canadian Auto Parts Manufacturers Association and the Canadian Auto Workers). Unlike restrictions on imports, such an approach permits compliance through balanced shipments between blocs—e.g., exports from North America to Japan.

The United States, Mexico, and Canada could alternatively or in addition propose a Global Auto Pact between Japan, the EC, and North America, perhaps under the auspices of the General Agreement on Tariffs and Trade (GATT). A global pact would seek to ensure balanced interbloc trade, and stabilize trade and investment rules for the world industry over an extended period.

Within North America, the proposed NAFTA would permit Mexico and Canada to retain a degree of protection for their national markets over transition periods of 8 to 10 years. In this context, the United States might consider seeking reciprocal

---

[37] The EC-Japan auto agreement combines restrictions on imports with local content requirements. *Competing Economies*, op. cit., footnote 17, pp. 205-208.

protections—e.g., local content rules for transplant assemblers—that would help assure independent U.S. parts firms that their sales would not continue to melt away. Such safeguards could help parts suppliers, in particular, construct dynamic industrial networks domestically, rather than simply move to Mexico.

2b: Continental Investment Policy—Since joining GATT, Mexico has been liberalizing its restrictions on trade and investment. With a NAFTA, this process would continue. One result may be accelerated investment in Mexico by Japanese firms. Although these investments might transfer Japanese technology and organizational practices to Mexico, they would also intensify the pressures on established U.S. and Canadian firms (and Mexican firms). If they could, Japanese companies with plants in Mexico would bring in components and capital equipment from Asia rather than the United States or Canada. And a Mexico open to Japanese investment could lead to bidding wars pitting country against country for Japanese plants.

The range of options for regulating direct investment on a continental basis includes:

1. limits on new investment when substantial excess capacity already exists, possibly coupled with incentives for Japanese investment in modernization of *existing* facilities;
2. establishment of continental discipline on subsidies for new investment, aimed at limiting bidding wars (and complementing Option 3 under Issue Area B); and
3. guidelines to ensure that Japanese manufacturers transfer technology-intensive, high value-added production to North America.

Because all three of these alternatives stop short of limits on Japanese market share, they would not directly reduce the competitive pressures on North American producers to improve their own performance.

2c: Link Trade and Worker Rights in the Apparel Industry—For several decades, low-wage competition in the labor intensive garment industry has been indirectly governed by the Multi-Fiber Arrangement (MFA, ch. 9). With liberalization of apparel trade

under the Caribbean Basin Initiative, NAFTA, and possibly GATT itself, apparel production could well gravitate to regions where workers are habitually exploited. Given the mobility and global dispersion of this industry, NAFTA would be too limited an instrument to have much effect. In this light, Congress could instruct the administration to pursue negotiations within the Organization of American States or GATT on trade and worker rights in the apparel industry. Any future liberalization of U.S. import quotas for apparel could be linked to the creation of multilateral institutions for monitoring worker rights in producing countries.

Option 3: Create a Binational Commission on Border Environment and Infrastructure

NAFTA negotiations focused attention on environmental problems along the U.S.-Mexico border, leading to parallel discussions on the environment and the *Integrated Environmental Plan for the Mexican-U.S. Border Area* discussed in chapter 6. The *Plan* is short on funding, vague on enforcement, and lacks deadlines. Estimates of the sums needed to clean up the region run in the billions of dollars, far more than either government has committed. To ensure that environmental issues continue to get high-level attention once the NAFTA debate is over, and that adequate funding for border improvements will be available, Congress could instruct the president to pursue an agreement with Mexico to establish a binational commission to determine needs and priorities and arrange financing. H. Con. Res. 325, for example, calls for a commission that would obtain funding by issuing bonds backed by both governments to be repaid by a mutually agreeable method, perhaps a tax on U.S. investment in Mexico's border area. Other alternatives include debt-for-nature swaps—basically, forgiveness of debt in exchange for a commitment to safeguard or improve the environment.[38]

Option 4: Technical Assistance on Workplace Health and Safety Issues

Mexico has fewer workplace health and safety regulations than the United States, and they tend to be considerably less detailed. In part, the differences reflect Mexico's more collaborative and less sanctions-

---

[38] In a private commercial swap, a nongovernmental group buys commercial bank debt at a discounted rate and returns it to the debtor country, which agrees to dedicate funds to environmental protection. In the public sector equivalent, such as the Enterprise for the Americas Initiative, the U.S. Government forgives debt—e.g., repayment for food sent to a foreign country. See H. Williams III, "Banking on the Future," *Nature Conservancy*, vol. 42, May/June 1992, pp. 24-26.

oriented approach to improving health and safety. In some cases, they also reflect lack of the expertise and resources needed to develop detailed standards and measure levels of workplace exposure. One noncontroversial way for the United States to foster higher health and safety standards in Mexico would be for the Occupational Safety and Health Administration (OSHA) to provide Mexico with technical assistance—for instance, through OSHA's training programs for workplace health and safety personnel.

Option 5: Provide Loans and Aid for Balanced Economic Development in Mexico

Mexico has high levels of unemployment and underemployment, a rapidly growing labor force, and a foreign debt of over $100 billion—a combination suggesting that Mexico might continue trying to attract capital inflows through lax social regulation and low-wage policies.

In the EC, the potential for economic integration to increase income inequality and spur migration from poor economies to wealthier regions precipitated two complementary policies:

1. increases in structural funds that redistribute money to poor or depressed parts of the community; and
2. an effort to implement minimum communitywide labor standards and communitywide labor-management negotiation to foster higher standards in less affluent countries.

The Bush administration has argued that the EC negotiated a wide range of supra-national political and social agreements because it is establishing an economic and political union, which includes free movement of labor. The United States, Canada, and Mexico, on the other hand, are proposing only a narrow trade agreement. But differences in per-capita gross domestic product (GDP) are greater within North America than within the EC. The United States and Canada have per-capita GDPs about 10 times that of Mexico, while the EC's richest 260 million people have incomes about 2.5 times those of its poorest 80 million. In addition, legal and illegal labor flows from Mexico to the United States are higher than emigration from Spain, Greece, and Portugal to the rest of the EC.

A North American Development Bank (NADB), launched with capital contributions from all three countries, could provide loans for infrastructure and social spending in Mexico, including environmental improvement, rural employment creation, labor market, and health and safety programs, that would accelerate upward harmonization of Mexican wages and social standards and permit appreciation of the Mexican peso.[39] A second possibility would be structural funds that distribute aid for similar purposes. In Europe, structural funds provide financial aid to poorer countries that have been asked to accept continent-wide minimum social standards (and gradual introduction of a single currency) that limit their ability to attract investment through low wages and lax environmental regulation.[40]

Congress may want to defer consideration of structural funds, both because of resource constraints in the United States and because Mexico may not be able to absorb and put to effective use substantial additional funds in the short run (and instead might be tempted to use them to maintain the power of the ruling *Partido Revolucionario Institucional*). In the medium term, structural funds would make it easier for Mexico to join in negotiating continental environmental and labor standards, while support for continental structural funds might emerge in the United States if they were understood as a mechanism for ensuring the improvement of standards in Mexico, thus relieving pressure on U.S. workers.

Option 6: Establish North American Works Councils

In light of EC 92, the European Commission has proposed establishing European Works Councils in companies that employ more than 1,000 workers in the community, and more than 100 in two or more member countries. North American Works Councils formed on a similar basis could have two major

---

[39] For one proposal along these lines, see Albert Fishlow, Sherman Robinson, and Raúl Hinojosa-Ojeda, "Proposal for a North American Development Bank and Adjustment Fund," *Business Mexico*, April 1992, pp. 47-50. While their proposal would include no direct aid, they suggest capitalizing the bank in a way that reduces Mexico's debt obligations. This could be done by giving commercial banks that hold Mexican debt NADB shares in exchange for writing off equal amounts of debt valued at the secondary market rate.

[40] Based on past formulas used to allocate structural aid to poorer European countries, Mexico would be receiving roughly $10 billion annually—about 4 percent of its GDP. Instead, Mexico has been paying debt service of roughly $10 billion annually, at the cost of infrastructure and social investments essential to raising its productivity and social standards. The EC has pledged to double the size of its structural funds between 1993 and 1997.

benefits. First, regular meetings between U.S., Canadian, and Mexican workers should be a help to independent union leaders in Mexico seeking to negotiate the consensual modernization of Mexican industrial relations. Second, continental works councils could lay groundwork for the harmonization of Mexican, U.S., and Canadian labor standards, helping allay fears by U.S. and Canadian workers of being undercut by Mexico, while giving Mexican workers confidence that they would share in the benefits of productivity growth. Continental wage rules might also help stabilize bargaining in smaller firms by establishing a target wage increase considered affordable by employers and fair by workers. Over the long term, sectoral wage agreements might evolve in Canada, the United States, northern Mexico, and the Mexico City region, with continental agreements establishing links between wage increases in each region.

Option 7: Trilateral Dispute Resolution on Labor Issues

Critics of Mexican labor relations argue that, despite the laws on the books, weak enforcement and arbitrary government action hold down wages and result in inadequate protection of basic rights and health and safety standards in Mexico. Over time, U.S. workers fear, weak labor protection in Mexico could lead to competitive erosion of U.S. practices. This concern has prompted proposals for bringing enforcement of labor rights and standards under a dispute resolution procedure established by or in parallel with a NAFTA.[41]

The present administrations in both the United States and Mexico oppose incorporating labor rights and standards into a NAFTA or a separate trilateral dispute resolution system, suggesting that this could infringe on national sovereignty. (Even critics of the Mexican Government's worker rights record sometimes state reservations about delegating authority on labor issues to a body that might be dominated by the United States.) Nonetheless, in other areas where the dividing line between domestic and continental issues is grey—e.g., the two major ''capital rights,'' protection for intellectual property and resolution of

investment disputes—issues of sovereignty did not prevent NAFTA negotiations over possible bilateral, trilateral, or third-party dispute resolution.

As a starting point for dispute resolution mechanisms, a panel could be established with at least three recognized authorities on labor relations from each country. The panel could hear cases from several categories of complainants—e.g., those who believe their rights have been violated, those who believe they face unfair competition because of inadequate labor protections in one of the other countries, or groups acting on behalf of either of these parties.[42] In addition, a small ''public defender's'' office could be set up to help those without other resources bring cases before the panel.

At the beginning, a panel might have little or no power to impose fines or other sanctions, but could be charged to review the consistency of labor enforcement with each country's own laws. Over time, a common set of principles—some of them defined by reference to standards of the International Labor Organization (ILO)—might be laid down in a NAFTA preamble, a parallel agreement on labor issues, or a continental social charter. With common principles in place against which cases would be reviewed, panels could then, following the precedent set by ILO committees of experts, issue periodic reports measuring each country's practices against those principles. Over time, dispute panels might take on enforcement powers. They might, for example, be given the authority to deny NAFTA trade preferences to a company or a sector in violation of labor standards. Alternatively, NAFTA signatories could delegate to panels the power to levy punitive or compensatory damages.

Option 8: Shorter Work Time

Reducing the length of the work week and increasing the length of vacations and other forms of leave—e.g., for training—could help increase the total number of North American jobs, reducing unemployment and increasing job security and promotion opportunities. These steps should increase productivity on a per-hour basis, because

---

[41] See, for example, Michael S. Barr, Robert Honeywell, and Scott A. Stofel, ''Labor and Environmental Rights in the Proposed Mexico-United States Free Trade Agreement,'' *Houston Journal of International Law*, vol. 14, fall 1991, pp. 1-84; also Ann Weston with Nona Grandea, ''Social Subsidies and Trade with Developing Countries,'' Working Paper, North-South Institute, Ottawa, Canada, December 1991.

[42] The details of this option are drawn from three sources, Barr, Honeywell, and Stofel, ibid., pp. 79-82; H.R. 4883, the North American Environmental, Labor, and Agricultural Standards Act of 1992; and the operating procedures of the Committees of Experts and Committee on the Freedom of Association of the International Labor Organization.

output generally declines more slowly than hours worked.[43] Training leaves or sabbaticals would contribute to lifelong learning, resulting in a more flexible workforce. Shorter work hours could confer environmental benefits by reducing the rate of economic growth necessary to achieve full employment—particularly desirable in Mexico, with its rapid labor force growth.

In recent years, work hours in the United States and Mexico have been *increasing*—a tendency that a NAFTA could reinforce because employers, workers, and officials in each country would fear a loss of production if they independently cut work time. Continental negotiations leading to sectoral agreements or legislation might solve this problem, and enable each country to shorten work hours without suffering a competitive disadvantage.

Option 9: A Commission on the Future of Political Democracy in North America

OTA's analysis indicates that the most fundamental threat to economic performance and social stability in North America stems from high levels of inequality in Mexico and the United States, and the possibility that neither country will invest adequately in the education and skills of its workers. A NAFTA could increase the danger if it led to further decline of political power among the lower income groups that lost the most ground during the 1980s.

While the future of political democracy in North America is an enormously sensitive issue, it is also an enormously important one. To address it, Congress could ask the administration to negotiate the establishment of a trilateral Commission on the Future of Political Democracy in North America.

Focusing on the long term, the commission could be asked to analyze prospects for enhancing democracy in each country. The commission could also be asked to examine the extent to which continental integration threatens to erode national political authority, as well as prospects for expanding authority at regional and continental levels.

In a high-productivity future, the importance of regional concentrations of production is likely to grow in all three countries. Regional-level associations—for example, groups of States in the United States—could prove critical to nurturing industrial networks. Many such groups—for example, the Northeast-Midwest Institute and the Western Governors' Association—already exist, and have shown interest in possibilities for regionally integrated production. The Western Governors' Association already meets on a regular basis with premiers from Canadian provinces and governors from Mexico's border states. At the same time, dispute resolution, continental managed trade, and other North American institutions that grow out of NAFTA and subsequent negotiations inevitably imply some redistribution from national to trinational authorities—issues that would have to be addressed at some point as economic integration proceeds.

In politics and culture, as in industrial development, economic integration can accentuate the weaknesses of trading partners or their strengths. By self-consciously seeking a North America that combines the commitment to individual liberties of the United States with the emphasis on social justice found in Mexico and Canada, it should be possible to ensure that the strengths, not the weaknesses, will predominate.

---

[43] Juliet Schor, *The Overworked American* (New York, NY: Basic Books, 1992).

Chapter 3

Mexico's Needs:
Growth and Development

Contents

Boxes

Figures

Tables

SUMMARY

This chapter gives a snapshot of Mexico's economy entering the 1990s, highlighting the differences between its export-oriented firms, many of them foreign-owned, and the much larger number of Mexican-owned companies that produce wholly or primarily for domestic consumption. The best companies are world class in productivity and quality; many of the rest have had trouble competing with the imports flooding into Mexico's markets since deregulation and the opening of the economy—fundamental changes in government policies responding to the devastating economic ''crisis'' of the 1980s. The chapter concludes with a brief exploration of possible economic futures for Mexico, all tied to political choices.

The United States is the wealthiest nation the world has ever seen. Mexico, though not one of the poorer countries in the Third World, still is only partially industrialized. During the 1980s, Mexico's inflation averaged more than 70 percent per year, the peso lost 99 percent of its value against the dollar, and real wages dropped by some 40 percent. Low wages and underemployment drove growing numbers of Mexicans across the border into the United States. Today, per-capita income in Mexico is little more than one-tenth of that in the United States.

Despite the vast differences between Mexico and the United States, one part of Latin America, the other with its political heritage and legal traditions rooted in England, their futures are inseparable. Millions of Mexicans have crossed the border to work. Already, the United States is home to the second largest Spanish speaking population in the world. U.S. companies ship parts south to be assembled for sale in the United States. Polluted air and water cross even more easily than people and goods. These links will grow, with or without a North American Free Trade Agreement (NAFTA), as will debate over the possible outcomes of the pact for the people and the economies of the United States and Mexico.

The debate over NAFTA reflects diverging views of Mexico's current industrial capabilities and future economic prospects. At one extreme are those who

believe Mexico will soon be able to produce most manufactured products as well as the United States, and will suck investment south to the detriment of U.S. workers. At the other extreme are those who believe that competition will decimate the bulk of once-protected Mexican industry. The truth is more complicated.

Without too much oversimplification, Mexico's industries and economy can be divided into traditional and modern sectors. The traditional sector includes:

1. Farmers who produce for home consumption and the local market, many of them on small plots of *ejido* land that was formally owned by the state and could not be sold prior to reforms now underway.

2. A very large number of smaller enterprises, employing less than 250 people each and accounting for about half of total employment.

3. An informal sector including many self-employed workers and unregistered micro-enterprises (1-15 employees)—street vendors, garbage pickers who reclaim glass and metals for recycling, and small retailers and manufacturers who avoid dealings with the government.

In recent years, the modern sector has expanded, including:

1. Export-oriented farmers who ship winter fruits and vegetables to the United States.

2. A number of relatively large and sophisticated Mexican firms and industrial groups, the best-known based in Monterrey.

3. Mexican subsidiaries of U.S. and third-country firms, most of them labor-intensive assembly plants registered under Mexican law as export-oriented *maquiladoras*. In addition, companies including Ford, Nissan, and IBM operate non-*maquila* plants producing high-quality goods to world standards for sale in Mexico and for export.

Mexico's economic future will be determined by the evolution of both the traditional and modern sectors. Important factors include:

1. The ability of Mexico to move beyond *maquiladora*-like manufacturing. As Mexico climbs

the ladder of development, it will become attractive as a production site to a broader group of U.S.-based firms—so long as Mexican wages remain low.

2. Mexico's imports from the United States, of both capital goods for its factories and consumer goods for those Mexicans with rising living standards.

3. Mexico's ability to provide jobs for millions of today's unemployed and underemployed, and absorb refugees from agriculture.

4. Rising wages that could dampen emigration to the United States, particularly if accompanied by more equal distribution of the benefits of economic growth.

5. The resolve, financing, and technical ability to curb pollution of air, land, and water on both sides of the border.

For more than 50 years, Mexico sought to guide economic development through trade protection, subsidies, state ownership, and controls on foreign investment. Business agreed to stay out of politics in return for the profits available in a sheltered economy. Labor provided votes for the ruling political party, the *Partido Revolucionario Institucional* (PRI); in turn, government helped PRI-affiliated ''official'' unions gain recognition from employers and gave them a share of PRI political positions. Agricultural workers were promised land.

Prospects for continued recovery from the 1980s economic crisis seem good, but Mexico still lacks many of the ingredients for a vibrant industrial economy. Shortages of skilled workers and experienced managers limit Mexico's ability to absorb and utilize technology from abroad, as do poor transportation and communications. Longstanding accomodations among government, business, and labor shattered during the crisis. The government has opened the economy, but in the process many smaller firms have failed. Declining real wages and the growth of the largely nonunion *maquiladora* sector have diminished the influence of organized labor. The government has abandoned its former policies, but it is not clear what the new policies will be.

Continued *laissez-faire* policies and reliance on low wages to attract investment would suggest a future Mexican economy that looks much like the current *maquiladora* sector. A second future would draw more heavily on Mexico's past history of government guidance and traditional views of social justice to encourage integrated manufacturing networks linking domestic and foreign firms in the name of better jobs for more workers. That might also mean better jobs for U.S. workers because Mexico would become a more attractive market for U.S. goods and services, rather than a haven for low-wage plants supplying the United States.

INDUSTRIALIZATION

Given rapid population growth, Mexico's labor force will double in the next 20 years. The birth rate has come down in recent years, but, as discussed in chapter 6, the Mexican economy will need to create more than a million jobs a year to stay even, and would need to grow even faster to make a dent in unemployment and underemployment. New jobs imply foreign investment, bringing technology, managerial skills, and linkages to the international economy through multinational firms. This is the fundamental reason Mexico's government seeks a NAFTA.

In 1990, Mexico's economy was the 13th largest in the world, slightly smaller than that of India, slightly larger than that of Korea, and about 4 1/2 percent as large as that of the United States.[1] The country's citizens live better than gross domestic product (GDP) figures and rankings suggest (box 3-A). But the averages also mislead. Large differences in quality of life separate rich and poor in Mexico, more so than in most countries, even the United States.

U.S.-Mexico Trade

Mexico trades primarily with the United States, while U.S. trade is spread among many countries. As figure 3-1 shows, Mexico currently supplies 6 percent of U.S. imports of manufactured goods (accounting for two-thirds of all Mexican exports), while taking 9.2 percent of U.S. exports (likewise accounting for about two-thirds of Mexican im-

---

[1] *World Development Report 1992: Development and the Environment* (New York, NY: Oxford University Press, May 1992), pp. 222-223. Because India has about 10 times as many people as Mexico, and Korea about half as many, Mexico's gross domestic product (GDP) per capita was about $2,500 (putting it in the World Bank's upper-middle-income developing country group), compared with $350 in India and $5,400 in Korea. (The rankings by size exclude the former Soviet Union.)

Box 3-A—Measuring Quality of Life

In recent years, the United Nations Development Program (UNDP) has sought to define indicators of socioeconomic development going beyond such measures as gross domestic product (GDP) per capita, life expectancy, infant mortality, education, and nutrition. The aim: to develop measures of personal choice, political freedom, gender equality, income distribution, and environmental quality that can stand alongside the more familiar indicators.[1] Not all have yet been incorporated in the UNDP's quantitative rankings: the Human Development Index (HDI) is composed of life expectancy at birth, average educational level, and purchasing power parity (a measure of GDP per capita weighted by the relative basket of goods the national currency will buy).

HDI values have been compiled for 160 countries. As discussed below, Mexico ranks substan-tially higher on HDI than on income (table 3-1). In contrast, the United States has about the same ranking on both measures.

Table 3-1—Development Indicators

	Rank among 160 countries[a]		GDP rank minus HDI rank
	Rank by GDP	Rank by HDI	
Japan.	3	1	2
United States.	6	7	- 1
Canada.	10	2	8
(West) Germany. . . .	11	14	- 3
Hong Kong.	25	25	0
Singapore.	26	37	-11
South Korea.	44	35	9
Mexico.	65	45	20
Thailand.	88	66	22
Egypt.	104	114	-10
India.	132	123	9
Nigeria.	138	129	9

[a]Based on data for 1988.

KEY: GDP=Gross Domestic Product; HDI=Human Development Index.

SOURCE: *Human Development Report 1991* (New York, NY: Oxford University Press, 1991), pp. 119-121.

Comparing rankings based on GDP per capita to those based on HDI gives a rough indication of how well governments translate economic growth into quality of life. The UNDP's 1991 report notes, for example, that the HDI rank of 26 countries is 20 or more places below their rank as measured by per capita income, suggesting that these countries have the wealth to provide better lives for average citizens. As table 3-1 shows, Mexico ranks 20 places higher in terms of HDI, meaning that when factors such as education and life expectancy are considered, quality of life in Mexico exceeds the level that would be expected based solely on national income. However, adjustments for equity in income distribution, which the UNDP has not yet calculated for the full set of countries, depress Mexico's ranking more than that of the United States; the top quarter of Mexicans have per capita incomes averaging 20 times those in the bottom quarter, compared with a disparity of 10 to 1 here. On the UNDP's recently developed Human Freedom Index, the United States ranks high, while Mexico falls in the medium group.

---

[1]*Human Development Report 1990* and *Human Development Report 1991* (New York, NY: Oxford University Press, 1990 and 1991, respectively).

---

ports). Table 3-2 includes the trade figures for agricultural products and oil and gas, as well as manufacturing. These figures show that United States has had a growing surplus in manufacturing since 1988, but an overall deficit until 1991 because of oil and gas imports. Agricultural trade has been small compared to manufacturing trade, although imports from Mexico have accounted for more than 10 percent of all U.S. agricultural imports in recent years, and U.S. exports to Mexico 5 to 6 percent of all U.S. agricultural exports.

Figures 3-2 and 3-3 plot the constant dollar trends for the sectors covered in more detail later in OTA's report, with table 3-3 showing the actual figures for selected years. Trade in apparel and in motor vehicles and parts is growing substantially faster than total trade in manufactured goods. Increases occur on both the import (figure 3-2) and export (figure 3-3) sides because much of the trade involves exports of parts to Mexico for assembly, followed by shipment back to the United States for final sale.

State-Led Development

Mexico's economy developed slowly before World War II and rapidly thereafter. Starting about 1940, Mexican industry grew behind a thicket of barriers to trade and foreign direct investment (FDI). Mexico sought to be self reliant, building its own industries and growing its own food. GDP grew faster than the population, with per-capita income rising at more

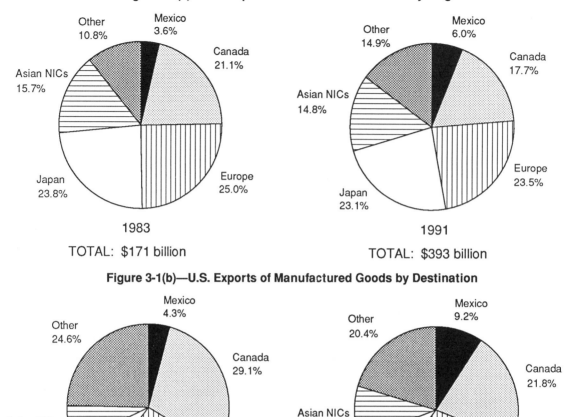

Figure 3-1(a)—U.S. Imports of Manufactured Goods by Origin

1983
TOTAL: $171 billion

1991
TOTAL: $393 billion

Figure 3-1(b)—U.S. Exports of Manufactured Goods by Destination

1983
TOTAL: $149 billion

1991
TOTAL: $345 billion

SOURCE: Office of Technology Assessment, 1992, based on official statistics of the U.S. Department of Commerce.

than 3 percent per year from 1940 to 1980 (about the same as the rate of population growth).[2] Sheltered businesses earned high profits, including foreign-owned companies (e.g., the major U.S. automakers) allowed to remain under grandfather clauses. If industries were inefficient, the government subsidized purchases of consumer goods including food and gasoline.

During the period of import substitution industrialization (ISI, box 3-B), millions of people moved from rural areas to cities, many of them taking jobs in manufacturing; more than 70 percent of Mexico's population now lives in urban areas.[3] As a stable working class emerged in larger cities, self- and family employment declined; the estimated fraction of the economically active population working in the

---

[2] GDP increased at an annual rate of 6 1/2 percent from 1965 to 1980, but from 1980 to 1990 averaged only 1 percent per year. *World Development Report 1992,* ibid., p. 221.

[3] Defined as having more than 2,500 inhabitants. Saul Trejo Reyes, ''Mexican-American Employment Relations: The Mexican Context,'' *U.S.-Mexico Relations: Labor Market Interdependence,* Jorge A. Bustamante, Clark W. Reynolds, and Raúl A. Hinojosa Ojeda, eds. (Stanford, CA: Stanford University Press, 1992), pp. 257-268.

Table 3-2—U.S.-Mexico Trade

	1983	1984	1985	1986	1987	1988	1989	1990	1991	First 4 months (January - April) 1991	1992
	Billions of current dollars										
U.S. imports from Mexico											
Manufacturing...................	$6.7	$8.9	$9.6	$10.8	$13.9	$17.5	$19.4	$21.3	$22.9	$6.7	$8.4
Agriculture......................	0.8	0.9	1.0	1.3	1.0	0.9	1.4	1.5	1.4	0.8	0.6
Oil and gas.....................	8.0	7.0	7.1	3.4	3.6	3.0	4.1	5.0	4.5	1.5	1.2
Other[a]........................	1.2	1.2	1.5	1.9	1.8	1.9	2.3	2.5	2.4	0.8	0.8
Total (all commodities)........	$16.8	$18.0	$19.1	$17.3	$20.3	$23.3	$27.2	$30.2	$31.2	$9.8	$11.0
U.S. exports to Mexico											
Manufacturing...................	$7.2	$10.0	$11.8	$11.3	$13.3	$18.6	$22.5	$26.1	$31.1	$9.0	$12.2
Agriculture......................	1.5	1.5	1.1	0.6	0.7	1.1	1.4	1.3	1.2	0.5	0.7
Oil and gas.....................	0.1	0.2	0.2	0.1	0.1	0.1	0.2	0.2	0.1	0.1	0.1
Other..........................	0.3	0.4	0.5	0.4	0.4	0.8	0.9	0.8	0.9	0.3	0.4
Total (all commodities)........	$9.1	$12.0	$13.6	$12.4	$14.6	$20.6	$25.0	$28.4	$33.3	$9.9	$13.3
Balance[b]											
Manufacturing...................	$0.5	$1.0	$2.2	$0.5	$(0.6)	$1.2	$3.0	$4.8	$8.2	$2.4	$3.8
Agriculture......................	0.7	0.6	0.1	(0.7)	(0.3)	0.2	(0.0)	(0.1)	(0.2)	(0.3)	0.1
Oil and gas.....................	(7.9)	(6.8)	(6.9)	(3.2)	(3.5)	(2.9)	(3.9)	(4.8)	(4.3)	(1.5)	(1.1)
Other..........................	(0.9)	(0.8)	(0.9)	(1.5)	(1.3)	(1.1)	(1.3)	(1.7)	(1.6)	(0.9)	(0.8)
Total (all commodities)........	$(7.7)	$(6.0)	$(5.5)	$(4.9)	$(5.7)	$(2.6)	$(2.2)	$(1.8)	$(2.1)	$ 0.1	$ 2.3

NOTES: Data series used in this table and elsewhere in this report begins in 1983 because trade figures for earlier years are reported by the U.S. Department of Commerce on a different, noncompatible basis. Because Mexico's economic crisis began before 1983, data for the late 1970s, if available, would provide a more informative set of statistics.

Totals may not add because of rounding.

[a]Includes raw mining materials and livestock.
[b]Parentheses denote negative U.S. trade balance (imports from Mexico greater than exports to Mexico).
SOURCE: Office of Technology Assessment, 1992, based on official statistics of the U.S. Department of Commerce.

Table 3-3—U.S.-Mexico Trade in Manufactured Goods

	All manufactures[a]			Autos and parts (SIC 37)			Electrical machinery, equipment, and supplies (SIC 36)			Apparel (SIC 23)			Food (SIC 20)		
	Imp.	Exp.	Bal.	Imp.	Exp.	Bal.	Imp.	Exp.	Bal.	Imp.	Exp.	Bal.	Imp.	Exp.	Bal.
	Billions of 1991 dollars														
1983...	$8.7	$8.5	$(0.1)	$1.0	$1.1	$0.0	$2.3	$1.6	$(0.7)	$0.3	$0.2	$(0.1)	$0.4	$0.4	$0.1
1984...	11.5	11.6	0.2	1.4	1.5	0.1	2.8	2.3	(0.5)	0.4	0.2	(0.2)	0.4	0.5	0.1
1985...	12.5	13.8	1.3	2.2	2.0	(0.2)	3.0	2.3	(0.7)	0.4	0.2	(0.2)	0.5	0.6	0.1
1986...	13.4	13.2	(0.3)	2.2	1.5	(0.7)	3.3	2.4	(0.9)	0.6	0.2	(0.4)	0.6	0.5	(0.1)
1987...	15.7	14.8	(0.9)	3.0	1.8	(1.3)	3.9	2.8	(1.1)	0.7	0.2	(0.5)	0.8	0.4	(0.3)
1988...	18.5	19.6	1.2	3.1	2.2	(0.9)	4.9	4.0	(0.9)	0.8	0.3	(0.5)	0.7	0.8	0.1
1989...	20.1	23.1	3.1	3.1	2.9	(0.2)	5.8	4.7	(1.0)	1.0	0.5	(0.5)	0.8	1.2	0.4
1990...	21.4	26.4	5.0	4.2	4.0	(0.2)	6.2	5.2	(1.1)	1.2	0.5	(0.7)	0.9	1.1	0.2
1991...	22.9	31.1	8.2	4.5	4.3	(0.2)	6.8	5.8	(1.0)	1.5	0.7	(0.8)	0.9	1.6	0.7
First four months:															
1991..	$6.6	$9.0	$2.4	$1.2	$1.0	$(0.2)	$1.9	$1.7	$(0.2)	$0.4	$0.2	$(0.2)	$0.3	$0.5	$0.2
1992..	8.4	12.2	3.8	1.7	1.8	0.1	2.4	2.2	(0.2)	0.6	0.3	(0.3)	0.3	0.6	0.3

NOTE: Parentheses denote negative U.S. trade balance.
[a]Includes SIC (Standard Industrial Classification) categories 20-39.
SOURCE: Office of Technology Assessment, 1992, based on official statistics of the U.S. Department of Commerce.

Figure 3-2—U.S. Imports from Mexico

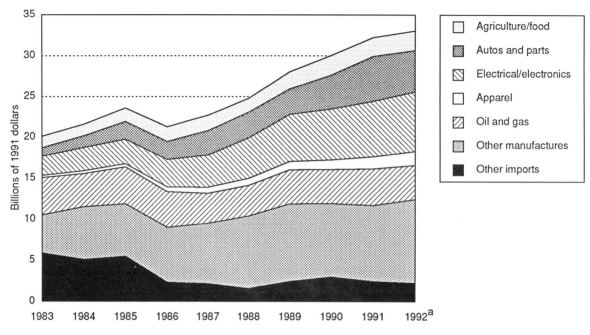

Figure 3-3—U.S. Exports to Mexico

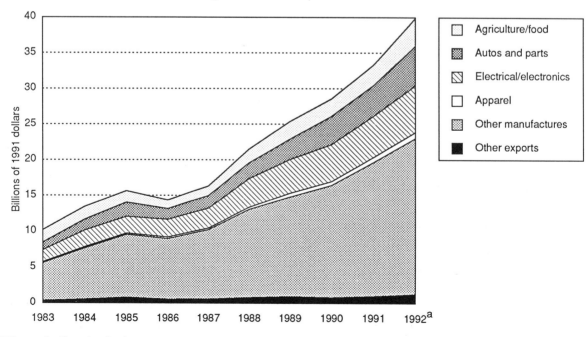

Box 3-B—Mexico's Industrial Policies: Import Substitution and After[1]

Most of Mexico's industrial policies originate in the executive branch; neither legislature nor the courts have much influence. During the period of import substitution industrialization (ISI), Mexico generally provided higher levels of protection to consumer products industries, particularly non-durables, than to capital goods firms. Licenses were required for many imports (indeed for *all*, by 1982). These barriers began to come down after Mexico joined the General Agreement on Tariffs and Trade (GATT) in 1986.

Table 3-4 includes selected examples of policies during the era of ISI and state-led growth lasting through the middle 1980s. Mexico nationalized (''Mexicanized'') many industries during the decades following the 1910-1917 revolution. In others, including automobile production, the government permitted foreign ownership under successive mandates, decrees, and plans. With few exceptions, foreign firms could enter only as minority partners in joint ventures with Mexican investors. Petroleum has been an extreme case, with prohibition of foreign ownership written into Mexico's constitution. Even here, however, downstream petrochemical production has been partially opened to foreign participation in recent years, as Mexico sought to tap foreign capital and know-how.

Table 3-4—Sectoral Policies in Mexico

Autos and parts

Mexico began requiring import licenses for automobiles in 1944. The first auto decree, issued in 1962, prohibited imports as of 1964, forcing companies that wanted to sell in Mexico to assemble locally. Successive decrees modified various requirements, limiting entry by additional firms, requiring high levels of domestic content, controlling prices, and establishing performance requirements—e.g., exporting in proportion to local sales (after 1978). "Official" imports of used cars have been tightly limited to encourage domestic production. Since the mid-1970s, these regulations have led to steadily increasing exports to the United States of autos and parts (mostly engines and wiring harnesses) from the Big Three U.S.-based firms, along with Nissan and Volkswagen. The latest decree, issued in 1989, liberalized the rules substantially (see ch. 7).

Electronics

For many years, Mexico relied on trade barriers to encourage local production of TVs and other consumer products. These barriers began to come down in 1987. Policies toward the computer industry were more complex. The first computer decree, issued unofficially in 1981, sought foreign investment in some segments of the industry (e.g., small computers and peripherals) through a combination of import barriers, investment restrictions, local content requirements, and incentives including tax credits and low-interest loans. Starting in 1985, policies were progressively liberalized (ch. 8).

TelMex, the monopoly telecommunications supplier, used its purchasing power to favor firms with domestic production facilities. Until 1987, TelMex's "Buy Mexico" policy was reinforced by a combination of tariffs and import licensing. At the same time, expansion of the telephone network and conversion to digital equipment created a market for advanced equipment. TelMex itself was sold by the government in 1991 to an international consortium.

Petrochemicals

Pemex, the state-owned oil monopoly, still has the exclusive right to produce "primary" petrochemicals (e.g., ammonia, propylene), but the definition of secondary products (e.g., polypropylene) has been expanded, permitting foreign firms up to 40 percent shares in joint ventures. By the end of 1991, the primary list, reserved for Pemex, had been cut to 19 products, compared with more than 100 in 1986. Wholly foreign owned firms can produce downstream tertiary products (such as antifreeze or molded polypropylene auto parts).

Agriculture and Food

Price supports and controls, production subsidies, and import barriers still apply to many food products, although government subsidies to agriculture (irrigation, low cost diesel fuel, fertilizers and pesticides) have been declining (ch. 10). *CONASUPO (Compañía Nacional de Subsistencias Populares)*, the government's agricultural marketing and food distribution arm, buys wheat and milk in the United States for sale at subsidized prices, purchases domestic production at supported prices, runs food processing plants, and distributes to nearly 2,000 retail food outlets. Despite the decline in subsidies, the costs for supporting production and consumption of corn and tortillas (staple crop of small farmers and staple food for lower income groups) came to about $1 billion in 1991.

SOURCE: Office of Technology Assessment, 1992.

---

[1]''Mexican Industrial Policy,'' report prepared for OTA under contract No. I3-0315 by Thomas H. Kelly, Dec. 28, 1991. Also see, in general, *Review of Trade and Investment Liberalization Measures by Mexico and Prospects for Future United States-Mexico Relations—Phase I: Recent Trade and Investment Reforms Undertaken by Mexico and Implications for the United States*, USITC Publication 2275 (Washington, DC: U.S. International Trade Commission, April 1990).

Table 3-5—Distribution of Mexico's Non-Agricultural Urban Employment

	1940	1960	1980	1989[a]
Higher nonmanual...........................	4.5%	9.4%	13.4%	14.0%
Employers, independent professionals	3.3	1.4	3.5	NA
Managers, technical/professional employees	1.2	8.0	9.9	NA
Lower nonmanual...........................	14.1	20.2	21.6	22.7
Office workers	8.5	12.9	16.7	15.7
Sales workers	5.6	7.3	4.9	7.0
Small entrepreneurs.........................	NA	0.5	4.6	3.7
Self-employed and family workers..............	37.9	20.5	18.6	22.0
Wage workers.............................	32.8	41.9	36.5	32.6
Transport	4.7	4.8	2.5	2.3
Construction	3.3	6.4	8.3	2.6
Industry	19.5	21.6	14.5	16.0
Services (personal, repair)	5.3	9.1	11.2	11.7
Domestics.................................	10.7	7.5	5.3	4.8
	100%	100%	100%	100%

NOTES: Totals may not add because of rounding.

NA = not available.

[a]Based on data from seven cities (Mexico City, Guadalajara, Monterrey, Tijuana, Ciudad Juarez, Nuevo Laredo and Matamoros), roughly comparable to earlier data from national censuses.

SOURCE: Bryan R. Roberts, "The Dynamics of Informal Employment," paper prepared under contract with the U.S. Department of Labor, Bureau of International Labor Affairs, January 1992, p. 19.

informal sector (or "underground economy") fell from 57 percent in 1950 to 40 percent in 1980.[4] During the 1970s, employment grew rapidly in social and producer services (table 3-5), contributing to the growth of a new white-collar middle class— managers and clerical workers, technicians and teachers, nurses and physicians—many in the public sector.[5]

Indigenous and Export-Oriented Industries

Today, Mexico has a relatively small but flourishing group of export-oriented firms, centered on the 2,000 or so *maquiladoras*, plus hundreds of thousands of mostly small firms producing for the domestic market. Monterrey, in northern Mexico, is home to a number of large conglomerates that dominate the country's steel, cement, petrochemical, consumer goods, packaging, and glass industries. But small companies—some 700,000, 85 percent of them tiny microenterprises—dominate Mexico's economy.[6] Leaving aside the "Monterrey Group," most of Mexico's large firms have been foreign owned (auto and computer manufacturers) or state owned (Pemex, TelMex until its recent privatization).

[4] Manuel Castells and Alejandro Portes, "World Underneath: The Origins, Dynamics, and Effects of the Informal Economy," *The Informal Economy: Studies in Advanced and Less Developed Countries*, Alejandro Portes, Manuel Castells, and Lauren A. Benton, eds. (Baltimore, MD: Johns Hopkins University Press, 1989), pp. 11-40. Leopoldo Solis, "Social Impact of the Economic Crisis," *Mexico's Search for a New Development Strategy*, Dwight S. Brothers and Adele E. Wick, eds. (Boulder, CO: Westview, 1990), pp. 43-52, gives a somewhat lower estimate for the size of the informal economy during the 1980s, putting it at about one-third the size of the official economy. In Guadalajara, one recent estimate is that 40 percent of those working in *manufacturing* may be doing so informally (including the self-employed). Bryan R. Roberts, "Employment Structure, Life Cycle, and Life Chances: Formal and Informal Sectors in Guadalajara," Portes et al., eds. *The Informal Economy* (above), pp. 41-59. A forthcoming volume prepared by the U.S. Department of Labor and the Mexican Ministry of Labor will provide an overview of estimates of the size of Mexico's informal sector according to various definitions.

[5] Agustín Escobar Latapi and Bryan R. Roberts,, "Urban Stratification, the Middle Classes, and Economic Change in Mexico," *Social Responses to Mexico's Economic Crisis of the 1980s*, Mercedes Gonzales de la Rocha and Agustín Escobar Latapi, eds. (La Jolla, CA: University of California, Center for U.S.-Mexican Studies, San Diego, 1991).

[6] Jaime Luis Padilla, General Director for Training and Productivity, Ministry of Labor, personal communication, January 1992.

Mexico resembles Taiwan in that large firms account for only a small fraction of total GDP (14.3 percent for the 10 largest firms in Taiwan, 14.7 percent in Mexico). Korea's *chaebol*, in contrast, dominate that country's economy, with the 10 largest accounting for 63.5 percent of GDP. Gary Gereffi, "Big Business and the State," *Manufacturing Miracles: Paths of Industrialization in Latin American and East Asia*, Gary Gereffi and Donald L. Wyman, eds. (Princeton, NJ: Princeton University Press, 1991), pp. 90-109.

The capabilities of Mexico's small-firm sector may not improve rapidly because there are few established channels for diffusing technical knowledge, managerial expertise, best practices, and other skills needed to become more competitive. Trade associations have so far been largely political and lobbying organizations; the government itself has no active technology policy. The multinational corporations (MNCs) that account for 45 percent of Mexico's exports function in isolated enclaves, training their workers but relying on imported materials and components.

Maquiladora Plants: Offshore Assembly in Mexico[7]

A number of large U.S.-based firms have manufactured (or at least assembled) in Mexico for the Mexican market for many years—Ford since 1925, General Motors since 1935. They have developed sales and distribution channels, sometimes buy parts locally, and make minor design changes for the Mexican market. In contrast, *maquiladora* plants operate like the offshore production facilities found in many other developing countries. Production tends to be simple and labor intensive. Workers need few skills, only a willingness to perform routine tasks at what is often an intense pace. Normally, MNCs seek to minimize their investments in such plants, transferring no more technology than necessary and retaining the ability to pull out quickly. Often, they simply contract with a local firm. Mexico has accepted this kind of investment, with the view that bad jobs are better than no jobs.

Mexico's government established the *maquiladora* program in 1965, intending to use the country's low-wage labor and proximity to the United States to build export platforms that create jobs and earn foreign exchange. *Maquila* plants could bring in equipment, raw materials, and semifinished items duty free as long as they were used to fashion products for shipment back to the United States, which in turn levied duties only on the value added in Mexico. (Ch. 9 describes how the tariff system works for apparel.)

At first, *maquiladoras* had to be located within 20 kilometers of the border; although there are several medium-sized Mexican cities along the border (from

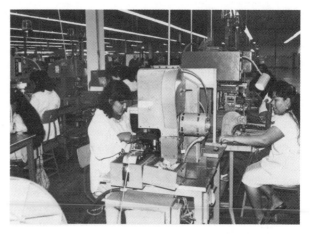

Photo credit: Twin Plant News

Workers crimping connectors in a TRW *maquiladora* in Reynosa.

Tijuana on the west coast, across from San Diego, to Matamoros on the east coast, next to Brownsville, Texas), this part of Mexico was largely undeveloped at the time. Later, restrictions on *maquila* location were relaxed. The *maquila* sector grew rapidly beginning in 1982, as devaluation of the peso depressed Mexican wages relative to U.S. wages. By the end of 1991, 2,000-plus *maquilas*, employing more than 450,000 people, produced more than a third of Mexico's exports of manufactured goods.

While *maquilas* produce for the U.S. market (they can now also sell some of their output within Mexico), they need not be U.S. owned. Mexican entrepreneurs operate many as contract facilities; about 70 are owned and operated by Japanese firms (see box 3-C), a somewhat larger number by European companies. As table 3-7 shows, electronics and auto parts—e.g., assembly of TV sets and automobile wiring harnesses—account for more than half of *maquiladora* employment and valued added.

Because *maquiladoras* serve primarily as branch or satellite plants, they have brought little in the way of technology and skills to Mexico. On average, they buy less than 2 percent of their parts and components from Mexican firms, and even import cardboard boxes for packaging from the United States, claiming that Mexican firms cannot meet quality (e.g.,

---

[7] M. Angeles Villarreal, *Mexico's Maquiladora Industry*, CRS Report 91-706 E (Washington, DC: Congressional Research Service, Sept. 27, 1991); "The Maquiladoras: Present Status, Future Potential," report prepared for OTA under contract No. H3-7040 by Leslie Sklair, December 1991; "NAFTA and the Electronics Industry in Mexico," report prepared for OTA under contract No. H3-7200 by Patricia A. Wilson, February 1992.

Box 3-C—*Japanese Maquiladoras*[1]

Cumulative Japanese direct investment in Mexico stands at about $1.8 billion, far less than U.S. investment ($19 billion) and also far less than Japanese firms have invested in, say, Brazil. The majority of the 100 or so Japanese *maquilas* assemble consumer electronics products, chiefly television sets for shipment to the United States, or else supply parts to these firms. Most of the plants operated by companies including Sanyo, Hitachi, Sony, and Matsushita are in Tijuana, in part for ease of shipping components from Asia and exporting finished products to the United States, but also because Japanese managers much prefer living in San Diego to the alternatives. (Many components for TVs come from newly industrializing countries in Asia, although Japan still supplies some parts and most production equipment.)

In consumer electronics particularly, Japanese investment in Mexico represents a response to U.S. trade policies as much as a search for low-cost assembly labor. When the United States negotiated import quotas in the form of "Orderly Marketing Agreements" (OMAs), first with Japan (in 1977)

Table 3-6—Perceptions by Japanese Managers on Producing in Mexico

Advantages
- Cheap labor
- Transportation cost savings for shipment of finished goods to the United States
- No unions or weak unions (in *maquiladoras*)
- Lack of labor market regulations regarding minorities, gender, age
- No lawyers
- Tax system more lenient than in the United States
- Improving network of Japanese suppliers (in Tijuana)
- Electricity costs one-third those in the United States
- Contribution to North American content
- Special tariff provisions

Disadvantages
- High workforce turnover and absenteeism
- Poor infrastructure
- Fear of possible political instability
- Shortages of managers, engineers, and technicians
- Border crossings time consuming
- High inventory levels needed
- Low educational levels and poor "socialization" of workers
- Hard to recruit Japanese managers to work in Mexico

SOURCE: "Japanese-Owned Maquiladoras in Mexico," report prepared for OTA under contract No. H3-7145 by Martin Kenney and Richard Florida, April 1992, table 9.

and later with South Korea and Taiwan, Japanese and other Asian TV manufacturers not only began shipping from existing plants in countries not covered by the OMAs, but also set up shop in the United States and in some cases Mexico. Sanyo, for example, entered U.S.-based TV production in 1976 by purchasing the private-brand manufacturer Warwick, a major supplier to Sears. At that time Warwick already had a *maquiladora* in Tijuana. A few years later, Zenith—today the only remaining U.S.-owned TV manufacturer—moved much of its production to Mexico and Taiwan. Both Sanyo and Zenith are now in the process of consolidating their North American TV operations in Mexico.

Despite the example of Sanyo, there are few signs that Japanese firms will substantially increase their rate of new investment in Mexico. In interviews, Japanese managers repeatedly stress the difficulties of producing high-quality output in Mexico, pointing to a workforce relatively poorly qualified compared to that in low-wage Asian countries, to the lack of suppliers and poor infrastructure, and to difficulties in communicating in either Spanish (which very few Japanese speak) or English (a second language on both sides). Few companies have tried to introduce a full range of production techniques associated with Japanese practices elsewhere (work groups, quality circles and *kaizen*, job security). Table 3-6 summarizes the views of Japanese firms on manufacturing in Mexico.

To solve the supplier problem, Japanese end-product manufacturers have encouraged their Asian suppliers to establish *maquilas* of their own, but these firms, too, have been reluctant. Japanese managers seem universally unhappy if asked to take posts in Mexico (and increasingly even to go to the United States, which many view as a detour from preferred career paths). At the same time, Japanese multinationals seem less willing than American firms to delegate to Mexican managers.

[1] "Japanese-Owned Maquiladoras in Mexico," report prepared for OTA under contract No. H3-7145 by Martin Kenney and Richard Florida, April 1992.

Table 3-7—Profile of Mexico's *Maquiladora* Sector, 1990

Products	Number of plants	Number of employees
Electronic and electrical equipment and components..................	501	161,000
Auto parts, transportation equipment...	158	100,000
Apparel...........................	289	42,000
Furniture........................	265	25,000
All other........................	707	118,000
	1,920	446,000

SOURCE: "The Maquiladoras: Present Status, Future Potential," report prepared for OTA under contract No H3-7040 by Leslie Sklair, December 1991, table 3, p 57 (based on data compiled by the Mexican Government).

printed graphics) and delivery standards.[8] The steel, insulation, piping, and furnishings in factory buildings—along with the production equipment—comes from abroad.

When the *maquiladoras* began growing rapidly, they drew on a rural labor force, in part comprised of migrants from southern Mexico, with little or no experience of industrial discipline.[9] Even in the mid-1980s, the average *maquiladora* employee had only 3 years of basic education. With further growth, rising wages, and a slow increase in the number of technical jobs, *maquiladoras* have drawn labor from a wider region and levels of education have increased to about the national average of 6-plus years. The proportion of white- and grey-collar workers (e.g., administrators, technicians, quality-control inspectors) in the *maquiladora* sector has increased from about 14 percent in the 1970s to 18 percent today—far lower percentages than common in U.S. industry. High turnover stems from low wages, poor working conditions, and the ease with which workers can get an equivalent job in another *maquila* or cross the border into the the United States. Generally

speaking, *maquila* owners and managers prefer to live with turnover rates that may exceed 20 percent per month rather than move away from the border, with its easy access to the United States.[10]

Maquila-like production will not solve Mexico's employment problems. Despite the labor intensive nature of their operations, *maquiladoras* created only about half a million new jobs during the 1980s, a period in which Mexico's labor force grew by a million people each year.

Agriculture

About 26 percent of Mexico's labor force remains in agriculture. Considering that agricultural output has fallen from 14 percent of GDP in 1965 to about 9 percent today, this high percentage indicates the low productivity of Mexican agriculture.[11] A long-standing policy of granting usage rights to small plots of land called *ejidos*, to which the state retained ownership, has helped preserve a fragmented and inefficient system. Through trade protection and price supports, the government sought to keep *ejidatarios*, small farmers, and agricultural laborers on the land. At least 2 million peasant farmers continue to grow corn and beans—staple foods before the Spanish arrived. More than two-thirds cannot produce enough for their own families.[12] Today, Mexico cannot feed itself; food imports tripled during the 1980s.

The changes to the *ejido* system will remove one of the government's principal sources of social control; the promise of expanded *ejido* lands (e.g., through expropriation of large private holdings) has for many years served to dampen unrest among the rural poor. By withdrawing its longstanding promise of land, the government will satisfy those who gain title to their *ejidos*, while leaving those still waiting—perhaps 2 1/2 million—with few prospects except to

---

[8] The primary exceptions are the petrochemical and food processing (or *agro-maquila*) sectors, both of which source more of their inputs in Mexico. See Jaime Zabludovsky, "Trade Liberalization and Macroeconomic Adjustment," *Mexico's Search for a New Development Strategy*, Dwight S. Brothers and Adele E. Wick, eds. (Boulder, CO: Westview, 1990), table 3, p. 196.

[9] This paragraph draws on Jorge Carillo, "*Mercados de Trabajo en la Industria Maquiladora de Exportación*" [Labor Markets in the Assembly Plant Exporting Industry], unpublished report, *El Colegio de la Frontera Norte*, Tijuana, 1991.

[10] A recent survey found little indication of plans to move to the interior in the event of a NAFTA. Jan Gilbreath Rich and David Hurlbut, *Free Trade With Mexico: What's In It For Texas?*, U.S.-Mexico Policy Report No. 1 (Austin, TX: University of Texas, Lyndon B. Johnson School of Public Affairs, 1992), pp. 40, 41. For exceptions to this pattern, see ch. 9 on apparel.

[11] *World Development Report 1992*, op. cit., footnote 1, p. 223; *Foreign Agriculture 1990-91* (Washington, DC: Department of Agriculture, Foreign Agricultural Service, August 1991), p. 82.

[12] Santiago Levy and Sweder van Wijnbergen, "Transition Problems in Economic Reform: Agriculture in the Mexico-US Free Trade Agreement," *Economy-Wide Modeling of the Economic Implications of a FTA with Mexico and a NAFTA with Canada and Mexico*, Addendum to the Report on Investigation No. 332-317 Under Section 332 of the Tariff Act of 1930, USITC Publication 2508 (Washington, DC: U.S. International Trade Commission, May 1992), pp. 299-357.

**Table 3-8—Mexico's Federal Spending on
Education and Health**

Share of all central government spending (percent)		
Year	Education	Health
1982...............	13.2%	1.3%
1983...............	10.9	1.2
1984...............	12.3	1.5
1985...............	11.5	1.4
1986...............	9.1	1.3
1987...............	8.3	1.2
1988...............	9.0	1.3
1989...............	11.7	1.5
1990...............	13.9	1.9

SOURCE: *Government and Financial Statistics Yearbook 1991* (Washington, DC: International Monetary Fund, 1992), Mexico table 3.

work as agricultural laborers or move to urban areas in search of other work.[13]

CRISIS AND AFTERMATH

Mexico's new middle class had a hard time during the 1980s, as did almost all Mexicans except the wealthy who could send capital abroad to protect against inflation.[14] The ''crisis'' began in 1981, when the price of oil—then Mexico's largest export—began to fall and interest rates on Mexico's foreign borrowings to rise. The price of Mexican crude had doubled between 1979 and 1981, when a barrel brought as much as $37. Projecting future prices as high as $50 a barrel for state-owned oil, the government increased spending levels faster than revenues, borrowing billions of dollars from foreign lenders.

Oil revenues began to slide, gradually at first, as the government's budget deficit rose. In 2 years, external debt more than doubled, from $40 billion in 1980 to $91 billion in 1982.[15] As the 1980s progressed, public sector spending dropped, squeezing social programs, including education and health, while the government steered scarce funds to managing the debt crisis (table 3-8). When then-President Lopez Portillo nationalized the banks, the progressive deterioration in relations between government and business reached a breaking point. Mexico's balance of payments went deeply negative. The peso fell from its 1981 value of about 25 to

the dollar, passing through 250 to the dollar in 1985 on the way to 3,100 to the dollar at the beginning of 1992. Unemployment and underemployment rose, while wages and living standards dropped. Mexico's stock market crashed in 1987, like many others, increasing the already high rate of bankruptcies, particularly among smaller firms.

Following an agreement with the International Monetary Fund in 1986, Mexico embarked on a stabilization program. The 1987 Economic Solidarity Pact (*Pacto de Solidaridad Económica*) and its successors provided for predictable devaluation of the peso. As the policies of austerity and opening (*apertura*) brought inflation rates down (to 17 percent in 1991), economic growth gradually resumed and capital began flowing back into the country. After 1989, commercial lenders forgave a small portion of Mexico's debt and extended new loans under a plan developed by U.S. Secretary of the Treasury Nicholas Brady. Other exports began taking the place of oil, which accounted for about 70 percent of Mexico's total exports in 1982, but only 30 percent in 1988.

Entering office in 1988, President Carlos Salinas de Gortari accelerated Mexico's opening to trade and investment, which had begun with accession to the General Agreement on Tariffs and Trade—a step that required an end to ISI policies. The PRI (box 3-D) had nearly lost the 1988 elections, despite its well-honed ability to ''manage'' the electoral process; Salinas knew that without economic recovery his party's control could end. In August 1990, he formally requested talks with the United States on a free trade agreement, hoping to encourage investment by foreign firms and create new jobs for a rapidly growing labor force.

A cautious fiscal and monetary policy and reductions in trade barriers leading to increased import competition reinforced the wage and price controls under the *Pacto* to contain inflation. Real wage declines slowed, and then wages began to rise, although unemployment remains in the range of 18 to 20 percent or higher and as much as half of the

---

[13] The 2 1/2 million figure is from Tim Golden, ''The Dream of Land Dies Hard in Mexico,'' *New York Times*, Nov. 27, 1991, pp. A1, A10.

[14] More than $11 billion left the country in 1981, and perhaps $40 billion during the period 1980-84. Estimates for the decade as a whole range up to $80 billion. For a comparison of five estimates of capital flight, see Rudiger Dornbusch, ''Mexican Debt,'' *Mexico's Search for a New Development Strategy*, Dwight S. Brothers and Adele E. Wick, eds. (Boulder, CO: Westview, 1990), table 11, p. 165.

[15] Ibid., pp. 141-169. Most of Mexico's external debt was owed by the government, and mostly to foreign commercial banks. The government suspended payments on its foreign debt in August 1982.

Box 3-D—Organized Labor and the PRI[1]

Mexico has been a one-party state since 1929, in part because of votes assured through the longstanding alliance between the PRI-affiliated (or ''official'') labor movement and the national political leadership. The post-revolutionary Mexican social pact provided the unions incorporated into the PRI with preferential treatment in union registration proceedings and a share of the PRI's elected offices. Union members received government-subsidized housing, health care, and basic foodstuffs. When opposition elements threatened PRI-affiliated unions, several Mexican presidents have employed force against them. For the government, the official unions provided a base of mass electoral support. In periods of economic instability, such as the 1980s, the labor leadership's capacity to contain rank-and-file wage demands and control worker opposition helped the government manage the macroeconomy and reduce inflation.

Since the 1930s, the PRI-affiliated labor movement has been dominated by the *Confederación Trabajadores de Mexico* (CTM), formed in 1936 by socialist Vicente Lombardo Toledano. The CTM drifted to the right when President Avila Camacho replaced Toledano with the more conservative Fidel Velasquez. Velasquez, now 92, remains the head of the CTM and the most powerful labor figure in Mexico. On various occasions since Velasquez came to power, radical or independent elements of the Mexican labor movement have challenged CTM dominance and advocated pressure on the PRI for policies more favorable to workers. On each of these occasions, divisions among dissident unionists, the use of state power to weaken opposition, and overtures to moderate elements in opposition coalitions served to re-establish the dominance of the pragmatic mainstream of the Mexican labor movement.

---

[1] This box draws from Kevin J. Middlebrook, ''State-Labor Relations in Mexico: The Changing Economic and Political Context,'' Unions and the State in Mexico, Kevin J. Middlebrook, ed. (La Jolla, CA: University of California-San Diego, Center for U.S.-Mexican Studies, 1991).

---

workforce may be underemployed.[16] Lacking unemployment insurance, and with such high levels of unemployment and underemployment, it is possible that half of Mexico's labor force lives below the official poverty line.

MEXICO'S ALTERNATIVE FUTURES

Politics and Policy

President Salinas, who cannot succeed himself, has until 1994 to lock in the new economic policies he helped put in place as planning and budget minister in the preceding administration.[17] If his policies are seen as failing, the government and the PRI risk political backlash. Although Salinas will probably pick his own successor—just as he was chosen in 1986 by then-President de la Madrid—a

NAFTA would help solidify his reforms, making it harder to return to past policies and practices.

Mexico is trying not only to open and modernize its economy, but also to define a new set of accomodations among government, business, and labor. The 30-year understanding between government and business, which broke down with the crisis, called for the private sector to stay out of party politics in return for trade protection, subsidies, and, in effect, guaranteed high profits. Under the 1987 *Pacto*, business interests acquiesced in the continued opening of the economy, while labor settled for wage increases that initially lagged behind inflation. For its part, the government promised to contain spending, raise controlled price levels for products including gasoline, electrical power, and fertilizer, and reduce the size of a state-owned sector that had

---

[16] The official unemployment figures are much lower, but do not include rural areas or discouraged job-seekers, while counting anyone who works an hour or more per week among the employed. Also see Michael J.D. Hopkins, ''Employment Forecasting and the Employment Problem: Conclusion,'' *Employment Forecasting: The Employment Problem in Industrialized Countries*, M.J.D. Hopkins, ed. (London: Pinter, 1988), pp. 210-247; and Trejo Reyes, ''Mexican-American Employment Relations: The Mexican Context,'' op. cit., footnote 3.

[17] That is probably enough time. The experiences of a wide range of developing countries suggest that after 5 or 6 years liberalized trade and industrial policies are unlikely to be reversed. Michael Michaely, Demetris Papageorgiou, and Armeane M. Choksi, *Liberalizing Foreign Trade, Volume 7: Lessons of Experience in the Developing World*, Demetris Papageorgiou, Michael Michaely, and Armeane M. Choksi, eds. (Cambridge, MA: Basil Blackwell, 1991), p. 33.

numbered more than 2,000 companies.[18] The *Pacto* has also given business greater and more formalized access to the policymaking process, for instance through representation on the *Comisión de Seguimiento y Evaluación del Pacto*, which monitors price and wage levels and administers the *Pacto*. While many in Mexico will probably continue to look to the government to lead if not guide the economy, it is not clear that government—at least under Salinas—will exercise the powers it retains. The *Pacto* has given Mexico a window of relative stability in which to rebuild, but the future form of Mexico's industrial policy has yet to take shape.

A long list of issues will demand the government's attention in the years ahead. With *apertura*, Mexican industry must learn to compete against imports and the products of new plants under foreign ownership. Productivity levels must rise, and costs fall. Mexican- and foreign-owned companies must generate new jobs to keep pace with a swelling labor force driven by the country's still-high birth rate and the reform of the *ejido* system, which will force subsistence farmers and farm laborers off the land and into Mexico's already overburdened cities. Mexico must depend on foreign enterprises for long-term investments in productive economic sectors and for inflows of technology. Finally, Mexico needs massive investments in infrastructure—roads, ports, and railroads; electrical power and communications networks; water and sewage facilities—if it is to attract the investments its economy needs to grow.

Infrastructure

In OTA interviews, many managers in Mexico reported that rail transportation bordered on unusable. Telephone service is expensive and unreliable, new lines take months to install, and businesses pay for more lines than they would otherwise need because repairs take so long. Rural areas, which are attractive to firms seeking low-cost labor and reduced turnover, often have little or no telephone service.[19]

Under such circumstances, larger Mexican firms and affiliates of U.S. producers have significant advantages. They can, for instance, operate their own fleet of trucks or set up private communication systems. Xerox's plant in Aguascalientes has a satellite link to Xerox's domestic communications network. Indeed, until the Mexican telecommunications network is upgraded, large companies will usually have better communications with the United States than with other parts of Mexico.

Infrastructure problems are more than annoyances. They raise the costs of doing business and thereby slow the development of Mexico's economy. The government has programs in place for upgrading the infrastructure, including large planned investments in the telecommunications grid (see ch. 8). Service has been improving. In interviews, managers noted that telephone repair personnel now may show up on the same day they are called. Despite complaints about the roads, shipments eventually get through. Many highways are being rebuilt, and private investors are financing a number of new toll roads.

Two Paths

Over the years ahead, Mexico (like the United States) could follow one of two broad development paths, as summarized in table 3-9. The first path, characterized by market-oriented policies and continued deregulation—and thus labeled *laissez-faire* in the table—would extend and expand the policies of the 1980s, when the Mexican Government sought to attract FDI through low wages. The second or "developmental" path would link elements of Mexico's recent market-oriented approach with policies that reflect the country's traditions of social policy and state intervention in the economy. Because the impacts on U.S. jobs and job opportunities will depend on how the Mexican economy

---

[18] By the end of 1992, Mexico hopes to have privatized all but about 30 companies. Susan Kaufman Purcell, "Mexico's New Economic Vitality," *Current History*, February 1992, pp. 54-58. Mexico's two largest banks, and a number of smaller financial institutions, were reprivatized in 1991, the rest in 1992. Tim Golden, "Mexico Sells Off Last Of 18 Banks at Big Profit," *New York Times*, July 7, 1992, p. D2. Favored Mexican businesses appear to have gained substantially from privatization. See, for example, "Benefits to Business Supporters of PRI Cited," *Daily Report: Latin America*, FBIS-LAT-92-049, Foreign Broadcast Information Service, Mar. 12, 1992, pp. 10-14, translated from *Este Pais*, January 1992.

[19] The manager of an apparel firm based in Aguascalientes visited for OTA had recently set up a factory in an adjacent rural area where there were no telephones. He kept in touch with his factory by radio. Another producer had built a plant in a small town with only one telephone—on the plaza in the center of town. At the time of the interview, he communicated with this factory by asking whoever answered to walk down the street and have the factory manager call him back. "The Effect of a North American Free Trade Agreement on US Apparel Employment and Industry Structure," report prepared for OTA under contract No. I3-0165 by Thomas Bailey and Theo Eicher, May 1992.

Table 3-9—Alternative Paths for Mexico's Economy

	Laissez-Faire	Developmental
Government role	Continues to shrink, as the influence of market-oriented technocrats and business interests grows.	Political forces, corporatist heritage, and social policy traditions lead to emphasis on quality of working life, human resource development, and diffusion of the benefits of economic growth to poorer groups and regions.
Parallels in other countries	United States, Britain.	Germany, Sweden, South Korea, Singapore.
Sectoral industrial policies	Limited to cases where broad consensus favoring government involvement exists (e.g., oil and petrochemicals, telecommunications).	Moderate degree of industrial targeting—e.g., to attract foreign investment, support small- and medium-sized firms, channel investment capital.
Trade policy	Continued lowering of barriers.	Selective trade protection within limits set by GATT and NAFTA discipline.
Regional policies	Left primarily to state and city governments.	Federal government steers resources and development assistance to poorer states and cities.
Human resource policies	Federal government continues to support basic education but does not pursue aggressive worker training programs.	Government provides steady increases in support for public education, with special programs for poorer regions and population groups (e.g., peasants, Indians). Vocational-technical education expands, along with training programs developed in cooperation with industry and unions, complemented by retraining for displaced workers, especially former agricultural workers.
Labor policy	Organized labor loses influence as union coverage declines, government selectively withdraws support, and employers co-opt existing unions.	Independent unions expand with government support; "official" unions become more democratic. Organized labor supports "negotiated flexibility" at the plant level (see ch. 4). Labor standards gradually rise.
Implications for Mexico	Industrial development follows a *maquiladora*-like model, with limited productivity growth and little rise in real wages. Mexico remains a site for labor-intensive branch plants operated by or for multinationals. Domestic firms, likewise, seek to compete with imports primarily through low-wage strategies.	Broader based development, with multinationals investing in a growing number of world-class plants relying on sophisticated technology and flexible forms of work organization, as well as labor-intensive production. Domestic firms pursue a greater range of strategies for growth and competitiveness, emphasizing technological upgrading and skill-based products/processes. With political opening, and growing technological and financial resources, environmental protection becomes a higher priority.
Implications for U.S. jobs and job opportunities	Threats to U.S. jobs greatest in labor-intensive sectors like apparel. Slow growth in Mexican market limits imports from the United States, hence creation of new jobs here. Large numbers of Mexicans continue to emigrate to the United States.	Some U.S. jobs and job opportunities lost in higher-wage, higher-skill sectors/occupations. Mexico buys more U.S. capital goods as well as consumer goods, thus creating some good new jobs here. With rising wages and living standards in Mexico, and better opportunities at home, emigration slows.

SOURCE: Office of Technology Assessment, 1992.

develops over the next several decades, the table serves as a guide to much of the rest of the report.

Two major variables distinguish the developmental path from *laissez-faire*. First, the Mexican Government would, over time, define a new but still activist role for itself in development. As a result, policy attention and financing would be directed to bottlenecks such as human resource limitations or backward organizational practices that might otherwise constrain development and leave Mexico heavily dependent on foreign firms. Second, Mexico would establish a new "social pact" with labor—one that would sustain commitment to flexibility, productivity, and quality improvement—rather than accept or accelerate labor's declining influence.

The path that Mexico ultimately follows will depend on which of two factors with deep roots in the country's history prevails. These two factors are the country's tradition of social solidarity, reflecting the heritage (and mythology) of revolution, and Mexico's older and still strong authoritarian and patriarchal traditions. The structure of the PRI, with its three "sectors"—labor, peasants, and an amalgam of middle-class interests called the popular sector—reflects the Mexican notion of society, in which the group takes precedent over the individual. The role of party and government leaders is then to define consensus among the groups. The strength of extended family ties also illustrates the country's social traditions, as does Mexico's high ranking on the quality of life indicators discussed earlier in the chapter (box 3-A). The hierarchical side of Mexico is reflected in high levels of income inequality, the subservient place of women and people of Indian ancestry, the many decades of one-party rule, and the lack of democracy in Mexico's labor unions (as discussed in the next chapter).

Mexico's social traditions are alive and well. Elaborate tripartite structures linking labor, government, and business oversee labor-management relations, the minimum wage system, and profit sharing. During the crisis, government called on its control mechanisms to enforce austerity. Afterwards, spending on education rose, some of it directed to making Mexico more competitive but some also at improving rural schools in poor villages. The government's new "Solidarity" program directs resources to social and infrastructure needs in poor and rural areas. With World Bank money, the Labor Ministry has established a training and industrial extension program to help Mexican workers and businesses adjust to international competition (ch. 5). The mayor of Mexico City has created an urban development program to bring commercial and clean industrial jobs to some of the poorest areas of the city. In the wake of *apertura*, modest programs have been established to help small-and medium-sized firms obtain financing or upgrade their technology. The Mexican government and the World Bank are discussing irrigation projects that would help more farmers move into labor-intensive fruit and vegetable production, thus easing the employment problems that might result from the combination of *edjido* reforms and freer trade in crops like corn.

But the central question—which path will Mexico take?—has no clear answer. Fifty years of regulation and protection have left the country with a bureaucracy accustomed to intervention. Although spending on education has risen, the government has not demonstrated a commitment to human resources—and to raising the necessary tax revenues—comparable to that in industrializing countries in Asia. Except for a few MNCs, neither government nor employers have paid much attention to the critical grey- and blue-collar technical and managerial skills essential to broad-based development. In labor relations, it is not clear whether Mexico will find a new consensus that generates virtuous circles of high worker commitment, high productivity, and rising wages. Achieving such a consensus requires a more independent union movement, hence loss of power by current union leaders—and government and PRI officials—particularly if independent unions join with other parts of civil society to demand political liberalization. Finally, the government and its market-oriented technocrats may believe that wage controls and weak unions are needed to limit inflation, attract foreign capital, and achieve long-term growth.

The pace of Mexican development remains uncertain. In contrast with Korea, Taiwan, and Hong Kong—whose economies are dominated by domestic enterprises—only a handful of Mexican-owned and -operated firms have proven themselves in world markets. There are few analogs in Mexico to Korea's *chaebol* (large conglomerates, including Hyundai and Samsung) or the many dynamic smaller firms in Taiwan. The dense, flexible networks of small companies in Taiwan and Hong Kong have helped those countries move into higher value-added production in response to changing demand. At the same time, government-initiated income redistribution and land reforms—part of post-World War II restructuring in Japan, Korea, and Taiwan—fueled domestic consumption and accelerated development in Asia. Taiwan also redistributed industrial assets that had been in the hands of the Japanese. Moreover, while popular wisdom links Asian development to labor repression, land reforms raised rural incomes, forcing manufacturing firms to pay higher wages to attract workers.

CONCLUDING REMARKS

To become a full-fledged participant in globalization, Mexico must help its workers learn to function in the sophisticated technological and organizational context of complex international production networks. Failing that, Mexico will remain primarily a site for labor-intensive branch plants. Today, Mexico competes for jobs with such countries as Thailand and Indonesia; if it fails to improve its human resources, it will find itself competing with a poorer group of Third World countries.

Mexico cannot develop through *"maquilazation."* Since his election, President Salinas has visited Europe and Japan, as well as the United States, seeking investments that can help modernize Mexico's economy. With European governments preoccupied with the new democracies of Central and Eastern Europe and the breakup of the Soviet Union, and with Japan focused on the Pacific Rim and its trade disputes with the United States, Salinas has found himself with little choice but to look northward. Hence his proposal for trade talks with the United States.

Chapter 4

Two Traditions, One Continent:
Labor Relations and Labor Markets in Mexico and the United States

Contents

Boxes

Figures

Tables

Two Traditions, One Continent:
Labor Relations and Labor Markets in Mexico and the United States

SUMMARY

This chapter compares labor relations and labor markets in Mexico and the United States. These will have a powerful influence on whether the two countries follow a high- or low-productivity path. The following conclusions result:

- The differences between the systems of labor protection in the United States and Mexico are systemic, linked to differences in political structure and history. No simple claim that Mexican labor protection is less adequate than U.S. protection or that Mexican labor protection is strong can capture the complex reality of interactions among government, labor, and business in Mexico.
- That said, there is a sense in which government intervention in Mexican labor relations violates U.S. conceptions of individual rights. To take the clearest example, Mexican workers rarely choose their own unions. In addition, the exercise of government power frequently compromises workers' freedom to bargain collectively and strike.
- From 1983 to 1988, the Mexican Government used its control over labor unions to achieve reductions in real wages of about 40 percent. While wages have recovered somewhat since 1988, if wage controls become part of a long-term strategy for attracting foreign investment, pressures on competing U.S. workers would increase.
- Despite the limitations on worker rights in Mexico, labor is more embedded in politics and society than in the United States. In the individualistic United States, unions are sometimes seen as a "third party," a remnant of a more primitive managerial era. In Mexico, workers collectively are viewed as one of the pillars of society. With some exceptions along the border, the presence rather than absence of a union is regarded in Mexico as normal and expected.
- In the United States, unions represent 16 percent of the workforce. This compares with 35 percent in the 1950s. While the proposed North American Free Trade Agreement (NAFTA) has so far focused the spotlight on Mexican labor rights, some observers view the decline in union membership in the United States as a consequence of inadequate protection of workers here from employer intimidation.
- Union decline and the globalization of the U.S. economy—of which NAFTA negotiations are a reflection—have hit U.S. workers hard. Imports and offshore production have displaced some directly. Displaced manufacturing workers frequently suffer substantial wage cuts. The future seems especially grim for workers with modest levels of educational attainment and skill.

It is in the context of the vulnerability of U.S. workers that a NAFTA and the prospect of accelerating economic integration with Mexico have become so controversial. OTA's analysis indicates that the growing interdependence of the labor relations systems of both countries could have mutually beneficial or mutually destructive results.

A mutually destructive interaction would hurt workers in both countries. In that scenario, employers and the state in Mexico would come to adopt the U.S. view that multiemployer unions are a "third party," while competitive pressure from Mexico further weakens the labor market position of less-skilled workers in the United States. Fueled by movement of capital to Mexico and Mexican workers to the United States, such an outcome would reinforce economic inequality in both countries and help entrench low-wage, low-productivity strategies throughout North America. Many of the policy options discussed in chapter 2 are intended to avoid these outcomes.

A mutually beneficial synthesis would combine U.S. views of individual rights with Mexican views of collective rights. U.S. recognition that elected representatives, including union officials, should be accountable to their constituents would be combined with the Mexican view that workers should have collective representation. Mexico's structures for

Box 4-A—The Origins of the Mexican System

Mexican industrial relations emerged from a series of political bargains struck during and after the 1910-1920 revolution. The alliance between worker organizations and the governing political coalition culminated in 1938 with labor's formal incorporation into what is now the *Partido Revolucionario Institucional* (PRI, see box 3-D, ch. 3). From labor's perspective, in the context of a predominantly agricultural economy and employer opposition, alliance with the state provided a more rapid means of gaining strength than collective action; if government intervention in union formation and dispute resolution implied loss of autonomy, the power of government to force employers to accept unions seemed to justify the trade-off. Moreover, labor's place in the dominant political coalition meant substantial influence in shaping the legal foundation of labor relations—the 1931 Mexican federal labor law (which builds on Article 123 of the 1917 Mexican constitution).

The principles embodied in Mexico's constitution and federal labor law include:[1]

* Labor standards are intended to provide a balance and social justice in the relations between employees and employers.
* Both workers and employers have the right to organize for the defense of their respective interests—e.g., by forming unions and professional associations.
* Strikes are legal when they have as their purpose the achievement of "equilibrium" among the factors of production.
* Work must guarantee employees and their families a decent living.
* Permanent (*planta*) workers (as opposed to temporary or *eventuales* employees) fired without cause are entitled to additional severance pay.
* Employers are obligated to train their workers.
* Discrimination is prohibited on the basis of sex, race, age, religious or political beliefs, and social standing.
* Social security should include protection against disability, old age, death, involuntary unemployment, sickness, and accidents. Child care services are also provided for in the social security article of Mexico's constitution.
* Labor standards are mandatory and workers' rights are irrevocable (i.e., may not be superseded by agreements between management and labor). Any renunciation of workers' rights is void. Ambiguities in labor standards are to be construed in workers' favor.

[1]This list is drawn from Art. 123 of the Mexican constitution and from the principles listed in Néstor de Buen Lozana and Carlos de Buen Unna, *A Primer on Mexican Labor Law* (Washington, DC: Department of Labor, Bureau of International Labor Affairs, 1991).

---

workplace labor-management consultation and national tripartite consensus-building on social issues would also contribute to a positive synthesis.

MEXICO'S LABOR RELATIONS SYSTEM

U.S. labor unions fear that low labor standards and weak enforcement in Mexico would divert post-NAFTA investments to Mexico, placing downward pressure on U.S. labor rights and standards. In response, the Bush administration argued in its "Action Plan" on labor and environmental issues that Mexico has "strong labor protections" that are "comparable to those in the United States, Europe, and other industrialized countries."[1]

Mexican laws cover a broader range of labor standards than U.S. laws, mandating severance pay, vacation pay, maternity leave, and profit sharing (Mexico does not have an unemployment insurance program). Mexico's federal labor law also establishes several basic principles that are more favorable to workers than U.S. statutes (box 4-A). The questions raised in the NAFTA debate concern the force of these laws and principles. NAFTA proponents offer the law itself as evidence that Mexico has adequate labor rights; critics argue that the law is irrelevant to the practice, in which, they claim, the government, "official unions" (e.g., the *Confedera-*

---

[1] "Response of the Administration to Issues Raised in Connection With the Negotiation of a North American Free Trade Agreement", May 1, 1991, sec. 3, p. 1. For a lengthier defense of Mexican labor rights, see "1991 GSP Annual Review: Worker Rights Review Summary, Case 001-CP-91: Mexico," Office of the U.S. Trade Representative, GSP Information Center, Washington, DC, November 1991.

ción de Trabajadores Mexicanos, or CTM, affiliated with the long-dominant *Partido Revolucionario Institucional*), and employers do not respect basic labor rights and standards.

Mexico's system of labor relations springs, not from the U.S. notion of society as an association of free individuals, but from a so-called "corporatist" view of society as comprised of groups: workers, peasants, employers, and the middle-class "popular sector."[2] In the United States, the group is seen as subordinate to the individual, while in Mexico the individual is seen as part of a group. It is the responsibility of the Mexican state to mediate among major social groups to achieve social peace and social justice.

Tripartite Structures and Labor-Management Committees

The Mexican view of society and the state-labor alliance of the 1920s and 1930s underly the tripartite structures which, together with the Ministry of Labor and Social Welfare (*Secretaría del Trabajo y Previsión Social*, STPS), have responsibility for implementing labor law and mediating conflicts. Conciliation and arbitration boards at federal and state levels, with equal numbers of labor and business members plus a government representative, have broad authority over union registration and strikes.[3] These powers give the boards considerable influence over the character and composition of the union movement as a whole.[4] To initiate an authorized strike, a union must file a petition with the appropriate conciliation and arbitration board, ad-dressed to the employer, 6 to 10 days in advance. The board may declare the strike illegal (*inexistente*) for a variety of reasons, including a finding that the union has not complied with registration requirements, or that a collective bargaining agreement already exists.

In addition to conciliation and arbitration boards, Mexican law provides for tripartite commissions that determine the minimum wage and annual profit sharing disbursements. Ad hoc commissions address issues such as labor law reform, discussed in a later section. In the workplace itself, federal law requires bipartite labor-management commissions on training and on health and safety.

In its tripartism and capacity for high-level consultation between unions and the government, the Mexican system of labor regulation resembles that of northern Europe (e.g., Sweden, Germany, Austria). However, Mexico's government has more power relative to labor than in Europe, while union leaders—with the support of the state—generally have more control over the rank-and-file. The end result, according to some analysts, has been that the Mexican labor-government link is more a means for enlisting lower class support for the governing elite than a means for social-democratic negotiation.[5]

Union Formation in Practice

Nearly all U.S. industries have some nonunion plants; unions gain their influence one workplace or one company at a time. In Mexico, manufacturing firms of any size (100 or more employees) outside

---

[2] Francisco Zapata, "Labor and Politics—The Mexican Paradox," *Labor Autonomy and the State in Latin American*, Edward C. Epstein, ed. (Boston, MA: Unwin Hyman, 1989); Kevin J. Middlebrook, "State-Labor Relations in Mexico: The Changing Economic and Political Context," *Unions, Workers, and the State in Mexico*, Kevin J. Middlebrook, ed. (La Jolla, CA: University of California, San Diego, Center for U.S.-Mexican Studies, 1991), pp. 1-25; and Graciela Bensusán, "Union Freedom: Real or Apparent Change in the Labor Scene," *Modernidad y Legislacion Laboral*, Graciela Bensusán and Carlos García, eds. (Mexico City: *Universidad Autónoma Metropolitana*, 1989) [translated by Deanna Hammond, Congressional Research Service].

[3] The labor memberships of the boards (and other tripartite structures above the plant level) reflect the dominance of the official unions. Victor Manuel Durand Ponte, "The Confederation of Mexican Workers, the Labor Congress, and the Crisis of Mexico's Social Pact," *Unions, Workers, and the State in Mexico*, Kevin J. Middlebrook, ed. (La Jolla, CA: University of California, San Diego, Center for U.S.-Mexican Studies, 1991), p. 91.

[4] On paper, registration requires only that a union present a membership list including at least 20 active workers, a copy of its by-laws, and a certified copy of the minutes of the general meeting at which the union was constituted and its board of directors elected. Nestor de Buen Lozano and Carlos de Buen Unna, *A Primer on Mexican Labor Law* (Washington, DC: Department of Labor, Bureau of International Labor Affairs, 1991), p. 28.

[5] Laurence Whitehead, "Mexico's Economic Prospects: Implications for State-Labor Relations," *Unions, Workers, and the State in Mexico*, Kevin J. Middlebrook, ed. (La Jolla, CA: University of California, San Diego, Center for U.S.-Mexican Studies, 1991), pp. 57-84. According to Middlebrook in the same volume, p. 9:

> . . . the postrevolutionary state's unchallenged control over coercive force and its well-developed administrative capacity place the national political leadership in a position to define (and redefine) the terms of the alliance, while the labor movement's structural weaknesses (comparatively small worker concentrations per firm and low overall levels of unionization . . .), and organizational weakness (poorly developed representational structures in many enterprise-level unions), and fractional divisions place labor in a generally subordinate position in decision making on wage levels, income policies, and economic development strategies—issues that directly affect workers.

the *maquila* sector are normally unionized.[6] The only question is which union will gain recognition, a choice usually made by national labor leaders, government officials, or employers, not by workers. In industries governed by a national, industrywide contract ("law contract" or *contracto ley*) the relevant national industrial union or regional federation becomes the representative. A *contracto ley* may be established at the request of unions representing at least two-thirds of the unionized workers in an industry in a given area. Once negotiated, it applies to all firms in the industry, including nonunion establishments. According to the Mexican Ministry of Labor, *contracto leyes* currently cover about 150,000 workers.

Where labor has been weak, as in much of northern Mexico, employers have more influence over union selection. Monterrey, the largest northern industrial center, has a tradition of "white" unions affiliated with individual enterprises or industrial groups. In *maquiladoras* on the northern border, a few cities—notably Matamoros, which has a strong, centralized CTM organization—are heavily unionized. Otherwise, labor authorities have generally accommodated *maquiladoras* that sought to operate nonunion or establish "protection unions."[7]

The evidence suggests that the Mexican Government and official unions have often used their power to block independent union formation.[8] In an OTA interview, an official of the Mexican Labor Ministry, while denying charges of manipulation, did acknowledge that independent unions often have difficulty in complying with registration requirements. In disputes over union registration, the threat of unemployment, coupled with lack of unemployment insurance, make independent activists vulnerable to legal delaying tactics and offers of severance pay. Official unions use contractual "exclusion clauses"—which require employers to fire workers who are forced out of the union—to forestall independent, rank-and-file challenges. One source estimates that only about 5 percent of unionized workers are free from control of the PRI.[9]

Wages and Wage Setting

From the 1940s until the crisis, Mexico had a stable relative wage structure, reflecting the influence of collective bargaining and minimum wages.[10] As well as wage increases from about 1950, Mexican unions obtained substantial improvements in non-wage benefits, including housing, education, health, and social security. But with large parts of the population in agriculture, and small firms in the informal sector not paying their social security obligations, Mexican health, pension, and housing funds cover only 40 to 50 percent of the population.[11]

---

[6] There are no reliable data on union membership in Mexico. Registration records held at federal and local conciliation boards and the unions' own membership figures both suggest that somewhat less than one-third of Mexico's workers belong to unions. Roughly one third work in the informal sector, with another third consisting mostly of managerial and technical workers. (OTA field visits suggest that skilled workers are more often defined outside the bargaining unit in Mexico than in the United States, reducing union leverage.)

[7] Protection unions provide employers with "protection contracts," under which, for a price, the union registers with the authorities—thereby impeding independent union registration—and then permits the employer wide latitude in setting wages, benefits, and working conditions. Workers might not even know they belong to a union.

Seeking to attract foreign investment, government officials have reportedly pressured national union leaders not to undertake major efforts to organize *maquiladoras*. According to OTA interviews with the managers of a *maquila* in a sparsely populated border area, "Companies choose the union when they start . . . . You're better off . . . . Otherwise you'll get one that will make trouble . . . ." In this case, management bought a union affiliated with one of the major federations; the managers of this *maquila* acknowledged that it was easier for them, as small independent contractors, to select their own union than it would be for larger, more visible plants.

[8] Kevin J. Middlebrook, "State Structures and the Politics of Union Registration in Post-revolutionary Mexico," *Comparative Politics*, vol. 23, 1991, pp. 459-478. Middlebrook also notes that the Mexican government has favored different union federations at different times to ensure that none, including the CTM, gained too much power. For details on formal rationales for denying independent union registration in 20 cases, see Arturo Alcalde, "State Obstacles to the Right of Union Association," *Modernidad y Legislacion Laboral*, Graciela Bensusán and Carlos García, eds. (Mexico City: *Universidad Autónoma Metropolitana*, 1989) [translated by Deanna Hammond, Congressional Research Service].

[9] Rodney D. Anderson, "Mexico," *Latin American Organizations*, G.M. Greenfield and S.L. Maran, eds. (New York, NY: Greenwood Press, 1987), p. 522.

[10] Before the crisis, the minimum wage directly determined paychecks for 40 percent of the workforce. From 1939 to 1950, average pay declined, as conservative union leaders accepted the need for savings and investment to stimulate economic growth. From the early 1950s to the early 1970s, wages rose steadily. Zapata, "Labor and Politics," op. cit., footnote 2, p. 176; Jeffrey Bortz, "The Effects of Mexico's Postwar Industrialization on the U.S.-Mexico Price and Wage Comparison" and Peter Gregory, "Comment," *U.S.-Mexico Relations: Labor Market Interdependence*, Jorge A. Bustamante, Clark W. Reynolds, and Raul A. Hinojosa Ojeda, eds. (Stanford, CA: Stanford University Press, 1992), pp. 214-242.

[11] Nora Lustig, "Mexico at the Threshold of Prosperity," unpublished draft, September 1991.

During the crisis, real wages fell dramatically. Devaluation raised the cost of imports and pushed consumer prices up by 60 percent in 1982 and 100 percent in 1983. As inflation accelerated, government officials looked to wage controls as a means of reducing inflation and expanding exports while limiting imports. The tripartite national minimum wage commission held increases below inflation so that real minimums—which had already declined 20 percent from 1977 to 1982—fell by a further 22 percent in 1983 and 50 percent from 1983 to 1988.[12]

Wage reductions led the CTM and independent unions to file some 14,000 strike petitions in 1983.[13] To contain the protests, federal officials persuaded other PRI-allied union federations to oppose CTM mobilization efforts; the government also withdrew recognition from some independent unions. Conciliation and arbitration boards generally ruled strike petitions *inexistente*.[14] The government also intervened against striking workers on highly visible occasions—at TelMex (the nationwide telecommunications company) in 1984 and 1987, at Mexicana de Aviation (one of two major airlines) in 1982 and 1987—in some cases resorting to violence.[15]

The 1987 economic solidarity pact (*Pacto*, ch. 3) ushered in a period of less openly conflictual efforts to control wages and bring down inflation. Under the *Pacto*, the Labor Minister sometimes calls in company and union negotiators to urge them to agree to noninflationary increases.[16] In the *maquiladora* sector, wages were controlled to a considerable extent even before the crisis—usually by local employers acting together. Instead of increasing wages to reduce turnover, many employers have taken the view that bidding up wages would simply mean similar turnover at higher wage levels—hence, according to *maquila* managers in Tijuana, employers agree to hold wages at low levels.[17]

Shopfloor Relations

Historically, Mexican manufacturing managers, like their U.S. counterparts, were content to push workers for greater effort. Committed to scientific management and mass production, they made no effort to improve productivity by tapping workers' skills. But rather than the "Fordist" practices common in the United States—machine-pacing, job standards set through time and motion study, and large numbers of supervisors—smaller, less bureaucratic Mexican firms often relied on piece rates. Supervisors, sometimes union members, agreed to a price and took responsibility for distributing wages and overseeing production.[18] Delegation of authority to supervisors and work groups gave union officials and informal shopfloor leaders in some plants a more central role in hiring and production management than their counterparts in the United States.

Mexican labor relations began to change in the 1960s and 1970s, as a result of independent unions and the growth of *maquiladoras*. Independent unionism emerged out of a complex of economic and political developments. Economically, when Mexico's rapid development and increasing scale of production intensified the pace of work and tightened shopfloor customs in large Mexican plants, workers sought to replace systems of informal control (augmented by one appointed union delegate per plant or several plants) with direct election of larger numbers of shop representatives. Politically,

---

[12] As wages fell, the wage share of national income declined from 40 percent in 1981 to 27 percent in 1989. Ibid., table III.3.

[13] Durand Ponte, "The Confederation of Mexican Workers, the Labor Congress, and the Crisis of Mexico's Social Pact," op. cit., footnote 3, p. 100.

[14] Alejandro Alvarez Bejar, "The Economic Crisis and the Labor Movement in Mexico," *Unions, Workers, and the State in Mexico*, Kevin J. Middlebrook, ed. (La Jolla, CA: University of California, San Diego, Center for U.S.-Mexican Studies, 1991), p. 45.

[15] Alvarez Bejar, ibid, p. 46, states that "Union activists were assassinated in Acer-Mex and Refescos Pascual in 1982, and in dissident teachers' movements near Mexico City in 1982, Oaxaca in 1985, and Chiapas in 1987."

[16] According to "The Auto and Electronics Sectors in U.S.-Mexico Trade and Investment," report prepared for OTA under contract No. I3-1815 by Harley Shaiken, May 1992, pp. 44-45:

> The Mexican Government also exercises considerable pressure both on the auto companies and the official unions not to violate the government's overall wage guidelines. . .''We even get help from the government making sure that we don't settle too high," a Verde [Verde is the pseudonym of an auto plant] manager commented, "because of the economic reforms and the fact that we are so visible." He also speculated that the government had pressured the union into granting the company an extension in the most recent round of bargaining in 1992. "We suspect . . .the government was putting [pressure] on the CTM to settle at a low level because of [our] visibility," he added. An industrial relations manager at Azul [another auto plant] confirmed a similar pattern. . .''The Labor ministry takes an active part in negotiations, especially in companies our size. And they steer the level of increases."

[17] Harley Shaiken, personal communication, July 1992.

[18] Francisco Zapata, personal communication, January 1992.

a wave of student unrest in the late 1960s, echoing that in other parts of the world, led to a bloody confrontation between students, the police, and the army. As part of later efforts to repair relations with the left, labor authorities more readily registered independent unions. In other plants, the threat of affiliating with independent unions enabled workers to pressure the CTM to accept greater local democracy.

During the same period, nonunion *maquiladoras* emerged in the north. In the 1980s, as Mexico sought to accommodate itself to the pressures of international competition, their labor practices seemed to some a possible direction for Mexican labor policy as a whole.

The economic crisis deepened the challenge to traditional Mexican industrial relations. In its wake, employers have sought greater flexibility to deploy workers and to lay them off. Some began seeking to include workers in programs to improve productivity and quality. Restructuring has taken place in different ways in different parts of the economy:

- Unilaterally in the face of worker and union resistance at traditional, often state-owned establishments.[19] With strikes protesting reorganization and privatization typically ruled illegal, workers and unions have eventually accepted privatization and bargained over severance pay. In the reorganized workplace, managers have taken at least some control from unions over hiring, work assignments, and promotions.
- Sometimes, though not commonly, through more negotiated, "consensual" restructuring, the best known example being at TelMex (box 4-B).
- Through new investment at greenfield sites— e.g., Japanese electronics *maquilas*, IBM's computer facility in Guadalajara, and a number of export-oriented automobile engine and assembly plants built in the 1980s. These plants have no unions or unions with little shopfloor presence.

At TelMex and elsewhere, employers and the government remain torn between the unilateral imposition of "flexibility" and negotiations over a more truly participative workplace that might ultimately prove more productive. The three paths by which Mexican companies have sought flexibility suggest three possible outcomes of restructuring:

1. autocratic shopfloor regimes, in which a rollback of union influence, protective labor laws, and work rules gives management unilateral control (as in the United States in the 1920s);
2. a durable regime of negotiated flexibility; and
3. Japanese-style "lean production" with employers seeking cooperative labor relations in a context of weak unions or no unions.

Box 4-C includes examples of each.

THE FUTURE OF MEXICAN INDUSTRIAL RELATIONS

For the past several years, Mexico has been debating labor law reform.[20] At its core, the debate is about which of the above models of workplace flexibility will predominate, and the future role of unions, if any, beyond the workplace. Employer proposals could be read as an attempt to generalize the practices found in *maquilas*. For companies, flexibility means relaxation of substantive labor standards such as severance pay and greater use of temporary labor. Employers' associations also seek an end to the legal priority given to more senior workers over more skilled ones. Reformist labor groups favor greater union independence from the government, mandated collective bargaining, and participation in personnel decisions by workplace committees, as found in most European countries.

Official unions, the government, and the PRI are divided about reform. Union independence and expanded worker associational rights could reduce labor support for the PRI. Some PRI leaders also fear instability if unions are granted greater autonomy too quickly. Other factions within government and the official unions believe they cannot maintain their legitimacy and rebuild the economy unless unions become more accountable to their members.

A commission on labor law reform created by President Salinas after his inauguration has yet to deliver public recommendations. Union and government sources in early 1992 suggested that "now is

---

[19] For details on several cases, see Daniel LaBotz, *The Mask of Democracy: Labor Suppression in Mexico Today* (Boston, MA: South End Press, 1992).

[20] This overview of the labor law reform debate is based on Bensusán, "Union Freedom," op. cit., footnote 2.

Box 4-B—Negotiated Flexibility at TelMex

During 1987, with preparations for the privatization of TelMex underway, government officials began negotiations with the Telephone Workers Union (the *telefonistas*), hoping to avoid the labor conflicts that had surrounded the sale of AeroMexico and other state-owned enterprises. In doing so, the government was able to take advantage of ties between the *telefonista* leader, Francisco Hernandez Juarez, and Mexican President Salinas, as well as the particular character of this union and the conditions in the industry.

Hernandez Juarez became president of the *telefonistas* in 1976, following a successful effort to dislodge the official leadership and establish an independent union. In the course of the next 12 years, the *telefonistas* called 8 strikes over wages and workplace issues. Towards the end of this period, confronted with the limits of working outside the system, the *telefonistas* joined the *Congreso del Trabajo* (CT), Mexico's umbrella union organization, to which all major federations and many nonaffiliated unions belong.

Since Salinas came to power, Hernandez Juarez and the *telefonistas* have had generally cooperative relationships with the government. From Hernandez Juarez's perspective, seeking accommodation with Salinas made sense because the union had little bargaining power. For the government, Hernandez Juarez represented a new brand of labor leader who might prove instrumental in modernizing state-labor relations. At the same time, TelMex appeared set for a period of substantial new investment following privatization. Cooperative relations with its skilled workforce would be needed to upgrade the nation's telecommunications system (see ch. 8, box 8-B).

In negotiations, the government was able to get the *telefonistas* to accept privatization and support efforts to improve productivity and service in exchange for several commitments:

1. workers would not be laid off without union consultation and, at a minimum, severance pay of 5 months plus 40 days per year of service for regular (*planta*) workers;
2. workers would be trained for new positions; and
3. workers would receive 5 percent of the stock of the privatized company.

Still unclear at TelMex is exactly what the rights and responsibilities of labor will be within a more flexible private company. In 1989, before privatization, a contractural provision giving the union rights to information and consultation on modernization (e.g., introduction of new technology, work reorganization) was "brutally mutilated," restoring unilateral management authority in most aspects of restructuring.[1] Since then, a new clause has given more limited rights back to the union.

---

[1]Enrique de la Garza Toledo, "Productive Restructuring of the Contractual Model and of Unionism in Mexico," *Sindicalismo Mexicano de Los 90's*, Jose Woldenberg and Carlos Garcia, eds. (Mexico City: *Instituto de Estudios Para La Transicion Democratica* and *Friedrich Ebert Stiftung*, 1990) [translated by Deanna Hammond, Congressional Research Service].

---

not the time" for reform. NAFTA, the opening to foreign investment, and the transformation of the *ejido* system give the government enough to worry about. No doubt the Salinas administration also fears that a reform proposal could be read in the United States as a weakening of labor standards or an implicit acknowledgement of the current extent of control over labor relations by the state and official unions.

Instead, the government, labor, employers, and peasant groups negotiated a National Accord on Raising Productivity and Quality.[21] Signed May 25, 1992, the accord emphasizes the need to improve human resources and calls for worker participation in efforts to improve productivity, equitable sharing of the benefits, and the acceptance of unions as "legitimate coparticipants in the development of companies." It stresses the role of the sectors—labor, business, and peasant organizations—in implementing "a broad social movement for production" and a "new work culture." On paper, the accord looks like the outline of a move towards negotiated flexibility. What remains unclear is whether Mexico's new set of principles will mean any more than its old set.

Developments in Mexico over the past two decades suggest two institutionally distinct systems spanning the range of possible outcomes. The first:

---

[21] "Accord on Productivity, Quality Concluded," *Daily Report: Latin America*, FBIS-LAT-42-119, Foreign Broadcast Information Service, June 19, 1992, translated from *Excelsior*, May 27, 1992.

Box 4-C—*Flexibility in the Mexican Auto Industry: Three Cases*

Autocratic Shop Floor Relations[1]

In the Mexican auto industry, ironically, a Japanese firm provides the clearest example of flexibility as a vehicle for authoritarian management. Hokkaido—a pseudonym for a factory complex northwest of Mexico City that produces engines, transmissions, transaxles, and stampings—performs nearly as well as sister plants in Japan. The facility employs an unusually high level of salaried, nonunion personnel—42 percent of the workforce of 2,700 (including several hundred Japanese nationals). A compliant CTM union with no shopfloor presence represents the rest of the workers, towards whom Hokkaido pursues what might be called a *maquila* strategy: workers perform narrowly defined jobs at an intense pace for wages one-third lower than at other Mexican auto plants.

Turnover in 1990 was 100 percent. Asked why workers quit, one manager answered, "The pay is poor, the work is heavy, and the company always asks for more." One Mexican executive said, "basically what we have in this plant is a modern form of slavery; it's a kind of peonage the way people are treated."

Negotiated Flexibility[2]

Sealed Power Mexicana (SPM), a joint venture between Sealed Power-U.S. and Condumex, a diversified Mexican auto parts firm, provides a sharp contrast to Hokkaido. SPM's Naucalpan plant, near Mexico City, makes piston rings—a product demanding high precision and consistent quality. For many years, supervisors had exercised arbitrary authority and demanded favors from workers in return for better treatment. The company frequently violated its CTM contract—sometimes failing, for instance, to pay for overtime and vacation periods—and was unresponsive when workers complained.

The local union cut its ties to the CTM in a 1979 election, voting 274 to 1 to become independent and to join the iron and steel industry section of FAT (*Frente Autentico del Trabajo*, the Authentic Front of Labor), setting the stage for several years of adversarial relations with SPM management. In the mid-1980s, under pressure from Ford, a major customer, the company tried to unilaterally impose a total quality control (TQC) program. Ten months before a deadline set by Ford for achieving top quality (Q1) status, SPM managers came to the union to ask for help. The union agreed to support TQC provided product quality targets were accompanied by quality of life for workers both on the job and outside the plant.

Reorganization at SPM included a shift to participative management, with workers taking more responsibility while supervisors acted as teachers and facilitators. The company achieved Ford's Q1 status and, in 1990, General Motors' "Level 3" classification qualifying SPM to export to the United States. For their cooperation, workers have achieved what a union leader in early 1992 termed "the best contract in Mexico."

Lean Production: Cooperation Without Negotiation?

Many managers, particularly in companies facing new competitive pressures, would prefer workers to support company goals, as at SPM, while management retains unilateral authority, as at Hokkaido. A number of export-oriented engine and assembly plants operated by U.S. automakers in northern Mexico began with the goal of emulating Japanese practices, transcending both Taylorism and the adversarialism of Big Three-UAW relations in the United States. Unlike Hokkaido, these plants have attempted to develop and diffuse skills on a scale unprecedented in Mexico—the classic example being Ford's Hermosillo facility, where managers have experimented with rotating production workers between the assembly line and skilled, craft jobs that would be held by 4-year apprentices in the United States.[3] At least initially, their unions have been compliant.

---

[1]"The Auto and Electronics Sectors in U.S.-Mexico Trade and Investment," report prepared for OTA under contract No. I3-1815 by Harley Shaiken, May 1992.

[2]This account is based on "Total Quality, Case 3: Sealed Power Mexicana," Mexico City, Mexican Institute for Total Quality Control, nd; an OTA interview with Benedicto Martinez, union leader at Sealed Power Mexicana, Jan. 31, 1992; and Maria de los Angeles Pozas, "Modernization of Labor Relations in Companies of Monterrey," University of California, San Diego, Center for U.S.-Mexican Studies, forthcoming [translated by Deanna Hammond, Congressional Research Service].

[3]"The Auto and Electronics Sectors in U.S.-Mexico Trade and Investment," op. cit., footnote 1.

an enterprise union/nonunion model, in which the role of labor atrophies beyond the workplace level. The second possibility is social corporatism on

European lines. The two possibilities differ along four dimensions: type of union; workplace relations; wage setting; and labor's role at sectoral and

Management control and worker cooperation may prove to be an unstable combination in Mexico, with auto plants—and Mexico as a whole—ultimately swinging toward negotiated flexibility or autocratic management. Workers achieving U.S. productivity and quality levels have argued that they should be paid more like U.S. workers. Conflicts over wages have contributed to high turnover and growing ambivalence about cooperation with performance improvement programs.[4] Another context where management has sought both cooperation and greater managerial authority is Ford's Cuatitlan factory, near Mexico City.[5] With the consent of the CTM, the company reorganized the plant along the lines of its flexible northern factories. As Cuatitlan reached full production, workers resisted what they saw as tighter discipline on the shop floor and an increase in workload. The leader of a group of 1,000 dissident workers, Raul Escobar, called the change one that "puts the union to the side and establishes a unilateral relationship where, in effect, the company imposes everything."[6] When workers sought to switch their union registration and gain the right to elect the leader of the national Ford union, conflict with the CTM followed, leading to the death of one of the dissidents in early 1990. A year and a half later, in a highly controversial election, Cuatitlan workers voted to reaffiliate with the CTM by 1,325 to 1,112.

No matter what version of the episode one accepts, the events at Cuatitlan point to three possible opponents of a transition to negotiated flexibility:

1. the leaders of official unions, many of whom would lose their place and power;
2. government officials, either because they believe autonomous unions would hurt the economy or because losing control over unions would jeopardize the PRI politically; and
3. employers reluctant to cede managerial prerogatives.

The recent discharge of 14,200 workers at Volkswagen's huge Mexican complex and the annulling of the contract between VW and the independent union there raise further questions about the prospects for negotiated flexibility.[7]

---

[4]Because *Pacto* wage controls make employers less willing or able to share the benefits of productivity with workers, increasing turnover of workers with scarce skills, and undermining worker commitment, some analysts see the *Pacto* as an increasing obstacle to the diffusion of cooperative workplace relations in Mexico—particularly in Monterrey. Pozas, "Modernization of Labor Relations in Companies of Monterrey," op cit., footnote 2; and Lourdes Melgar, "Emerging Alternative Forms of Economic Development," paper presented to the Annual meeting of the Latin American Studies Association, Washington, DC, Apr. 4-6, 1991.

[5]This account is based on Pozas, ibid., p. 18; an OTA interview with a former elected representative at the plant, Jan. 31, 1992; and Daniel LaBotz, *The Mask of Democracy: Labor Suppression in Mexico Today* (Boston, MA: South End Press, 1992).

[6]Pozas, ibid., p. 15.

[7]"Mexico: Mending the People's Car," *The Economist*, August 22, 1992, p. 31. According to this article, "management, having talked to the Labor Ministry, said it would rehire most, but not all, of the sacked workers, on the company's terms."

---

national levels. The two outcomes carry differing implications for U.S. workers who might find themselves competing for jobs with Mexico.

In the enterprise union/nonunion alternative, the number of nonunion firms and employer-dominated unions would grow under the influence of conservative government labor policies and foreign investment. Large firms would emulate lean production practices pioneered in Japan, although worker commitment and training might be limited to a minority of workers (as at Hokkaido, box 4-C). Smaller firms would pursue low-wage strategies with autocratic shopfloor relations. Wages would be set at the enterprise, not the industrial or national level. In retrospect, wage regulation during the crisis—with falling minimum wages, together with greater inter-industry wage differentials—would come to be seen as a stepping stone from the rigid wage system of the 1970s to decentralized "market-determined" wage setting. A diminished role for labor nationally would mean less stress on equity in education and training, social security, labor market, and regional development policies.

In the social corporatist alternative, government would encourage unions that were more responsive to their members. The negotiated flexibility seen emerging at TelMex, Sealed Power Mexicana, and some companies in Monterrey would spread. Companies and workers would benefit from increasing productivity and rising wages. Unions would regain influence over sectoral, regional, and national wage setting. As well as minimum wages, modified forms of sectoral *contracto leyes* might emerge. At the national level, democratic social corporatism would mean greater distributional equity in labor and social policies.

Despite the current emphasis on the market as Mexico deregulates, and the defensiveness of unions, social corporatism remains a possibility because labor is so deeply embedded in Mexican society. Even among employers, the U.S. notion that unions are a "third party" is uncommon. Moreover, Mexico has a much broader set of concertation structures—from mixed commissions in the workplace, to *contracto leyes*, to tri-partite minimum wage and profit sharing commissions and the new productivity accord itself—than the United States. In the *Congreso del Trabajo*, Mexico also has an umbrella labor organization that might, if democratized, provide a unified voice for labor at national political levels, as in European social democracies. But it is not clear whether business and especially the political elite will grant labor the independence necessary for such an outcome; union democracy and social corporatism could mark the end of the one-party state.

The U.S.-Mexico economic relationship would be easier to manage if Mexico develops in a social corporatist direction. Rising wages and greater equity, along with better education and training leading to greater opportunities at home, would help slow emigration and increase demand for U.S. exports. (In Spain, infrastructure and human resource investments paid for in part by European Community structural funds created opportunities and expectations sufficient to reduce emigration nearly to zero, even while the German-Spanish wage ratio remained around three to one.) By contrast, an enterprise union model with stagnant wages would cause even more Mexicans to cross the border and slow market growth in Mexico. The enterprise union outcome also implies low labor standards for a greater portion of the Mexican economy. Under social corporatism, in contrast, Mexican workers would seek industrywide or national policies to keep small firms and the informal sector from undercutting their standards—and by extension, U.S. standards in labor-intensive industries. The strength of unions in a democratic social corporatist Mexico would also facilitate negotiation of continental rules discouraging low-wage strategies.

LABOR RELATIONS IN THE UNITED STATES

The New Deal and After: Labor Relations in the Era of Mass Production

Like Mexico, the United States is in transition from a mass production economy driven by domestic demand to a new structure adapted to competition in a regionally and globally integrated economy. This entails changes in the industrial relations system that developed from legislative initiatives and political conflicts in the New Deal and World War II eras. That system included the following features:[22]

- *Employer hostility to unions.* Many U.S. employers are more strongly opposed to unions than their counterparts in Western Europe, Mexico, and even Canada.
- *Adversarial labor-management relations.* Rhetorically, and often in practice, relations between employers and unions have been governed by an implicit assumption that one side's gain is the other's loss.
- *Exclusion of workers from efforts to improve performance.* Compared to Japanese, European, and even Mexican employers, U.S. firms tend to be more deeply committed to the principles of scientific management and to systematic efforts to deskill jobs.
- *Decentralized bargaining.* Collective bargaining generally takes place at the firm or plant level, rather than on a sectoral or geographic basis.
- *Exclusive representation and a rigid union/ nonunion distinction.* Laws in Mexico and in many industrialized countries grant union representation on the request of small numbers of workers and/or provide legal support for sector-wide collective bargaining. Such an approach limits wage competition between union and nonunion firms, and thus employer opposition to unions. By contrast, U.S. policies calling for exclusive representation by majority vote, along with decentralized bargaining, heighten competition between union and non-union firms.
- *A relatively weak and decentralized union movement.* Labor in the United States is farther

---

[22] This summary draws heavily from Ray Marshall, "Unions and Competitiveness," *Empowering Workers in the Global Economy: Conference Proceedings* (Toronto, Ontario: United Steel Workers, October 1991).

removed from centers of political power than in most Western European countries and Mexico. Together with a recent tendency to label unions as just another special interest group, this limits potentials for political trade-off at the national level (e.g., wage restraint in exchange for more active labor market policies).

- *Limited government involvement in labor-management issues.* The U.S. Government rarely seeks centralized bipartite or tripartite consultation on policies affecting the labor market or the economy as a whole.

The Legislative Framework

With the Great Depression of the 1930s creating demands for action to alleviate economic distress and counter the power of large corporations, Congress passed the three legislative pillars of postwar U.S. labor regulation:

1. *The National Labor Relations Act of 1935* (NLRA, also known as the Wagner Act) provided Federal protection for workers' rights to organize and bargain collectively, barred firing of workers for union activity, and outlawed company unions.
2. *The Fair Labor Standards Act of 1938* (FLSA) established national standards for hours of work, minimum wages, and child labor.
3. *The American Social Security Act of 1935* (ASSA) created a national contributory old-age pension system, the foundation of the current social security system. This legislation also established state-provided unemployment insurance (UI) and Aid to Dependent Children (ADC, later Aid for Families with Dependent Children, AFDC).

New Deal labor and social security legislation reflected a balance between the preferences of northern liberals and the emergent labor movement on one side, and southern Democrats and low-wage employers on the other. In the case of the minimum wage and UI, employers in the industrial north joined with labor to win a uniform national standard that protected both groups against low-wage, southern competition.[23]

Conflict between advocates of national standards and "states rights" recurred periodically, shaping the 1946 revision of the NLRA, when Republicans and southern Democrats passed the Taft-Hartley Act over President Truman's veto. Taft-Hartley provided a legal basis for intraindustry wage differentials that are large compared to other countries, making it easier for employers to pursue low-wage strategies in small, rural, and southern plants. With limited exceptions for the construction industry, the law barred "secondary pressure" such as boycotts or picketing by employees of one establishment aimed at others, as well as collective agreements restricting sourcing from nonunion firms. These prohibitions on secondary pressure contrast with Mexican *contracto ley* provisions and European legislation facilitating sectorwide collective bargaining or the extension of the terms of major collective agreements to other employers (nonunion as well as union) in the same sector. Taft-Hartley also allowed States to prohibit the union shop (collective agreements requiring all workers in an establishment to join the union) and removed first-line supervisors (e.g., foremen) from bargaining units, ensuring, at least formally, that these pivotal "men in the middle" would remain on the side of management.

Postwar Shopfloor Relations and Wage Bargaining

Most large U.S. manufacturing firms eventually made pragmatic decisions to recognize unions, shifting their attention to shaping labor relations in ways that would preserve their freedom of action. They had two major priorities: ensuring that unions did not infringe on management's prerogative to run the business; and avoiding the work stoppages that were so expensive in interconnected, mass production industries. To achieve these goals, U.S. manufacturers, led by General Motors (GM), made two primary concessions to unions. Large employers granted annual increases in real wages roughly paralleling productivity increases, while supple-

---

[23] In some southern industries, the new minimum wage was higher than the previous wages of 70 percent of the workers. Gavin Wright, *Old South, New South* (New York, NY: Basic Books, 1987). When it came to social security provisions, southern opponents of national standards managed to retain considerable discretion for States over benefit levels, eligibility, and administration. They also supported health care providers in pressuring President Roosevelt to withdraw health insurance provisions from the 1935 social security act.

menting these with periodic improvements in non-wage benefits. Employers also accepted contracts specifying detailed job classifications and seniority-based work rules that limited scope for arbitrary supervision.

Employers accepted this system because it meshed with business strategies of the mass production era:

- Contractual increases in real wages complemented mass production by sustaining consumer demand. Despite the absence of European-style centralized bargaining, real wage increases diffused through "pattern bargaining," in which unions in individual plants or companies sought to match the gains achieved at core firms like GM. Periodic increases in the minimum wage helped low-wage workers maintain their incomes relative to those in unionized manufacturing sectors.

- So long as expanding markets limited need to lay off workers or move them among jobs, contractual work rules tied to narrow job classifications did not appear to impair efficiency. Enforcement of work rules off the shop floor via a multistep grievance procedure and third-party arbitration—rather than via work stoppages—minimized disruptions of production.

While they won restrictions on arbitrary supervisory actions, unions gained no role in management. Rather, the United States adopted the doctrine of "retained management rights"—that management had full prerogatives over matters not explicitly covered in the contract. The axiom "management acts and the union grieves" captured the essence of postwar U.S. labor relations. With unions in a reactive role and production workers confined to a narrow range of deskilled tasks, the adversarial system left labor out of efforts to improve productivity. Government, moreover, had a more limited role in collective bargaining, dispute resolution, and wage regulation than in many European countries or Mexico.[24]

Table 4-1—Union Coverage in the United States

	Union members as percentage of employed workers	
	1983	1991
Industry group		
Agriculture	3.4%	2.1%
Mining	20.7	15.0
Construction	27.5	21.1
Manufacturing	27.8	20.3
Durable goods	29.2	21.9
Nondurable goods	25.9	18.0
Transportation and public utilities	42.4	31.2
Wholesale and retail trade	8.7	6.7
Finance, insurance, and real estate	2.9	2.4
Services	7.7	5.7
All private nonagricultural wage and salary workers	16.8%	11.9%
Occupational group		
Managerial and administrative	8.1%	6.4%
Professional	24.0	21.7
Technical and support	13.3	11.7
Sales	6.7	5.2
Administrative support, including clerical	15.0	13.5
Service occupations	15.3	13.9
Precision production, craft, and repair	32.9	25.9
Operators, fabricators, and laborers	35.5	26.3
Machine operators, assemblers, and inspectors	36.9	26.8
Transportation, materials moving	38.5	28.4
Handlers, equipment cleaners, helpers and laborers	29.5	23.6
Agriculture, forestry and fishing	5.5	5.0

SOURCE: Department of Labor, Bureau of Labor Statistics, March 1992.

The Decline of the Post-War Structure

Since the 1960s, the institutional framework of U.S. labor relations has frayed badly. Beginning with difficulty in organizing workers in the expanding service sector and in the South, union coverage has fallen to only 12 percent of the private nonagricultural labor force (table 4-1). Facing growing international competition, U.S. firms took advantage of widening gaps between union and nonunion wages to locate new, nonunion plants in low-wage, rural areas. Given the decline of union coverage to pre-Wagner Act levels—and the possibility that this

---

[24] Although some presidents resorted to jawboning to end strikes or curb wage increases, routine involvement by the executive branch entailed little more than appointments to the National Labor Relations Board (NLRB) and the judiciary. One observer argues:

The fact that the role of government in this country remains largely hidden . . . means that the rules dominate the spirit—there is no forum for building of public agreement or shared vision. Indeed, the NLRB avoids public involvement or debate in its proceedings. Unlike most regulatory agencies, it holds no hearings . . . the NLRB is resolutely unreflective, and the framework as a whole continues to develop by patchwork additions.

Charles Heckscher, *The New Unionism: Employee Involvement in the Changing Corporation* (New York, NY: Basic Books, 1988), p. 52.

Box 4-D—Labor Rights and Union Decline: A U.S. Representation Gap?

Does declining union coverage reflect worker preferences, employer opposition, or both? Since the mid-1950s, U.S. employers have campaigned more aggressively prior to elections, taking advantage of the scope permitted them under the NLRA. By the 1970s, advising corporations on how to remain "union-free" had become a thriving cottage industry.[1] Paul Weiler has argued that employer intimidation has played a substantial role in generating what he calls the "U.S. representation gap."[2]

A 1988 Gallup poll found that 70 percent of workers believed that "employers sometimes harass, intimidate, or fire employees who openly speak up for a union." Forty percent believed their own employer would use such tactics on them. Employer campaigns against unions rely on a combination of legal delays, extensive use of management free speech rights to discourage union support, and—whether deliberately or not—violations of Wagner Act protections ("unfair labor practices"). One common delaying tactic is to dispute the bargaining unit defined by a union. "Free speech" rights give employers many avenues for persuading workers that union formation would not serve their interests; unions, in contrast, have very limited rights of access to workers.[3] Weiler has estimated the fraction of union supporters fired illegally during certification campaigns at 1 in 20.[4] Penalties are light if the courts find employers have violated the law: workers fired for union activity are entitled only to back pay minus earnings in the interim. Back pay awards average around $2,000; if the company seeks delays, reinstatement can take years.

Other analysts have challenged Weiler's emphasis on management opposition in explaining union decline, pointing out that charges of unfair labor practices are filed against employers in only about 30 percent of elections that unions lose.[5] They argue that union decline reflects worker preferences: once unions became large bureaucratic organizations, their appeal as a rank-and-file movement for social justice diminished, while male-dominated industrial unions did not adapt well to increases in working women and an expanding service sector.

[1]Richard B. Freeman and James L. Medoff, *What Do Unions Do?* (New York, NY: Basic Books, 1984).

[2]See, most recently, Paul C. Weiler, *Governing the Workplace: The Future of Labor and Employment Law* (Cambridge, MA: Harvard University Press, 1990).

[3]Unions may enter employer property during certification campaigns only when they have "no other reasonable" means of communication—e.g., to contact isolated groups of loggers working and living on company land. In January 1992, the Supreme Court ruled that the opportunity to run local radio ads or hold up signs from an adjacent highway constituted "reasonable" means of communication with workers at a retail store in a shopping center. Thus, the union could not campaign from the parking areas held in common by employers in the center. While union supporters among the workforce have access to their fellow workers during break time and at the beginning and end of a shift, open campaigning exposes them to possible recriminations.

[4]Weiler, *Governing the Workplace*, op. cit., footnote 2, pp. 238-239.

[5]Robert J. Lalonde and Bernard D. Melzer, "Hard Times for Unions: Another Look at the Significance of Employer Illegalities," *University of Chicago Law Review*, vol. 58, 1991, p. 953. Lalonde and Melzer also argue that Weiler overstates the prevalence of illegal discharge for union activity. A response by Weiler follows their article.

may reflect employer intimidation—some observers have suggested that the NAFTA debate concerning labor rights is one-sided, and that scrutiny of Mexico should be complemented by a hard look at the rights of U.S. labor to associate, organize, and bargain collectively (box 4-D).

As union membership fell, other pieces of the postwar labor market structure eroded. Industrywide pattern bargaining gave way to wages set in local and regional labor markets, with growing variations within sectors. The process took three decades in some cases (auto parts), only a few years in others. Real wages in meatpacking dropped by nearly 30

percent from 1981 to 1987 as the industry restructured around nonunion plants (ch. 10, box 10-C).

Union decline also contributed to erosion of the social policies supported by labor. Between 1968 and the mid-1980s, the U.S. minimum wage declined by one-third in real terms. UI payments and spending on labor market adjustment, never high by international standards, declined to levels well below those in most other industrial nations (table 4-2).

On the shop floor, as union power declined and international competition rose, companies restructured in ways paralleling recent changes in Mexico. Large, nonunion firms pioneered the "managerial-

Table 4-2—Government Spending on Labor Market Programs

	Government spending as a fraction of gross domestic product, 1990-91				
	Unemployment insurance	Employment services	Youth programs	Training	Total[a]
United States..........	0.60 %	0.08 %	0.03 %	—	0.85 %
Canada[b]..............	1.57	0.21	0.02	0.09	2.08
West Germany[c]........	1.14	0.22	0.04	0.38	2.18
Britain................	0.90	0.14	0.18	0.22	1.49
Sweden..............	0.59	0.21	0.05	0.47	2.25
Spain[d]................	2.33	0.12	0.08	0.10	3.21
Japan................	0.32	0.02	—	0.03	0.45

[a]Includes other categories not listed individually.
[b]1989-90.
[c]1990.
[d]1989.

SOURCE: *OECD Employment Outlook* (Paris: Organization for Economic Cooperation and Development, 1991), pp. 239-249.

ist'' model, seeking greater flexibility.[25] By broadening job responsibilities, creating work groups, and investing in training, such firms seek employee contributions to performance improvement. Managerialist firms also place limits on the arbitrary exercise of administrative power to avoid undermining worker commitment to the firm's goals. Some have created internal job ladders and made explicit or implicit promises of job security. As in Mexico, questions remain about the durability of cooperation in the absence of independent worker representation and about the proportion of employees to which management-led cooperation would apply.

In other sectors of the economy, growing numbers of immigrant workers and the vulnerability of less-educated native-born U.S. workers have reinforced low-wage strategies. Examples include not only meatpacking, but many service sector jobs, which, if less routine and less dangerous, pay wages near the legal minimum and offer little prospect of upward mobility.

Among unionized firms, competition from imports and nonunion rivals and emulation of Japanese production methods have spurred departures from traditional models. As in Mexico, substitution of flexible work arrangements for traditional union protections has sometimes followed negotiation, sometimes been unilaterally imposed in the context of plant closing threats.

As unions' capacity to protect workers on the job declined, the U.S. Government expanded its regulation of the labor market, beginning with passage of civil rights and antidiscrimination laws in the 1960s.[26] The Occupational Safety and Health Act (OSHA) followed in 1970 and the Employment Retirement Income Security Act (ERISA), intended to safeguard pensions, in 1974. More recently, the courts have expanded employee rights by reinterpreting existing legislation (e.g., reading freedom from sexual harassment into the law). Through wrongful dismissal litigation, they have also scrutinized personnel practices such as mandatory random drug testing. In theory, expanding individual employee rights has the advantage over unionism of protecting all workers. In practice, close and detailed regulation by government may offer the worst of both worlds: for employers, it creates uncertainty and expense; for most workers, who lack the resources and knowledge to enforce their rights, it provides little meaningful protection.

---

[25] Ibid. See also Thomas Kochan, Harry Katz, and Robert McKensie, *The Transformation of American Industrial Relations* (New York, NY: Basic Books, 1986), ch. 3.

[26] Paul C. Weiler, *Governing the Workplace: The Future of Labor and Employment Law* (Cambridge, MA: Harvard University Press, 1990), pp. 14-17.

Figure 4-1—Income by Level of Education and Occupation

Figure 4-1(a)—Annual Earnings by Level of Education[a]

Figure 4-1(b)—Annual Earnings by Occupation[a]

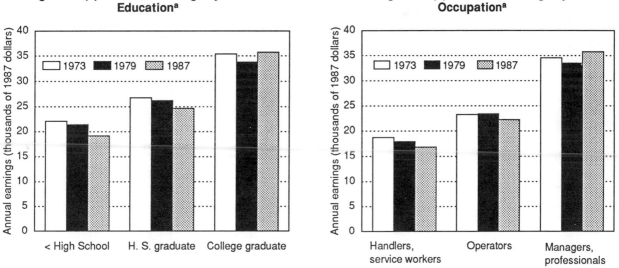

[a]White males with full-time, year-round jobs.

SOURCE: McKinley L. Blackburn, David E. Bloom and Richard B. Freeman, "The Declining Position of Less Skilled American Men," *A Future of Lousy Jobs? The Changing Structure of U.S. Wages*, Gary Burtless, ed. (Washington, DC: Brookings, 1990).

Workers in Trouble: Consequences of Labor Market Restructuring

Wages

By nearly any measure, living standards for most Americans have fallen over the past several decades.[27] Wage declines have been greatest for the over half of the workforce without a college education. Real hourly wages for production and nonsupervisory workers—currently 63 percent of the employed civilian workforce—peaked in 1972, and have since dropped back to the levels the of mid-1960s. Wages for men without a high school diploma declined by 23 percent between 1979 and 1991, for women by 11 percent. Wages fell for male college graduates, too, by 2.3 percent.

At the same time, income inequality has grown: managers and professionals have done relatively better than blue-collar workers; so have those with higher levels of education (figure 4-1). Wage gaps have also opened within the ranks of the blue-collar workforce. The range in earnings among people with similar levels of education (and age) in similar occupations and similar industries grew during the 1980s. With the breakdown of pattern bargaining in industries like auto parts, workers in independent firms earn much less than those in captive suppliers operated by the automakers themselves (ch. 7).

Unemployment and Underemployment

For four decades, unemployment and underemployment have been slowly increasing. A little over 3 percent in 1951, unemployment stood at close to 8 percent in mid-1992—nearly 10 million people in a labor force of 128 million. The United States also has a growing number of underemployed—including those who take part-time jobs because that is all they can get and casual workers in the informal economies of large cities. Most "contingent" workers—without formal or long-term ties to an employer—live without health insurance and retirement plans.

In 1990, the total of the unemployed (6.8 million); involuntary part-time workers (5.4 million); and those earning wages insufficient to support a family of four at the poverty level (14.4 million) came to 26.6 million, some 21 percent of the labor force.

The total has risen since then, and would be higher still if workers who had involuntarily accepted temporary jobs were included. (The government

[27] *Competing Economies: America, Europe, and the Pacific Rim* (Washington, DC: Office of Technology Assessment, October 1991), p. 4; W. Norton Grubb and Robert H. Wilson, "Trends in Wage and Salary Inequality, 1967-88," *Monthly Labor Review*, June 1992, p. 35.

Table 4-3—Worker Displacement[a]

Industry	Displacements		Duration of unemployment			Change in earnings[c]		
	Number per year	Annual rate	Less than 6 months	Greater than 6 months	Reemployed at time of survey[b]	Greater than 50% decline	Up to 50% decline	Increase
	(thousands)	(percent)	(percentage of displaced workers)			(percentage of workers)		
All industries.	2,026	NA	75%	25%	78%	14%	46%	41%
All manufacturing.	834	3.7%	70	30	77	15	48	37
Agriculture.	24	0.9	80	20	71	11	47	42
Meat products and canned fruit.	24	4.1	72	28	76	11	53	36
Apparel, excluding knits. . . .	49	4.9	68	32	73	7	61	33
Computers and peripherals.	16	2.5	83	17	82	10	54	35
Communication equipment.	17	3.1	61	39	69	14	45	40
Electrical machinery.	51	3.7	72	28	72	12	40	48
Autos and parts.	51	4.8	60	40	75	25	51	23

NA = Not available.

[a]Over the period 1979-1989.

[b]Within 0-5 years.

[c]Among workers who found new jobs.

SOURCE: Office of Technology Assessment, 1992, based on data from Michael Podgursky, "Changes in the Industrial Structure of Job Displacements: Evidence from the Displaced Worker Surveys," final report to the U.S. Department of Labor, Bureau of International Labor Affairs, August 1991.

collects information neither on such workers nor on those in the informal economy.)

Displacement

Between 1985 and 1989, 9.2 million workers lost their jobs due to plant closings or layoffs.[28] Workers in industrial sectors threatened by a NAFTA have already been hit hard (table 4-3). The displacement rate (total displacements divided by average industry employment) was 4.1 percent in durable goods manufacturing during the 1979-1989 period, 4.8 percent in autos and parts, and 4.9 percent in the apparel industry.

Falling wages, inequality, and a decline in good entry-level jobs have aggravated the problems faced by displaced U.S. workers. Only half of those who lose their jobs due to plant closings or permanent layoff get unemployment insurance; of those that do, about 40 percent exhaust their UI benefits before finding a new job.[29] Large-scale layoffs create waves of disruption in surrounding communities. Local businesses and supplier firms cut back,

eliminating job opportunities that might otherwise exist and weakening the local economy so that redevelopment becomes more difficult.[30] Unemployment takes a heavy toll on individuals and families, including physical and mental stress, which can lead to spouse and child abuse, substance abuse, and illness. As many as one-quarter of displaced workers lose their health insurance along with their job. Local governments may be trying to increase social services in response to individual and family stress at a time when their tax base is shrinking.

Although many displaced workers quickly find new jobs, others face lengthy periods of unemployment. As shown in table 4-3, one-quarter of all workers (including managers and professionals) laid off between 1979 and 1989 were unemployed for more than 6 months. Displaced workers with substantial prior job experience took two to four times longer to find new employment than others.[31] Nearly 15 percent of displaced workers surveyed in 1988

---

[28] Michael Podgursky, "Changes in the Industrial Structure of Job Displacements: Evidence from the Displaced Worker Surveys," final report to the U.S. Department of Labor, Bureau of International Labor Affairs, August 1991. Workers also quit their jobs voluntarily. In the third quarter of 1990, for example, the total of 6.8 million unemployed included 3.3 million who had been laid off, plus nearly 1 million more who had quit to search for a better job despite the recession and a difficult labor market; the rest of the unemployed were people seeking to enter or reenter the job market. Joseph R. Meisenheimer II, Earl F. Mellor, and Leo G. Rydzewski, "Job Market Slid in Early 1991, Then Struggled to Find Footing," *Monthly Labor Review,* February 1992, p. 15.

[29] Podgursky, ibid., p. 42.

[30] *After the Cold War: Living with Lower Defense Spending* (Washington, DC: Office of Technology Assessment, February 1992), p. 153.

[31] Michael Podgursky and Paul Swaim, "Duration of Joblessness After Displacement," *Industrial Relations,* vol. 26, 1987, pp. 213-226.

Box 4-E—Worker Aspirations, Labor Market Opportunities, and Social Stability

Social stability depends in part on job opportunities that correspond at least roughly to aspirations. Such a match no longer exists in most U.S. cities, leading to high levels of unemployment among young, less-skilled male workers, many of whom earn their living in the informal economy or turn to crime. The mismatch between aspirations and employment opportunities could worsen in the future for two reasons: the number of high-wage jobs for which less-educated workers can qualify will continue to dwindle, and, by comparison with their parents, fewer immigrants and women may be willing to accept "secondary jobs"—low-wage, low-prestige jobs with little prospect for advancement.

Traditionally, first-generation immigrants filled many of these secondary jobs, along with young people and married women. For all three groups, the social connotations of secondary jobs matter relatively little. The identity of new immigrants tends to remain linked to their status at home (and to dreams of return migration).[1] Unlike their parents, the children of first-generation immigrations have few dreams of going home and no first-hand memories of an even poorer life; they often reject secondary jobs that their parents found acceptable. As a result, labor force participation rates in poor, immigrant Hispanic neighborhoods, which have typically been high (in contrast to ghettos), will probably fall. One example comes from the Houston neighborhood of Magnolia Park, where today the children of Mexican immigrants, as well as new immigrants, are stuck in jobs as gardeners, janitors, and babysitters.[2] Labor force participation rates have declined, drug use is beginning to rise, and the birth rate among Hispanic teenagers in Houston is now three times that for whites and 15 percent higher than that of black teenagers.

There are two ways to reduce the social strains resulting from mismatch between worker aspirations and the jobs being created in the U.S. economy. During the 1980s, the United States tried, with only limited success, to force workers to accept secondary jobs by cutting unemployment benefits and social support for able-bodied workers. The second is to turn toward the kinds of policies OTA analyzes in chapter 2, seeking to transform secondary employment opportunities into better-paying, more stable jobs with meaningful prospects for on-the-job training and advancement. Because the service sector is very large and still growing, any such approach would have to focus on this part of the economy (see box 2-B in ch. 2).

---

[1]Michael J. Piore, *Birds of Passage* (New York, NY: Cambridge University Press, 1979).

[2]See the two-part series, "Without a Ladder: the Mexican Immigrants. Part One: Mexicans Come to Work, but Find Dead Ends. Part Two: Generational Chasm Leads to Cultural Turmoil for Young Mexicans in U.S.," *New York Times*, Jan. 19, 1992, sec. 1, p. 16 and Jan. 29, 1992, p. A-16.

---

had become so discouraged that they withdrew from the labor force.[32]

Sixty percent of all displaced workers who find new jobs suffer losses in earnings compared with their previous employment (again including managers and professionals). Manufacturing workers lose more than others, on average earning 10 percent less when re-employed. Workers displaced from high-wage, semiskilled jobs in former union strongholds—such as auto and steel—tend to lose the most. Over a 10-year period, manufacturing workers laid off during the mid-1980s suffered income losses averaging $36,000 each, including lost wages during periods of unemployment and lower wages and benefits once reemployed.[33]

Implications

Taken together, the trends outlined above point to growth in low-wage labor markets offering little prospect of job security or on-the-job training and advancement. If these trends continue, they will aggravate social ills already widespread in the United States (box 4-E). More workers will become discouraged and drop out of the labor market, while others will be unable to support their families. Welfare dependency, crime, and social unrest will increase.

CONCLUDING REMARKS

Over the last several years, rhetoric in both the United States and Mexico has pictured workers as

---

[32]Diane E. Herz, "Worker Displacement Still Common in the Late 1980's," *Monthly Labor Review*, May 1991, p. 8. Herz, unlike Podgursky (footnote 28), removes displaced workers with less than 3 years tenure from the displaced workers survey sample.

[33]Podgursky, "Changes in the Industrial Structure of Job Displacements: Evidence from the Displaced Worker Surveys," op. cit., footnote 28.

valued resources whose cooperation is needed for improving productivity. The reality for workers in both countries has included falling real wages, displacement, greater pressure to produce, and the loss of formal and informal protections against arbitrary management authority. From the company perspective, declining wages and benefits, and the loss of on-the-job protections, reflect necessary adjustments to new competitive forces—in effect, the end of earlier, more isolated industrial economies. Few firms see much contradiction between asking workers to make concessions and calling on them to participate in a team effort to compete. Employers have felt that, once workers understand the new realities of international competition, they will accept the compromises necessary to protect their jobs and future income. In the background, for many managers, is a vague idea of Japanese enterprise unionism.

But Mexico and the United States are not Japan. It is hard to envision Mexico's traditions of social solidarity transformed into some notion of "company as family," and just as hard to see U.S. individualism transformed in this way. Each country has a history of broad-based unionism—usually adversarial, periodically militant—that will endure even if the institutional power of organized labor continues to decline. Most important, economic conditions in Mexico and especially the United States are nothing like those in Japan in the early 1950s, when the model of enterprise unionism emerged. Japan's phenomenal growth rates brought employment security, promotion opportunities, and rapid wage increases for workers in large, core firms. These rewards will not be available to cement a management-led model of labor-management cooperation in the United States.

The danger in the United States and Mexico is that employer efforts to have it both ways—unchallenged control as well as worker cooperation—will end up reinforcing North American adversarialism. Workers without the power to negotiate differences in constructive ways will withdraw their effort and cooperation in ways that may not be visible. A NAFTA that contributed to the recognition of this danger and initiated a concerted attempt to avoid it could prove a turning point in North American development.

Chapter 5

Mexico's Workers:
Bonanza for U.S. Companies?

Contents

Mexico's Workers: Bonanza for U.S. Companies?

SUMMARY

This chapter compares Mexico's workers with their counterparts in the United States and Asia. Mexican workers have generally poor levels of education and training. But so do many millions of U.S. workers, both older blue-collar workers and young people with a high school education or less. The proposed North American Free Trade Agreement (NAFTA) is controversial in part because of fears that it would aggravate the impacts of "globalization" on U.S. workers, especially those in traditional manufacturing jobs.

From Mexico's perspective, the fundamental intent of a NAFTA is to attract new foreign investment. This could affect U.S. workers both directly and indirectly. It might encourage U.S.-based firms to:

1. transfer existing production from the United States to Mexico, or
2. build new factories in Mexico that would otherwise have been located at home.

At the same time, firms based in Japan, Europe, and elsewhere might find it attractive to locate plants in Mexico to serve the U.S. market, some of which might otherwise have been built in the United States. In doing so, some U.S. jobs and job opportunities would inevitably be lost. While a NAFTA would also stimulate job creation in U.S. firms that serve Mexican markets through exports, the rate at which exports grow will depend in part on the ability of Mexican workers and unions to win wage increases reflecting true productivity improvements (ch. 4). Immigrants from Mexico, finally, compete with U.S.-born workers for jobs. As discussed in the next chapter, a NAFTA could increase immigration in the short and medium terms before rising wages and living standards in Mexico slowed the flow of migrants northwards.

Mexico's future development will depend heavily on its capacity to absorb technology and management practices accompanying foreign investment, and Mexico's human resources will be critical in this process. After decades of import substitution industrialization (ISI), Mexican industry is backward and Mexican workers are poorly prepared by U.S. standards. A NAFTA would force Mexican firms to become more efficient or go out of business. As Mexican productivity improves, the labor market will absorb fewer new entrants relative to output. At the same time, increasing productivity will make Mexican workers better able to compete with U.S. workers. If wages increase to reflect productivity improvement, Mexican workers will become better customers for U.S. goods and services. But if an excess supply of labor holds down wage increases while productivity improves, more jobs will flow to Mexico at the expense of U.S. workers.

So far, Mexico has made only limited progress in building the foundations for continued development. By Third World standards, Mexico has a reasonably well-educated labor force, but compared with Asian countries like South Korea, Mexico has not put a high priority on human capital. Today, Mexico is short of skilled workers, experienced managers, and entrepreneurs. Most fundamentally, Mexico confronts the dilemma of all industrializing countries: its advantages lie in cheap labor at a time when cheap labor is becoming less important in many types of manufacturing—which is no consolation for U.S. workers who find themselves competing for the same kinds of lower skilled jobs.

No one knows what the balance of the job creating and job destroying effects of a NAFTA might be. As explained in appendix 5A, at the end of this chapter, there are too many uncertainties for quantitative predictions. For example, the impacts in the United States will depend in part on how work is organized. Currently, many U.S. manufacturers rely on low-skilled workers in narrowly defined jobs, exactly the kind of jobs most at risk. None of the many economic models that have attempted to predict the impacts of a NAFTA include the full range of relevant factors, which go well beyond those mentioned above. All suffer from assumptions that cannot be independently validated—notably, future levels of investment and its impacts on Mexico's productivity growth. Thus, the models provide little insight useful for policymakers seeking to understand the ways in which a NAFTA might be "good" or "bad" for the United States.

COMPETITION FOR JOBS: MEXICO AS A LOCATION FOR PRODUCTION

U.S.-based firms produce in Mexico for two major reasons—access to markets and access to cheap labor. Table 5-1 summarizes industry views of Mexican investments. The advantages and disadvantages listed in the table will shift, for instance, as educational levels in Mexico improve, or environmental enforcement becomes more stringent (ch. 6). The dynamic nature of these changes is one reason future levels of investment cannot be predicted with any confidence.

Why Companies Go Abroad

U.S.-owned firms locate plants abroad for two primary reasons: to serve foreign markets and to reduce costs of delivered products (box 5-A). Companies put up plants for processing tomatoes or freezing broccoli near growing regions (ch. 10). Governments may require companies to manufacture locally in order to sell into their markets, as Mexico did during the years of ISI. Or a company may feel it necessary to manufacture inside a market to understand what customers want and need; as noted in chapter 8, Hyundai is moving most of its personal computer operations from Korea to the United States—the world's most demanding market for such products.

For commodity-like products where little differentiation is possible, price competition has driven many labor-intensive operations to developing countries. Offshore production has been common not just for low-end television receivers (many of which are now made in Mexico), but for high-technology integrated circuit chips (for which assembly moved to Southeast Asia in the 1960s and 1970s). Little high-technology work has gone to Mexico because the country's infrastructure (water, electricity, transportation) and workforce skills and discipline are poor compared to countries like Singapore, and because products like chips can easily be shipped by air. Now, with automation, some assembly has moved back to the United States. For other products, bulky or heavy in relation to their value (e.g., TV sets), transportation costs are a major factor in location of production (ch. 8).

Table 5-1—Production in Mexico as Viewed by U.S.-Based Firms

Advantages	Disadvantages
• Low wage/benefit costs for "unskilled" and "semiskilled" workers.	• High turnover and lack of previous industrial experience among production workers.
• Trainable workforce averaging about 6 1/2 years of schooling, with higher educational levels among younger workers in urban areas.	• Can be difficult to hire grey-collar technical workers, administrators, and managers with training and experience.
• Unions pliable in many parts of the country.	• In principle, Mexican labor law gives unions considerable power.
• Proximity to United States eases many logistics problems.	• Poor transportation, communications, utilities, and other services.
• Lax enforcement of environmental and workplace health and safety regulations, at least until recently.	• Traditionally intrusive government contributes to uncertain business climate.
• Growing domestic market.	• Lack of local suppliers.

SOURCE: Office of Technology Assessment, 1992.

Choice of Technologies

Technological change also affects jobs and job opportunities, in both number and skill requirements. Productivity improvements—greater output with fewer workers—can entail much more than simply automation of the production process. Companies redesign products so they are easier to build. They reorganize to improve efficiency, product quality, and responsiveness to customer needs—on the shop floor and through corporate wide reorganizations involving computer-aided manufacturing and "lean production."

Make-or-buy decisions—whether a company chooses to produce parts, components, and subassemblies itself or purchase them outside—depend on a company's technological capabilities and strategic choices. Generally speaking, end-product manufacturers prefer to reserve high value-added production for themselves, while purchasing relatively standardized items. Nonetheless, in recent years these familiar patterns have been in flux. Automakers have been asking first-tier suppliers to undertake more design and development work, and to deliver parts of guaranteed high quality on a just-in-time basis. Electronics firms develop products in which the essential functions are incorporated in chips purchased from suppliers, so that the end-product manufacturer of, for example, a desktop computer or a FAX machine is best viewed as a

Box 5-A—Globalization and Offshore Production

Put simply, globalization entails:

- "Offshore" *production in low-wage locations* consistent with needs for quality, flexibility, and on-time delivery. Mexico is the only large, low-wage economy close to the United States.
- Development of *products for worldwide rather than national markets.*

Factory location decisions require balancing production costs (including wages and benefits for skilled workers, administrators, and managers, as well as production workers) against transportation, communications, and other indirect expenses. To the extent that products must be tailored for local markets, costs of technical and marketing activities must be considered as well. Energy costs differ from country to country, along with environmental regulations and political stability. Multinational corporations (MNCs) seek to manage their exposure to currency fluctuations. Local and national governments sometimes grant tax holidays to attract jobs.

Generally speaking, Mexico has suffered in its ability to attract manufacturing investment because of its poor infrastructure and lack of local suppliers and service firms (e.g., tool and die shops). It may take twice as long to build a factory and get it into production in Mexico as in the United States, even though the total costs are about the same.

Only in unusual cases does cheap labor in a country like Mexico make it attractive to shut down an efficient U.S. plant and move. But when companies have excess capacity, perhaps because of declining market share, they close less productive facilities. Inefficient capacity can normally be traced to some combination of:

- outmoded equipment and/or plant layout and design, driving up costs and/or driving down quality;
- outmoded managerial, organizational, and labor practices, so that productivity, up-time, quality, and/or delivery suffer (even though hourly direct labor costs might be competitive);
- long distances to customers and/or suppliers, which raises transportation costs and precludes just-in-time production.

Strategy as well as costs guide location decisions. Within the United States, companies have moved south and west not only in search of lower wages, but also in search of "right-to-work" laws and a labor force likely to remain nonunion. Internationally, a company may believe that early entry into a country will enable it to preempt rivals, preserving a large part of the market for itself. This was one motive for investments by U.S. auto firms in Mexico during the 1920s and 1930s.

Today, firms adding production capacity to serve the North American market might see strategic advantages in placing efficient new capacity in Mexico. OTA's interviews indicate that this is a particular concern for some companies in the U.S. auto parts industry. Many parts suppliers have old plants and find themselves with excess capacity because their traditional customers—the Big Three U.S. auto firms—have lost sales to Japanese automakers who buy primarily from suppliers at home or transplant suppliers in the United States (ch. 7). If a parts firm sees itself as burdened with poor labor-management relations and an inflexible workforce, and believes it can organize production more efficiently in a new plant, it might well choose to invest in Mexico. In OTA interviews, managers of auto parts firms characterized by limited economies of scale, high capital costs per unit of output, easily shipped products, excess U.S. capacity, little proprietary technology, and corporate cultures resistant to change expressed considerable concern over the threat posed by new entrants setting up in Mexico.

Overseas production operations take many forms. Table 5-2 outlines three of these.

Table 5-2—International Production

Type	Motives	Mexican examples
Unaffiliated—contract with local firm.	Take advantage of low-cost foreign labor while preserving flexibility through short-term contracts.	Many *maquiladoras* engage in contract production for U.S. companies, while U.S.-based agribusiness firms contract with Mexican farmers.
Wholly owned affiliate.	Market access—to avoid trade barriers, provide responsive delivery and customer service, or tailor product attributes to local conditions. Labor cost advantages may be secondary or irrelevant.	Automobiles and computers during import substitution industrialization.
Strategic partnership (or alliance).	Partners typically motivated by differing combinations of costs, market access, financing, and technology. Strategic alliances may or may not involve equity links.	Joint venture announced in 1991 between Vitro (Mexico) and Corning (U.S.) to make and market household glassware products.

SOURCE: Office of Technology Assessment, 1992.

systems integrator—in the extreme as little more than an assembler of purchased components. As such examples suggest, the collection of skills and capabilities needed in a world-class manufacturing firm extends well beyond low-wage production labor. It is in technologically based skills and managerial expertise that the United States excels compared to Mexico. The question then becomes: how fast can Mexico improve?

MEXICO'S HUMAN RESOURCES

Given the competitive imperatives of cost, quality, and flexibility, employers increasingly balance labor quality against labor costs in deciding where to locate plants. MNCs seek workers with basic skills, acquired through education, good enough that they can be trained in the firm's production technologies and operating procedures. To compete for foreign direct investment (FDI) with other low-wage countries—and to compete through local production with the imports now entering its own markets—Mexico will need to improve its human resource base.

Because no more than 50 to 60 percent of Mexican children enroll in secondary school, compared with 95 percent here, the disparity in workforce skills between Mexico and the United States will not close in the near future.[1] But education is only a starting point. On the shop floor and in the front office, practical skills and experience count for more than years of schooling.

Some of the needed skills are relatively easy to learn. A factory technician may be reasonably good at his or her job after 3 or 4 years. For other kinds of work—planning and managing factory production, developing new products, negotiating with distributors or bankers—3 or 4 years is only a start. Because Mexico has relatively small numbers of people entering these kinds of career paths, the country will be limited for years by lack of experienced people.

That is one reason why know-how acquired through FDI is so important for Mexico.

Historically, Mexico has voiced strong commitments to education, but it has not followed through with sustained efforts to improve the quality of its workforce. Recent policy initiatives have been modestly funded, partly because of the economic crisis. Current education and training programs seem inadequate to deal with a large and complex problem—one that will continue to grow because of Mexico's rapidly increasing labor force.

To improve its human resource base, Mexico must:

- raise the average level of education of its population, improving literacy and other basic skills for those already in the blue-collar workforce, as well as young people;
- increase its pool of workers with vocational-technical training in grey-collar skills (tool-making, equipment repair and maintenance, quality control); and
- train more college graduates for white-collar jobs in engineering, administration, and management (computer programmers, accountants, financial planners).

Education and Training

Average educational levels of Mexican workers are much lower than those here (box 5-B). Mexico spends about $70 per elementary school student per year, compared with $4,070 in the United States.[2] While U.S. employers and politicians are concerned about "functional" or "marginal" literacy, Mexico still has a large number of absolute illiterates who cannot read or write their own name. In 1992, 12 percent of the population was illiterate, 14 percent of children of school age were not in school, and 6.7 million adults had no education at all.[3] Despite a long series of government literacy programs, Mexico's 1990 report to United Nations Educational,

---

[1] *Digest of Education Statistics* (Washington, DC: Department of Education, Office of Educational Research and Improvement, 1988), pp. 340-341.

Only about 6 percent of young Mexicans enter college, although admissions standards are almost nonexistent and tuition at the national university the equivalent of about 6 cents. "Students Close U. of Mexico to Protest Tuition Increase," *Chronicle of Higher Education*, July 8, 1992, p. A35. A proposed increase to nearly $700 per year would close off higher education to many students from the lower classes.

[2] "Staff Appraisal Report: Mexico Primary Education Project," World Bank, Washington, DC, Aug. 28, 1991, p. 41; *Digest of Education Statistics, 1991* (Washington, DC: Department of Education, National Center for Education Statistics, 1991), p. 155. The U.S. figure is the average for both elementary and secondary students.

[3] Andrew Cawthorne, "School Reforms Spark Debate," *The News* [Mexico City], May 21, 1992, p. 4. Also see "Report on Education in Mexico," Mexico Ministry of Public Education, paper prepared for Forty-Second Meeting of the International Conference on Education, Geneva, Switzerland, September 1990. Illiteracy in the United States is about 1/2 percent. Estimates for both countries are based on self-reporting of complete inability to read and write, and probably understate true levels of illiteracy.

Box 5-B—Basic Education in Mexico

The Federal Education Ministry controls Mexico's system of free public schools, paying 70 percent of the costs (with the rest paid by the states). Education is not only free but in principle compulsory for all children aged 6 to 15, although, as shown in table 5-3, educational attainments do not yet reflect that much schooling. The crisis of the 1980s forced many children out of school and into the labor market.[1] Public expenditures on education fell (see ch. 3, table 3-8), and teachers' salaries along with them.

Table 5-3—Average Educational Levels for Mexicans Aged 15 and Above

Year	Years of schooling completed
1970/71	3.4
1980/81	5.4
1989/90	6.3

SOURCE: Nora Lustig, "Mexico at the Threshold of Prosperity," unpublished draft, September 1991, table III.8.

The figures in table 5-3 conceal considerable variation by age (younger people have more schooling than older people), socioeconomic status (children in poor families often leave school at an early age to help earn money for the family), gender (boys get more education than girls), geography (urban children stay in school longer), and race (Indian and *mestizo* children get less education). Thus, a U.S. automaker opening a new engine plant in Mexico was able to hire the cream of the local labor force—half of the 1,500 people applying for 149 slots as technician trainees had had 9 or more years of school.[2]

Like many other countries, Mexico continues to suffer from discrimination against women and minorities. Unless educational opportunities improve, Mexican women will continue to find work predominantly as domestics, in personal services, in the apparel industry, and doing simple, unskilled jobs in *maquilas* or *maquila*-like plants. Closing the gender gap would help Mexico tap the skills it needs to industrialize rapidly. Better educational opportunities for farmers and farm workers, many of whom are Indians—and practical training in agricultural technologies—could help Mexico improve its agricultural productivity and cope with the problems that reform of the *ejido* system will bring. But differences in wealth and population density between northern and southern states will make this difficult. Although millions of poor families have moved to Mexico's large cities, the worst poverty remains in the countryside. Low population densities in rural areas hamper efforts to maintain adequate schools. Teachers prefer urban areas, and sometimes resign if assigned to a village school. For U.S. firms considering Mexico as a production site, variation in levels of education creates an incentive to locate in the northern two-thirds of the country.

[1]Nora Lustig, "Economic Crisis, Adjustment and Living Standards in Mexico, 1982-85," *World Development*, vol. 18, 1990, pp. 1,325-1,342. In interviews, teachers note that the cost of school materials and uniforms are a burden for many families, while primary-aged students sometimes work to help with family finances. Susan Rippberger, "Insiders' Perspectives on Strengths and Weaknesses of the Mexican Education System," unpublished report, 1988, pp. 5-6.

[2]Harley Shaiken and Stephen Herzenberg, *Automation and Global Production* (La Jolla, CA: Center for U.S.-Mexican Studies, University of California, San Diego, 1987), p. 10. The MIT International Motor Vehicle Project found cars produced at Ford's Hermosillo, Mexico, factory had the best quality of those from any high-volume assembly plant in the world; it was, they said, the result of a young, motivated, and intensively trained workforce that "embraced lean production with the same speed as American workers at the Japanese transplants in North America." James P. Womack, Daniel T. Jones, and Daniel Roos, *The Machine That Changed The World: The Story of Lean Production* (New York, NY: HarperCollins, 1991), p. 87.

Once up and running, multinationals that had initially looked for high school graduates started hiring junior high school graduates more typical of the Mexican labor force as a whole. "The Auto and Electronics Sectors in U.S.-Mexico Trade and Investment," report prepared for OTA under contract I3-1815 by Harley Shaiken, May 1992, p. 5.

Scientific and Cultural Organization stated that "illiteracy is a serious problem to which a solution has not yet been found."[4]

The Vocational-Technical System

During the 1980s, Mexico's government declared an "Educational Revolution," with special attention

[4] "Report on Education in Mexico," ibid., p. 90. President Echevarria (1970-1976) renewed and refocused government efforts to combat illiteracy, but his National System of Adult Education (SNEA) failed to attract absolute illiterates, and dropout rates were high. SNEA programs included "cultural missions" to rural communities involving local teachers, telesecondary school offerings, and mobile libraries. Daniel A. Morales-Gomez and Carlos Alberto Torres, *The State, Corporatist Politics and Educational Policy Making in Mexico* (New York, NY: Praeger, 1990), pp. 107-135.

Echevarria's successor, President Lopez Portillo launched a new initiative, the National Program for Literacy Training (PRONALF), which relied heavily on temporary employees and volunteer university students to avoid the teachers union. Reductions in illiteracy over this period appear to result more from the growing reach of the public school system than from PRONALF.

to vocational education.[5] But technical training in Mexico remains weak. Many young people drop out or fail in primary and middle school, reducing the numbers who get advanced training of any sort, while most Mexicans—like their U.S. counterparts—view vocational training as inferior to academic education. Despite heavy investments in secondary vocational education over the past two decades, about 60 percent of Mexico's 2 million high school students take college preparatory courses, while another 20 percent attend dual-track vocational and preparatory high schools (most of whom then go on to a university). Only 20 percent enroll in vocational schools leading directly to work.[6]

The current vocational education system evolved from crafts schools created in the 19th century and agricultural schools established in the 1920s. Today, three groups of vocational-technical schools coexist somewhat uneasily:[7]

1. Dual-purpose technical high schools. Some are operated by the National Technological Institute (established in 1937) and its network of colleges, while others are overseen by the Secretariat of Public Education (SEP). Graduates of these schools can go on to attend college and most do so.

2. Schools known as *Centros de Enseñanza Terminal* (CETS, dating from 1958), originally intended for those going directly into the labor market. Most of the 163 CETS centers have evolved to become similar to the dual-purpose technical high schools. Only 40 percent of the young people enrolled in these two types of schools are preparing to go directly to work, while 60 percent are on a dual-purpose track (table 5-4).

3. In 1978, with fewer than 5 percent of Mexican students (at all levels) enrolled in technical

Table 5-4—Vocational-Technical Education in Mexico

School or program	Enrollment (1989/90)	Graduates (1989/90)
Dual-purpose technical high schools.	383,200	82,400
Terminal technical schools (CETS and others).	262,100	72,900
CONALEP.	155,300	33,200
Total.	800,600	188,500

SOURCE: *Staff Appraisal Report: United Mexican States, Third Technical Training Project (CONALEP III)* (Washington, DC: World Bank, 1991), p. 8.

fields, the government established a quasi-autonomous agency under SEP known as CONALEP. A network of 250 CONALEP centers offers 3-year training programs in about 90 occupations (in fields ranging from agriculture to health care and tourism). CONALEP training qualifies graduates for work, rather than advanced education. Three World Bank loans, totaling $323 million, have helped CONALEP grow rapidly.[8] By the 1989/90 school year, CONALEP enrolled nearly 20 percent of the 800,600 young people enrolled in one of Mexico's three vocational education programs (table 5-4). Recently, CONALEP has offered more short courses and evening courses, in part because many young people cannot afford to spend 3 years studying rather than working.[9]

Despite the growth in CONALEP, both Mexican and foreign firms complain of inadequate skills in the workforce. Shortages of technical and professional workers have pushed up salaries in *maquiladoras*.[10] In Guadalajara, electronics firms have been unable to hire mid-level technicians trained in quality control methods.[11] To alleviate such shortages and cope with the rising unemployment, the

---

[5] Wayne Riddle, "Education Concerns," *North American Free Trade Agreement: Issues for Congress* (Washington, DC: Congressional Research Service, July 12, 1991), p. 46.

[6] "Report on Education in Mexico", op. cit., footnote 3, p. 91.

[7] Victor L. Urquidi, "Technical Education in Mexico: A Preliminary Appraisal," *Prospects*, vol. 12, 1982, p. 115.

[8] Jaime Luis Padilla, Director General for Training and Productivity, Ministry of Labor and Social Welfare, personal communication, Jan. 16, 1992; Juan Pravda, World Bank, personal communication, Feb. 6, 1992.

CONALEP programs are closely job-related, overseen by industry boards and employ part-time teachers from industry. The Ministry of Education claims that 62 percent of CONALEP graduates find jobs within 3 months of graduation, 84 percent in the specialties for which they have trained, compared with 52 percent of CETS graduates and 25 percent of university engineering graduates.

[9] Ing. Diodoro Guerra, Director General, CONALEP, personal communication, May 19, 1992.

[10] "The Maquiladoras: Present Status, Future Potential," report prepared for OTA under contract No. H3-7040 by Leslie Sklair, December 1991, p. 22.

[11] "NAFTA and the Electronics Industry in Mexico," report prepared for OTA under contract No. H3-7200 by Patricia A. Wilson, February 1992.

Ministry of Labor and Social Welfare (STPS) launched a pilot program in 1984 to retrain displaced workers, expanded the next year with the help of an $81 million World Bank loan. About half of all retraining has taken place at CONALEP centers, with STPS paying tuition and the minimum wage for enrollees in 1 to 6 month courses.

Worker Training

Most company training in Mexico takes the form of on-the-job instruction and short in-plant courses (box 5-C). Although the Mexican constitution guarantees workers the right to employer-provided training, the government did not follow through on this promise until 1978, when it enacted Article 153-A of the federal labor law. This article requires companies and their employees (through unions, where they exist) to jointly develop training plans, to be submitted to STPS for approval, and provide graduates with certification of their skills. During the first several years after passage of Article 153-A, STPS concentrated on informing companies of the new law and urging compliance.[12]

With the opening of the economy, and the anticipation of pressure on small and medium-sized firms, STPS officials decided that active training assistance would be needed; as in the United States, most smaller firms did little or no training and had no experience to draw on. In addition to the CONALEP program for retraining displaced workers mentioned above, STPS initiatives included:

- upgrading of the Public Employment Service;
- research on the impact of retraining and on-the-job training programs; and
- the CIMO program described in box 5-C.

STPS put more than $100 million into these efforts. About 12,000 small and medium-sized firms have participated in the CIMO program, in sectors including metalworking, electronics, garments, textiles, shoes, furniture, and tourism. Some 70,000 people have received training, and the government is planning to expand the program. Funding promises to be the principal obstacle: large numbers of workers, supervisors, and managers need training in depth, requiring longer and more costly programs than have been common in Mexico. In 4 years, when a new World Bank loan for CIMO runs out, given the Mexican Government's limited resources, the private sector would almost certainly have to pay much of the cost.

Higher Education

Except for inexpensive consumer goods, Mexican firms make few products of their own design. To move into more complex production and more demanding markets, both indigenous firms and the subsidiaries of MNCs will need capable engineers and managers. During the past decade, engineering enrollments in Mexico's public and private colleges and universities grew faster than enrollments in any other field, reaching 342,000 in 1990—nearly as many as in the United States.[13] It takes 5 or 6 years to earn the equivalent of a bachelor's degree in engineering, and attrition is high. Even so, Mexico graduated 28,200 engineers in 1989, two-thirds more than in 1979—and nearly half as many as the United States (table 5-5).[14] Mexico lags further behind in its stock of engineers, with 4.3 engineers per thousand people in 1989, compared with 11.6 in the United States.

About half of Mexico's engineering students enroll in polytechnic institutes; the remainder study at colleges and universities. The National Polytechnic Institute was intended to supplement a university system strongly oriented toward the humanities. Graduates of either polytechnics or universities become *licensorios* in an engineering discipline (or in such related areas as marine technology, business administration, architecture, or economics).

---

[12] Large firms—and unionized firms—are more likely to comply than smaller establishments. Agustín Ibarra, General Director of Employment, Ministry of Labor and Social Welfare (STPS), personal communication, January 1992. Article 153-A requires that labor contracts in unionized companies specify training to be provided.

[13] Undergraduate enrollments in U.S. engineering schools have been declining since 1983, when they peaked at 441,000. The 1989 total was 378,000, to which some 128,000 engineering technology students should probably be added for comparisons with other countries. *Science & Engineering Indicators 1991*, 10th ed. (Washington, DC: National Science Board, 1991), p. 234.

[14] *El Estado del Arte de la Ingenieria en México y en el Mundo* (Mexico City: *Academia Mexicana de Ingenieria*, 1991). Graduation rates for engineers in Mexico are the lowest among all academic disciplines, with, in 1989, only 8.4 percent of the students enrolled in engineering programs graduating, compared with 11.8 percent in nonengineering fields.

Mexico compares less well with the United States if scientists are included, graduating 31,900 at both undergraduate and graduate levels in engineering and the natural sciences in 1990, compared with almost 250,000 in the United States. This comes to about 3.9 graduates per 10,000 in the Mexican population, compared with about 10 per 10,000 in the United States.

Box 5-C—Training and Industrial Adjustment

Skills and Training of Mexican Manufacturing Workers

A 1988 survey of Mexican manufacturing establishments found that most workers had quite limited skills.[1] The profile:

- unskilled workers, 20.1 percent;
- semiskilled workers, 24.9 percent;
- skilled workers, 32.5 percent;
- technicians, 14.9 percent; and
- professionals, 7.5 percent.

Half the workforce (49.9 percent) reported no more than a primary school education (i.e., 6 years or less of schooling), one-quarter had had some secondary school, and just 15.6 percent had earned a high school diploma. Another 8 percent reported college or university degrees (with 0.6 percent having completed postgraduate studies). The study concluded that about 20 percent of those surveyed lacked adequate training, with 23 percent of semiskilled workers and 27 percent of unskilled workers rated as poorly prepared for their jobs. Small companies reported the largest skill deficits.

Plant managers commonly responded to skill deficiencies with short courses on an ad hoc basis for selected employees. Forty percent of workers surveyed had received some job-related training.[2] Three out of five workers reported courses lasting less than a month, 26 percent courses lasting 1 to 3 months, and the remainder 4 months or longer. Mexican firms rely primarily on internal trainers (51 percent) and other workers (37 percent) for instruction; there has been little involvement by private training centers (6 percent), secondary schools and technical institutes (2 percent), or government training centers (1 percent).[3]

Training and Adjustment: The CIMO Program

During the ISI period, when customers had no choice but to accept the goods produced by Mexican firms, neither employers nor government worried much about training. Most large firms, as in the United States, organized work around simple, unskilled tasks. Today, Mexican companies not only face competition from imports, but many would like to export their goods. This means achieving world-class standards. To help them, STPS, backed by World Bank loans, created the *Capacitación Industrial de la Mano de Obra* (CIMO) program.[4] CIMO operates 26 training centers, staffed by a total of 90 "promoters," whose job is to analyze the needs of local industry and identify companies' immediate training needs.

In Tlaxcala, for example, Mexico's least populous state, CIMO promoters have worked with small firms, including a number of apparel shops in which managers had little familiarity with modern production practices. The promoters found volunteers willing to allow a consultant into their shops. In two shops visited by OTA, the consultant had helped managers master the basics of standardized garment production under the "bundle system" (ch. 9).

In a very different setting, the large industrial city of Puebla, local promoters worked with Volkswagen to upgrade the local supplier base. The first stage of this undertaking, funded jointly by VW, the suppliers, and CIMO, focused on defining training needs for supervisors, skilled workers, and key production employees (e.g., total quality control, just-in-time inventory management). Most of the subsequent training programs lasted a few days to a few weeks. A planned second stage may evolve into a more comprehensive industrial extension program, including technical and business assistance.

---

[1]*"Características del Personal Ocupado y Requirimientos de Capacitación en Establecimientos Manufactureros Mexicanos,"* Instituto Nacional de Estadística, Geografía e Informática (INEGI), Mexico City, 1991. The survey covered 3,189 plants in sectors including textiles and apparel, paper, printing, plastics, metal fabrication, and food products.

[2]This figure exceeds the 35 percent of U.S. workers who reported in a 1983 survey by the Bureau of Labor Statistics that they had received some training for their current job. See *Worker Training: Competing in the New International Economy* (Washington, DC: Office of Technology Assessment, September 1990), pp. 227-228. Moreover, training was more evenly distributed among occupational groups than in the United States, where managers and professionals are more likely to get training than unskilled or semiskilled workers.

[3]*Maquiladoras* report substantially lower skill levels than found by the survey discussed above. See, for example, Jorge Carillo, *"Mercados de Trabajo en la Indústria Maquiladora de Exportación"* [Labor Markets in the Assembly Plant Exporting Industry], unpublished report, *El Colegio de la Frontera Norte*, Tijuana, 1991. Carillo's 1991 survey of *maquila* plants in the auto parts, electronics, and apparel sectors, located in Juarez, Tijuana, and Monterrey, found that more than three-quarters of workers had no qualifications and were performing unskilled tasks, half of them assembly. Most training was done internally; only 29 of 43 technical schools surveyed had any relationship with local *maquiladoras*.

[4]Agustín Ibarra, General Director of Employment, Ministry of Labor and Social Welfare (STPS), personal communication, January 1992.

Table 5-5—Engineering Graduates by Country, 1989

	Number of graduates[a]	Graduates per 10,000 population
South Korea............	28,141	6.70
Japan.................	77,009	6.62
Singapore..............	1,452	4.84
Taiwan................	7,994[b]	4.0
Mexico................	**28,193**	**3.32**
France.................	16,658	2.97
United States...........	67,214	2.70
West Germany..........	9,579	1.55
India.................	28,500[b]	0.34

[a]Bachelor's level equivalent.
[b]1988.

SOURCES: *El Estado del Arte de la Ingenieria en México y en el Mundo* (Mexico City: *Academia Mexicana de Ingenieria*, 1991), p. 153; and *Science & Engineering Indicators 1991*, 10th ed. (Washington, DC: National Science Board, 1991), p. 263.

At the graduate level, about 5,300 students were enrolled in engineering programs in Mexico in 1990, compared with 109,000 in the United States.[15] U.S. graduate engineering programs enrolled some 38,000 foreign nationals in 1990, but most came from Asia and very few from Mexico. Data from the U.S. National Science Foundation (NSF) indicate that as a fraction of national populations, Mexican students received only one-tenth as many doctoral degrees in engineering and science from U.S. institutions between 1960 and 1988 as Korean students, and one-fortieth as many as those from Taiwan.

Academic training is only a starting point for the development of industrial competence. OTA's interviews with managers in Mexican firms—MNCs like IBM or Hewlett-Packard (H-P), as well as Mexican-owned companies—indicate that the country's universities and technical institutes graduate capable bachelor's level engineers.[16] H-P's plant in Guadaljara, once strictly an assembly site for impact printers and personal computers, now conducts some design and development. Graduates of local universities fill most of H-P's engineering positions.[17]

But there are relatively few such jobs in Mexico today. A recent survey in Guadalajara found that IBM and H-P were the only two foreign-owned electronics firms conducting R&D.[18] In 1988, 350 students applied for internships at IBM; the company found 150 qualified for positions, but could only hire 20. It appears that, while Mexico graduates engineers in considerable numbers, many have trouble finding technical positions and leave engineering. Some go to work as skilled production workers or enter nontechnical fields such as accounting and marketing.

Effective deployment of Mexico's engineers must seemingly await demand. Mexican industrial policies and tax laws provide few incentives for MNCs to conduct R&D locally, while Mexican-owned firms rarely pursue technology-intensive lines of business (with the primary exception of the steel and petrochemical industries). Mexico's R&D expenditures are significantly lower than other developing countries. According to NSF, Mexico invested 0.2 percent of its gross national product in R&D in 1987, compared with 1.4 percent for Taiwan and 1.8 percent for South Korea. The government pays for almost all of Mexico's R&D, often in educational institutions that have little contact with industry. So far, then, it appears that Mexico has not been able to generate a self-sustaining technological infrastructure; the country has a surplus of academically educated engineers and a shortage of those tested and tempered by experience.

Mexico Compared with Developing Countries in Asia

Might Mexico nonetheless follow the trajectory of East Asia's newly industrializing countries (NICs)—Korea, Taiwan, Hong Kong, Singapore—which moved rapidly from reliance on low-wage, low-skill production into more sophisticated manufacturing? How does Mexico match up today with Indonesia, Thailand, and Malaysia (sometimes referred to as the newly industrializing economies, NIEs, to distin-

---

[15] *El Estado del Arte de la Ingenieria en México y en el Mundo*, ibid., p. 151; *Science & Engineering Indicators 1991*, op. cit., footnote 13, p. 239. Eighty-seven percent of the Mexican students were enrolled in master's level programs, the rest at the doctoral level. Whereas engineering students comprise 32 percent of total enrollments in Mexican universities, graduate engineering students comprise only 12 percent of the graduate student population, a percentage that has declined in recent years.

[16] Almost half of IBM's permanent workforce in Guadalajara consists of engineers, mostly electrical and mechanical, many of whom have been recruited from local universities. Harley Shaiken, *Mexico in the Global Economy: High Technology and Work Organization in Export Industries* (La Jolla, CA: University of California, San Diego, Center for U.S.-Mexican Studies, 1990), p. 110.

[17] "NAFTA and the Electronics Industry in Mexico," op. cit., footnote 11; and OTA interviews.

[18] "NAFTA and the Electronics Industry in Mexico," ibid.

Table 5-6—Education in Mexico Compared With Asian Developing Countries

	Mexico	Korea	Singapore	Malaysia
Spending on education				
As a percentage of GNP (1986)	2.8%	3.0%	5.0%	7.9%
As a percentage of federal budget (1989/90)	11.7	19.6	18.1	5.3
Percentage of age group enrolled (1986-88)				
Primary grades	99%	100%	100%	NA
Secondary (all)	53	86	69	57
Secondary technical	12.6	15.9	NA	1.7
College/university	15.2	37.7	NA	6.7
Science and engineering majors as percent of higher education students	36%	31%	29%	34%
Average years of schooling in the adult population (1988)	6.2	8.0[a]	6.0[a]	7.0

NA = Not available.

[a]1980.

SOURCES: **Average years of schooling**—George Psacharopoulos and Ana Maria Arriagada, "The Educational Composition of the Labor Force: An International Update," unpublished paper, January 1992.
Government spending— Mexico, *Government and Financial Statistics Yearbook 1991* (Washington, DC: International Monetary Fund, 1992), Mexico table 3; others, Steven Schlossstein, *Asia's New Little Dragons: The Dynamic Emergence of Indonesia, Thailand, and Malaysia* (Chicago, IL: Contemporary Books, 1991), p. 24.
Other entries—*Human Development Report 1991* (New York, NY: Oxford University Press, 1991), pp. 146, 148.

guish them from the more advanced NICs)? The NIEs, in particular, have developed in large part through foreign investment, much of it Japanese, while the Salinas administration hopes that welcoming foreign capital will speed Mexican development.

Education

Table 5-5 showed that Mexico graduates as many engineers as Korea, and many more than Taiwan or Singapore (though not on a per-capita basis). Table 5-6 shows that Mexico also compares reasonably well with Asian NICs and NIEs in primary and secondary education, although it spends the least. Mexico's dropout rates also tend to be high—45 percent from elementary school, 48 percent from technical secondary education—while Taiwan and Hong Kong graduate 80 percent of those enrolled in secondary education.[19]

Industrial Structure

In the Asian NICs, in several European countries, and in Japan, communication and cooperation within corporate organizations (for example, between manufacturing engineers and production workers) and among companies have been critical factors in the spread of best practices and in the development of flexible networks of manufacturing firms.[20] Generally speaking, these channels and networks are poorly developed in Mexico.

Monterrey, home of many of Mexico's most dynamic companies, is one exception. There, long-standing family ties have contributed to the formation of manufacturing networks.[21] At the same time, foreign firms have pushed local enterprises to improve quality through reorganization and training. Monterrey firms that have been leaders in flexible work organization include Conek, a Caterpiller affiliate, and Metalsa, a supplier to Mexico's foreign-owned automakers. But most companies that reor-

[19] Jose Dominguez, World Bank, personal communication, April 1992; Steven Schlossstein, *The End of the American Century* (New York, NY: Congdon & Weed, 1989), p. 250. On the relationship between education and economic growth, see Robert J. Barro, "Economic Growth in a Cross Section of Countries," *Quarterly Journal of Economics*, vol. 106, 1991, pp. 407-443.

[20] See, for example, Paul Hirst and Jonathan Zeitlin, eds., *Reversing Industrial Decline? Industrial Structure and Policy in Britain and Her Competitors* (Oxford, UK: Berg, 1989); Robert E. Cole, *Strategies for Learning: Small-Group Activities in American, Japanese, and Swedish Industry* (Berkeley, CA: University of California Press, 1989).

[21] Lourdes Melgar, "Emerging Alternative Forms of Economic Development: The Industrialization Process of Monterrey, Nuevo Leon," paper presented at the Annual Meeting of the Latin American Studies Association, Washington, DC, Apr. 4-6, 1991, pp. 11-12; Maria de los Angeles Pozas, "Modernization of Labor Relations in Companies of Monterrey," University of California, San Diego, Center for U.S.-Mexican Studies, forthcoming [translated by Deanna Hammond, Congressional Research Service].

Figure 5-1—Indicators of Technological Capacity[a]

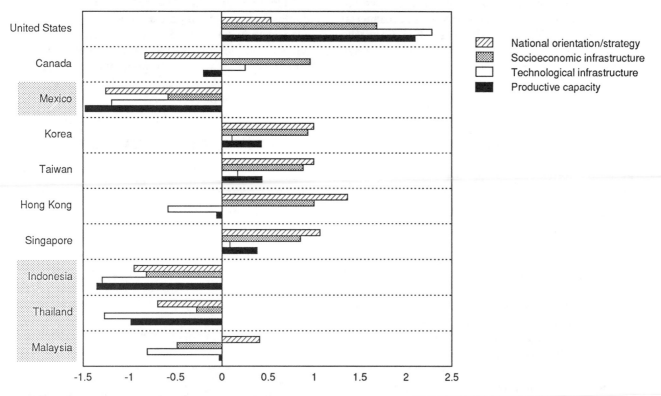

National orientation/strategy is intended to indicate "directed action to achieve technological competitiveness" based on government policies, government-business relations, and social values.

Socioeconomic infrastructure incorporates measures of capital formation, inward direct investment, and spending on education.

Technological infrastructure incorporates measures of R&D spending, alliances involving multinational enterprises, technical personnel in the labor force, and investments in capital stock (e.g., telecommunications infrastructure, computers).

Productive capacity is based on such measures as manufacturing productivity and investments in machine tools and other manufacturing equipment.

[a]Normalized to median values of zero for 29 countries, based on surveys of expert opinion conducted in 1990 and statistical data for the late 1980s.

SOURCE: Alan L. Porter and J. David Roessner, "Indicators of National Competitiveness in High Technology Industries," Executive Summary, Phase I Report, and Phase II (Final) Report under National Science Foundation Award Number 8808909, Georgia Institute of Technology, May 1991.

ganized work or introduced modern quality control practices have done so on a piecemeal basis, and remain committed to methods rooted in Taylorism and "scientific management."

Although manufacturing networks are poorly developed, Mexico's institutional structures—labor unions, business and industrial chambers at the local, State, and national levels—could become vehicles for dissemination of government-to-business assistance and interfirm cooperation. Along

these lines, the Ministry of Commerce (SECOFI) recently initiated economic development planning, in cooperation with business chambers and labor, in each of the 31 Mexican States.[22]

Technological Capacity and Organizational Competence

Figure 5-1 presents a set of broad comparisons of technological capability among Mexico, the United States and Canada, and the NICs and NIEs. Each of the four indicators is itself a normalized composite

---

[22] The Technological Institute of Monterrey supported development of the plan for the state of Chihuaha by evaluating the needs of business and industry sector by sector. Labor unions, the state government, and CANACINTRA (the association of small manufacturers) participated in formulating the plan itself, and have signed a formal agreement to implement it. Luis Miguel Pando Leyva, General Director, CANACINTRA, personal communication, May 20, 1992.

based on statistics (e.g., levels of education, capital stock in industry) and expert opinion (e.g., evaluations of openness to foreign investment, managerial capabilities). While any such set of indicators will be open to question on almost innumerable grounds, there is little alternative for attempting extensive cross-country comparisons.

Mexico's profile on the four indicators in figure 5-1 is much like that of the NIEs but indicates that Mexico is well behind the Asian NICs. To the extent that competition for jobs depends on level of economic development, Mexican workers will be competing against their counterparts in Indonesia and Thailand rather than those in the United States or Japan.

To improve its capabilities, Mexico must improve its human capital at many levels. The country needs capable farmers and bankers, skilled production workers, experienced technicians and engineers, able managers, and sensible administrators. Japan's postwar economic performance reflects a stress on skills over knowledge, and on organizational knowledge and skills over those of individuals. This is a lesson that the Asian NICs appear to have learned, but Mexico has not yet grasped. Traditionally, a small elite received a good education on classical European lines, with much of the rest of Mexico's school-age population largely neglected. This pattern has begun to change, but countries like Korea have viewed education and training in more nearly "universal" terms for decades, and thus built strong foundations for continuing development.

The pacing factors in Mexico's development thus promise to be institutional and organizational. Human capital must become embedded, taking on the form of organizational capital, before it can contribute to productivity growth. The recent troubles of the domestically oriented portion of Mexico's economy suggest that it will take time for Mexico to move beyond the "branch plant" stage of development, regardless of how much know-how might be available in principle through direct investment by multinational firms.

CONCLUDING REMARKS

With or without a NAFTA, Mexico's economic structure promises to change rapidly in the years ahead. New jobs will require new skills. Companies will have to adapt to competition or close their doors. The adjustment pressures on Mexico will be even greater than those on the United States. Mexico's government has launched a series of initiatives aimed at improving workforce skills through adult literacy programs, modernization of the vocational education system, and worker training. However, it is not clear whether these programs will succeed.

Mexico's earlier choices in education and training leave it in the 1990s with a relatively modest capacity to absorb sophisticated technologies and business practices. This means that large numbers of Mexicans will have to improve their knowledge and skills as the economy develops. It also means that whatever impacts economic integration with Mexico has had on U.S. workers in the past, these are likely to be dwarfed by future effects—positive or negative—particularly if Mexico succeeds in improving its capabilities in relatively sophisticated manufacturing.

Economic Models as Predictors of NAFTA Impacts[1]

More than a dozen economic models have been used to estimate how trade agreements among the United States, Mexico, and Canada might affect national income, exports and imports, and jobs gained or lost. Such models can be constructed in a variety of ways. Some deal with two of the three countries, some with all three, some with three plus the rest of the world. At best, the results are suggestive. None of the quantitative models and predictions reviewed by OTA provide a useful guide to policy choices.

Predictions from all the models depend on arbitrary assumptions—e.g., the prices that Mexico can expect for its oil in the future, or levels of investment in industry. The predictions of the models are no better than the assumptions. It can be very difficult to decide whether a given assumption is ''good'' or ''bad.'' Of the necessary assumptions, those dealing with investment are by far the most important. There is no way to model or otherwise generate quantitative predictions for future levels of either foreign or domestic investment (with or without a NAFTA). Investment levels can only be assumed. In fact, many of the models have assumed there will be no change in Mexican investment after a NAFTA, even though Mexico wants an agreement in large part to attract new investment.

Many of the models also suffer from dependence on input data that are old or of questionable accuracy or both. These problems are particularly severe on the Mexican side. For instance, Mexico's government reports values for imports from and exports to the United States that differ substantially from the U.S. figures; some of the reasons are known, and adjustments can be made, but this accounts for only a portion of the discrepancies.[2]

Results

Most of the modeling suggests relatively little impact on U.S. or Canadian gross domestic product (GDP), trade, or jobs as a result of lower tariffs, with greater changes in Mexico because its economy is so much smaller. Typical results suggest that a NAFTA would have broad if small benefits—growth in both (or all three) countries, with only minor negative impacts. Several sets of results—particularly those that disaggregate the economies into a number of sectors, so that impacts on, say, the apparel industry can be isolated—show larger impacts, including losses in U.S. jobs.

When predicted impacts are small, one of the reasons is usually that potentially important factors have been omitted (usually because the model cannot incorporate them). Many models, for example, fail to account for nontariff barriers (NTBs), even though Mexico has relied heavily on these over the years, and they have become even more important with reductions in Mexico's previously high tariffs. In principle, non-trade-related government policies—e.g., dealing with domestic price controls, subsidies, taxation, preferential credit, and the many other tools of economic and industrial policies—should also be incorporated, but rarely are. Again, given that Mexico has had a heavily regulated economy until recently, such factors carry particular weight; a NAFTA should properly be viewed in the context of a larger package of economic reforms in Mexico.

Types of Models and Limitations

A simple extrapolation of past trends is itself a model. But such a model can say nothing about what would happen if the United States and Mexico reduce their tariff levels, lower NTBs, or otherwise alter

[1] This discussion is based primarily on presentations at the Symposium on Economy-Wide Modeling of the Economic Implications of a FTA with Mexico and a NAFTA with Canada and Mexico, U.S. International Trade Commission, Washington, DC, Feb. 24-25, 1992. For the conclusions of the staff of the U.S. International Trade Commission concerning models and results presented at that symposium, see *Economy-Wide Modeling of the Economic Implications of a FTA with Mexico and a NAFTA with Canada and Mexico*, Report on Investigation No. 332-317 Under Section 332 of the Tariff Act of 1930, USITC Publication 2516 (Washington, DC: U.S. International Trade Commission, May 1992). The papers themselves are included in *Economy-Wide Modeling of the Economic Implications of a FTA With Mexico and a NAFTA with Canada and Mexico*, Addendum to the Report on Investigation No. 332-317 Under Section 332 of the Tariff Act of 1930, USITC Publication 2508 (Washington, DC: U.S. International Trade Commission, May 1992). For a useful review, see also Gregory K. Schoepfle and Jorge F. Perez-Lopez, ''U.S. Employment Effects of a North American Free Trade Agreement: A Survey of Issues and Estimated Employment Effects,'' draft dated Feb. 12, 1992 prepared for 1992 Joint Meeting of the Association of Borderland Scholars and Rocky Mountain Council of Latin American Studies, El Paso, TX, Feb. 20-22, 1992. Also see the papers presented at the conference on NAFTA: An Assessment of the Research, Brookings Institution, Washington, DC, Apr. 9-10, 1992.

[2] Mexico leaves shipments to and from *maquila* plants out of its accounts. For a discussion of misreporting of trade data in the context of capital flight, see David Barkin, *Distorted Development: Mexico in the World Economy* (Boulder, CO: Westview, 1990), pp. 58-71.

policies affecting trade and investment: after all, the purpose of the policy changes is to change the trend.

More sophisticated models represent the economies through systems of equations—sometimes more than a thousand. These equations relate variables such as investment, productivity, employment, exports and imports, and GDP to one another. Models involving only a few equations can sometimes be solved without a computer. Such models rarely make use of empirical data, or indeed numbers of any sort; they are purely theoretical.

Computer-based models come in a number of varieties. Their common characteristic is that they involve too many equations—or equations of too much complexity—to be solved except with a computer. These equations might, for example, specify the relationships between rising income levels in Mexico and demand for goods ranging from autos to ice cream. The more an economy can be disaggregated—i.e., the greater the number of sectors the model treats independently—the more detailed the predictions. The price is greater complexity. Even the most complicated U.S.-Mexico models include only two dozen sectors or so. High levels of aggregation mean that the model may not distinguish demand for mainframe computers from that for chemical process equipment.

Some computer models are static, meaning that they produce estimates of the one-time change resulting from, say, a reduction in tariffs. A static model, in other words, calculates the increment in GDP or trade or employment resulting from the tariff change, without saying anything about the *process* of adjustment to the new tariff levels within either economy, or about the continuing path of either economy afterwards. The results are limited to a before-and-after comparison.

Dynamic models, in contrast, can include representations of ongoing adjustment processes. A prediction of, for example, a 1 percent annual increase in Mexico's GDP expected to continue (and compound) indefinitely is far more meaningful than a prediction of a one-time increase. But dynamic modeling is much more difficult; almost all NAFTA predictions have been based on static models. For an indication of the complexities encountered in the dynamic case, consider the effects of a NAFTA on FDI in Mexico. First, it would be necessary, or at least desirable, to have a model that would predict FDI as a function of NAFTA provisions (e.g., North American content requirements), real interest rates in Mexico and elsewhere, and other relevant variables. New investment, in turn, would bring with it new technology and improved managerial practices. As a result, Mexico's rate of productivity growth should increase. This, in turn, would make some Mexican industries more competitive, altering Mexico's patterns of trade with both the United States and third countries. No current model incorporates these dynamics, even in crude approximation.

Moreover, many computer-based models, because of their structure, make use of only a single year's data for "calibration." While other types of models incorporate equations fit to lengthy time series, models calibrated on a single year cannot hope to reveal the impacts of a change in underlying conditions.

Finally, even the simpler computer-based models are complicated enough that only an expert, with considerable expenditure of time, can interpret the results. The more complicated models, which one would expect to be more useful because they are able to account for more variables, tend to be opaque even to those who have developed them. That is, the results simply emerge; the analyst must take them or leave them. If predictions seem counter-intuitive or otherwise surprising, and the model incorporates hundreds of equations—any of which might change under a given NAFTA scenario—it will generally be impossible to explain these predictions. The only choice is to try to make sure that the equations are individually correct, properly linked, and the computer coding free of errors. Because no one can understand a complex economic model in its entirety, it can be difficult or impossible to tell whether a particular model-based forecast of NAFTA impacts has been "tweaked" to give results supporting a particular advocacy position.

Note that there is a major difference between economic modeling and the equally complex mathematical models employed in the physical sciences. In most cases, models representing physical systems can be checked, debugged, and validated by comparing their predictions against empirical results. The very complex computer programs used to simulate flow around an airplane wing are verified and tuned based on both wind tunnel experiments and flight tests of prototype aircraft. It is true that, in a sense, a NAFTA would be an "experiment." However, it would be an experiment that ran only once, with many of the critical parameters outside the control of the modelers (e.g., decisions made by private investors). Under these circumstances, it is difficult to determine how well a given model actually performed.

Assumptions

The results of economic models are highly sensitive to assumptions. These may be hidden to all except those skilled in complex computer calculations and intimately familiar with the particular model. Many economists who work with models are more interested in theory and/or in modeling itself than in a NAFTA or its impacts; they may have little interest in realistic assumptions if that would make other tasks more difficult. But even where modelers seek realism, the structure of the model often works against this. Development of more sophisticated models will permit some of the restrictive assumptions listed below to be relaxed or removed. But even then, the problem of validating the results will remain.

In addition to investment levels, discussed above, many other assumptions must be made even in the most sophisticated models currently available.[3] Not all of these assumptions feature in every model; but every model is subject to some of them:

- *Perfect Competition.* The model assumes many firms, none of which have market power. In reality, only a few firms compete in many of the industries in question—for instance, automobile production. In such cases, companies have considerable power to engage in strategic behavior and to set prices, whereas in a perfectly competitive setting, all companies become price takers.

- *Homogeneous Products.* While gasoline is gasoline (within grades), automobiles differ, and automakers develop strategies based on product differentiation. Few models incorporate such behavior.

- *Exchange Rates.* The slow unexpectedly response of the U.S. current account to dollar depreciation during the latter part of the 1980s shows how poorly exchange rate shifts are understood. But even if the effects of changes in the value of the peso relative to the dollar could be incorporated into a model linking the two economies, no one knows how to predict the future value of either currency (which will depend on factors including, for instance, the U.S. budget deficit).

- *Employment.* Many models require restrictive assumptions concerning labor markets. For instance, the model may be able to calculate the number of jobs created or destroyed only at an assumed fixed percentage of unemployment—not a very useful result.

- *Migration and Demographics.* A NAFTA could result in large numbers of Mexicans leaving the agricultural sector to seek other jobs. Some may migrate to the United States. If U.S. firms found it easier to hire low-cost, unskilled Mexican immigrants, this might reduce their incentives to shift production to Mexico. None of this can be modeled at present. When migration or immigration can be included at all, this is through more or less arbitrary assumptions (e.g., that the number of Mexicans entering the United States after a NAFTA will increase or decrease by a certain number).

If economic models seem of little use for forecasting, one reason is that many were not developed for such purposes. Many models have been built to explore the ramifications of this or that set of theoretical postulates. Economists who build and exercise models could help policymakers by running their models with differing sets of assumptions chosen to investigate the significance of factors such as investment levels, oil prices, or migration. Few have attempted this, in part because their interests are in modeling rather than in policy outcomes.

Summary

By and large, the results of economic models suggest little reason to fear overall loss of large numbers of U.S. jobs. Few analyses have suggested large impacts of any sort, particularly on the United States—as opposed to Mexico, with its much smaller economy. But to a considerable extent, such results are built into the theoretical frameworks and assumptions of the models.

Nor can models reveal much about sectoral impacts, still less regional impacts. Almost anything that economic models say about NAFTA outcomes that seems plausible might be said without their aid. But because only a few experts can comprehend the innards of such models, their results too easily acquire an air of scientific authority. In the future, modeling of complex economic systems may lead to results of use to decisionmakers concerning events such as a NAFTA. This is not the case today.

---

[3] Most NAFTA-related projections have been based on computable general equilibrium (CGE) models, a relatively new species of great power but with the corresponding drawback of highly restrictive assumptions built into the theories on which the models are based. For an extensive discussion of the limitations resulting from these assumptions, see James O. Stanford, ''C.G.E. Models of North American Free Trade: A Critique of Methods and Assumptions,'' Testimony to the U.S. International Trade Commission Public Hearing on Economy-Wide Modeling of the Economic Implications of Free Trade, Investigation No. 332-317, April 1992.

Chapter 6

The Border:
A Boundary, Not A Barrier

Contents

Boxes

Figures

Tables

The Border: A Boundary, Not A Barrier

SUMMARY

This chapter deals with immigration from Mexico to the United States and environmental problems along the border. The boundary between the United States and Mexico stretches for 2,000 miles; at most points, people can cross almost as easily as polluted air. It will be easier to improve the environment than to slow immigration; short of establishing a police state along the border, there is no way the United States can stop the flow of migrants. Only socioeconomic development in Mexico that reaches into the lowest classes will slow that flow appreciably.

For many years, large numbers of Mexican workers have been coming to the United States, legally or illegally, in search of higher wages and a better life. If economic growth in Mexico leads to meaningful gains in wages and living standards, some of the pressure to emigrate will abate. But Mexico's income distribution is heavily skewed toward the wealthier classes. Should the benefits of a North American Free Trade Agreement (NAFTA) go to those who are already well off, there might be little if any slowing of emigration. Moreover, a NAFTA could lead to increased emigration in the short-term by creating rising expectations in Mexico that could not be quickly satisfied—or simply by creating new jobs near the border to serve as jumping-off points for migrants.

Improvements in wages and living standards promise to take decades rather than years, given Mexico's rapidly growing population and already high levels of unemployment and underemployment. The Mexican economy would have to grow at rates in the vicinity of 10 percent annually to create enough well-paying jobs to keep people content at home. This is substantially faster than the country was able to achieve even in the relatively prosperous 1950s and 1960s. The United States has little choice but to prepare to absorb and put to work continuing inflows of Mexican immigrants. When people have moved to the United States and want to work, it makes sense to maximize their productive contributions to the U.S. economy.

Serious environmental problems exist on both sides of the U.S.-Mexican border. Although the United States is far from blameless, most pollution sources lie in Mexico. Mexican cities, for example, dump some 20 million gallons of raw sewage each day into the Rio Grande—a river the two countries share. Similarly, much of El Paso's polluted air comes from Ciudad Juarez. Because Mexico is poor and the United States is rich, because pollution sources in the 250,000 square mile Border Area affect residents in both countries, and because Mexico's pollution problems are worse in other parts of the country, it seems likely that over the next several decades the United States will have to bear a majority of the border clean-up costs.

Mexico has announced an ambitious program to deal with environmental degradation, both along the border and in its large interior cities. Generally speaking, the country has relatively strict standards on the books (although officials are still writing regulations to implement a comprehensive environmental protection law passed in 1988). As in so many cases in Mexico, the salient questions concern enforcement and financing, rather than the letter of laws and regulations. Today, the country lacks capabilities for enforcement: the government employs fewer than 200 environmental inspectors, and budgets less than 1 percent as much for its environmental agency as does the United States. Public pressure for environmental protection and improvement is just beginning to build.

Stricter controls and enforcement will almost certainly accompany industrial development in Mexico. Countries that can afford to protect their environments and their populations generally do so; there is no reason to expect Mexico to be an exception. If the country was something of a haven for polluters in the past, that will change. But even the United States, which spends a great deal of money on environmental protection, and which has many years experience, has failed to do a very good job of setting priorities and managing cleanup. Still, there is much the United States could do to help Mexico with technical assistance and money, particularly where pollution spills across the border.

Because Mexico is only beginning to attack its environmental problems, and lacks technical expertise, in many cases there is not even baseline

Figure 6-1—Country Sources of U.S. Immigrants

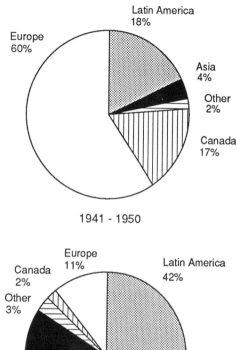

1941 - 1950

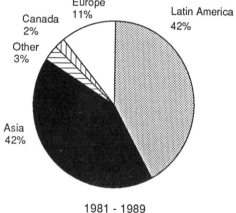

1981 - 1989

NOTE: Totals may not sum to 100 percent due to rounding.

SOURCE: *Statistical Yearbook of the Immigration and Naturalization Service* (Washington, DC: U.S. Immigration and Naturalization Service, 1990), pp. 3-4.

information on the severity of existing pollution problems and pollution sources. By providing technical and financial assistance, the United States can help ensure that a NAFTA will serve to raise, not inadvertently lower, Mexico's levels of environmental protection. The greatest need is for a steady, predictable stream of funds for control and cleanup in the border region, so that planners will not be hostage to the vagaries of the budgetary processes in the two countries. The greatest danger is that government bodies in both countries might turn away from their commitments to improving the border environment once a NAFTA were implemented.

Table 6-1—Foreign-Born U.S. Residents by Major Sending Country

	Number of U.S. residents[a] (thousands of people and percentage of all foreign-born residents)			
	1980		1990	
Mexico.	2,199	15.6 %	4,447	20.6 %
Germany.	849	6.0 %	1,163	5.4 %
Philippines.	501	3.6 %	998	4.6 %
Canada.	843	6.0 %	870	4.0 %
United Kingdom. . .	669	4.8 %	765	3.5 %
Cuba.	608	4.3 %	751	3.5 %
Korea.	290	2.1 %	663	3.1 %
Italy.	832	5.9 %	640	3.0 %
Vietnam.	231	1.6 %	556	2.6 %
China.	286	2.0 %	543	2.5 %
Total[b].	14,080	100 %	21,632	100 %

[a]The 10 countries listed comprised the 10 largest senders as determined by both the 1980 and 1990 censuses. The census does not ask whether immigrants have legal status, but appears to count one-half to two-thirds of undocumented resident aliens (see Jeffrey S. Passel, "Undocumented Migration," *Annals of the American Academy of Political and Social Science*, vol. 487, 1986, p. 187).
[b]Total represents *all* foreign-born U.S. residents.

SOURCE: 1980 and 1990 U.S. Census Special Tabulations.

IMMIGRATION[1]

The United States, a nation of immigrants, continues to admit more migrants than any other country. In earlier years, most came from Europe (figure 6-1). Today, they come predominately from Latin America and Asia, most of all from Mexico (table 6-1). Many enter illegally (table 6-2).

Immigrants may fill jobs that would otherwise go to native-born citizens; on the other hand, they may accept work that natives refuse, such as some kinds of agricultural labor, or provision of household services. Whether or not Mexican immigrants compete for jobs with native-born citizens, immigrants

Table 6-2—Legal and Illegal Immigrants

Decade	New immigrants (from all countries) (millions)		Immigrants as percentage of labor force at beginning of decade
	Legal	Illegal[a]	
1970s.	4.5	1.3	6.7%
1980s.	5.9	2.5	7.3%

[a]Estimated.

SOURCE: John M. Abowd and Richard B. Freeman, "Introduction and Summary," *Immigration, Trade, and the Labor Market*, John M. Abowd and Richard B. Freeman, eds. (Chicago and London: University of Chicago Press, 1991), table 1, p. 5.

---

[1] This section draws heavily on ''Trends in Mexican Migration and Economic Development,'' report prepared for OTA under contract No. H3-7140 by Susan Christopherson and Marie R. Jones, December 1991. Information not otherwise cited comes from this report.

who work contribute directly to the U.S. economy through their labor. They also pay taxes, while absorbing social services—health care, welfare payments, public schools, and so on.[2] Although immigrants with high levels of education, skill, and experience tend to raise overall U.S. human capital levels, most of those entering from Mexico have low levels of education.

Immigrants From Mexico: Legal and Illegal

U.S. laws limit entry by people wishing to live and work here through a complicated system of numerical quotas based on national origin, family relationships, and occupational skills. The Immigration and Naturalization Service registered about 600,000 new residents during each of the first 8 years of the 1980s.[3] The level rose to about 1 million in 1989 and 1.5 million in 1990 as a result of the amnesty provisions of the Immigration Reform and Control Act (IRCA) of 1986, which permitted many undocumented immigrants to qualify for permanent residency (box 6-A). With the amnesty in effect, Mexican immigrants grew from around 10 percent of newly registered immigrants to 37 percent in 1989 and 44 percent in 1990 (table 6-3).

Estimates of undocumented immigration are by nature far less reliable, but the total number of illegal residents is thought to be in the range of 2 to 3 million, increasing at about 200,000 annually. Mexicans make up an estimated two-thirds to three-fourths of the undocumented population, with many of the others from elsewhere in Latin America.[4] As discussed below, there is little evidence that IRCA has reduced illegal entries.

While the stereotypic undocumented Mexican is male, the proportion of single women has increased in recent years, and U.S. Government estimates indicate that women comprise about half the undoc-

Photo credit: Roberto Cordoba for the New York Times

In the Tijuana River levee preparing to climb the metal barricade under the lights; hundreds cross this barrier into the United States every night.

umented population. Moreover, IRCA has made it easier for men who entered in earlier years to bring their families here.

As indicated by table 6-4, most legal entrants from Mexico settle in California, with Texas a distant second. Moreover, most reside in a few large metropolitan areas, especially Los Angeles. Undocumented workers tend to stay closer to the border; indeed, some commute to work in the United States daily from homes in Mexico. More than half a million undocumented aliens may be sojourners who live and work in the United States for a time, save money, then return to Mexico.[5]

---

[2] Most estimates suggest the net of payments to and claims on government by immigrants is small. Undocumented aliens in Texas, for example, were found to contribute a net surplus to the State treasury, while six city governments, which bore the burdens of health care and educational costs, showed net drains on revenues. Since the State surplus exceeded the deficits incurred by local governments, the overall impact was positive. Sidney Weintraub, "Illegal Immigrants in Texas: Impact on Social Services and Related Considerations," *International Migration Review*, vol. 18, 1984, pp. 733-747. Other studies have found a net loss. See R. W. Gardner and L. F. Bouvier, "The United States," *Handbook on International Migration*, W. J. Serow et al., eds. (New York, NY: Greenwood Press, 1990), p. 356.

[3] *Statistical Yearbook of the Immigration and Naturalization Service, 1990* (Washington, DC: U.S. Immigration and Naturalization Service, 1991), p. 52.

[4] K.A. Woodrow and J.S. Passel, "Post IRCA Undocumented Immigration to the United States: An Assessment Based on the June 1988 CPS," *Undocumented Migration to the United States: IRCA and the Experience of the 1980s*, F.D. Bean, B. Edmonston, and J.S. Passel, eds. (Washington, DC: Urban Institute Press, 1990), pp. 33-76. Also D.G. Papedemetriou, "South-North Migration in the Western Hemisphere and U.S. Responses," paper prepared for the Ninth Seminar on Migration of the International Organization for Migration (IOM), Geneva, Dec. 4-6, 1990, p. 11.

[5] See Jeffrey S. Passel, "Undocumented Migration," *Annals of the American Academy of Political and Social Science*, vol. 487, 1986, pp. 181-200.

Box 6-A—Evolution Of U.S. Immigration Law[1]

1882

High unemployment on the west coast in the late 1870s leads to passage of the Chinese Exclusion Act, barring entry by Chinese laborers. Little prior law or policy had dealt explicitly with immigration.

1906-1907

A "Gentlemen's Agreement" signed with Japan limits entry to family members of Japanese residing in the United States.

1920s

1921 brings the Quota Act, followed by the National Origins Act of 1924. New entrants permitted in proportion to distribution of residents by birth or national origin as determined in the 1920 census, subject to an annual ceiling of 154,000 total immigrants. Northern and Western European nations get 82 percent of the quota, Southern and Eastern Europe 16 percent.

1952

The Immigration and Nationality Act (INA) reaffirms quotas based on national origin, with very restrictive annual limits for some countries (e.g., 185 Japanese, 105 Chinese, and 100 persons each from Egypt and New Zealand). INA also establishes a preference system based on skill levels and family ties.

Mid-1960s

Amendments to INA passed at the height of the civil rights movement replace the previous quota system, based on the existing racial, ethnic, and national origin composition of the U.S. population, with three major preference groups:

- Immediate relatives of U.S. citizens, exempt from numerical limits.
- Refugees, subject to numerical limits determined annually through consultation between Congress and the administration.
- Up to 270,000 entrants based on a 6-category preference system emphasizing family reunification, with a ceiling of 20,000 from any one country.[2]

1986

With a great deal of public attention focused on illegal immigration, Congress passes the Immigration Reform and Control Act. IRCA penalizes employers who knowingly hire undocumented workers, while allowing qualifying undocumented aliens already in the country to apply for amnesty and eventual citizenship. To qualify, undocumented aliens must have lived in the United States since January 1, 1982, or have worked harvesting perishable crops at least 90 days during specified periods from 1983 to 1986. About 3.1 million people, three-quarters of them Mexicans, applied for legalization.[3]

1990

In another major revision of the law, the Immigration Act of 1990 (P.L. 101-649) raises the immigration ceiling to 700,000 for fiscal years 1992-94, then sets a cap of 675,000 beginning in fiscal 1995 (480,000 family-sponsored, 140,000 based on employment needs, and 55,000 to increase "diversity").[4]

---

[1] See R. W. Gardner and L. F. Bouvier, "The United States," *Handbook on International Migration*, W. J. Serow et al., eds. (New York, NY: Greenwood Press, 1990), pp. 341-362.

[2] The preference system put more weight on family reunification than on labor market qualifications. Professionals and their immediate family (spouses and children) were limited to 10 percent of the total (27,000 visas). Skilled or unskilled workers in short supply in the United States (and their immediate family) fell in another category, also subject to the 10 percent limitation. The remaining four categories included people claiming various kinds of family relationships; for example, unmarried adult children of U.S. citizens and their children, a category allocated 20 percent or 54,000 visas.

[3] Sergio Díaz-Briquets and Sidney Weintraub, *Regional and Sectoral Development in Mexico as Alternatives to Migration* (Boulder, CO: Westview, 1991), p. xi.

[4] *Statistical Yearbook of the Immigration and Naturalization Service, 1990* (Washington, DC: U.S. Immigration and Naturalization Service, 1991), p. A.1-20.

As a percentage of the total, the employment-based preference under the 1990 revisions remains about the same as established in the mid-1960s—close to 20 percent—but the qualifications in terms of education and skill have been raised.

Table 6-3—Legal Immigrants From Top Five Countries

1985			1989			1990		
	Number (thousands)	Percent of total		Number (thousands)	Percent of total		Number (thousands)	Percent of total
Mexico.........	61	11%	Mexico........	405	37%	Mexico..............	679	44%
Philippines......	48	8%	El Salvador.....	58	5%	El Salvador..........	80	5%
South Korea.....	35	6%	Philippines.....	57	5%	Philippines...........	64	4%
Vietnam........	32	6%	Vietnam.......	38	3%	Vietnam.............	49	3%
India..........	26	5%	South Korea....	34	3%	Dominican Republic...	42	3%
Total[a]........	570	100%	Total[a]......	1,090	100%	Total[a]............	1,536	100%

[a]Totals represent *all* legal immigrants.

SOURCE: *Statistical Yearbook of the Immigration and Naturalization Service, 1990* (Washington, DC: U.S. Immigration and Naturalization Service, 1991), pp. 52-53.

Competition for Jobs

Mexicans with schooling and skills have little incentive to emigrate because wage structures in Mexico reward skilled and professional workers disproportionately.[6] It is mostly the less skilled who tend to migrate. Three-quarters of Mexican immigrants have less than a high school education, compared to one-quarter of native-born U.S. citizens; only 2 percent of Mexican immigrants have completed college. Although the differences are slight, undocumented aliens tend to be younger than legal immigrants, less literate in Spanish, and less likely to speak or read English.

Direct competition for jobs with native-born workers takes place primarily in the local labor markets of cities with large immigrant populations. Within these areas, competition centers on low-skilled jobs, as suggested by table 6-5.[7] Native-born men appear to be competing with Mexican immi-

Table 6-4—Intended Residence of Legal Immigrants From Mexico Entering in 1990

	Number (thousands)	Percent of all legal Mexican immigrants
Total.....................	679	100%
Top five States.............	626	92
California...............	420	62
Texas..................	131	19
Illinois.................	47	7
Arizona................	18	3
New Mexico............	8	1
Top five metropolitan areas...	426	63
Greater Los Angeles[a].....	303	45
Chicago................	42	6
Houston...............	35	5
San Diego..............	26	4
Dallas.................	19	3

[a]Including Los Angeles/Long Beach, Anaheim/Santa Ana, and Riverside/San Bernadino.

SOURCE: *Statistical Yearbook of the Immigration and Naturalization Service, 1990* (Washington, DC: U.S. Immigration and Naturalization Service, 1991), pp. 79, 83.

---

[6] George J. Borjas, ''The Economic Consequences of Migration,'' paper presented at Annual Meeting of the American Association for the Advancement of Science, Chicago, Feb. 7, 1992. In countries like Sweden, with relatively flat income distributions, it is skilled workers that have the greatest motivation to migrate.

Incentives to migrate from Mexico to the United States depend not only on income but on income relative to others in a local area. See Oded Stark and J. Edward Taylor, *Demography*, vol. 26, 1989, pp. 1-14. While immigrants are responding to the wage differential between the two countries, most migrants do not come from the poorest regions in Mexico, and most have jobs in Mexico before they emigrate.

[7] Indirect effects can also be significant. For instance, fewer native-born citizens may migrate to Los Angeles if they conclude that immigrants have depressed the job market there. Migration within Mexico can also affect U.S. jobs. For example, migration from Mexico's interior to *maquila* plants on the border can cut into U.S. jobs and job opportunities directly, as well as provide a stepping stone on a journey whose final destination is Los Angeles or Houston.

Labor force participation rates are higher for undocumented aliens than for either legal immigrants or natives, They are especially high for illegal immigrant women, 64 percent of whom work outside the home. Leo Chavez, ''Settlers and Soujourners: The Case of Mexicans in the United States,'' *Human Organization*, vol. 47, 1988, pp. 5-108.

Occupational distributions appear to be similar for legal and illegal immigrants. More than a third of undocumented Mexican males and some 40 percent of undocumented Mexican females work in manufacturing (but only 10 percent of native-born women), while agriculture and mining together employ only about 15 percent of male and 10 percent of female undocumented immigrants. Increasing numbers of undocumented Mexican workers, both men and women, have also found work in personal services and in restaurants. See Passel, ''Undocumented Immigration,'' op. cit., footnote 5.

Many U.S. farmers, especially those growing fruits and vegetables, claim they depend heavily on undocumented workers to fill jobs no one else will take. ''Agricultural Issues in U.S.-Mexico Economic Integration,'' report prepared for OTA under contract No. I3-0310 by B. Kris Schulthies and Gary W. Williams, April 1992.

Table 6-5—Occupational Profiles for Mexican-Born and Native Workers

| | Mexican-born workers | | | | | Native workers | | |
| | 1980, All | 1988 | | | Percent change, 1980-88 (All) | 1988 | | |
		Men	Women	All		Men	Women	All
Operators, fabricators, and laborers............	44%	35.1%	37.3%	35.8%	-19%	21.7%	8.7%	15.8%
Service workers............................	18	15.6	25.0	18.5	5	9.5	18.3	13.5
Precision production, craft, and repair..........	15	22.5	6.4	17.5	19	20.0	2.3	11.9
Farming, forestry, fisheries....................	13	17.6	8.2	14.7	11	5.1	1.3	3.4
Technicians, sales, and administrative support....	7	4.7	17.3	8.6	17	19.1	44.8	30.8
Managers and professionals..................	3	4.5	5.9	4.9	63	24.5	24.6	24.6

SOURCES: **Mexican-Born Workers, 1980** - *Census of the Population, 1980* (Washington, DC: Bureau of the Census, 1980, table 255(b); 1988 -*Special Studies Series*, p-23, No. 17 (Washington, DC: Bureau of the Census, 1988). **Native Workers**, "Current Population Survey," unpublished tables, Bureau of the Census, Washington, DC, June 1988.

grants for manufacturing jobs. The picture is somewhat different for women. Mexican-born women tend to find work in sectors where overall employment is declining, including personal services and nondurable goods industries such as apparel. Because many native-born women have moved into sales and administrative or "super-clerical" positions in service industries, competition between Mexican-born and native-born women for jobs may be diminishing.

On average, wages for recent immigrants are more than 20 percent below those for native workers, and Mexicans earn lower wages than immigrants from other countries (figure 6-2).[8] It makes little difference whether or not the new immigrants have legal status. In local labor markets, Mexican immigrants depress wages to some degree. (New immigrants are most likely to depress wages for older immigrants, since both old and new are likely to seek similar work.) But competition for jobs in local labor markets is not the only source of impacts on U.S. jobs and job opportunities.

Immigration increases the overall supply of low-skilled workers in the United States directly. Trade (with Mexico and with other countries) has the same effect indirectly if the United States imports goods produced by low-skilled foreign workers while exporting goods produced by higher skilled labor. Under these circumstances, trade will displace low-skilled jobs in the United States, creating an

Figure 6-2—Wage Differentials Between Immigrants and Native-Born U.S. Workers

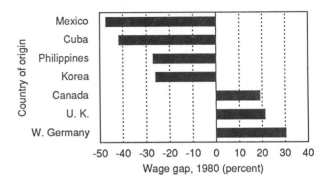

SOURCE: George J. Borjas, *Friends or Strangers: The Impact of Immigrants on the U.S. Economy* (New York, NY: Basic Books, 1990), p. 232.

"excess" of low-skilled labor. Both immigration and trade can thus drive down wages for low-skilled U.S. workers. Estimates based on input-output tables suggest that, in 1988, immigration (from all countries) and trade (with all countries) had, together, increased the effective supply of high school dropouts in the United States by 28 percent for men and 31 percent for women.[9] Combining these estimates with reasonable assumptions about the substitutability of dropouts and graduates indicates that trade and immigration flows may explain 30 to 50 percent of the approximately 10-percent decline in the relative weekly wage of high school dropouts between 1980 and 1988 (see ch. 4, figure 4-1). Because Mexico is the largest source of U.S.

---

[8] The wage gap between immigrants and native workers similar in age and educational attainment was 22 percent in 1980: it has been increasing; immigrants earned 2.6 percent less in 1940, 11 percent less in 1960, and 15 percent less in 1970. One reason is that earlier waves of immigrants from developed countries in Europe were more likely to have skills in high demand in the U.S. labor market. George J. Borjas, "Immigrants in the U.S. Labor Market: 1940-80," *American Economic Review*, vol. 81, 1991, pp. 287-291.

[9] George J. Borjas, Richard B. Freeman, and Lawrence F. Katz, "On the Labor Market Effects of Immigration and Trade," Working Paper No. 3761, National Bureau of Economic Research, Cambridge, MA, June 1991. In 1988, immigrant workers increased the supply of high school dropouts by approximately 25 percent, the supply of high school graduates by 6-7 percent, and the supply of college graduates by 10-11 percent.

Figure 6-3—Age Distributions in Mexico and the United States

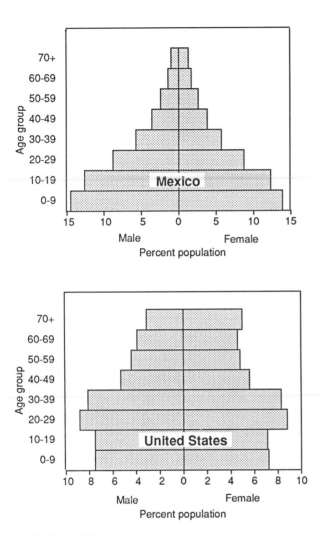

SOURCE: United Nations.

immigrants, and because Mexican immigrants have lower skills on average than immigrants from elsewhere, immigration from Mexico would probably account for something over half of the effect of all immigration on the relative wages of U.S. high school dropouts.[10] Immigration thus appears to have had significant impacts on employment and wages for U.S. workers, even if those impacts can be estimated only roughly.

Factors Influencing Immigration From Mexico

Migration from Mexico to the United States responds to three major influences:

- income inequalities within Mexico, plus demographic and socioeconomic differences between the two countries;
- migration networks that have matured and become entrenched over the past several decades; and
- U.S. immigration policy.

Given the cumulative impacts of these factors, there seems little likelihood that migration will slow appreciably over the next two decades. The United States could not unilaterally stop entry by illegals short of militarizing a 2,000-mile border. There is little the Mexican Government can do to stop migration without dramatically improving living standards for the many millions of poorer Mexicans at the bottom of a highly unequal social pyramid.

Demographic and Socioeconomic Factors

Mexico will have great difficulty creating new jobs for the many people who will enter the labor force in the years ahead. More than half of all Mexicans are under the age of 20, reflecting high birth rates in past years. The population is currently increasing at about 2.3 percent per year, doubling every 30 years or so.[11] The pyramidal age distribution shown in figure 6-3 creates a high degree of momentum for further growth: even if fertility dropped to replacement levels, Mexico's population would continue to increase for several decades as young people entered their reproductive years.

Unless unemployment and underemployment come down, and wages rise, pressures to emigrate could grow rather than diminish.[12] After World War II and

---

[10] Except for 1987, the United States has exported more manufactured goods to Mexico than it has imported in every year since 1983 (ch. 3). The $22.9 billion in U.S. imports from Mexico during 1991 would probably have required more less-skilled labor to produce than the $31.1 billion in exports in that year. Thus trade with Mexico, despite being in substantial surplus, could also have had negative effect on the relative earnings of less skilled U.S. workers.

[11] *1992 WP Data Sheet* (Washington, DC: Population Reference Bureau, 1992). In contrast, the U.S. population is growing at only 0.8 percent per year (including growth due to immigrants), for a doubling time of 90 years.

[12] While relative wages in Mexico and the United States will be a major force in determining future rates of immigration, there is much more to socioeconomic development—and to peoples' propensity to migrate in search of a better life—than their money incomes, as discussed in box 3-A in chapter 3.

until about 1980, Mexico's gross domestic product (GDP) grew at about 6 1/2 percent annually, before dropping during the 1980s. If GDP growth averages 3 percent over the period 1985-2000, Mexico can expect some 10 million "excess" workers by the turn of the century; if GDP growth averages 5 percent, the predicted excess would still reach 6 million.[13] It seems highly unlikely that Mexico's economy could expand fast enough to absorb all new labor force entrants: this would take an unprecedented growth rate of more than 10 percent annually.

Because Mexico's future growth will depend heavily on foreign investment, failure to reach a free trade agreement would ensure more immigration to the United States. On the other hand, socioeconomic improvements in Mexico may initially result in an increase in migration to the United States rather than the decrease expected over the long term. The reason is that expectations could well rise faster than economic improvements in Mexico can be realized.[14]

Migration Networks

Flows of immigrants from particular regions in Mexico to particular regions in the United States have become strongly established over several generations. Mexicans crossed the border to work on railroads at the turn of the century, then to work on farms, still later to work in the growing Los Angeles garment industry.

Currently, the two major migrant streams come from the border region and from rural areas and small towns in Mexico's interior. Immigrants from the border region typically shuttle between jobs in U.S. cities and homes in Mexico. Aided by family and friends, they make repeat trips to the same U.S. city and often the same job. Migrants from the interior are more likely to be undocumented and more likely to end up staying in the United States because of the distance from their home. Having, on average, less education, they generally start lower on the job ladder, but show somewhat more upward mobility than border migrants.[15] The longer migrants from either group stay in the United States, the more likely they are to move into better jobs, bring in family members, and become permanent U.S. residents.

U.S. Immigration Policy

IRCA was intended to slow illegal immigration by requiring employers, for the first time, to verify the legal status of those they hired. But because forged papers are cheap and easily available and because employers have little incentive to closely question those they hire, or to give their papers more than a cursory look (they need not even keep copies on file), the law has been easy to circumvent.[16] Apprehensions of illegals (the only routinely available indicator of entry) dropped sharply after passage of IRCA in 1986, but rose again to 1.2 million in 1990—the same as in 1983.[17] Not only does it seem impossible for the United States to appreciably slow the flow of undocumented workers, but as Mexico continues to industrialize, more workers will develop skills in demand in the United States, increasing their attractiveness to U.S. employers (for some of whom, undocumented workers are not only cheap, but easier to control, and less likely to complain than legal immigrants or native-born workers).

Pressures to migrate grow with rapid population increases in many parts of the Third World. Even if wealthy nations provided considerable development assistance to their poorer neighbors, these pressures seem bound to increase. It may be time to rationalize migration on an international level; as a first step, for instance, the United States could initiate discussions aimed at international agreement on the definitions of such migrant categories as political refugees. It would also seem desirable to establish an interna-

[13] Saul Trejo Reyes, "Mexican-American Employment Relations: The Mexican Context," *U.S.-Mexico Relations: Labor Market Interdependence*, Jorge A. Bustamante, Clark W. Reynolds, and Raúl A. Hinojosa Ojeda, eds. (Stanford, CA: Stanford University Press, 1992), table 6, p. 265. By Reyes's definition, Mexico has about 2 1/2 million excess workers today.

[14] *Unauthorized Migration: An Economic Development Response*, Report of the Commission for the Study of International Migration and Cooperative Economic Development (Washington, DC: U.S. Government Printing Office, July 1990).

[15] In the rural towns of Texas and California, immigrants from the interior find work in agriculture or sawmills, as craftsmen or service workers; in urban areas, they tend to work in construction or service jobs. Richard Jones and William Murray, "Occupational and Spatial Mobility of Temporary Mexican Migrants to the U.S.: A Comparative Analysis," *International Migration Review*, vol. 20, 1986, pp. 973-985.

[16] Robert L. Bach and Howard Brill, "Impact of IRCA on the U.S. Labor Market and Economy," Final Report to the U.S. Department of Labor, Institute for Research on Multiculturalism and International Labor, State University of New York at Binghampton, April 1991.

[17] Borjas, "The Economic Consequences of Migration," op. cit., footnote 6.

tional migration policy body, perhaps under the United Nations.

ENVIRONMENTAL ISSUES

Mexico's most serious environmental problems are in the Federal District (Mexico City and vicinity), Guadalajara, and Monterrey, but it is pollution along the border that most affects air and water quality in the United States.[18] NAFTA opponents have argued that an agreement would spur still more rapid and uncontrolled development along the border, with U.S. firms exporting dirty factories to Mexico. Supporters counter that Mexico can improve its environment only if economic growth generates new revenues that can be put toward cleanup and prevention of pollution.

The Scope of the Problem

Some of the driest land in North America is found in the Border Area, although the region also includes forest and irrigated farmlands.[19] Most of the Border Area is sparsely populated. High salinity of both soil and river water limits food production and human settlements. The total population is about 9 1/2 million, three-quarters of whom live in 14 pairs of sister cities located on each side of the international boundary. Tijuana-San Diego, with nearly 2 million people, and Ciudad Juarez-El Paso with 1 1/2 million, are the two largest city pairs. More people cross the border each day than any other national boundary in the world, with over 200 million entries from Mexico into the United States recorded at 10 crossing stations in 1989 and again in 1990.

Much of the growth on the Mexican side of the border has been recent, paralleling industrial expansion—especially the *maquiladoras*, which have been growing at about 16 percent annually as measured by number of plants and employees. Nearly half of those employed in the Border Area in Mexico work in *maquiladoras*, more than half of which are located in just two cities—Tijuana and Ciudad Juarez.[20] Rapid growth without land use and urban planning has resulted in severe strains on services and infrastructure. Mexican border cities do not have enough drinking water, sewage capacity, housing, or transportation. While San Diego is one of the wealthiest cities in the United States, 40 percent of households across the border in Tijuana have no running water, and 28 percent no electricity.[21]

Environmental problems in the Border Area run the gamut: soil erosion, unmanaged solid and

---

[18] Air pollution in Mexico City is believed to cause hundreds of deaths each year. *U.S.-Mexico Trade: Information on Environmental Regulations and Enforcement*, GAO/NSIAD-91-227 (Washington, DC: U.S. General Accounting Office, May 1991), p. 3. Mexico City's air pollution comes mostly from cars, trucks, and buses (80 percent), with industry contributing 15 percent. Fecal dust comprises most of the balance, because the city's sewage treatment capacity is too small by a factor of three. N. Gardels and M. B. Snell, ''Asphyxiation by Progress,'' *Columbia Journal of World Business*, vol. XXIV, spring 1989, p. 43.

One set of estimates ranks the relative costs of four classes of environmental problems in Mexico in descending order as follows:

- diarrheal diseases arising from water and solid waste pollution, coupled with lack of sanitation and poisoning of foodstuffs;
- health effects of air pollution in Mexico City;
- groundwater depletion; and
- soil erosion.

S. Margulis, *Back-of-the-Envelope Estimates of Environmental Damage Costs in Mexico*, Policy Research Working Paper No. 824 (Washington, DC: World Bank, January 1992).

Because OTA's assessment focuses on the potential effects of increased trade with Mexico on U.S. jobs, the discussion of the environment is necessarily limited. A detailed review of the relationships between international trade and environmental protection can be found in U.S. Congress, Office of Technology Assessment *Trade and the Environment: Conflicts and Opportunities*, OTA-BP-ITE-94 (Washington, DC: U.S. Government Printing Office, May 1992), part of the ongoing study, American Industry and the Environment: Implications for Trade and U.S. Competitiveness. That assessment will examine international markets for environmental services and technology, including Mexico's, and the impact of environmental regulations on U.S. industry.

[19] Factual information on the Border Area comes from *Integrated Environmental Plan for the Mexican-U.S. Border* (Washington, DC: U.S. Government Printing Office, 1992) and *Review of U.S.-Mexico Environmental Issues*, Interagency Task Force coordinated by the Office of the U.S. Trade Representative, Washington, DC, February 1992, unless otherwise noted.

The ''Border Area'' was itself defined in the 1983 ''Agreement between the United States of America and the United Mexican States on Cooperation for the Protection and Improvement of the Environment in the Border Area,'' usually called the U.S.-Mexico Border Environmental Agreement or sometimes the La Paz Agreement, as the region extending 100 kilometers (62 miles) on each side of the boundary between the two countries. Covering about 250,000 square miles, the Border Area is nearly as large as Texas (267,000 square miles).

[20] *Summary: Environmental Plan for the Mexican-U.S. Border Area, First Stage (1992-1994)* (Washington, DC: U.S. Environmental Protection Agency, February 1992), p. 8.

[21] C. Cooper, ''Ecological Exchanges in a Bi-national Metropolis: San Diego and Tijuana,'' paper presented at the Annual Meeting of the American Association for the Advancement of Science, Chicago, Feb. 8, 1992.

Box 6-B—Conservation

Biodiversity in Mexico is exceptionally high. The country ranks fourth in the world in total number of species (first in species diversity for reptiles, second for mammals, and fourth for amphibians).[1] More than half of Mexican reptilian, amphibian, and plant species are found only in Mexico, as are almost half of its freshwater fishes and about one-third of its mammals.

Economic development and population growth inevitably threaten wildlife habitats. Mexico cannot feed its people, and will seek to expand its agricultural lands. If a NAFTA reduces U.S. barriers to imports of Mexican fruits and vegetables, areas that are now marginal for farming could come under cultivation. Careful planning will be needed if the highways, roads, and railway lines needed to transport a growing volume of trade are not to cut into fragile wetlands and desert habitats. But perhaps most threatened are the Gulf of Mexico and its estuaries, major commercial fishing areas and unique resources.

The Gulf of Mexico

Gulf wetlands provide habitat for at least three-quarters of North American migrating waterfowl.[2] Many species of fish and shellfish breed in these same wetlands. The gulf and its estuaries have already been seriously damaged by U.S. oil and gas production, the associated petrochemical industries, and agricultural runoff, together with industrial wastes and sewage from Mexico. Oil spills and wastes associated with shipping also pose continuing threats. Examples of the damage include:

- polluted estuaries, with adverse consequences for commercial fishing (including closure of millions of acres to harvesting of shellfish because of human health concerns);
- the deaths of an estimated 2 million seabirds and 100,000 marine mammals each year in the United States alone because of marine debris, often plastic, which entangles the animals or is mistaken as food; and
- the loss of marine vegetation from dredging, urbanization, toxic industrial wastes, and sewage.

---

[1] *Mexico Environmental Project,* Report No. 10005-ME (Washington, DC: World Bank, 1992).

Threats to biodiversity go back at least to the European colonization of North America and the westward expansion of the United States. The estimated 60 million bison, which in 1700 roamed much of what is now Mexico as well as the central United States, had been reduced to a few dozen by 1900. F. O. Monasterio, ''Confronting Environmental Degradation: A Problem Without Borders,'' *FAO Review,* vol. 20, Sept./Oct. 1987, pp. 35-37.

[2] *Summary: Environmental Plan for the Mexican-U.S. Border Area, First Stage (1992-1994)* (Washington, DC: U.S. Environmental Protection Agency, February 1992), p. 8.

---

hazardous waste, pesticides and other agricultural chemicals, pollution of air and water, and squandering of natural resources (box 6-B). Damage occurs both directly (e.g., contamination of rivers and ground water with industrial solvents) and indirectly (e.g., as a secondary consequence of unpaved roads and poor housing). The current situation can be summarized as follows:

- *Air quality.* The limited data available from monitoring stations on the U.S. side indicate that most of the larger U.S. border communities, including San Diego and El Paso, fail to meet one or more national air quality standards. Air quality monitoring, often limited on the U.S. side, has only recently begun on the Mexican side of the border, but it seems clear that Mexico is the source of much of the air pollution in the Border Area as a whole.

- *Water quality.* Border Area water comes from major river systems including the Colorado, Tijuana, and Rio Bravo/Rio Grande, and from ground water sources. Threats to the quality of Border Area water supplies, and to the marine environment of the Pacific Ocean and the Gulf of Mexico, come both from industrial pollution and from inadequate sewage treatment. For example, the common ground water aquifer serving Nogales, Mexico and Nogales, Arizona has been contaminated with industrial solvents from *maquila* plants.[22]

Many Mexican border cities have no sewage treatment plants of any kind. Ciudad Juarez, for

---

[22] Mary E. Kelly, Dick Kamp, Michael Gregory, and Jan Rich, ''U.S.-Mexico Free Trade Negotiations and the Environment: Exploring the Issues,'' *Columbia Journal of World Business,* vol. XXVI, summer 1991, pp. 43-58.

Cooperation and Conflict

The United States and Mexico are signatories to both bilateral and multilateral wildlife conservation agreements covering migratory birds, game mammals, and endangered species. The agreements provide for animal surveys, information exchange, training of technicians, enforcement of prohibitions against trade in wildlife, and preservation of wetlands and wintering sites.[3] Bilateral agreements also provide for establishment of national parks, firefighting, and management of forest resources.

While cooperative efforts go back many years, so do conflicts—over water rights, and recently over tuna fishing. With the 1972 Marine Mammal Protection Act, the United States set strict standards for the protection of dolphins, which were frequently killed or injured during commercial fishing operations.[4] Failure by Mexico to meet these standards led the United States, in 1991, to ban imports of tuna from Mexico.[5] Mexico protested to the General Agreement on Tariffs and Trade (GATT), arguing that the U.S. ban was an unfair trade practice. Subsequently, a GATT dispute resolution panel found the U.S. action to be in violation of GATT codes. The matter remained unresolved as of mid-1992, the next step being consideration of the panel's findings by the GATT Council.

Similar issues have surrounded the incidental death of sea turtles during Mexican shrimp fishing operations in the Pacific and the Gulf of Mexico. Seven of the eight species of marine turtles lay their eggs on Mexico's beaches.[6] U.S. shrimping vessels use special devices to keep sea turtles out of their nets, practices that Mexican officials state will be adopted within 3 years. Mexico has also promised to stop fishing for the olive ridley sea turtle, an endangered species found on the Pacific Coast of southern Mexico.

---

[3] Bilateral agreements include the 1936 Convention for the Protection of Migratory Birds and Game Mammals and the 1984 Agreement for Cooperation in the Conservation of Wildlife. Multilateral agreements include, among others, the 1941 Convention on Nature Protection and Wildlife Preservation in the Western Hemisphere, the 1988 U.S.-Mexico-Canada Tripartite Agreement on the Conservation of Wetlands, and the Convention on International Trade in Endangered Species of Wild Fauna and Flora (CITES), a treaty addressing illegal trade in wildlife that Mexico recently signed. *Review of U.S.-Mexico Environmental Issues,* Interagency Task Force coordinated by the Office of the U.S. Trade Representative, Washington, DC, February 1992, p. 49-50.

[4] Tuna and dolphins often swim together, especially in the eastern tropical Pacific, where a quarter of the world's tuna are taken. Fishermen who saw herds of dolphins surfacing to breathe would set their nets for tuna, entangling dolphins who then suffocated because they could not reach the surface. With passage of the 1972 law, modifications to nets and new fishing practices reduced estimated dolphin deaths from about 130,000 in 1986 to 25,000 in 1991.

[5] *Trade and the Environment: Conflicts and Opportunities* (Washington, DC: Office of Technology Assessment, May 1992), pp. 15-16, 18-19. Between 1986 and 1989, Mexican fishermen reduced the number of dolphins killed per net deployed by more than half. R. Howard, "U.S.-Mexican Cooperation Goes Far Beyond Trade," *Business America,* Apr. 8, 1991, p. 9.

[6] *Mexico Environmental Project,* op. cit., footnote 1, p. 4.

---

example, produces 22 million gallons of raw sewage daily.[23] With an estimated 8 to 10 million gallons of raw sewage pumped daily into the Tijuana River, a 2.5-mile section of San Diego beach has been closed since 1980, with the quarantine temporarily extended to 6 miles in 1983 and again in 1985 because of shifts in ocean currents.[24] Besides the major river systems, Border Area fresh water comes from renewable and nonrenewable ground waters. The quality of recharging water will affect the quality of water later pumped from underground aquifers. Inadequate or nonexistent sewage treatment has contaminated wells with coliform bacteria and viruses, leading to concern over sewage-associated diseases including typhoid and hepatitis, which are more common on the Mexican side of the border.[25]

---

[23] D. Solis and S. L. Nazario, "U.S., Mexico Take on Border Pollution," *Wall Street Journal,* Feb. 25, 1992, p. B1.

[24] J. Ladou, "Deadly Migration: Hazardous Industries' Flight to the Third World," *Technology Review,* July 1991, p. 50; *Summary: Environmental Plan for the Mexican-U.S. Border, First Stage (1992-1994),* op. cit., footnote 20, p. 12. San Diego, which has treated some of Tijuana's waste water since the 1960s, now plans to build a new sewage plant for Tijuana's sole use.

An estimated 20 million gallons of raw sewage enters the Rio Grande each day; the New River receives 17 million gallons. "A Permanent US-Mexico Border Environmental Health Commission," *Journal of the American Medical Association,* vol. 263, June 27, 1990, p. 3320.

[25] The Pan American Health Organization places the incidence of typhoid at 100 times higher on the Mexican side. Solis and Nazario, "U.S., Mexico Take On Border Pollution," op. cit., footnote 23. Hepatitis in San Elizario, TX, which affects 35 percent of children by the age of 8 and 90 percent of residents by the age of 35, has been attributed to a sewage-polluted aquifer shared across the border. "Environmental Impact of NAFTA Investment Provisions: Problems and Solutions, Memo to Ambassador Carla Hills, U.S. Trade Representative, from J. D. Hair, President, National Wildlife Federation," Nov. 20, 1991, p. 2.

- *Municipal solid waste*. Mexican border cities generate about 3,500 tons of garbage each day; only half is collected, two-thirds of which goes to open air dumps.
- *Hazardous waste. Maquiladoras* generate unknown but evidently large amounts of hazardous waste. Mexico's environmental regulations require that hazardous waste generated in *maquila* plants from raw materials imported from the United States either be returned or ''nationalized'' (e.g., recycled and retained in Mexico). Compliance appears to be low: records collected by the U.S. Environmental Protection Agency (EPA) show only 9 shipments (totaling 190 tons) of hazardous waste from *maquila* plants through U.S. Customs ports in Texas in 1987, and 356 shipments (2,390 tons) in 1990. Mexico's environmental agency, SEDUE, has put the compliance of *maquiladoras* with requirements for hazardous waste return at about 30 percent in 1991, twice as high as the previous year.[26]
- *Soil erosion*. An estimated two-thirds of Mexican land suffers from moderate erosion (losses of up to 4 tons of soil per acre per year), and 13 percent from severe erosion (losses of 4 to 6 tons annually).[27] For the farmer, erosion reduces land productivity and raises costs if more fertilizer is used to replenish nutrients. Erosion also leads to increased runoff, slowing the recharge of aquifers, and causes silting of dams and waterways.

Environmental Protection in Mexico

Mexico passed its first environmental law in 1971, establishing a Subsecretariat of Environmental Improvement under the Secretariat of Health, but the agency got little money and did not accomplish much.[28] Under President de la Madrid, who took office in 1982 after making the environment a campaign theme, Mexico created SEDUE, with responsibilities similar to those of the U.S.

EPA. SEDUE's budget remained small, if only because of Mexico's debt crisis, but the 1980s brought acknowledgement that Mexico City's air pollution was becoming intolerable and saw the beginnings of a grassroots environmental movement. So far, environmental groups have been small, scattered, and concerned with local issues, most of them in Mexico City, although citizen involvement is also growing in the Border Area.

The comprehensive Federal Law of Ecological Equilibrium and Environmental Protection followed in 1988, covering both environmental protection (water, air, pesticides, hazardous wastes) and conservation of natural resources.[29] SEDUE was given considerable powers to, for example, shut down plants—powers not unusual in Mexico (box 6-C). But Mexico's government announced in April 1992 that SEDUE itself would be absorbed into a new Secretariat for Social Development (SEDESOL), along with the huge social welfare agency known as PRONASOL. SEDESOL will be a large and powerful agency, thanks to the former PRONASOL; it also becomes heir to a long-established tradition of patronage and porkbarreling. In the U.S. context, merging SEDUE into PRONASOL could be compared to merging EPA into the Department of Health and Human Services. In the Mexican context, on the other hand, the shift might be taken as a signal of a higher priority for the environment. If nothing else, a wait-and-see attitude seems called for. Much the same holds for Mexico's announced plans to give more responsibility for environmental enforcement and clean-up to state governments.

Mexican environmental laws state general objectives rather than specific criteria that must be met. These broad objectives must be codified in regulatory language and technical standards, a process that is underway but not complete. Regulations and technical norms issued so far cover aspects of environmental impact assessment, air pollution, hazardous waste disposal, vehicle emissions in

---

[26] P. Chirinos, Secretary of Urban Development and Ecology, ''Mexican Integrated Environmental Border Plan,'' speech, Ciudad Juarez, Oct. 23, 1991.

SEDUE (*Secretaría de Desarollo Urbano y Ecologia*, the Secretariat for Urban Development and Ecology) has recently merged with another agency, as discussed later in the chapter. For convenience, the chapter refers to SEDUE throughout.

[27] *Back-of-the-Envelope Estimates of Environmental Damage Costs in Mexico*, op. cit., footnote 18, pp. 7-8.

[28] This summary of events before passage of Mexico's comprehensive environmental law in 1988 is based on S.P. Mumme, ''Clearing the Air: Environmental Reform in Mexico,'' *Environment*, vol. 33, December 1991, pp. 9-10.

[29] The text was drafted by the then head of SEDUE, a close associate of Mexico's current President Salinas. Seventeen separate U.S. statutes deal with the comparable range of issues. See *Review of U.S.-Mexico Environmental Issues*, op. cit., footnote 19, pp. 17-23.

As in the United States, the laws and regulations of the 31 Mexican states must be at least as stringent as federal law.

Box 6-C—Enforcement[1]

In the United States, legal maneuvers and litigation can substantially slow regulatory enforcement. By the same token, environmental groups have been able to use the U.S. legal system to force reluctant firms and government agencies to follow the law. Neither polluters nor citizen groups have as much recourse in Mexico, where government agencies have substantially more independence of action and freedom from oversight.[2] Enforcement takes place primarily through administrative proceedings, rather than litigation.

Like the United States, Mexico relies on a system of permits (now requiring environmental impact assessments for new facilities and expansions, and, if there are possible hazards, a risk assessment) and inspections to ensure compliance with laws and regulations. SEDUE can levy fines, close plants (partially, temporarily, permanently, or in combination), and order administrative detention of corporate officers for up to 36 hours (usually served in periods of several hours per day until an agreement on compliance is reached). SEDUE not infrequently shuts plants before negotiations to force a quick settlement.[3] Criminal prosecutions have been rare.

Despite SEDUE's theoretical powers, enforcement of Mexico's environmental regulations has been lax. The agency's budget was only $39 million in 1991 (compared with a U.S. EPA budget of about $5 billion), and at that had increased by more than six times from a 1989 total of $6 million.[4] Mexico had only 19 inspectors to monitor some 120,000 industrial facilities until 1991, when the authorized level went to 100.[5]

---

[1] For further detail, see *Review of U.S.-Mexico Environmental Issues*, Interagency Task Force coordinated by the Office of the U.S. Trade Representative, Washington, DC, February 1992, pp. 38-42.

[2] Mexico's civil law tradition gives the executive considerable power to take unilateral action and to itself resolve disputes; the public at large has little standing or influence. S.S. Jarvis, "Preparing Employees to Work South of the Border," *Personnel*, June 1990, p. 60.

[3] Plant closings by SEDUE in the winter of 1990-91 spurred multinationals operating in Mexico to begin environmental audits in preparation for negotiations with SEDUE inspectors, so as to avert the possibility of costly shutdowns. R.S. Jones, "Learning from Experience," *Business Mexico*, October 1991, p. 26.

Reportedly, more than 1,000 plants have been closed since 1989—82 permanently, including a state-owned refinery in Mexico City that employed 5,000 people. A.R. Dowd, "Viva Free Trade with Mexico!" *Fortune*, June 17, 1991, p. 100.

[4] "Mexican Environmental Laws, Regulations and Standards: Preliminary Report of EPA Findings," U.S. Environmental Protection Agency, Office of Enforcement, Office of the General Counsel, May 3, 1991, revised June 19, 1991, p. 2.

The World Bank is currently evaluating Mexico's application for a $90 million loan for SEDUE. T. Atkeson, Assistant Administrator, Office of International Activities, Environmental Protection Agency, *Hearings on the North American Free Trade Agreement*, Serial No. 102-15, House Committee on Energy and Commerce, Subcommittee on Commerce, Consumer Protection, and Competitiveness, Mar. 20, May 8 and 15, 1991, p. 104.

[5] S. Fletcher and M. Tiemann, "Environment and Trade," Issue Brief IB92006, Congressional Research Service, updated Mar. 4, 1992. Fifty of the new inspectors are intended for the Border Area.

Mexico City, and contamination of the sea. Environmental impact and risk assessments are not required for existing industrial facilities, but plants must register with SEDUE and apply for air, water, and hazardous waste permits, as appropriate.[30] Three areas regulated in the United States but not yet covered in Mexico are: land disposal of hazardous waste; leaking underground storage tanks; and cleanup of abandoned hazardous wastesites.[31]

Environment and the NAFTA

Mexico and the United States have negotiated over issues at least tangentially related to the

---

[30] The percentage of *maquiladora* plants meeting the requirements for licensing under the 1988 federal law reportedly rose from 6 percent in 1989 to 55 percent in the fall of 1991. Chirinos, "Mexican Integrated Environmental Border Plan," op. cit., footnote 26.

U.S. labor and environmental groups have argued, with some justification, that lax environmental enforcement in Mexico attracts U.S. plants that might otherwise stay at home. Most of the documented cases involve inherently dirty industrial processes, where U.S. regulations have become increasingly stringent. For example, three-quarters of furniture companies that relocated from Los Angeles to Mexico during 1989 cited tough California standards for emissions associated with paint and solvents, although labor costs appeared to be at least as important as a reason for moving. U.S. General Accounting Office, letter to the Honorable John Dingell, *Hearings on the North American Free Trade Agreement*, Serial No. 102-1-5, House Committee on Energy and Commerce, Subcommittee on Commerce, Consumer Protection, and Competitiveness, March 20, May 8 and 15, 1991, p. 237.

A study by the U.S. International Trade Commission found that labor costs ranked first and environmental controls last in a list of 21 factors influencing locational decisions. T. Atkeson, Assistant Administrator, Office of International Activities, Environmental Protection Agency, *Hearings on the North American Free Trade Agreement* (above), p. 87.

[31] *U.S.-Mexico Trade: Information on Environmental Regulations and Enforcement*, op. cit., footnote 18, p. 6.

Box 6-D—*Major U.S.-Mexico Agreements Related to the Environment[1]*

1889 - International Boundary Commission (IBC)

Created to settle boundary disputes.

1906 - Convention Providing for the Equitable Distribution of the Waters of the Rio Grande for Irrigation Purposes

Governed allocation of water from the upper 90 miles of the Rio Bravo/Rio Grande.

1944 - Treaty on the Utilization of Waters of the Colorado and Tijuana Rivers and of the Rio Grande (Water Treaty of 1944)

Replaced the IBC with the International Boundary and Water Commission (IBWC) and modified the 1906 convention. In cooperation with SEDUE and EPA, the IBWC identifies and seeks to correct cross-border water pollution problems. Currently, the IBWC is overseeing construction or expansion of waste water treatment facilities in five pairs of Border Area cities.

1983 - U.S. Mexico Border Environmental Agreement (La Paz Agreement)

First formal agreement to improve the environment in the Border Area. Provides a ''basis for cooperation for the protection, improvement, and conservation of the environment and the problems that affect it . . . and a framework for development of a system of notification for emergency situations.'' Defines responsibilities for governmental bodies including EPA, SEDUE, and the IBWC. Provides for study of air pollution along the border.

1989 - Mexico City Agreement on Pollution

Commits both countries to solving air and water pollution, hazardous waste, and environmental health problems in Mexico City.

Integrated Environmental Plan for the Mexican-U.S. Border Area (First Stage, 1992-1994)

The *Plan*, as it is referred to in this chapter, was released in February 1992. It is discussed in the text of the chapter.

---

[1]*U.S.-Mexico Trade: Information on Environmental Regulations and Enforcement*, GAO/NSIAD-91-227 (Washington, DC: U.S. General Accounting Office, May 1991); *Integrated Environmental Plan for the Mexican-U.S. Border Area (First Stage, 1992-1994)* (Washington, DC: U.S. Government Printing Office, 1992).

---

environment—notably use of water from the Rio Grande—for more than a century. During the 1980s, the agenda expanded to include the full panoply of environmental issues (box 6-D).

In May 1991, when Congress granted the administration ''fast track'' negotiating authority, it called for the administration to address the environmental consequences of a NAFTA (on both sides of the border) on a parallel track.[32] In response, Presidents Bush and Salinas charged EPA and SEDUE to jointly prepare the *Integrated Environmental Plan for the Mexican-US. Border Area*. Intended as a master plan for dealing with border environmental problems, the *Plan* was released at the same time as a parallel *Review of U.S.-Mexico Environmental Issues* (the ''*Review*''), prepared by the Office of the U.S. Trade Representative. Neither the *Plan* nor the *Review* is an environmental impact statement; such a document could not be prepared without a NAFTA text in hand.

Both reports, and especially the more important *Plan*, have come under intense criticism for lacking specific goals for environmental improvements and

---

[32] In a letter to President Bush, Senator Lloyd Bentsen, Chairman of the Committee on Finance, and Representative Dan Rostenkowski, Chairman of the Committee on Ways and Means, also requested the president to indicate how differences in health and safety standards and the rights of workers in the two countries would be addressed. See *Exchange of Letters on Issues Concerning the Negotiation of a North American Free Trade Agreement*, Committee on Ways and Means, U.S. House of Representatives, May 1, 1991.

cost estimates for achieving them.[33] EPA and SEDUE conducted 17 public hearings in September 1991, following release of a draft of the *Plan* the preceding month. Seven of the hearings took place in Mexico, where they attracted great attention as unique events in a country lacking a tradition of citizen involvement on environmental matters.[34] The final version of the *Plan* addressed some (but not all) of the issues raised at the hearings. It does not, for example, call for *maquiladoras* to submit plans and timetables for meeting environmental standards, or require SEDUE to disclose information on environmental and health hazards, a matter of great concern to many of those who participated in hearings on the Mexican side of the border.[35]

Congressional concern has continued to mount. In House Resolution 146, Congress reserved the right to rescind fast-track authority if the administration failed to act decisively on border environmental problems, and in at least four other resolutions (H. Res. 149, H. Res. 151, H. Res. 227, and H. Res. 246), Congress requested the administration to include environmental provisions within the NAFTA it-

self.[36] In response to mounting criticism and this spate of resolutions, the administration began to negotiate for "green language" in a NAFTA. U.S. Trade Representative Carla Hills, in a June 1992 letter to Senator Max Baucus, listed the following environmental goals for NAFTA:[37]

1. To ensure that U.S. environmental laws and regulations, if applied in a nondiscriminatory manner, can be defended against unfair trade challenges.

2. To provide that the NAFTA not interfere with U.S. measures taken to comply with international environmental agreements.

3. To make clear that there is to be no "downward harmonization" of U.S. environmental and health and safety standards, and to explicitly recognize, in the text of the NAFTA, the right of States and other subnational governmental bodies to set their own environmental and health protection standards.

4. To place the burden of proof on the party challenging any environmental measure as constituting an unfair trade measure.

[33] In response to critiques of a draft of the *Review*, released in October 1991, the final version included further discussion of public health and maritime issues, among other additions. The additions can best be characterized as background information. See, for example, "Comments on the Draft Review of U.S.-Mexico Environmental Issues," Natural Resources Defense Council, *Instituto Autónomo De Investigaciones Ecológicas, A.C.*, and *Grupo de los Cien*, December 1991. The authors took issue with the draft *Review* because it concentrated on the Border Area, assumed that environmental improvement would automatically follow from economic development, and did not consider alternatives to a NAFTA versus no-NAFTA choice.

[34] For discussion of the criticisms of the 1991 draft *Plan* based on testimony at eight of the hearings, interviews with environmental specialists in the Border Area, and other sources, along with briefer comments on the final *Plan*, see J.G. Rich, *Planning the Border's Future: The Mexican-U.S. Integrated Border Environmental Plan*, U.S.-Mexican Occasional Paper No. 1 of the U.S.-Mexican Policy Studies Program, LBJ School of Public Affairs (Austin, TX: University of Texas at Austin, March 1992). This report summarizes criticisms of the draft *Plan* in 17 areas, ranging from inadequacies in the planning process itself (border communities complained of exclusion from the process, including inadequate notice of hearings) to vagueness on measures for improvement in all areas of environmental protection. Lack of funding drew the most criticism.

[35] Rich, *Planning the Border's Future*, ibid.

In a another analysis of the *Plan*, the Texas Center for Policy Studies stated that it "still falls far short of the needs of the border area today." After examining 87 action items for 1992 in the *Plan*—none constrained by financing—the Center concluded that:

• more than half (53 percent) consisted of information exchange during meetings, training programs, and plant visits;

• 10 percent of the remainder "amounted to a promise to enforce existing laws"; and

• 17 percent called for a study or for further planning. See "A Response to the EPA/SEDUE Integrated Border Environment Plan," Texas Center for Policy Studies, Austin, Mar. 1, 1992.

Another critic in Texas, the Governor's environmental policy advisor, included in the *Plan*'s deficiencies that it is: short on funding; lacks deadlines; is vague on enforcement and on mechanisms for coordination between State agencies and EPA; and calls for unnecessary needs assessments. She also criticized the U.S. funding commitment compared to that of Mexico. See *International Trade Reporter*, Mar. 4, 1982, p. 401.

Further criticism of the *Plan* and/or the *Review* has come from the Community Nutrition Institute, the National Wildlife Federation, the Fair Trade Campaign, and the Environmental Defense Fund. See, for summaries, "NAFTA: Flaws in Free Trade, Border Plans Seen Drawing Environmentalists' Opposition," *International Trade Reporter*, Mar. 11, 1992, p. 452; and "Environmental Community Cites Flaws in Border Plan, Environmental Review," *International Environmental Reporter*, Mar. 11, 1992, pp. 136-137.

[36] Congress also raised these issues in hearings—e.g., *Issues Relating to a Bilateral Free Trade Agreement with Mexico*, hearings, Subcommittee on Western Hemisphere and Peace Corps Affairs, Committee on Foreign Relations, U.S. Senate, Mar. 14, 22 and Apr. 11, 1991, and *North American Free Trade Agreement*, hearings, Subcommittee on Commerce, Consumer Protection, and Competitiveness, Committee on Energy and Commerce, U.S. House of Representatives, Mar. 20, May 8 and 15, 1991.

[37] "Hills Lays Out Administration Plans on Environmental Initiatives in NAFTA," *Inside U.S. Trade*, June 19, 1992, pp. S-1 - S-5.

5. To include technical and scientific experts in dispute resolution concerning environmental issues.

Though such a response might seem comprehensive, it fell far short of what Senator Baucus sought. For example, Senator Baucus had asked for an explicit declaration that existing U.S. Federal and State environmental laws and regulations be immune from challenge under NAFTA. He also called for uniform North American environmental protection standards, which all new manufacturing facilities would have to meet; for financial commitments within the NAFTA text; and suggested that a permanent advisory body be created to monitor environmental conditions in the years following implementation of a NAFTA.

Cleaning up the Border Area will take a great deal of money. Keeping it clean will require serious commitment to regulatory enforcement, particularly in Mexico. Estimates of the sums needed run well into the billions of dollars.[38] The final version of the *Plan* provides relatively little reassurance on the central issue of long-term funding by the two governments (or other means of financing clean-up such as taxes on polluters). The United States has agreed to pay $379 million during fiscal years 1992 and 1993, and Mexico $466 million over the 3 years 1992 to 1994. These are modest sums. They may not be enough even to begin arresting the deterioration of the Border Area environment, much less to begin improving conditions there. Since the Border Area is still industrializing rapidly on the Mexican side, greater expenditures in all likelihood will be needed in the years ahead just to keep up with growth.

Mexico's budgetary commitment is commendable, but it is hard to be sanguine about the government's decision to eliminate SEDUE as an independent agency, and to merge it into a Secretariat for Social Development. Moreover, should a NAFTA be implemented, some of the pressure would be off the Mexican Government, because environmental groups are not strong enough, as yet, to have much influence. Ensuring border cleanup requires financing methods in both countries that do not depend on government appropriations. As discussed in chapter 2, a binational commission could be created to finance environmental improvement and infrastructure projects (e.g., sewage treatment plants) along the border.[39] The commission might issue bonds, backed by both governments, to be repaid, for example, by the proceeds from user fees or "green taxes." These fees could be levied on business profits in the Border Area or on exports from *maquiladoras*.

CONCLUDING REMARKS

Signs of the growing momentum behind environmental protection in Mexico include the comprehensive federal law passed in 1988, a growing number of environmental inspectors, stronger ties between the environmental protection agencies in Mexico and the United States, spending promised by Mexico for implementation of the *Integrated Plan for the Mexican-U.S. Border Area*, and growing citizen awareness. But the problems are massive, and the *Plan* has been widely criticized as inadequate, particularly in its lack of timetables and guaranteed long-term funding sources. Despite its own limited success in setting priorities, the United States has far more experience than Mexico in environmental cleanup and control, and could, with Mexico's agreement, take a more prominent role in improving environmental conditions in the Border Area, where pollution affects people in both countries.

In contrast, the United States has relatively little ability to control the flow of Mexican immigrants seeking to cross the border. Draconian policies would be necessary to slow undocumented immigration appreciably; only with improvements in wages and income distribution in Mexico will the pressures that drive migration moderate. There is little reason to expect a NAFTA, by itself, to slow migration to the United States.

---

[38] An EPA official recently estimated that meeting current needs simply for sewage treatment and drinking water in the Border Area would cost $3.5 billion. "U.S. Working With Mexico to Develop Way to Track Maquiladora's Hazardous Wastes," *International Environment Reporter*, July 1, 1992, p. 431. Also see "Down Mexico Way," *The Economist*, Apr. 18, 1992, p. 24; "The Environmental Impact of NAFTA Investment Provisions," op. cit., footnote 25, p. 5.

[39] Representatives Bill Richardson and Ron Wyden have introduced a resolution (H. Con. Res. 325) calling for a U.S.-Mexico environmental commission with 13 members from each country having such responsibilities. Such a commission could also determine needs and priorities. This approach has the advantage that funds would be independent of federal budget processes in both countries. See *Congressional Record*, May 27, 1992, p. H 3834.

Chapter 7

Autos and Parts

Contents

Boxes

Figures

Tables

SUMMARY

Mexico has an automobile industry today as a direct result of government policies that forced companies to produce in Mexico in order to sell there. General Motors (GM), Ford, Chrysler, Nissan, and Volkswagen (VW), the major firms in the Mexican industry, viewed their original investments as the price of admission to Mexico's market. Because sales were too low to support efficient plants, the companies would have preferred to supply Mexico through imports. But today all five operate engine and assembly plants oriented to both the domestic and export markets.

Most of the companies have assembly plants near Mexico City that primarily serve the domestic market. Historically, these have been profitable only because of trade barriers; if a North American Free Trade Agreement (NAFTA) sharply lowered those barriers, these plants would have to reduce their costs and improve their productivity to remain viable. Newer export-oriented plants have good to excellent performance records. The automakers now view them as part of their continental production base. In contrast to engine and assembly plants, most *maquiladora* investments for assembling wiring harness, electrical and electronic parts, and seats would have been made regardless of the Mexican Government's auto decrees.

In the highly integrated U.S.-Canadian industry, trade friction and the threat of protection by the United States accelerated investments by Japanese automakers in U.S. "transplants." These, along with imports, have permanently altered the dynamics of the industry, for GM, Ford, and Chrysler—the Big Three—and for the independent firms that supply them with parts (box 7-A).

Transplant assemblers, and the transplant suppliers that sell to them, have significant cost advantages over their U.S.-based rivals; even if they pay similar wages, their benefit costs are much lower. Independent U.S. suppliers will come under severe pressure in the next few years. Some may see their hope for survival in moving to Mexico.

A NAFTA that forced Mexico's Government to abandon its protectionist policies would leave auto-makers free to locate plants in Mexico based on the same criteria they use in the United States and Canada. But Mexico offers limited strategic options for the Big Three: while direct production costs are sometimes lower in Mexico, shipping can eat up the savings and then some. Only for engines and labor-intensive *maquila* parts production do low labor costs consistently outweigh the additional costs of operating in Mexico. Thus, OTA finds little reason to believe that *existing* efficient capacity with a high utilization rate in the United States or Canada would be closed and replaced by production in Mexico. But plants with old equipment, poor productivity/quality records, or low utilization (e.g., because they make vehicles whose sales have declined) will be at risk regardless of a NAFTA.

Companies that need *new* capacity in North America will find Mexico more attractive as they continue to gain experience there, as the Mexican market grows, and as local suppliers become more numerous and capable. So far, a weak Mexican supplier base has made it difficult for automakers to meet existing local content requirements. Mexican-owned and operated parts firms can rarely match their U.S. and Canadian counterparts in terms of cost or quality, much less engineering capability; small size, low productivity, and poor management offset their low labor costs.

In the short term, then, neither the Big Three nor transplant assemblers can expect to substantially improve their competitive positions by moving production to Mexico. Some parts suppliers can do so, particularly if they have labor-intensive production processes. Parts firms are putting more sophisticated production into Mexico, and Mexican suppliers are entering strategic alliances with U.S. and European firms to improve their own capabilities. Even so, the overall risks to U.S. jobs and job opportunities in this industry stem more from contraction and restructuring by the Big Three and their independent suppliers, who have not only lost sales to transplants and imports but must improve productivity to achieve and maintain profitability. As these companies become leaner, they need fewer workers. Meanwhile, most of the transplants have located in different parts of the country than the

---

Box 7-A—North American Auto Production: An Overview

A car or truck has thousands of parts made by many different companies. The industry can be viewed as a pyramid consisting of assemblers, their internal or captive suppliers, and independent suppliers in several tiers. The assemblers sit at the apex, designing, developing, assembling, marketing, and distributing vehicles—which today include a wide variety of light trucks (e.g., vans and jeep-like utility vehicles), as well as passenger cars (1991 U.S. sales included 5 million light trucks, along with 9.5 million cars), typically, the assemblers make most major components themselves—engines, transmissions, and large stampings (fenders, hoods, body structure). But they buy other parts, components, and subsystems, ranging from brakes and engine electronics to seats and window glass.

The 1965 auto pact with Canada led to the integration of the U.S. and Canadian industries and a single market for vehicles and parts. In addition, GM and Ford have extensive overseas operations, especially in Europe, while each of the Big Three has equity links and/or strategic alliances with automakers in the Far East. GM was and is highly integrated vertically, making many more of its own parts than Ford and Chrysler.

As Japanese automakers increased their sales in the United States, helped by superior manufacturing and organizational know-how (lately labeled ''lean production'') that enabled them to keep their prices low and their quality high, the Big Three lost market share and in some years lost money. Sales dropped (figure 7-1), they found themselves with more engine, assembly, and parts plants than needed, and began to close some. Continuing trade friction, exemplified by the long-running ''voluntary'' restraint agreements on imports from Japan, spurred investments in U.S. plants by Japanese automakers. As they began to assemble vehicles in the United States and Canada, many of their parts suppliers, often members of the same *keiretsu*, followed. At the same time, despite the intense rivalries among the major automakers, they have formed a growing number of joint ventures and cooperative marketing agreements.

Today, the U.S. industry employs about a million people. Some 600,000 work for assembly firms, about half in their parts operations, and 400,000 for independent suppliers. Roughly 100 first-tier suppliers—many of them large companies with such familiar names as United Technologies and TRW—sell to the automakers, sometimes in competition with captive suppliers like GM's Delco division. Thousands of lower tier suppliers and subcontractors sell to first-tier suppliers, to the automakers themselves, and in the aftermarket.

Over the last decade, Ford and Chrysler have cut back their internal parts production, seeking to reduce costs and increase flexibility by buying more on the outside, and relying more heavily on suppliers for technology. At the same time, they have streamlined their purchasing, reducing the number of suppliers they deal with directly. Transplant assemblers import many parts from Japan or purchase from transplant suppliers here, which has increased the overcapacity in the traditional supplier base.

---

plants being closed by U.S. firms, aggravating displacement problems.

MEXICO'S AUTO INDUSTRY

Policy decrees issued by Mexico's government have shaped its automobile industry since 1925 (box 7-B). Over time, the objectives shifted from import substitution through assembly of knock-down kits to, most recently, investments by multinational auto firms in world-class assembly and engine plants that would export to the United States and elsewhere. Today, Mexico produces almost as many cars for export—mostly to the United States—as for domestic sale (table 7-1).

Assembly

Because of the policies summarized in box 7-B, automakers operate two types of assembly plants in Mexico—those supplying the domestic market, and those producing for export, primarily to the United States. With Mexico's economic upturn, domestic sales more than doubled from 274,000 passenger cars and trucks in 1989 to 643,000 in 1991. OTA's interviews suggest that sales could reach a million units by 1995. Because trade barriers remain in force, imports take less than 2 percent of the market.

For many years, sales in Mexico were relatively low. Plants were small, built mostly in and around Mexico City. Today these plants are old and difficult to expand because they are in locations that have

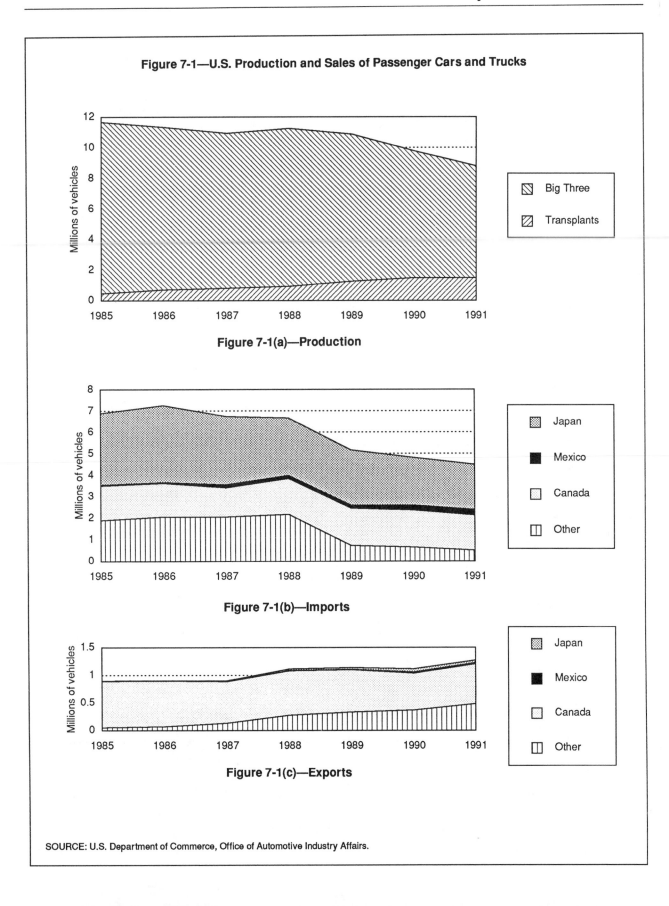

Figure 7-1—U.S. Production and Sales of Passenger Cars and Trucks

Figure 7-1(a)—Production

Figure 7-1(b)—Imports

Figure 7-1(c)—Exports

SOURCE: U.S. Department of Commerce, Office of Automotive Industry Affairs.

Box 7-B—Mexico's Auto Decrees[1]

Mexico's first auto decree remained in force, largely unchanged, from 1925 until 1962. This period featured the screwdriver assembly of knockdown kits behind a tariff wall. No more than 20 percent of parts content came from Mexican suppliers. Assembly plants proliferated, numbering 12 by 1960, although the industry's annual output never exceeded about 60,000 cars. Most were built and sold by U.S. firms.

The 1962 decree called for 60 percent domestic content, requiring that powertrains (engines, transmissions) be made in Mexico. Foreign firms could continue to own assembly and engine plants but were limited to minority shares in parts producers. The government also prohibited all imports of finished vehicles. While a supplier base began to develop, the Mexican market was much too small for economic production of either vehicles or components. Output reached 188,000 units in 1970, well below the capacity of a single efficient assembly plant. Costs and prices were high. Mexico continued to import many parts, and ran a trade deficit in the motor vehicle sector.

Further decrees in 1969, 1972, and 1977 addressed the trade deficit by requiring assemblers to export in proportion to their production for sale within Mexico. Despite rising exports of engines, the trade deficit worsened. But by the end of the decade, U.S. automakers, under pressure from Japanese imports, began looking at Mexico as a possible site for low-cost production capacity.

In 1982, Mexican demand plummeted as a result of the economic crisis. A new auto decree followed in 1983. Given strong U.S. demand, the automakers, led by Ford, built a number of new export-oriented engine and assembly plants that proved to be competitive in cost and quality with those elsewhere in North America. Production in *maquiladora* parts plants also rose. At the end of the decade, Mexican sales resumed their upward climb (table 7-1).

The latest auto decree, issued in 1989 and still in effect, includes the following provisions:

- Foreign-owned assemblers are permitted 100-percent ownership of parts plants producing for export, but only 40-percent ownership in suppliers serving the Mexican market.
- Local content rules require that Mexican firms (defined as 60 percent Mexican-owned) provide 36 percent of the value of the components used in vehicles sold within Mexico.
- Assemblers must maintain a positive balance of trade.
- Beginning in 1991, finished cars and light trucks could be imported into Mexico, limited to a 15 percent market share in the first two years, rising to 20 percent in 1993. A further provision requires that exports counterbalance these imports in 2.5:1 ratio (1991), declining to 2:1 in 1992-93 and 1.75:1 in 1994. Tariffs on imported vehicles were set at 15 percent, with a 13.2 percent duty on parts. Imports of used cars and trucks continue to be barred.
- *Maquila* plants may sell some of their output within Mexico.

[1]For details, see Douglas C. Bennett and Kenneth E. Sharpe, *Transnational Corporations Versus the State: The Political Economy of the Mexican Auto Industry* (Princeton, NJ: Princeton University Press, 1985); Wilson Perez Nuñez, *Foreign Direct Investment And Industrial Development In Mexico* (Paris: Organization for Economic Cooperation and Development, 1990), pp. 109-135; James P. Womack, "A Positive Sum Solution: Free Trade in the North American Motor Vehicle Sector," *Strategic Sectors in Mexican-U.S. Free Trade*, M. Delal Baer and Guy F. Erb, eds. (Washington DC: Center for Strategic and International Studies, 1991), pp. 31-65. The decrees also covered heavy trucks and buses, subjects outside the scope of this chapter.

Table 7-1—Mexican Car and Truck Production, 1981-1991

	1981	1982	1983	1984	1985	1986	1987	1988	1989	1990	1991
	(thousands of units)										
Production for sale in Mexico											
Passenger cars..........	340	287	192	218	242	167	154	211	275	354	379
Trucks and buses........	231	180	81	113	149	98	94	132	171	196	245
Production for export.......	14	16	22	34	58	72	163	173	196	279	366
Total.................	585	483	295	355	449	337	411	406	642	829	990

SOURCE: *World Motor Vehicle Data, 1991 Edition* (Detroit, MI: Motor Vehicle Manufacturers Association, 1991); *Automotive News 1992 Market Data Book* (Detroit, MI: Crain Communications, May 27, 1992).

Table 7-2—Assembly Plants in Mexico

	Location	Annual capacity[a]	Target markets
Ford............	Cuautitlan		
	cars	60,000	Mexico
	trucks	50,000	Mexico
	Hermosillo (cars)	160,000	U.S. and Canada
General Motors....	Ramos Arizpe (cars)	100,000	U.S. and Canada, Mexico
	Mexico City (trucks)	60,000	Mexico
Chrysler..........	Toluca (cars)	120,000	Mexico, U.S., and Canada
	Mexico City (trucks, some cars)	75,000	Mexico, U.S., and Canada
Nissan...........	Cuernevaca		
	cars	80,000	Mexico, Spain, Latin America
	trucks	50,000	Mexico, Spain, Latin America
Volkswagen.......	Puebla		
	cars	200,000	Mexico, U.S., and Canada
	trucks	15,000	Mexico, U.S., and Canada

[a]Based on recent production levels and industry interviews.
SOURCE: Office of Technology Assessment, 1992.

become congested and are subject to stiffening environmental controls (table 7-2). With some exceptions, including a number of foundries and glass plants, neither assembly nor supplier facilities oriented towards the Mexican market could survive an immediate and complete elimination of protective barriers. The companies that built these plants to gain a place in the Mexican industry sought a lengthy post-NAFTA adjustment period to preserve their positions while they install more modern equipment and reorganize production to meet world standards of cost and quality. Both GM and Chrysler have announced plans to close assembly plants in Mexico City. Replacement capacity, when added, will probably be nearer the U.S. border or close to ports suited for shipping to the rest of Latin America.

Export-oriented plants are newer and larger. Until these plants came on stream, few industry executives were sanguine about Mexico as a potential site for any but simple operations. Modern assembly and engine plants with state-of-the art production equipment were viewed as risky investments that had to be made to satisfy the government and tap a growing market. The concern was that low productivity and quality would offset low wages. This view has changed with the success of modern, export-oriented

Mexican plants.[1] Even so, of the five assemblers with operations in Mexico, only VW and Nissan are adding significant capacity. Both are doing so to increase their exports to other countries in the Americas as well as to the United States.

The Mexican Parts Industry

The supplier industry can also be divided into plants that produce solely or primarily for the Mexican market and *maquiladora* operations that export products such as wiring harnesses to U.S. and Canadian assembly plants. Few Mexican-owned parts suppliers have achieved levels of cost and quality necessary to sell into the United States and Canada, largely because they have been unwilling to invest sufficiently in plant, equipment, and technology. Most would not be viable without protection. As table 7-3 shows, *maquiladora* plants buy only about one-quarter of their parts content from Mexican suppliers, even though the *maquilas* rarely engage in technologically demanding production.

Assemblers in Mexico report continuing difficulty in meeting local content requirements because they cannot get what they need from Mexican firms; some have made their own investments in Mexican

---

[1] "The Auto and Electronics Sectors in US-Mexico Trade and Investment," report prepared for OTA under contract No. I3-1815 by Harley Shaiken, May 1992.

Table 7-3—Mexico's Auto Parts Market, 1990

	Value (billions of dollars)	Share of total (percent)
Consumption by assemblers		
Purchases from Mexican suppliers.............	$ 3.2	27%
Imported parts.............................	2.9	24
Captive (self-supplied)........................	0.6	5
Consumption by *maquiladora* component plants		
Purchases from Mexican suppliers.............	0.4	3
Imported parts.............................	1.0	8
Aftermarket sales		
Produced by Mexican suppliers	2.5	21
Imported parts.............................	1.0	8
Direct export sales by Mexican suppliers........	0.5	4
Total......................................	$ 11.9	100%

NOTE: Total does not add because of rounding.

SOURCE: Norman Stoller, "The Mexican Automotive Parts Industry: Challenge and Need of Capital Expansion," paper presented at the 46th Annual Plenary Meeting of the Mexico-U.S. Business Committee, San Diego, CA, Nov. 22, 1991, figure 10, p. 20.

parts plants to earn required export credits.[2] Some Mexican firms have entered strategic alliances with U.S. or European firms to bring in new technology and management know-how (table 7-4). This trend suggests that, given a suitable transition period, a growing Mexican market, and outside investments, post-NAFTA restructuring could be relatively rapid.

THE U.S. INDUSTRY: ASSEMBLERS AND SUPPLIERS

Industry in Trouble

At the end of World War II, the U.S. automobile industry was an oligopoly dominated by a single firm, General Motors. By 1964, imports (excluding those from Canada) exceeded half a million vehicles— a market share of 6 percent. By 1991, the Big Three's passenger car market share had fallen to 64 percent. Japanese firms had nearly 30 percent of the market under their own names, plus another 5 percent through cars sold under Big Three nameplates (and included in the Big Three's 64 percent) that were built in Japan or by transplants.[3]

Japanese automakers broke into the U.S. market by designing and developing vehicles that appealed to U.S. consumers through styling, functional performance, and long-term reliability as well as initial quality.[4] They differentiated their products, developed highly efficient manufacturing systems and extensive dealer networks, and now command levels of brand loyalty that often exceed those of the Big Three, especially among younger consumers—in large measure because of perceived advantages in quality.[5]

---

[2] Managers in one firm visited by OTA reported that they had recently begun to purchase steel tubing locally. The Mexican supplier had achieved competitive quality. Prices were 15 percent higher than in the United States, a difference less than the tariff and transportation costs for bringing in tubing from the United States.

Ford buys from about 250 suppliers in Mexico, GM from about 150, and Chrysler from 120. Nissan and VW buy from fewer than 100 each. *The ELM Guide to Mexican Auto Sourcing* (East Lansing, MI: ELM International, 1992), pp. C1-C14.

[3] U.S. firms retain more than 80 percent of the light truck market. VW, which opened the first transplant, ceased U.S. manufacture in 1988, and now supplies low-end vehicles from Mexico. European firms accounted for 4.1 percent of 1991 U.S. passenger car sales. *Automotive News 1992 Market Data Book* (Detroit, MI: Crain Communications, May 27, 1992), p. 17.

[4] *U.S. Industrial Competitiveness: A Comparison of Steel, Electronics, and Automobiles* (Washington, DC: Office of Technology Assessment, July 1981).

While Japanese auto firms benefited from lower wages during the years in which they began exporting to the United States, today total compensation (wages and benefits) in Japanese assembly plants is about 96 percent of the U.S. level. Kevin Done, "Japanese Earn Highest Motor Industry Pay," *Financial Times*, Feb. 22, 1992, p. 4.

[5] Fred Mannering and Clifford Winston, "Brand Loyalty and the Decline of the American Automobile Firms," *Brookings Papers On Economic Activity: Microeconomics*, 1991, pp. 67-103.

Table 7-4—Mexico's Major Auto Parts Manufacturers and Their Strategic Alliances

Firm	1990 Sales (million of dollars)	Principal products	Partners
Spicer.	$ 480	Engine parts, clutches, transmissions, axles, universal joints, gaskets, electrical parts	Dana, Kelsey-Hayes GKN, Perfect Circle, TRW, many others
Vitro Crinamex.	256	Auto glass	
ICA Autopartes.	250	Manual transmissions, clutches, brakes	Clark, Budd, Borg Warner
Condumex.	170	Wiring harnesses, shock absorbers, pistons, piston rings	Sealed Power, Packard Electric, Maremont
Proez/Metalsa.	120	Stampings, chassis parts	A.O. Smith, Solvay Automotive
Grupo Rassini.	100	Springs, seats and upholstery	NHK, Lear Seating
Grupo Tebo.	80	Brake and steering parts	Alfred Teves, TRW
Cifunsa.	80	Iron castings	Teksid
Nemak.	71	Aluminum castings	Ford, Teksid

SOURCE: Norman Stoller, "The Mexican Automotive Parts Industry: Challenge and Need of Capital Expansion," paper presented at the 46th Annual Plenary Meeting of the Mexico-U.S. Business Committee, San Diego, CA, Nov. 22, 1991, table 4, p. 22.

Perceived quality commands a substantial price premium in the U.S. market. The pricing policies of Japanese automakers reflect this: they rely less on rebates and find it easier to raise prices. As table 7-5 shows, Big Three rebates averaged $380 more than those for Japanese vehicles in 1991. Between 1985 and 1991, Japanese automakers were able to raise their prices by an average of 43 percent, while the Big Three could raise prices by only 25 percent.[6] These differences have had huge impacts on profits and losses.[7] For the Japanese firms, premium pricing in the United States has helped offset the losses inherent in rapidly developing a large-scale North American manufacturing base. In 1990, Japan's

Table 7-5—Retail Incentives in the U.S. Market

	1986	1987	1988	1989	1990	1991
Big Three average. . . .	$300	$490	$485	$760	$990	$910
Japanese average. . . .	—	—	—	355	370	530

SOURCE: "Statement of Ronald R. Boltz, Vice President, Product Strategy and Regulatory Affairs, Chrysler Corporation, Before the Joint Economic Committee," Dec. 10, 1991, chart 7.

automakers earned an average of about $1,300 for each car sold in their home market, while losing about $1,100 per vehicle sold in the United States.[8] Although their profitability at home has fallen since 1990, the major Japanese automakers have more latitude for reducing prices in the United States than the Big Three.

---

[6] "Statement of Ronald R. Boltz, Vice President, Product Strategy and Regulatory Affairs, Chrysler Corporation, Before the Joint Economic Committee," Dec. 10, 1991, chart 6.

[7] In 1991, GM had a net loss of $4.5 billion and an operating loss in automotive products of $3.5 billion. According to its annual report, the company lost $7.1 billion in the United States, made $600 million in Canada, $1.8 billion in Europe, and $460 million in Latin America, while losing $150 million in other parts of the world. North American losses came to $1,800 per car sold; GM spent an average of $1,100 per car for dealer and retail incentives. See Frank Swoboda and Warren Brown, "GM's Wrenching Task: Remaking Itself," *Washington Post*, Feb. 26, 1992, pp. G-1, G-2.

Ford lost about $2 billion in 1991, a year in which it paid out $6 billion in rebates. Ford's chairman has stated that "as long as there is excess capacity there will be rebates." Kathy Jackson, "Foreign Operations Put Ford Deep in the Red," *Automotive News*, Oct. 28, 1991, pp. 6, 41; Kathy Jackson, "Rebates Here for Long Term, But Ford May Spend Less," *Automotive News*, Jan. 20, 1992, p. 19.

[8] "Statement of Ronald R. Boltz," op. cit., footnote 6, chart 9. The leading Japanese automakers all experienced declines in profitability in 1991. OTA's interviews suggest that one result may be an extension of product life cycles from about 4 to 6 years. This would save the companies large sums in engineering and startup costs.

Table 7-6—U.S. Passenger Car Sales by Nameplate and Location of Production, 1991

| | Location of assembly plant | | | | | |
Nameplate	United States	Canada	Mexico	Japan	Other	Total
	(thousands of units)					
General Motors.......	3,609	550	35	91	35	4,320
Ford...............	2,329	370	105	—	63	2,867
Chrysler............	999	295	144	70	—	1,508
Toyota.............	299	36	—	676	—	1,010
Honda.............	409	74	—	321	—	803
Nissan.............	175	—	—	409	—	584
Mazda.............	89	—	—	255	—	344
Mitsubishi...........	70	—	—	121	—	191

NOTE: Totals may not add because of rounding.
SOURCE: *Automotive News*, Mar. 2, 1992, p. 3.

No longer do Japan's automakers rely almost entirely on manufacturing cost advantages and a reputation for making small cars with high quality. They have moved steadily up-market, established new nameplates, and taken the lead in many aspects of product engineering. One way or another, it seems the United States will have to become comfortable with a substantial Japanese presence in this industry through transplants and strategic alliances, as well as imports. Three factors underlie the emerging structure:

1. A growing number of market niches (minivans, new luxury nameplates).

2. Joint ventures, coproduction agreements, and other forms of alliances, including sales of vehicles produced in the Far East or by transplants and marketed under U.S. brand names (table 7-6) and U.S. sales by Japanese firms of products made for them by the Big Three.[9]

3. Rapidly rising imports of parts from the Far East, primarily to supply transplant engine and assembly facilities, along with investments in the United States by Japanese parts firms to supply the transplant assembly operations of their traditional Japanese customers.

The transplants and joint venture operations that began to open during the 1980s, largely in response to U.S. policies aimed at limiting imports, significantly increased North American assembly capacity (table 7-7). The new plants have high levels of productivity and quality, placing growing pressures on older U.S.-owned facilities.[10]

Costs

Automobile production facilities typically become profitable when operating at relatively high fractions of capacity (e.g., 85 percent or more).[11] In 1991, the Big Three averaged 63 percent, while the transplants operated at an estimated 67 percent of capacity.[12] The transplants are projected to reach 76 percent in 1992, with the Big Three at only 66 percent. If these projections prove even roughly accurate, U.S. automakers will continue losing money on their North American operations while Japanese firms, although also making losses, would improve their relative positions.

As a result, Japanese automakers would continue to have greater freedom of action. For example, they

---

[9] Single-firm transplants have been more successful than joint ventures. In October 1991, Chrysler sold its share in Diamond-Star Motors to its former partner, Mitsubishi. The Subaru-Isuzu transplant lost $31 million in 1991, while CAMI (GM-Suzuki) has been embroiled in a dispute over dutiable content with the U.S. Treasury. Nonetheless, Ford purchased a half-share in Mazda's Flat Rock facility, which already builds cars for both companies. In cooperative agreements, illustrated by Mazda's production of Ford Probes at Flat Rock, one company builds similar vehicles for sale under both nameplates. In another example, Nissan produces the Mercury Villager for Ford, while Ford builds the Nissan Pathfinder. Lindsay Chappell, "Joint Ventures Falter," *Automotive News*, Dec. 16, 1991, pp. 1, 45; Richard Johnson, "Mazda to Have 'American' Cars," *Automotive News*, Dec. 16, 1991, pp. 1, 43.

[10] Toyota, Honda, Mazda, and Nissan are believed to have automobiles that are on average significantly better designed for manufacturability than Ford, the best of the Big Three on this measure. But not all transplant factories have achieved productivity levels superior to the best plants operated by the Big Three. See James P. Womack, Daniel T. Jones, and Daniel Roos, *The Machine That Changed The World* (New York, NY: Harper Perennial, 1991), pp. 84-87.

[11] *U.S. Industrial Outlook '92* (Washington, DC: Department of Commerce, January 1991), p. 36-6.

[12] "Statement of Ronald R. Boltz," op. cit., footnote 6, chart 12.

Table 7-7—North American Passenger Car Assembly Plants, 1992

	Location			Total
	United States	Canada	Mexico	
	(number)			
Big Three				
General Motors.............	16	2	1	19
Ford.......................	7	2	2	11
Chrysler..................	4	1	1	6
Wholly Owned Transplants				
Honda.....................	2	1	—	3
Nissan.....................	1	—	1	2
Toyota.....................	1	1	—	2
Hyundai....................	—	1	—	1
Mitsubishi[a].................	1	—	—	1
Volkswagen................	—	—	1	1
Volvo......................	—	1	—	1
Joint-Venture Transplants				
CAMI (GM-Suzuki)..........	—	1	—	1
Mazda[b]....................	1	—	—	1
NUMMI (GM-Toyota)[c].......	1	—	—	1
Subaru-Isuzu..............	1	—	—	1
Total.....................	35	10	6	51

[a]Joint venture with Chrysler dissolved in October 1991.
[b]Ford purchased 50 percent share in 1992.
[c]Consent decree with U.S. Department of Justice calls for dissolution in 1996.
SOURCE: *Automotive News 1992 Market Data Book* (Detroit, MI: Crain Communications, May 27, 1992), p. 13.

might be able to avoid or delay layoffs and contraction in Japan, where profits have declined, while continuing to invest in North America and Europe. They could afford more aggressive pricing/incentive policies that would serve to further drain resources from the Big Three, undermining the latter's ability to overhaul their product lines and continue moving to lean production. Or Japanese firms could choose to continue rapidly introducing new models.

The transplants may have manufacturing cost advantages of up to $1,000 per car.[13] Productivity is only one of many reasons for this difference, and indeed may account for less than $200 of the total. Other factors include incentive packages provided by State and local governments to attract transplants and a new, young workforce with low pension and health care costs.

As table 7-8 shows, transplant assemblers pay about the same wages as the Big Three, but have benefits costs that are lower by roughly $5 per hour, corresponding to $400 per car. Transplant suppliers pay lower wages than traditional U.S. suppliers, while having lower benefits costs in addition; thus they have an even larger labor cost advantage. Lower benefits costs are a direct result of younger workers. The transplants pay much less for funding pensions because they have no retired employees to support; their medical insurance costs average less than half those for the Big Three because their younger workforces are healthier (table 7-9).

Largely because of differences in national approaches to health care, medical insurance cost differentials are at least as great when U.S. costs are compared with those in Canada, Germany, or Japan. Ford puts its 1990 health insurance expenses at $65 per vehicle produced in Canada, compared with

---

[13] ''Testimony by Candace Howes before the Joint Economic Committee hearing on The Future Of U.S. Manufacturing: Auto Assemblers and Suppliers,'' Dec. 10, 1991, p. 12.

A recent report from the Economic Strategy Institute (ESI) argues that, with favorable exchange rates, parts produced in the United States cost significantly less than parts shipped in from Japan, and that, largely for this reason, Ford has the lowest delivered costs per vehicle in the U.S. market (and, indeed, lower production costs than Japanese automakers in Japan). But when differences in capacity utilization, benefits, and capital costs are taken into account, the average U.S. automaker still has costs about $1,000 greater than the average Japanese automaker. ESI also acknowledges that Ford needs significantly more labor hours for assembly than Toyota, Honda, Nissan, or Mazda, and that GM and Chrysler take substantially more hours than Ford. *The Future Of The Auto Industry: It Can Compete, Can It Survive?* (Washington, DC: Economic Strategy Institute, 1992).

Table 7-8—Comparative Wage and Benefit Levels, 1986[a]

	Average hourly wage	Index	Total compensation (including benefits)	Index
Big Three assembly and in-house parts.......	$ 15.00	100	$ 22.50	100
Transplant assembly......................	15.00	100	17.50	77
Parts				
Independent U.S. suppliers...............	10.40	69	13.00	58
Transplant suppliers....................	8.00	53	10.00	44

[a]No comprehensive data are available for later years; although wages and benefits have increased considerably since 1986, with Big Three wages and benefits currently exceeding $35 an hour, OTA's interviews indicate that the ratios in the index columns remain about the same.

SOURCE: Candace Howes, "The Benefits of Youth: The Role of Japanese Fringe Benefit Policies in the Restructuring of the US Motor Vehicle Industry," *International Contributions to Labour Studies*, vol. 1, 1991, table 4, p. 125.

Table 7-9—Pension and Health Insurance Costs

	Big Three	Transplants
	(dollars per hour)	
Pension contributions..........	$ 2.75	$ 0.75
Health insurance..............	5.29	2.10
Total.....................	$ 8.04	$ 2.85

SOURCE: "Statement of Ronald R. Boltz, Vice President, Product Strategy and Regulatory Affairs, Chrysler Corporation, Before the Joint Economic Committee," Dec. 10, 1991, chart 15.

$300 in its U.S. plants.[14] Health care costs for auto firms are lower by half in Germany, and by three times in Japan.[15] Countries with national health plans and different approaches to pensions thus gain significant cost advantages. The problem is much greater for the Big Three than the transplants because Ford, GM, and Chrysler must pay the full costs of health and benefits packages for an older and still aging workforce.

Suppliers

U.S. parts suppliers are in as much trouble as the assemblers. Imports of parts from Japan have been increasing rapidly (figure 7-2). The majority of these parts go to transplant assemblers, which import an estimated 52 percent by value of the components in their vehicles (table 7-10). Transplants source the other 48 percent internally, from transplant suppliers, and from independent U.S. parts suppliers.

Figure 7-2—U.S. Imports of Auto Parts by Source

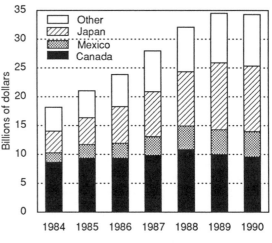

SOURCE: Stephen A. Herzenberg, "The North American Auto Industry At the Onset of Continental Free Trade Negotiations," Economic Discussion Paper 38, U.S. Department of Labor, Washington, DC, July 1991, table 13.

Japanese-owned parts firms followed their customers to the United States, operating about 300 plants here and in Canada by 1992. Transplants buy mostly simple, low-value-added parts from independent U.S. suppliers—gaskets and hoses, not gears and bearings.[16]

Because transplant suppliers pay less than traditional U.S. suppliers, a transplant assembler can save

---

[14] William C. Symonds, "It's Not Perfect, But It Sure Works," *Business Week*, Mar. 9, 1992, p. 54.

[15] "Auto Firms Need Both Trade Help, Domestic Reforms, Industry Experts Say," *International Trade Reporter*, Dec. 11, 1991, p. 1,803.

[16] A recent (and controversial) study estimated that Honda's Marysville plant—often thought to purchase more from the traditional U.S. supplier base than other transplants—sources only 53 percent (by value) of its parts content in the United States, not far above the average of 48 percent given in table 7-10. Of this 53 percent (the rest comes from Japan), Honda buys 20 percent from traditional U.S. suppliers. The other 33 percent comes from transplant suppliers and internal Honda production in North America. Sean P. McAlinden, David J. Andrea, Michael S. Flynn, and Brett C. Smith, *The U.S. Japan Automotive Bilateral 1994 Trade Deficit*, Report Number UMTRI 91-20 (Ann Arbor, MI: University of Michigan, Transportation Research Institute, May 1991). Also see, "Honda: Is It An American Car?" *Business Week*, Nov. 18, 1991, pp. 105-112.

Table 7-10—U.S. Content

	Estimated percentage value of U.S. parts[a]
Vehicles imported from Japan.........	1%
Transplant production...............	48
Big Three U.S. production............	88

[a]To determine whether a given model qualifies as "domestic" or "imported" for purposes of fuel economy standards, the U.S. Environmental Protection Agency (EPA) uses a formula for determining North American content that gives substantially different results. EPA content figures bear little relationship to the dollar values of U.S. and foreign parts.

SOURCE: "Statement of Ronald R. Boltz, Vice President, Product Strategy and Regulatory Affairs, Chrysler Corporation, Before the Joint Economic Committee," Dec. 10, 1991, chart 13.

a substantial sum on its total component costs simply by purchasing from low-wage transplant suppliers.[17] But even if Japanese automakers could buy equivalent parts more cheaply from a U.S. firm, they might gain by sourcing within their *kieretsu*. Supplier profitability, and with it the ability to contribute engineering support, depends on capacity utilization. The Japanese assemblers have no wish to weaken their traditional suppliers, while weakening their rivals' supplier base could help them.

Mounting pressure on the traditional supplier base has led companies to close unionized plants, add capacity in low-wage southern states, and in some cases relocate to Mexico. The principal countervailing force has been demand by assemblers for nearby parts plants to meet "just-in-time" (JIT) delivery requirements. Still, lean production does not automatically require that critical components and subassemblies come from tightly grouped plants. The need is for low inventories so that potential bottlenecks—for instance, a batch of bad parts—surface before they disrupt downstream production. Automakers continue to weigh transportation costs, economies of scale, currency exchange risks, political factors, labor costs and workforce capabilities, and regulatory requirements in deciding where to locate assembly and captive parts plants.

Transportation and inventory costs make it unlikely that imports to North America will incorporate significant content purchased from independent U.S. suppliers. Suppliers would have to offer exceptional advantages in cost, functional performance, or quality to win such business.[18] Critical components for transplants will likely continue to be made by the assembler (in Japan or in North America) or by the transplants' traditional suppliers, either in their Asian plants or here. The high proportion of components and subassemblies currently being imported or made in transplant supplier facilities, suggests that, even if all the vehicles now being imported from Japan were to be replaced by North American transplant production, many independent U.S. suppliers would continue to find it difficult to win the business of transplant assemblers.

State and Local Government Incentives

State and local governments have bid aggressively for transplant assembly and parts facilities, offering tax deferrals and abatements, new highways and industrial parks, training grants, and low-cost financing for plant and equipment. Subsidies provided by State governments to assembly transplants alone have been placed at $50 to $75 per vehicle.[19]

State and local government pay for these incentives from tax revenues that come in part from existing plants, which are thus supporting the creation of new competitors. Once fully established, the new competitors can expect to be more efficient, if only because they will have new equipment and factories laid out in accord with the latest practices. They may have better prepared workers, particularly if incentives include training grants. By reducing capital outlays and startup costs, incentives shorten the time it takes a new entrant to become profitable and challenge existing firms.

---

[17] Candace Howes, "The Benefits of Youth: The Role of Japanese Fringe Benefit Policies in the Restructuring of the US Motor Vehicle Industry," *International Contributions to Labour Studies*, vol. 1, 1991, pp. 113-132.

[18] Toyota claims that, in 1990, the "defect ratio for parts imported from 75 North American and European companies was 100 times greater than the ratio for parts supplied by 147 Japanese makers—1,000 defects per million imported parts versus 10 for locally produced parts." Richard Johnson, "Quality Still the Key, Toyota Tells Parts Makers," *Automotive News*, Nov. 11, 1991, p. 42.

[19] "Testimony by Candace Howes," op. cit., footnote 13, p. 9.

For a summary of incentive packages provided transplants, see *After the Cold War: Living with Lower Defense Spending* (Washington, DC: Office of Technology Assessment, February 1992), table 6-11, p. 181. Some U.S.-owned manufacturers also benefit from incentives. Thomas J. Leuck, "Business Incentives: A High-Priced Letdown," *New York Times*, Mar. 8, 1992, sec. 4, p. 16.

Table 7-11—U.S. Auto Industry Employment

	1978	1987	1991
	(thousands)		
Total employment.........	1,311	1,131	1,036
Total production workers.....	1,032	889	799
Big Three.............	693	536	436
Assembly.............	263	242	191
Parts................	428	293	245
Transplants.............	—	13	26
Union...............	—	4	11
Nonunion............	—	9	16
Independent parts........	296	320	325
Union...............	155	84	81
Nonunion............	141	236	244

NOTE: Totals may not add because of rounding.

SOURCE: Office of Technology Assessment, 1992.

The Labor Market

Employment

In 1991, a little over a million people held jobs in the U.S. auto industry (table 7-11). Seventy-seven percent worked in direct production—30 percent in assembly (including transplants and truck assembly) and the rest in parts production. The Big Three, including their parts divisions, employed 55 percent of all production workers, independent parts suppliers a little over 40 percent, and transplants 3 percent.

As the table shows, since 1978, employment has declined more than 20 percent, with Big Three employment dropping by 37 percent overall and fully 42 percent in captive parts divisions; as Big Three firms bought more parts from independent U.S. suppliers—and from Mexican *maquiladoras*—they shed 180,000 jobs in parts production. Nonunion U.S. parts suppliers, including transplants, have added roughly 100,000 production jobs since 1978, while employment in unionized independent parts suppliers has declined by an estimated 74,000 jobs. As a result, union coverage in independent U.S. parts plants has fallen from something over half to between one-sixth and one-third.[20]

Wage Setting and Wage Trends

From the late 1940s to the late 1970s, real hourly wages rose steadily as a result of United Auto Workers (UAW) contracts that stipulated annual increases of roughly 3-percent plus inflation. A pattern-setting agreement negotiated between the UAW and one or the other of the Big Three became the basis for subsequent negotiations at the other U.S. assemblers and major unionized suppliers. By 1982, competitive pressures ended the tradition of annual real wage increases; average hourly wages for assembly workers fell in real terms by 3 percent from 1985 to 1991. In exchange for wage moderation and acceptance of the automakers' demands for more flexible work rules on the shop floor, the UAW has gained guarantees for most workers of almost full-time pay even if laid off during the 3-year contract period.

Transplant assemblers, union and nonunion, have typically matched or almost matched Big Three wages, but real wages in the independent parts industry have declined steeply because of falling union coverage and the breakdown of pattern bargaining in parts companies that remain unionized. Since the mid-1980s, Big Three contracts have had little influence on bargaining at unionized independents. Contract outcomes depend on local labor market conditions, wage levels at competing companies, including nonunion and foreign producers, and the employer's financial position. By 1989, wages at unionized independents were only two-thirds those in assembly companies, and were nearly identical to the average in all U.S. manufacturing. At nonunion parts suppliers, wages had fallen to 77 percent of the U.S. manufacturing average.

MEXICAN AUTO PRODUCTION TODAY AND TOMORROW

Mexico as a Location for Production

Assembly

To build and equip a modern new assembly plant in Mexico, capable of producing 250,000 cars per year for the U.S. and Canadian markets, would cost at least $500 million—more if a stamping facility were included. Construction and plant startup would take at least 3 years. As table 7-12 shows, shipping in components would impose a substantial cost penalty over a U.S. plant. In OTA interviews, one

---

[20] There are no U.S. Government statistics on employment in independent parts firms, which has been estimated as total industry employment minus assembler employment. Union members in independent parts plants are estimated as auto industry union members minus assembly company union members, using figures on union membership collected in the Current Population Survey. Alternative estimates of union coverage over time based on membership figures from the United Auto Workers and on the Industry Wage Surveys of the Bureau of Labor Statistics give comparable totals.

Table 7-12—Cost Structure for Auto Assembly in the United States and Mexico[a]

	United States	Mexico
Labor[b]	$700	$140
Parts, components, subassemblies	7,750	8,000
Component shipping costs	75	600[c]
Finished vehicle shipping	225	400
Inventory costs[d]	20	40
	$8,770	$9,180

[a]Illustrative only.
[b]Assumes 20 hours of assembly labor per vehicle in the United States, 30 hours in Mexico, representative of good but not best current practice.
[c]Includes shipment of stampings from the United States; component shipping costs would come to about $400 for a plant that did its own stamping.
[d]Assumes 10 percent cost of funds.

SOURCE: Office of Technology Assessment, 1992, based on industry interviews.

Photo credit: Ford Motor Co.

Assembly line at Ford's Hermosillo, Mexico plant.

Big Three firm put these costs at $500 to $700 per vehicle, roughly 10 percent of the cost of the components. Shipping costs could be reduced by about one-third if the Mexican plant did its own stamping (sheetmetal parts are hard to handle and easily damaged in transit). But an integral stamping plant would raise the initial investment by about $250 million. Shipping completed vehicles would also incur a cost penalty in major U.S. markets that are distant from Mexico.

Table 7-12 indicates that cheap labor currently provides little or no incentive to build a new assembly plant in Mexico, unless a substantial proportion of the output were to be sold there or in Central and South America. Predictable future developments would work both for and against Mexico. A stronger Mexican supplier base, able to produce many of the components that must now be imported, would reduce the transportation cost penalty somewhat. OTA's industry interviews indicate that it would probably take 10 to 15 years to broaden and deepen the supplier base sufficiently.

Over this period, the automakers will redesign most of their vehicles twice, in the process reducing labor content through improved design-for-manufacturability and design-for-assembly. By the time Mexico's supplier base develops—and its transportation system improves, so that shipping costs decline—lower labor content will reduce the advantages Mexico can expect from low wages.

Table 7-13 illustrates, comparing three vehicles that differ in assembly labor requirements. In the first case ("Future"), assembly labor in the United States has fallen to 13 hours, about the best achieved anywhere in the world today. The second case ("Current") requires 20 hours—not far from the best achieved by the Big Three at present, and the same as assumed in table 7-12. The third case requires 30 hours, not uncommon today and representative of many cars still built in Mexico. In all three cases, stampings come from an integral plant,

Table 7-13—Illustration of the Effect of Design-for-Assembly on Costs[a]

Vehicle design case	U.S. assembly plant				Mexican assembly plant							
					Current productivity[b]				Equal productivity			
	Assembly hours	Costs (dollars)			Assembly hours	Costs (dollars)			Assembly hours	Costs (dollars)		
		Labor	Shipping	Total		Labor	Shipping	Total		Labor	Shipping	Total
Future	13	$455	$300	$755	19.5	$91	$750	$841	13	$61	$600	$661
Current	20	700	300	1,000	30	140	750	890	20	93	600	693
Older designs	30	1,050	300	1,350	45	210	750	960	30	140	600	740

[a]Assumes: integral stamping (no shipping costs for stampings); equal component and inventory costs; wage/benefit costs at $4.67 per hour in Mexico and $35 per hour in the United States; finished vehicles shipped to U.S. markets.
[b]Labor hours assumed 50 percent higher in Mexico.

SOURCE: Office of Technology Assessment, 1992.

avoiding the cost penalties of shipment from the United States to Mexico, while about 40 percent of the vehicles' components continue to be imported. The table includes two scenarios for Mexico. In the first, or current scenario, productivity is lower than in the United States, requiring 50 percent more assembly hours for vehicles of the same design— about the norm today. In the second scenario, Mexican productivity equals that in the United States; in addition, shipping costs decline from $750 to $600 as a result of improvements in Mexico's transportation system.

Table 7-13 indicates that Mexican assembly plants will have significant cost advantages in the future only if they incorporate integral stamping facilities and their productivity increases. If vehicle designs improve, reducing labor content, shipping costs will continue to offset much of the labor cost differential. If the Mexican supplier industry improves, assembly in Mexico will become more attractive. It is no surprise, then, that none of the Big Three's announced new capacity is planned for Mexico, with the exception of replacements for existing plants in Mexico City (table 7-14).

Engines

All five automakers active in Mexico elected to export engines to satisfy the government's trade balancing requirements. Engines are easy to ship; after transportation costs and tariffs, Mexican engine plants have proven able to deliver into the United States at costs perhaps 7 percent below those of U.S. plants.[21] The complex equipment required in engine plants means that workers must have good skills; while training is time consuming, it has not proved a major hurdle.[22] Engine production is high in value-added but not in labor intensity. A high-volume plant employs about a thousand people, about a third as many as a typical vehicle assembly plant. Companies can afford to pay a wage premium to reduce turnover and retain workers they have trained. They can also afford to bring in components from outside Mexico because parts like pistons and valves have low shipping costs relative to their value. Mexico has several foundries capable of producing complex castings at competitive cost and quality levels.

Table 7-14—New Assembly Plant Investments by Big Three Automakers[a]

	Location	Investment (millions of dollars)	Planned startup
Ford.........	Avon Lake, OH	$ 900	1992
Ford.........	Oakville, Ontario	900	1993
Ford.........	Louisville, KY	650	1995
Chrysler.......	Detroit, MI	1,000	1992
Chrysler.......	Bramalea, Ontario	600	1992
Chrysler.......	Mexico[a]	To be determined	
General Motors.	Silao, Mexico[a]	400	1994

[a]Replacement for existing plant.

SOURCE: Office of Technology Assessment, 1992, based on industry interviews.

Would companies put engine plants in Mexico in the absence of the government's trade-balancing requirements? Today, a new world-class plant with an annual capacity of 400,000 to 450,000 engines would cost around $700 million to build, about the same as a new assembly plant.[23] Such a factory, built in Mexico, could supply engines to the United States at unit cost savings (after transportation) of perhaps $50 to $70. In the United States, it would take about 2 years to build and equip the plant. It would be a further 2 years before it was running at full capacity. Construction would take longer in Mexico. It would also take an additional 1 to 2 years to reach full production because of the need to train the entire workforce, and because start-up would be slowed by lack of experience even given a well-trained workforce.

A firm that contemplated replacing an existing (high-wage, efficient) U.S. engine plant with a new factory in Mexico would calculate financial break-even at more than 30 years after construction began. The picture would look better if the existing U.S. plant was old and inefficient, or suffered from poor labor relations. The performance records of existing Mexican engine plants mean that when automakers consider location decisions in the future, Mexico will be viewed on its merits rather than in terms of meeting the requirements of the Mexican Government.

Parts

Powertrain assemblies have high value and are critical for customer satisfaction. Automakers make these themselves, with some exceptions for engines

---

[21] OTA interviews.

[22] "The Auto and Electronics Sectors in US-Mexico Trade and Investment," op. cit., footnote 1.

[23] OTA interviews.

Table 7-15—Cost of Typical Wiring Harness

Selling or transfer price.	$ 250
Expected profit.	$ 10-20
Assembly cost (40 minutes)	
Mexico.	$ 1-2
United States	
Big Three internal supplier (@ $35 per hour). . . .	23
Independent unionized supplier (@ $26 per hour).	17
Independent nonunion supplier (@ $18 per hour).	12
Added shipping costs for Mexican assembly.	$ 7
Extra inventory costs for Mexican production.	$0.50

SOURCES: Industry interviews; Candace Howes, "The Benefits of Youth: The Role of Japanese Fringe Benefit Policies in the Restructuring of the US Motor Vehicle Industry," *International Contributions to Labour Studies*, vol. 1, 1991, table 4, p. 135.

and more frequent exceptions for transmissions. Finish parts such as exterior sheetmetal or dashboard assemblies are easily damaged in shipping and critical for customer perceptions of quality. Automakers also control this production, either through internal production or subcontracting to trusted suppliers, and seek to keep it close to the point of final assembly. Specialists, either internal parts divisions or first-tier suppliers, design, develop, and manufacture many other vehicle subsystems—brakes, sunroofs, catalytic converters. Economies of scale are important, proprietary technology significant, and transportation costs typically low relative to value. Today, Mexican suppliers have little hope of competing for this business without a partner that has an established track record.

The situation is quite different for the labor-intensive *maquiladora* plants. Table 7-15 shows that Mexico has far lower costs for wiring harness assembly. Much the same is true for airbags and cut-and-sew operations on seats. Difficult to automate, this sort of work can be performed by low-skilled labor with little or no training. Production went to Mexico because of labor costs, not because of the government's trade balancing requirements. JIT means a potential distance handicap that *maquiladora* plants must overcome, but supply pipelines from Mexico are much shorter than those from the Far East. In combination with the other forces at play in this industry, a NAFTA would encourage further transfers of production.

Figure 7-3—U.S.-Mexico Auto Trade

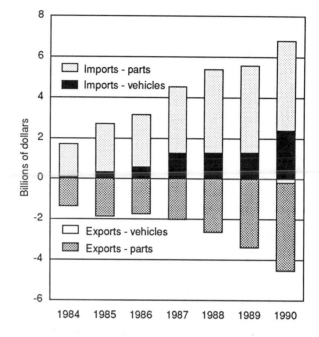

NOTE: Engines included under parts.

SOURCE: Stephen A. Herzenberg, "The North American Auto Industry At the Onset of Continental Free Trade Negotiations," Economic Discussion Paper 38, U.S. Department of Labor, Washington, DC, July 1991, table 2.

Employment in *maquiladora* parts production, less than 10,000 in 1980, reached 100,000 in 1990 and 130,000 by the end of 1991. Already, GM is Mexico's largest employer, with, for example, 27,000 workers assembling wiring harnesses in *maquiladoras* operated by the company's Packard Electric Division.[24] Of 64 Big Three-owned plants in Mexico, 40 are near the border; 26 of the border plants assemble wiring harnesses and 6 export upholstery and soft trim parts to the United States.[25]

NAFTA Impacts

Assembly

Figure 7-3 illustrates the speed with which U.S. imports of vehicles and parts from Mexico have increased. This is largely a result of Mexico's trade-balancing policies. Almost all of the vehicle imports are passenger cars, because light trucks face tariffs of 25 percent when imported into the United States, while tariffs on passenger cars are only 2.5 percent.

---

[24] OTA interviews and GM annual reports.

[25] *The ELM Guide to Mexican Auto Sourcing*, op. cit., footnote 2, pp. C1-C20. Many of the other border plants assemble electrical components such as relays and motors.

If a NAFTA led to the removal of Mexico's export-balancing requirements, U.S. imports of passenger cars from Mexico would probably stabilize, unless the relative cost picture changed a good deal. As discussed above, this seems unlikely; there is little or no advantage in locating assembly plants in Mexico today, and newer vehicles will require less assembly labor. Investments in new assembly capacity in Mexico will be driven primarily by Mexican demand. A NAFTA that removed the tariff on light trucks could encourage new Japanese investment in Mexico.

There is one further consideration. Mexican plants, because they use less automation, can be very flexible. This makes them attractive for assembling older designs with high labor content, low-volume niche vehicles such as convertibles (which likewise have high labor content), or as a means of increasing production when capacity limits have been reached in the United States and Canada. Thus, in some cases it might be profitable to close an older U.S. plant making such vehicles and transfer production to Mexico. Furthermore, if automakers continue to pursue niche marketing strategies, assembly in Mexico could become more attractive. However, the proliferation of new models during the 1980s strained the financial resources of a number of companies, and this trend has at least temporarily peaked.[26]

Engines

Mexico has demonstrated cost advantages in engine production. Nonetheless, while all five automakers active in Mexico have been adding engine capacity, their favorable experiences with export-oriented Mexican plants have not led them to put new capacity there. Ford, for instance, will have built or renovated three engine plants in the United States, one in Canada, and one in Mexico over the period 1990 to 1995. The existing Mexican plant, in Chihuahua, was closed for 2 years to be retooled for Ford's new Zeta engine. This is the only new or renovated Big Three engine plant that will come on stream in Mexico during these years. Nor have any of the Big Three announced major new investments in transmissions or other powertrain components in Mexico, although the economics for such plants are similar to those for engines.

A NAFTA that eliminated the current 2.5 percent tariff would reduce the costs of a typical engine delivered into the United States by $15 to $20. This would increase the cost advantage compared with U.S. production by as much as one-third, a significant amount. Automakers would be more likely to put new engine plants into Mexico after a NAFTA than they would new assembly plants. Nevertheless, the financial penalty of slower startup would likely outweigh the advantage of lower labor costs.

Parts

Relaxation of Mexico's investment requirements could attract more first-tier suppliers to Mexico, along with lower tier firms that have not considered Mexico in the past because their manufacturing processes are not especially labor intensive. Although Mexico could not become a design and development center within the next two decades (Canada has not managed that, after all), the growing role of suppliers in development suggests that some Mexican component firms would begin to take on more engineering-intensive work.

For labor-intensive parts production, a NAFTA, by itself, would do little to either encourage or discourage relocation. Mexico has sought to attract *maquiladora* parts plants for years. A good deal of the work suited to these plants has already moved, but more could be relocated in the years ahead, particularly if small U.S. parts manufacturers, many of whom are losing business, believe they can remain viable with lower wages. If more of these companies do flee to Mexico it will not be because of NAFTA provisions themselves, which should not change the economics of producing in Mexico significantly. An agreement might have its greatest impacts simply by publicizing the opportunities, so that smaller companies that might otherwise not think of moving begin to consider Mexico.

The Mexican Market

Given very substantial excess capacity in both the assembly and parts sectors in North America, immediate ''free trade'' would decimate Mexican suppliers. An end to local content requirements and import restrictions would also render much of Mexico's assembly capacity uncompetitive. If assemblers were permitted to supply Mexico by

---

[26] The number of models available in the U.S. market grew from about 400 in 1980 to a high of 614 in 1987, and now stands at 555. ''Number of Car Models Drops For '92: U.S. Builts Pass Imports,'' *AutoWeek*, May 18, 1992, p. 11.

importing vehicles, they would close some of these plants because they could thereby increase their capacity utilization and profitability in the United States and Canada. Nissan could supply Mexico from both the United States and Japan. Only VW needs its Mexican plants to continue servicing the rest of North America.

In the absence of trade restrictions, other Japanese and Korean automakers would quickly begin exporting to Mexico as well, reducing the market shares of the five firms that now sell there and cutting into their profits. If all but VW closed their assembly plants, the Mexican auto industry would be left with little beyond export-oriented engine plants, several modern assembly plants, and *maquiladoras*. Such an outcome would be unacceptable to the Mexican government—thus the negotiated NAFTA transition period, with rules of origin that vehicles or components would have to meet to qualify for favorable tariff treatment. Given a North American rule-of-origin of 62.5 percent, two-way trade in finished vehicles should increase during and following the transition period. Modernized Mexican assembly plants would produce fewer models in higher volumes to achieve economies of scale, and Mexico would import other models.

Sales in Mexico could approach those in Canada after 10 years or so, provided wages and living standards rise, enabling more Mexicans to buy cars. New capacity would probably go into Mexico in step with increases in sales. If infrastructure improvements continue at the pace currently planned, per-mile transportation costs would converge with those in the United State. Even so, if wages increased, shipping cost penalties would probably continue to make it unprofitable to assemble vehicles in Mexico for export unless the country's supplier base became much stronger. On balance, a NAFTA, if accompanied by growth in the Mexican market, should provide additional sales and profits for the Big Three firms and their suppliers as excess capacity in the United States and Canada came on line to replace higher cost assembly plants in Mexico.

NAFTA and U.S. Jobs

If a NAFTA benefits U.S. automakers by opening up the Mexican market, it is not likely to do much for U.S. auto workers. In the 1970s, the UAW represented the vast majority of workers in the industry,

and wages had been largely taken out of competition. Today, the industry is evolving toward a core of assembly companies, mostly unionized and paying high wages, surrounded by first-tier suppliers, some unionized, that pay somewhat lower wages, and by lower tier suppliers that are mostly nonunion and pay much lower wages.

Restructuring along these lines will continue. The high-wage core will shrink as the assemblers become more efficient and buy more of their components from independent suppliers. The rate at which the core shrinks will depend on the fortunes of the Big Three relative to the transplants. It depends particularly on the fate of GM, which remains much more vertically integrated than its competitors, employing about 150,000 production workers in its parts plants.

In this context, a NAFTA would affect U.S. jobs and job opportunities in two primary ways:

1. To the extent that Mexico relaxes its trade balancing and local content rules, U.S. companies would be able to increase their exports of vehicles and parts to Mexico. This would save a modest number of U.S. jobs, and a greater number if the Mexican market expands as a result of NAFTA.
2. A NAFTA would also influence business strategy and wage setting in the independent parts sector. By locking in more liberal policies in Mexico, a NAFTA could lead to increased investments in Mexico by first-tier U.S. and Asian suppliers and to plant relocations by lower tier U.S. suppliers pursuing low-wage strategies. A larger, more competent Mexican supplier base would in turn mean increased competition for suppliers that remained in the United States, putting downward pressure on U.S. wages.

Figure 7-4 shows one set of projections, based on output growth at 1.5 percent per year coupled with productivity improvements of 3 percent per year. Over a 15-year period, industry employment falls by 20 percent, from its current level of about 1 million workers to 800,000. If, over this same period, Mexican plants producing for the U.S. market added another 130,000 jobs—about the number working in *maquiladora* parts production at the beginning of 1992—and these jobs represented a one-for-one replacement of U.S. jobs—the U.S. total would fall to 650,00.

Figure 7-4—Projected U.S. Auto Industry Employment[a]

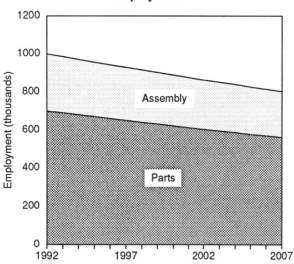

[a]All workers; assumes output increases at 1.5 percent per year, productivity increases at 3 percent per year.

SOURCE: Office of Technology Assessment, 1992.

Contraction and competition will probably mean continued real wage losses even for workers who keep their jobs. And few of those who lose semi-skilled jobs in the auto industry can expect to find comparable employment. Long-tenure, high-wage auto workers suffer longer unemployment spells and greater earnings losses than other displaced workers (see ch. 4, table 4-3). In a sample including engineers, managers, and skilled workers, as well as direct production employees, 40 percent of those displaced from auto industry jobs over the period 1979-89 were unemployed for more than 6 months. Of those who found new work, 55 percent suffered earnings loses of 25 percent or more. Restructuring in this industry will continue to place a heavy burden on the individuals who lose their jobs and the communities in which they live. And the reliance by independent parts suppliers on low-wage, low-skill strategies increases the likelihood that they will relocate to Mexico.

Even so, a NAFTA is unlikely to have the devastating effects on U.S. workers that the UAW has charged. To some extent, NAFTA has become a lightning rod for fears over the future of jobs in a shrinking industry with declining real wages. These trends have their origins in the globalization of the auto industry, a development in which Mexico has, as yet, played only a small part. But if NAFTA is not the root of U.S. auto workers' problems, it could

aggravate them or contribute to their solution. To contribute to solutions, a NAFTA would have to address four issues alongside liberalization of Mexico's government polices:

1. measures for limiting net imports into the North American market, so that some production now taking place in Asia would move to the United States, Canada, and Mexico;
2. to the extent that vehicles and components continue to enter from outside North America, measures for improving competitiveness here to achieve a rough trade balance with the rest of the world;
3. help for U.S. plants, particularly suppliers, in pursuing high-productivity strategies; and
4. measures for dampening downward pressure on wages in the United States and Canada, particularly in independent parts firms.

Chapter 2 includes a number of policy options that address these issues.

CONCLUDING REMARKS

Over the past three decades, U.S.-based automakers have seen their share of domestic sales decline from 95 percent to about 65 percent. They first lost market share to imports, later to Japanese-owned transplants. Transplant production provides some jobs for U.S. workers that would otherwise have been lost to imports. But transplant suppliers pay lower wages than traditional U.S. suppliers, and independent U.S. suppliers face a difficult future unless transplant assemblers begin buying from them in greater volume.

Mexico's auto decrees have sheltered the five participating assemblers, providing higher profits than they could otherwise expect. These profits came at a cost—the requirement for a positive trade balance, even at the expense of operating inefficient assembly plants and buying parts from inefficient Mexican suppliers. A NAFTA that reduced Mexico's local content and trade balancing requirements and included a reasonable transition period before new entrants could freely sell in Mexico should provide some additional sales, profits, and jobs in the United States. But this will be a very small effect superimposed on long-term employment decline. Despite widespread plant closings and layoffs, the Big Three as a group have yet to complete the transition to lean production. Auto industry employment will continue to fall as productivity improves.

Chapter 8

Electronics

Contents

Boxes

Figures

Tables

SUMMARY

As in the auto industry, government policies have shaped growth, development, and foreign investment in Mexican electronics. By controlling access to its domestic market, Mexico has attracted foreign-owned multinationals who have set up local manufacturing plants. Low-wage labor and preferential tariff treatment have also helped Mexico attract many *maquiladora* plants producing electrical equipment and electronic products such as TVs and telephones. In 1990, *maquiladora* factories sent 4.4 million color television sets to the United States— more than any other producing nation and half of all U.S. imports of color TVs. Growth in Mexican TV production has gone hand in hand with a continuing shift of production out of the United States in search of lower labor costs. In 1991, Zenith, the only remaining U.S.-owned TV maker, began moving its remaining U.S. assembly operations to Mexico.

Limitations in technology, worker skills, and infrastructure will, however, limit development of a more robust electronics industry in Mexico. Electronics firms, particularly those producing computers, telecommunications equipment, and process control systems for business and industry, compete on technological excellence, as do producers of some advanced consumer products like videocassette recorders (VCRs) and projection TVs. These businesses depend on skilled labor, along with design, development, and marketing.

Responsiveness to rapidly changing market demand is also essential in electronics. Production facilities belong near design and marketing teams so that new ideas can be quickly incorporated into products that are often specialized or customized. Mexico's proximity to the United States gives it some advantages over Asian competitors in this respect, but limited skills and research capacity detract from that advantage.

Better technical and managerial capabilities would enable Mexico to move up the development ladder over time. The Mexican university and technical training systems are producing large numbers of graduates, but relatively few can find jobs that provide the kind of experience needed for Mexico to improve its industrial competence. Furthermore, the Mexican Government has all but eliminated incentives for multinationals to produce sophisticated electronics products locally, which promises to slow the pace of development.

In the near term, Mexico will continue to attract mostly labor-intensive electronics production, such as TVs and other standardized consumer electronics products, telephones, and answering machines. There are still many of these kinds of jobs in the United States. U.S. plants employ about 230,000 electrical and electronics assemblers and over 150,000 precision assemblers. The Bureau of Labor Statistics (BLS) estimates that more than 40 percent of these jobs could disappear by the turn of the century. The jobs are at risk from automation and other forms of productivity improvement, including redesigned products that require less labor, as well as transfers of production to low-wage offshore plants. Production of many more-or-less standardized products has already moved out of the United States to the Pacific Rim, Mexico, and the Caribbean. A North American Free Trade Agreement (NAFTA) might accelerate movement of jobs to Mexico somewhat, but Mexico has been pursuing policies to attract labor-intensive production for years; a NAFTA would have only a limited effect on the dynamics in this sector.

MEXICO'S ELECTRONICS INDUSTRY: DEVELOPMENT AND CAPABILITIES[1]

The electronics industries in the United States and Mexico are becoming increasingly interrelated through trade and investment. U.S. electronics firms have invested in Mexico to take advantage of cheap

---

[1] This section draws in many places on "NAFTA and the Electronics Industry in Mexico," report prepared for OTA under contract No. H3-7200 by Patricia Wilson, February 1992. The Wilson report is based on surveys of *maquiladoras* and interviews covering the period 1988 until late 1991, and recent interviews at non-*maquila* electronics plants. This section also draws on "Japanese-Owned Maquiladoras in Mexico," report prepared for OTA under contract No. H3-7145 by Martin Kenney and Richard Florida, April 1992, which reports on site visits and interviews with Japanese-owned electronics firms in Mexico, both end-product manufacturers and component suppliers, and on interviews in Japan with high-level executives of electronics firms.

Table 8-1—Government Policies Affecting Electronics Production in Mexico

Sector	Policy tools	Outcome
Consumer Electronics......	• Import substitution through trade barriers, later liberalized. • *Maquiladoras.*	Export-oriented assembly industry dominated by foreign-owned multinational corporations (MNCs). Limited use of local suppliers. Limited domestic sales.
Computers..............	• Targeting through informal computer decrees in 1981 and 1987, which created a protected market for MNCs willing to invest in local manufacture.	Production within Mexico by companies including IBM and Hewlett-Packard. Limited integration of local component suppliers. Export of production in excess of Mexican demand, coupled with imports of products not locally produced.
Telecommunications.......	• State ownership of TelMex, the national telecommunications company, accompanied by "buy national" policies. • Market protection through tariff and non-tariff barriers.	Local production by two foreign-owned MNCs, Ericsson and Indetel, with limited imports and exports of finished products.
Electrical Equipment.......	• *Maquildadoras.*	Export-oriented firms supplying U.S.-based manufacturers.
Suppliers...............	• Local content provisions in computer decrees.	Extremely limited supplier network.

SOURCE: Office of Technology Assessment, 1992.

labor and gain access to a market that was heavily protected until recently. In 1989, the United States was Mexico's leading trading partner in electronics products; Mexico was the sixth largest trading partner of the United States, behind Japan and a number of other Asian countries, but ahead of Canada.[2] In 1991, the sum of U.S. electronics imports from Mexico and U.S. electronics exports to Mexico totaled $12.5 billion, with the United States posting a $1.0 billion deficit.

Electronics generates about 3 percent of Mexico's gross domestic product. There has been a good deal of foreign direct investment (FDI), especially in telecommunications, computers, consumer electronics, and electrical equipment. Factory shipments totaled $6.5 billion in 1989, and employment topped 250,000 workers.[3] But the Mexican industry is dwarfed by that of the United States, which had domestic shipments of over $190 billion in 1989 and employed more than 2 million workers. While employment in U.S. electronics is 8 times that in Mexico, U.S. output is almost 30 times greater,

indicating much higher productivity, for reasons that range from higher levels of automation to differences in the types of products manufactured in the two countries.

Government Policies

The Mexican Government has long considered electronics a key industry for the nation's overall economic development and created programs to attract investment. Unlike the auto industry (ch. 7), there was no single comprehensive policy. Instead, the government implemented a shifting mix of policies tailored to different segments of the industry and ranging from strict import substitution to the promotion of exports (table 8-1).

Government efforts to build a domestic industry by simple import substitution were generally ineffective. In consumer electronics, for instance, Mexico found itself with 10 small companies competing to sell components to domestically-oriented TV manufacturers. Total demand could have been supplied by a single producer. With the removal of

---

[2] *The Likely Impact on the United States of a Free Trade Agreement with Mexico*, USITC Publication 2353 (Washington, DC: U.S. International Trade Commission, February 1991), p. 4-27.

[3] Ibid., p. 4-26.

trade barriers in 1987, imported components flooded in. The percentage of locally manufactured components used by domestically-oriented TV manufacturers dropped from almost 90 percent during the mid-1980s to 10 percent in 1988.[4]

More effective were Mexico's computer programs which used restrictions on local sales in combination with import barriers to attract foreign investment (box 8-A). A number of U.S. companies established facilities in Mexico to gain access to the growing Mexican market—which would otherwise have been denied them—and to other Latin American countries with which Mexico had favorable trade agreements. Major U.S. computer manufacturers, including IBM, Hewlett-Packard, Digital Equipment Corp., and Tandem, established plants in Mexico.

In telecommunications, the government pursued its ends through state ownership, until 1990, of TelMex, the sole provider of telephone service. TelMex limited its purchases of switching and terminal equipment to domestic producers. Together with high trade barriers, this policy attracted investments by Ericsson and Indetel, the first based in Sweden, the second owned by the French company Alcatel.

In keeping with Mexico's overall transition away from an import substitution strategy, trade barriers in electronics have been reduced significantly in recent years. The market for computers has been opened to imports, TelMex has been privatized, tariffs have been lowered to a maximum of 20 percent, and import licensing requirements have been eliminated on many goods. These changes promise to enhance U.S. access to Mexico's markets for electronic products.

Mexico's export-oriented policies—notably the special treatment afforded *maquiladoras*—also attracted FDI in electronics. Many U.S. companies, in particular, invested in *maquila* operations to assemble standardized, labor-intensive products including TVs, transformers, and power supplies. Japanese TV manufacturers have done the same. Because the *maquiladora* program did not include provisions on local content, the sector developed in almost total isolation from Mexican suppliers.

The Mexican Industry Today

Largely as a result of these policies, Mexico's electronics industry consists of two groups of firms with quite different business objectives and capabilities. Both groups are dominated by foreign capital and technology. One produces goods such as computers and telecommunications equipment primarily for the Mexican market (although some computers are exported to meet trade-balancing requirements). The other group produces in *maquiladora* plants almost exclusively for export to the United States. Non-*maquiladora* electronics producers pose relatively little threat to U.S. jobs because they are inefficient, limited in skills, and/or focused on the Mexican market. They produce goods that might, but for the past policies of Mexico's government, be shipped in from the United States. Mexico's domestically oriented consumer electronics industry illustrates this point. As figure 8-1 shows, it is very small, with insignificant exports and considerable imports.[5]

Mexico's production and exports of computers have grown rapidly since 1985, but from a tiny base, so that the industry remains small and many products must still be imported (figure 8-2). Most of the multinational corporations (MNCs) operating in Mexico produce state-of-the-art products (the IBM PS/2, for example), but Mexican manufacturing tends to be limited to routine assembly of final products with components brought in from the United States and the Far East. While Mexico's computer decrees required foreign firms to transfer technology to Mexican suppliers, local content rules were necessarily loose enough to permit imports of critical components. Mexican suppliers provide simple, low-technology parts—housings, printed circuit boards, metal and plastic mechanical parts, cable harnesses, some power supplies, and some discrete electronic components.

The Mexican components industry is small—only about 50 firms, employing some 7,000 people. Local manufacture of semiconductors is limited to discrete

---

[4] Wilson Perez Nuñez, *Foreign Direct Investment and Industrial Development in Mexico* (Paris: Organization for Economic Cooperation and Development, 1990), pp. 92-93.

[5] Tariffs on imported consumer electronic goods were reduced dramatically in 1987. By the middle of 1988, Mexico had stopped producing car radios, audio turntables, and tape decks; speaker production had declined 92 percent. Gray Newman, ''Industries vs. Imports: The Gloves are Off,'' *Business Mexico*, March 1989, pp. 14-19.

Box 8-A—Mexico's Computer Programs

In 1981, following a near doubling of computer imports between 1979 and 1980, Mexico's government issued a set of unofficial guidelines intended to draw in foreign investments to the computer industry. Modified in 1987, these "computer decrees" helped Mexico attract foreign manufacturers of computers and peripherals.[1] The goals included:

- domestic production of computers sufficient to meet 70 percent of demand within 5 years;
- a greater number of domestically-owned component suppliers;
- promotion of exports to achieve economies of scale and generate foreign exchange; and
- increased spending on R&D.

Firms wishing to participate in the Mexican market were required to begin manufacturing in Mexico, meeting specified targets for employment, local content, and trade balancing, and to establish job training programs. Prices were limited to 15 percent above those charged in the firm's home country to prevent manufacturers from taking advantage of the protected market.[2] Microcomputer manufacturers could enter only through minority ownership in joint ventures with Mexican firms. (Apple refused to participate for fear of losing control over its proprietary Macintosh technology in a country with weak intellectual property protection.) The government permitted full foreign ownership of minicomputer operations so long as export requirements were met. Companies could import large computers provided they maintained local production of smaller machines. In return for their investments, companies were protected from import competition through tariffs and import licensing requirements. They also benefited from investment tax credits, low-interest loans, and subsidized utility rates.

Partly in response to pressure by IBM, the government relaxed some of its rules in 1985, codifying the changes in the 1987 decree. Foreign firms were permitted to establish wholly owned affiliates in Mexico for producing microcomputers, provided they complied with foreign exchange, export performance, training, and local content requirements. Import licensing requirements on some components and subassemblies were eased. Later changes eliminated many incentives, while permitting firms operating outside the plan to bring in larger numbers of assembly kits.

In April 1990, the Mexican Government effectively dismantled its previous computer decrees, replacing them with a "Program for the Modernization of the Computer Industry" scheduled to run through March 1993. Under the new program, Mexico will move in stages toward an open market. Import licensing requirements will be further eased, tariffs reduced to 20 percent on assembled computers and 5 to 10 percent on parts, and trade balancing requirements removed. Manufacturers with plants in Mexico will be allowed to import computers and components duty free up to a limit determined by the level of local content in their Mexican production and their level of investment in fixed assets and R&D.[3] Companies must maintain at least 30 percent local content by value and perform some R&D in Mexico.

---

[1]"The Program for Promoting the Manufacturing of Electronic Computer Systems, Their Main Modules and Their Peripheral Equipment" was never formally adopted by the Mexican government, but administrative authorities followed its guidelines, often modifying them on a case-by-case basis. See *Economic and Social Progress in Latin America: 1988 Report* (Washington, DC: Inter-American Development Bank, 1988), p. 166. Also, Susan Walsh Sanderson and Ricardo Zermeño-Gonzales, "Trade Liberalization in Mexico's Electronics Industry," *Strategic Sectors in Mexican-U.S. Free Trade*, M. Delal Baer and Guy F. Erb, eds. (Washington, DC: Center for Strategic and International Studies, 1991), p. 72.

[2]In OTA interviews, some firms stated that they can produce computers at somewhat lower cost in Mexico than in the United States. For others, however, higher prices for locally purchased components lead to increased manufacturing costs. See Wilson Perez Nuñez, *Foreign Direct Investment and Industrial Development in Mexico* (Paris: Organization for Economic Cooperation and Development, 1990), pp. 92-93.

[3]For instance, companies with local manufacturing facilities established under the old decrees can now import computer equipment and components duty-free up to 80 percent of the level of value added in their Mexican plants. *Review of Trade and Investment Liberalization Measures by Mexico and Prospects for Future United States-Mexican Relations*, USITC Publication 2275 (Washington, DC: U.S. International Trade Commission, April 1990), p. 4-8.

---

components such as transistors and diodes (not integrated circuits) and occurs in *maquiladoras* for export back to the United States. While Mexican-owned firms make parts for locally produced radios, TVs, and other consumer goods, they generally cannot meet requirements for close tolerances and high stability laid down by MNCs for industrial applications. Lack of experienced engineers and

Figure 8-1—Production and Trade in Mexico's Consumer Electronics Sector[a]

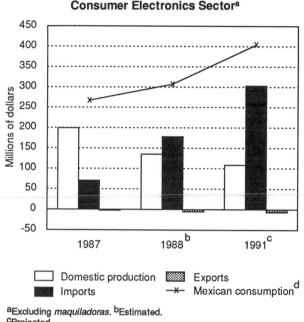

[a]Excluding *maquiladoras.* [b]Estimated.
[c]Projected.
[d]Production plus imports minus exports.

SOURCE: Edith Houston, "Mexico: Electronic Consumer Goods Market Assessment," U.S. Department of Commerce, International Trade Administration, 1988.

Figure 8-2—Production and Trade in Mexico's Computer Sector[a]

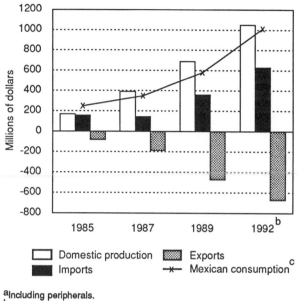

[a]Including peripherals.
[b]Projected.
[c]Production plus imports minus exports.

SOURCE: "Trade and Event Research: Mexico—Computers, Peripherals, Software, and Services," U.S. Department of Commerce, International Trade Administration, August 1990.

technicians will limit expansion into more sophisticated components, and indeed into more sophisticated electronics products of all types. Mexican suppliers currently provide one-third to one-half of the quantity of computer parts, but this corresponds to only about one-quarter by value (table 8-2).[6] Color monitors, disk drives, and most power supplies are imported from Asia. Integrated circuits come from the United States or Asia.

Few Mexican-owned firms have established themselves in the computer industry. U.S.-based companies, for example, account for about 80 percent of the personal computers (PCs) made in Mexico. While a few Mexican companies (Printaforma, for one) have designed PCs around components available on the open market, they are not exported. Companies producing peripherals have been somewhat more successful, but they typically produce simple assemblies such as keyboards, power supplies, and displays; in 1991, these three items comprised nearly all of Mexico's total exports of peripherals to the United States, with keyboards alone totaling 82

percent (table 8-3). U.S. imports from Japan and newly industrializing countries (NICs) in Asia, in contrast, center on more sophisticated peripherals such as disk drives and laser printers.

Computer production in Mexico poses little threat to U.S. jobs. If Mexico's economy grows, domestic production will be needed to serve the growing local

Table 8-2—Value-Added by Country for Personal Computer Production in Mexico

	Value (percent)
Components:	
From Mexico...........................	30%[a]
From the United States[b]................	30
From Asia.............................	30
In-plant value added (Mexico).............	10

[a]Overstated because many subassemblies purchased in Mexico include parts imported from the United States and Asia.
[b]Includes all internal production of components by the computer manufacturer in countries other than Mexico.

SOURCE: Harley Shaiken, *Mexico in the Global Economy: High Technology and Work Organization in Export Industries* (La Jolla, CA: University of California, San Diego, Center for U.S.-Mexican Studies, 1990), p. 112.

---

[6] Wilson, "NAFTA and the Electronics Industry in Mexico," op. cit., footnote 1, p. 7; Susan Walsh Sanderson and Ricardo Zermeño-Gonzales, "Trade Liberalization in Mexico's Electronics Industry," *Strategic Sectors in Mexican-U.S. Free Trade*, M. Delal Baer and Guy F. Erb, eds. (Washington, DC: Center for Strategic and international Studies, 1991), p. 79.

Table 8-3—U.S. Imports of Computer Peripherals and Subassemblies by Country, 1991

	Mexico	Taiwan	Singapore	Japan
	(thousands of units)			
Hard disk drives...	4	90	7,460	4,080
Floppy disk drives..	1	410	210	12,960
Printers..........	8	10	290	6,140
Displays.........	146	4,550	300	3,000
Power supplies....	370	1,870	670	450
Keyboards........	2,450	3,630	510	1,280

SOURCE: Office of Technology Assessment, 1992, based on official statistics of the U.S. Department of Commerce.

market. Imports from the United States and Asia will supply demand for products not locally produced. U.S. computer manufacturers have little incentive to establish additional manufacturing facilities in Mexico; they have already established production facilities primarily to serve the Mexican market. A NAFTA would not change this pattern.

In telecommunications, Mexico is nearly self-sufficient, due to local production by two large European-owned manufacturers, Ericsson and Indetel (figure 8-3). Other multinationals, including Siemens, Philips, and NEC sell some products including transmission equipment (e.g., cables) to TelMex. With Mexico investing heavily in its telephone network, imports have increased because local producers cannot expand rapidly enough. Little telecommunications hardware has been exported, with the exception of terminal equipment made in *maquiladoras*, in part because Mexican production has not offered economies of scale.

Telecommunications manufacturers in Mexico buy about one-third of their inputs locally, typically housings, low-end passive components, transformers, circuit boards, connectors, and relays for customer premises equipment. In recent years, both Ericsson and Indetel have established joint ventures with Mexican firms to produce printed circuit boards, connectors, and power equipment. One of Indetel's joint ventures makes advanced circuit boards using surface-mount technology. While Mexican firms export some of these components, volumes are small and sales have been mostly in Latin America.

Mexican telecommunications producers will probably continue to concentrate on domestic demand, which is expected to grow rapidly during the next decade. Mexico now has only about 6.3 telephone

Figure 8-3—Production and Trade in Mexico's Telecommunications Equipment Sector

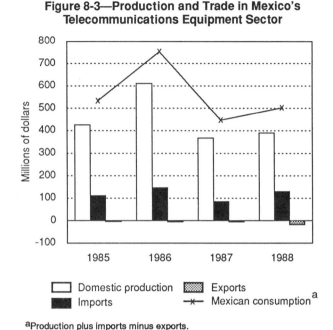

Domestic production   Exports
Imports   Mexican consumption[a]

[a]Production plus imports minus exports.

SOURCE: "Market Research Summary: The Mexican Market for Telecommunications Equipment," U.S. Department of Commerce, International Trade Administration, 1990.

lines per 100 inhabitants, compared with 50 to 60 lines per 100 in the United States. Over the next 5 years, TelMex expects to spend $10 billion to $14 billion to expand its telephone network (box 8-B), a task that will absorb most local production and also require increased imports.

Maquiladora Electronics

Electronics represents the largest sector of the *maquiladora* industry. In 1990, over 500 electronics *maquiladoras* produced goods valued at $6.1 billion, accounting for 44 percent of *maquiladora* output and 37 percent of employment (table 8-4). This is the segment of Mexico's electronics industry that presents the greatest threat to U.S. jobs, particularly in the manufacture of standardized, labor-intensive goods.

Unlike investments in Mexico's domestic-oriented electronics industry that were dictated by restrictions on market access, expansion in the *maquila* sector has been driven by cost considerations. U.S. companies have sought to reduce production costs and fend off competition from overseas rivals, particularly those in the Far East, by investing in Mexico or contracting with existing *maquilas*. Hourly wages in electronics *maquiladoras* averaged about $1.10 for direct laborers in 1991, approxi-

Box 8-B—Upgrading Telecommunications in Mexico

As part of the privatization agreement, the new owners of TelMex must expand and improve the Mexican telecommunications system. For example, by 1994, TelMex must:

- provide long distance service to all towns with over 500 inhabitants, 10,000 of which have no service at present;
- improve reliability and provide faster repairs; and
- answer all operator-assisted calls within 10 seconds (only 70 percent meet that mark at present).

TelMex is committed to increase network line density to 10 lines per 100 people by 1994, and 20 per 100 by 2000. This will require installation of about 800,000 new lines per year through 1994, rising to 1.6 million lines per year afterwards. New telephones (as opposed to lines) will go in at a rate of 3.3 million per year, to reach a level of 25 million installed phones by 1994. Much of the expansion will consist of digital systems.

Table 8-4—*Maquiladora* Electronics Production

	1982	1984	1986	1988	1990
Number of plants.........	223	244	302	411	519
Employment (thousands)...	74	109	113	153	170
Output (billions of dollars)...............	$1.7	$2.6	$2.6	$4.6	$6.1
Value added (billions of dollars)...............	$0.44	$0.57	$0.58	$0.97	$1.36
Share of electronics in all *maquila* production (by value).............	62%	53%	47%	45%	44%

SOURCE: *Maquiladora Industry Analysis*, CIEMEX-WEFA Mexican Service, September 1991, pp. 68-73.

cost-driven investments likely to be seen in Mexico in the wake of a NAFTA than the investments that have taken place in computers or telecommunications.

THE U.S. ELECTRONICS INDUSTRY

While the United States still has the largest electronics industry in the world in terms of output and employment, growth has been slower than in Japan and a number of Asian NICs. Competition has increased in all segments of the industry, but it is in commodity goods that the United States has fallen behind.

In the analysis that follows, OTA divides U.S. electronics into seven sectors:

1. consumer electronics, including household audio and TV equipment (Standard Industrial Classification (SIC) code 3651);
2. computers and peripherals (SIC 357);
3. semiconductors (SIC 3674);
4. electronic components other than semiconductors, including capacitors, resistors, and connectors (SICs 3671, 3672, 3675, 3676, 3677, 3678, and 3679);
5. telephone and telegraph equipment, including central office (CO) switches, private branch exchange (PBX) equipment, and customer premises equipment such as telephone sets and answering machines (SIC 3661);
6. radio communication and navigation equipment, including radio and television broadcasting and cellular telephone equipment (SICs 3663, 3669, and 3812); and

mately one-seventh to one-tenth their level in the United States and half the typical level in the Asian NICs.[7] Over 99 percent of the components used in these *maquiladoras* are imported from abroad.

Electronics *maquiladoras* rely heavily on low-skilled workers (box 8-C), which limits production to two types of assembly: finished products with high labor content and low profit margins, and labor intensive components or subassemblies to be shipped to the United States for incorporation into final products. The first category includes consumer goods such as telephones and small- to medium-sized TVs, along with electrical equipment such as transformers and power supplies; the second includes circuit boards and other subassemblies for large-screen TVs and for telecommunications switches. Such products can be assembled by unskilled or semiskilled workers with little or no sacrifice in product quality.

Thus, *maquiladora* electronics firms can be viewed as competing directly with both U.S. and Asian workers. They are more representative of the

---

[7] *Maquiladora Industry Analysis*, CIEMEX-WEFA Mexican Service, September 1991, pp. 75-78. In South Korea, Taiwan, and Singapore, production workers in electronics averaged $3-$3.25 per hour (including benefits).

Box 8-C—Workers in Electronics Maquiladoras[1]

Because of the high labor turnover rate in border area *maquilas*, itself a consequence of low wages and generally poor working conditions, managers are continuously hiring new workers and putting them on the production line. In Ciudad Juarez, a city with a high concentration of electronics production, *maquiladoras* report monthly turnover rates of 7 to 8 percent. Managers report that workers will leave a job for as little as 20 more pesos a week (there are about 3,000 pesos to a dollar). Workers object to the pace of assembly and to the continual pressure to increase output; managers claim that workers lack the discipline needed for industrial production. In the densely packed *maquiladora* parks in Juarez, plants actively solicit new employees. Many have large banners outside advertising that they are hiring. Others send sound trucks to rival *maquiladoras* during breaks to solicit workers, although in some parks managers have agreed to halt such practices.

Today, the typical *maquila* worker has little or no industrial experience beyond jobs in other *maquiladora* plants. Education levels are low (ch. 5), in part because *maquiladoras* in electronics tend to hire a large percentage of women, most of whom have little formal education. Direct production labor accounts for nearly 80 percent of employment, a figure that has declined only slightly in recent years. This is a much higher fraction than is typical in the United States, where production workers account for only 38 percent of employment in computers and peripherals and 68 percent in consumer electronics.[2]

Given low skills and high turnover, companies sometimes de-automate or otherwise modify tasks for Mexican workers, reducing productivity, often harming quality, and slowing production changeovers. Others have looked to automation as a means of coping with turnover, paying higher wages to retain a core of skilled workers able to keep the machines running while accepting high turnover in the rest of their workforce. In this way, one TV plant in Juarez reduced its workforce from 6,000 in 1974 to 3,800 in 1991.

Even in plants with automated equipment, most new workers get only a day or two of training. In OTA interviews, a manager in a *maquila* making transformers stated that production methods had been simplified compared to U.S. operations to accommodate workers lacking basic skills so that half the workforce needed only manual dexterity and good hand-eye coordination to do their jobs. Other workers did need skills such as soldering or tracking production statistics. The plant manager noted that it had taken 3 years to get the plant operating properly.

So far, these patterns have kept *maquiladoras* from moving into more complex forms of production. But with time and experience, the capabilities of the *maquiladora* labor force will improve. According to the manager of a TV plant, production skills and industrial discipline are now beginning to be passed down through families, so that young people entering the labor force have a better idea of what to expect. Willingness to pay higher wages would enable *maquilas* to reduce turnover and upgrade their workforces more rapidly. If they did so, they might begin attracting more demanding production, thereby putting Mexican workers in head-to-head competition with a larger number of U.S. electronics workers.

---

[1]Based on OTA interviews and "The Auto and Electronics Sectors in U.S.-Mexico Trade and Investment," report prepared for OTA under contract I3-1815 by Harley Shaiken, May 1992.

[2]*U.S. Industrial Outlook '92* (Washington, DC: Department of Commerce, January 1991), pp. 27-1, 37-14.

7. electrical equipment such as transformers, electric lighting equipment, motors, and generators (SICs 361, 362, and 364).

Competitive Status

Import Pressure

Since 1981, U.S. imports of electronic goods have increased from about $20 billion to $80 billion. U.S. exports, while increasing, have not kept pace, and since 1983, the United States has run a trade deficit in electronics.[8] In 1991, the deficit totaled over $11 billion, with consumer electronics leading the way (table 8-5). Only two segments of the industry recorded a surplus in 1991—components, which sends most if its exports to Mexico, Canada, and Asia to support offshore assembly operations, and radio communication and navigation equipment, much of which is defense-related.

Import penetration has been particularly high in standardized, labor-intensive products. As shown in table 8-6, the U.S. computer industry posted a trade deficit only in peripherals, for which direct labor constitutes up to 50 percent of production costs; the

---

[8] *1991 Electronic Market Data Book* (Washington, DC: Electronic Industries Association, 1991), p. 104.

Table 8-5—U.S. Electronics Trade, 1991

Sector	Shipments	Imports	Exports	Balance[a]
	(billions of dollars)			
Computers.....................	$ 58.5	$25.6	$24.0	($ 1.6)
Radio communication and navigation equipment[b].................	57.5	3.8	6.5	2.7
Electronic components...........	34.5	5.9	6.0	0.1
Semiconductors................	27.9	12.3	11.8	(0.6)
Electrical equipment[c]............	22.3	3.9	3.5	(0.5)
Telephone and telegraph.........	15.2	4.3	2.5	(1.9)
Consumer electronics............	7.7	12.3	2.1	(10.1)
Total.......................	$223.6	$68.1	$56.3	($11.9)

[a]Parentheses denote negative balance (imports greater than exports).
[b]Industry shipment data estimated from product shipment data for 1991.
[c]Trade figures estimated from 1990 data.

NOTE: Totals may not add because of rounding.

SOURCE: Office of Technology Assessment, 1992, based on official statistics of the U.S. Department of Commerce.

Table 8-6—U.S. Trade in Computers and Telecommunications Equipment, 1991

	Imports	Exports	Balance[a]
	(billions of dollars)		
Computer equipment			
Computers..................	$ 4.0	$ 7.6	$3.6
Peripherals.................	13.6	6.7	(6.9)
Parts and accessories.........	8.0	9.7	1.7
	$25.6	$ 24.0	($1.6)
Telephone and telegraph			
Network and transmission......	$0.5	1.9	1.4
Customer premises equipment..	3.5	0.8	(2.7)
Parts......................	0.5	0.7	0.2
	$2.1	$1.4	($1.2)

[a]Parentheses denotes negative balance (imports greater than exports).

NOTE: Totals may not add because of rounding.

SOURCE: Office of Technology Assessment, 1992, based on official statistics of the U.S. Department of Commerce.

computers and parts segments posted surpluses in 1991. Similarly, the deficit in telecommunications resulted from imports of customer premises equipment (telephones, FAX machines, and the like), of which little production exists in the United States, and for which direct labor is approximately 30 percent of production costs. For these products, competition hinges on costs, and low-wage Mexican labor can help improve the competitiveness of U.S. manufacturers. In capital goods such as large computers or CO switches, technological capability counts for more than manufacturing costs. Successful firms must continually develop new hardware and software. Because of its underdeveloped R&D base, Mexico offers little to U.S. manufacturers of capital goods and will compete only marginally with U.S. workers in these sectors.

Competition from low-wage nations has hurt U.S. manufacturers of standardized electronics products. For example, of 27 U.S.-owned companies that made TVs in 1960, only Zenith survives. The others have vanished or been purchased by Japanese and other foreign firms. Zenith has 16 percent of the U.S. television market, but, unlike its primary competitors, does not compete on a world scale. As of 1990, nine Japanese corporations assembled color TVs in the United States; four of these companies produced picture tubes here as well. Most of the TV manufacturers that sell in the United States assemble some of their sets in Mexico, and bring in circuit boards and other subassemblies from *maquiladoras* for those assembled in the United States.

In the computer industry, U.S. firms have managed to maintain their primacy, but competition has intensified as the industry has fragmented into submarkets for machines ranging from notebooks and laptops to workstations to supercomputers. Price competition for PCs has become almost as intense as for home entertainment products, with Asian and some U.S. firms seeking to undercut U.S.-based product leaders by offering competitive, but less sophisticated, machines. Low-cost clones have further segmented the PC market into a lower end, that can be satisfied with readily available technology and is thus less responsive to brand names, and an upper end that demands sophisticated technologies, such as active matrix liquid crystal displays, where brand names still help differentiate products.

Competitive pressures in end-product markets have been transferred to U.S.-based suppliers of electronic components and electrical equipment, driving down prices and profit margins. Faced with rising capital investments required to keep up in new technologies, many manufacturers sought merger partners or simply exited. In the recession year of 1991, more than two dozen manufacturers of circuit boards left the industry or went bankrupt, while Japanese firms bought out three large component producers. Nearly all component imports once originated in the offshore plants of U.S. firms, but now more than half come from foreign-owned companies.

U.S. Government Policies

U.S. electronics markets are considerably more open than foreign markets, including the European Community and Japan. The United States has led the world in deregulating telecommunications, for example. Other countries have been slow to follow, with governments reluctant to stop sheltering their manufacturers and service providers.[9] Foreign firms have captured over half the U.S. market for CO switches (in essence huge special-purpose computers, many of which sell for tens of millions of dollars) and PBXs, while U.S. telecommunications manufacturers have not done nearly as well abroad.

Deregulation and divestiture have had equally profound effects on household telephone equipment. As a monopoly, AT&T leased telephones to its customers. But, once customers could buy their own telephones, answering machines, and so on, many chose cheaper products from abroad. AT&T produced 14 million phones in 1982, less than 2 million in 1984. All telephones for home use, cordless phones, and answering machines sold in the United States—and almost all FAX machines (some are made here by foreign-owned "transplants")—are now imported, most from Asia and some from Mexico. Some office telephones are still made in the United States.

U.S. trade policies have preserved some domestic jobs in television production. After a long series of complaints alleging dumping and other "unfair" trade practices, U.S. officials negotiated Orderly Marketing Agreements (OMAs) in the late 1970s to limit imports. Japanese firms responded by investing in U.S. plants for assembling TVs, preserving some

Table 8-7—Employment in the U.S. Electronics Industry, 1991

	Total employment (thousands)	Production workers	
		(thousands)	(percent)
Electrical equipment......	430	300	70%
Electronic components....	320	220	69
Consumer electronics....	60	40	65
Telephone and telegraph..	120	70	54
Semiconductors.........	230	90	40
Radio communication and navigation........	390	140	37
Computers.............	420	130	32
Total...............	1,970	1,000	51%

NOTE: Totals and percentages may not compute because of rounding.

SOURCE: Office of Technology Assessment, 1992, based on figures from *Employment and Earnings*, March 1992.

U.S. jobs in an otherwise declining industry.[10] The structure of U.S. import duties also encourages domestic production of the picture tubes. Completed TVs are subject to a 5 percent tariff; picture tubes are subject to a 15 percent tariff. But picture tubes—the most costly component in a TV, representing some 40 percent of component costs—can be produced in the United States, shipped to a Mexican *maquiladora*, and then re-enter as part of an assembled TV with only a 5-percent tariff on the value added in Mexico, thus helping U.S. picture tube plants compete with Asian plants.

The Labor Market in Electronics

Jobs, Wages, and Displacement

The U.S. electronics industry employed nearly 2 million people in 1991, about 1 million of them classified as production workers (table 8-7). In computers, semiconductors, and radio communications and navigation equipment, production workers make up less than 40 percent of total employment. In electrical equipment, components, and consumer electronics, production workers represent 65 to 70 percent of employment.

Generally speaking, parts of the industry producing high-technology equipment in low to moderate volumes have the smallest percentages of production workers. Examples include military electronics and mainframe computers, where large numbers of engineers, software specialists, and skilled techni-

[9] After the AT&T breakup, the United States opened its equipment market more-or-less unilaterally to foreign manufacturers, losing leverage that might have helped U.S. firms gain access to foreign markets. See *International Competition in Services* (Washington, DC: Office of Technology Assessment, July 1987), ch. 9.

[10] *International Competitiveness in Electronics* (Washington, DC: Office of Technology Assessment, November 1983), pp. 446-447.

cians are needed to design and develop new products. Companies in these businesses sometimes move labor-intensive operations offshore, as do mass producers of semiconductor chips.[11] The sectors with high percentages of production workers tend to have lower rates of technological change and manufacture mature consumer products in large volumes or engage in customized assembly of standardized components (e.g., small-volume production of specialized power supplies). High-volume assembly is more footloose because so much production is controlled by MNCs that operate globally. Smaller U.S. companies producing specialized electronic equipment often depend on a core of experienced employees, from production workers and technicians to engineers and salespersons, working under one roof. Proximity to one another and to customers is important in this part of the industry.

U.S. electronics employment peaked in 1984. Since then, jobs have been disappearing more or less uniformly across the industry. In the five segments for which continuous data are available from the Labor Department, employment declined 16 to 19 percent over the period 1984 to 1991, for a total of 307,000 jobs (table 8-8). Production workers have suffered a disproportionate share of the decline. Employment in all of U.S. electronics was nearly the same in 1991 as in 1978, having risen before falling. But, with the exception of the highly diversified components industry, the labor-intensive segments of the industry have been shrinking since the late 1970s. Between 1978 and 1991, 194,000 production worker jobs were lost, 145,000 of these in consumer electronics and electrical equipment alone.

At the same time, employment in service industries related to electronics—notably computer and data processing services (SIC 737)—has been on the rise. BLS forecasts that employment in computer and data processing services will grow faster than in any other major industry, reaching 1.2 million jobs by the year 2000 compared with 224,000 in 1978.[12] Growth in software and computer services firms could create more jobs than are lost in electronics manufacturing over the next decade, but few people who lose production jobs in electronics are likely to find new work in computer services without considerable retraining.

Real wages have been relatively stable in electronics as a whole over the past 15 years (table 8-9). But in consumer electronics and electrical equipment, the two sectors with the longest history of job losses, wages have fallen by 7 to 10 percent since the mid-1980s. For most of the post-World War II period, unions represented workers at many large companies in these labor-intensive parts of the industry. Over time, the movement of production offshore and to nonunion plants in the United States diminished union influence on wages. To keep some jobs in the United States, unions have been willing

Table 8-8—Employment Trends in U.S. Electronics

Sector	Number of employees (in thousands) and percentage of production workers					
	1978		1984		1991	
Electrical equipment....	570	73%	520	71%	430	70%
Electronic components..	280	73	380	72	320	69
Consumer electronics...	90	73	70	69	60	65
Semiconductors........	170	47	270	43	230	40
Computers............	340	45	520	40	420	32
Total..............	1,450	64%	1,770	58%	1,460	54%

NOTE: Totals may not add because of rounding.

SOURCE: Office of Technology Assessment, 1992, based on data from *Employment and Earnings*, March 1992; and *Employment, Hours, and Earnings, United States, 1909-1990*, vol. 1, BLS Bulletin 2370, (Washington, DC: Department of Labor, Bureau of Labor Statistics, March 1991).

---

[11] Semiconductor firms employ many engineers in the design of new products, and more complex manufacturing during front-end wafer fabrication has increased the need for technicians. Much of the labor-intensive assembly required to package "commodity" semiconductors such as memory chips moved offshore beginning in the late 1960s. Unlike consumer electronics firms, which went to Asia and Mexico in efforts to match the costs of foreign firms, U.S. semiconductor firms shifted assembly operations to Asia at a time when they had little meaningful competition. Competitive forces *within* the U.S. industry drove these transfers of production, as firms sought to cut their costs in order to gain market share and move down learning curves ahead of their domestic rivals. *International Competitiveness in Electronics*, ibid., pp. 192-193. Design and production of application-specific integrated circuits (ASICs) has remained in the United States because these products must be tailored more closely to the needs of individual customers.

[12] Many more software specialists work in other parts of the economy, including the computer manufacturing sector and other durable goods industries. BLS expects employment of software professionals to increase by over 400,000, to 1.4 million by the end of the decade. George Silvestri and John Lukasiewicz, "Projects of Occupational Employment, 1988-2000," *Monthly Labor Review*, November 1989, pp. 42-65.

Table 8-9—Hourly Wages in the U.S. Electronics Industry and in Mexican *Maquiladoras*

	1978	1984	1988	1990	1991
	(1991 dollars)				
Electrical equipment[a]...............	$11.54	$11.55	$11.03	$10.51	$10.39
Electronic components...............	9.42	9.72	9.68	9.51	9.51
Consumer electronics................	10.95	12.16	11.35	10.58	10.97
Telephone and telegraph[b]............	NA	NA	13.25	12.09	12.20
Semiconductors....................	10.93	12.21	12.74	12.74	12.78
Radio communications and navigation[b]...	NA	NA	13.82	13.53	13.38
Computers........................	11.29	11.90	12.19	11.97	12.16
Average, U.S. manufacturing..........	$12.39	$12.24	$11.67	$11.26	$11.18
Average, electronics *maquiladoras*[c].....	NA	$1.06	$0.87	$0.92	$1.09

NA = Not available.

[a]Hourly wage data for electrical machinery (SIC 362) are not reported for 1978-1987. Wage estimates for this sector are therefore based upon wages in SIC 3621, motors and generators, which comprises 50-60 percent of production worker employment in SIC 362.

[b]Due to changes in SIC categories, wage data for telephone and telegraph and radio communications and navigation prior to 1987 is not comparable with that after 1987, and thus are not included in this table.

[c]Data not available for 1978. Data for 1991 forecast by CIEMEX-WEFA.

SOURCE: *Employment and Earnings*, March 1992; *Employment, Hours, and Earnings, United States, 1909-90*, vol. 1, BLS Bulletin 2370 (Washington, DC: Department of Labor, Bureau of Labor Statistics, March 1991). Base wages in Mexican maquiladoras estimated from data in *Maquiladora Industry Analysis*, CIEMEX-WEFA Mexican Service, September 1991, p. 75.

to accept wage reductions.[13] Members of the International Brotherhood of Electrical Workers (IBEW) at the Zenith plant in Springfield, Missouri, for example, agreed to an 8-percent wage cut and a 5-year wage freeze in order to dissuade the company from moving operations out of the United States. Nonetheless, the Springfield plant's production later went to Mexico.

Rates and impacts of displacement due to plant closings or other permanent layoffs reflect the variations in sectoral labor and product markets. On average, electronics workers lost jobs less often, found new jobs faster, and experienced smaller and less frequent wage losses between 1979 and 1989 than did workers in other durable goods industries. Workers in the labor-intensive portion of electronics (electrical equipment, consumer electronics, and components) fared slightly better than those in other durable goods industries, while workers in other electronics sectors fared significantly better (see ch. 4, table 4-3). For example, in electronic machinery,

equipment, and supplies, an average of 3.7 percent of workers were displaced each year over the 1979 to 1989 period, a rate about 10 percent below the average for durable goods manufacturing. About 28 percent of these workers experienced periods of unemployment greater than 6 months. Of those that had found new jobs by the time of the displaced worker survey, almost one-half earned their previous wage or higher (in nominal terms).

Mexico and NAFTA

The IBEW estimates that 25,000 of its members lost their jobs between 1985 and 1989 because of transfers of production to Mexico.[14] Electronics *maquiladoras* now employ more than 160,000 Mexican workers. But it is difficult to assess the true impact of Mexican production on U.S. electronics employment. In many cases, the only alternatives for electronics firms that moved manufacturing to Mexico were to shut down or move production to Asia. Moving production to Mexico has less impact

[13] OTA interviews. Recent wage declines in the electrical equipment, consumer electronics, and telephone and telegraph sectors have been accompanied by the growth of a low-wage, small-firm sector making specialized products in small volumes. Clusters of these firms exist in several parts of the country, including Southern California, where they rely heavily on Hispanic workers and have been cited for violations of wage and hour regulations almost as frequently as garment factories. Maria Patricia Fernandez Kelly, "Labor Force Recomposition and Industrial Restructuring in Electronics: Implications for Free Trade," draft report prepared for the U.S. Department of Labor, Bureau of International Labor Affairs, Washington, DC, July 1992.

[14] "Robert Wood, Director, Research and Economics Department, International Brotherhood of Electrical Workers, before the Office of the U.S. Trade Representative, Covering the Desirability, the Scope, and the Economic Effects of a North American Free Trade Agreement," Sept. 3, 1991, p. 18.

on U.S. employment than these alternatives. By staying in business, firms can retain U.S. jobs in engineering, marketing, and "headquarters" operations that would otherwise disappear as well. A move to Mexico rather than Asia, may not disrupt supplier networks. Electronics *maquilas* import some 99 percent of their components, many from the United States; factories in Asia buy mostly from Asian suppliers.

Until the mid-1980s, growing sales, defense production, a regulated telecommunications industry, and union influence combined to cushion U.S. electronics workers from the layoffs and wage losses that affected other blue-collar workers. Now, many of these cushions are gone. A NAFTA would find production workers in electronics increasingly vulnerable to competition from imports and the threat of offshore production. Regardless of NAFTA, however, employment in high-volume, standardized electronics manufacturing will continue to shrink in the years ahead due to automation. At the same time, cost pressures in a highly competitive industry dominated by Asian companies with worldwide marketing strategies and correspondingly large economies of scale will drive smaller U.S. companies to seek lower costs through low-wage offshore labor. Labor-intensive work will continue to migrate to Mexico, Asia, and the Caribbean. Even when production does not move, the option of producing in Mexico will restrain U.S. wage increases.

There is an alternative: production of differentiated, high-quality goods with varied product attributes and features. With flexible organizational forms, high levels of worker skill and training, and corresponding commitment to the job, firms could pay high wages in U.S. plants to supply such markets. Small, high-technology firms have used these methods for years, especially in defense electronics. Sony expects that such an approach will justify locating its new TV assembly (and picture tube) plant near Pittsburgh, bucking the pattern of movement of assembly to Mexico. The company plans to take over a former Volkswagen plant, receiving a substantial incentive package from State and local governments. To take advantage of the skilled and experienced labor pool in the area, Sony will replace traditional assembly lines with self-directed work teams responsible for tasks such as cabinet-making and installation of picture tubes. The groups will be responsible not only for assembly and quality assurance, but for scheduling and inventory

control and for maintaining their equipment. Workers will be trained in multiple skills and share responsibility for the group's work. Because the groups will be self-directed, Sony plans to dispense with first-level supervisors.

U.S.-MEXICO LINKAGES IN ELECTRONICS

Mexico has attracted foreign investment in electronics because of its low wages and because of government policies that controlled access to its markets. Mexico may continue to have cheap labor for many years, but market access has already been liberalized. Investment decisions will then depend more on Mexico's suitability as a location for manufacturing relative to alternatives. Production costs, skill levels, and the rate of growth of Mexico's domestic market will be primary considerations.

Location Decisions in Electronics

Mexico's advantages are most visible in labor-intensive consumer electronics production. Nearly all the major TV manufacturers that sell in the United States have assembly facilities in Mexico—Zenith, Thomson-RCA, Philips, Sony, Matsushita, and Hitachi. Zenith is consolidating its TV assembly in Mexico; Philips has half its North American production in Mexico. Production of smaller TVs went to Mexico first; now many companies assemble at least some of their large-screen TVs there as well.

Production Costs

In the low-margin consumer electronics business, a few dollars saved in production can make the difference between profit and loss. Compared with manufacturing in the United States, reduced labor and overhead costs from Mexican production can save as much as $80 per set (table 8-10). Some *maquiladora* TV plants have now invested in considerable automation, seeking to drive costs down still further.

Cost savings of the magnitude summarized in table 8-10 are compelling: a new TV assembly plant can be built for about $100 million; with production of 1 million sets per year, this initial investment could be paid back from the savings in production costs in about a year. Zenith, which posted a $52 million loss in 1990, claims that its Mexican

Table 8-10—TV Assembly Costs in Mexico and the United States

	Cost per TV (dollars)	
	Mexico	United States
Labor..........................	$ 15	$ 90
Overhead....................	60	70
Components..................	225	225
Additional duty................	3.75	NA
Additional inventory cost[a].......	0.60	NA
Additional transportation.......	1.50	NA
	$305.85	$385.00

[a]Assumes 10 percent cost of funds.

NA = Not applicable.

SOURCE: Office of Technology Assessment, 1992, based on industry interviews.

Table 8-11—Cost Breakdown for a Typical Personal Computer

Direct labor.........................	less than 5%
Overhead...........................	10%
Mechanical parts....................	5%
Tooling, etc.........................	2%
Electronic parts and components........	30-60%
Disk drives..........................	15-30%
Monitor............................	5-10%
Keyboard...........................	2-5%

SOURCE: Benjamin Gomes-Cassares, "International Trade, Competition, and Alliances in the Computer Industry," paper presented at the World Trade and Global Competition Colloquium, Harvard Business School, Boston, MA, December 1991 (based on company estimates).

operations will save $400 million a year once its remaining U.S. production has been relocated.[15]

But such savings are not possible in other parts of the electronics industry. Much of the cost of electronics equipment is in fact the result of mechanical, rather than electronic components. The disk drives in computers, for example, are complex electro-mechanical assemblies. Good design practices can reduce labor content, and, particularly if automation becomes feasible, make it cost-effective to produce in the United States. Design for manufacturability and design for assembly—e.g., reducing the number of parts and designing each for ease of handling, either manually or with automated equipment—can dramatically simplify production processes. For example, fasteners such as screws, may account for 5 percent of parts cost but 75 percent of assembly cost if they must be inserted by hand. Reducing the number of fasteners or replacing them with snap-fit assemblies or adhesive bonding eliminates much of this labor. Better yet, two or three pieces can be replaced by one. In redesigning its ProPrinter, for example, IBM reduced the number of parts by two-thirds, cutting assembly time by 90 percent and improving the reliability of the finished product.

Miniaturization—especially in semiconductors—also contributes to reductions in labor content by putting greater functional capability on each chip, so that fewer chips are needed in each system. With reductions in the total number of components and interconnections, assembly becomes less important,

component manufacturing more important. As a result, electronic devices for which assembly labor represented 40 percent of manufacturing costs a few years ago, such as computers, now have direct labor content of 5 percent or less (table 8-11). A PC that costs $1,000 to manufacture in the United States might cost $950 in Mexico. It would take many years to recover the costs of a new plant in Mexico. Moreover, import duties on computers produced in Mexico would negate most of the potential savings. Under a NAFTA that eliminated these duties, computer assembly in Mexico could become more attractive. But other costs of manufacturing in Mexico—e.g., the more complicated logistics of production management—might nonetheless outweigh the savings in direct labor.

Suppliers and Just-In-Time (JIT) Production

As a low-wage production site, Mexico competes directly with Asia. Mexico has the advantage of being near the United States, which simplifies the coordination of design and production for U.S. firms (box 8-D). Products shipped from Mexico can reach retail outlets in about a week, compared to 8 weeks if shipped from Asia. Reductions in inventories of goods in transit contribute to cost savings. On the other hand, for companies that currently manufacture in the United States, shifting production to Mexico can add considerably to inventory costs.

Where product cycles are short and companies must react quickly to changes in consumer demand, as in the PC industry, offshore production, even in Mexico, can penalize responsiveness and disrupt JIT production systems. Many firms in such markets, Dell Computer for one, carry very small inventories

---

[15] Zenith recently announced that it will close its Springfield, MO plant. In total, 1,200 jobs will be lost—600 in assembly and 600 in a cabinet finishing plant. John Burgess, "TV-Maker Zenith Will Move Assembly Operations to Mexico," *Washington Post*, Oct. 30, 1991, p. F3.

Box 8-D—*Making Telephones in Mexico*[1]

Direct labor represents 30 percent of manufacturing costs for standard telephones. Assembly requires just a few steps—manual insertion of the circuit pack, assembly into the housing, and testing to make sure the phone rings, followed by packaging for shipment. These tasks can be easily conducted with unskilled labor in Mexico or elsewhere.

With deregulation and the opening of the U.S. market, AT&T shifted production of telephones to Asia. Inventory costs for parts and finished goods erased much of the savings the company hoped to achieve, keeping prices high and costing the company market share. Phones sometimes had to be shipped back to Asia for repair. By moving production and repair operations to Mexico, AT&T reduced its inventory and shipping costs, lowered prices, and regained lost market share. The company now makes about 9 million phones each year in Mexico, up from 2 million before the move. Success with phones led AT&T to make answering machines to Guadalajara, after unsatisfactory experiences with contract production in Asia. The company claims it would have been unable to stay in the answering machine market without its manufacturing operations in Mexico, which it expects will produce several million answering machines in 1993.

[1]This box is based on industry interviews.

Table 8-12—Personal Computer Production Costs in the United States and Mexico

	Cost per computer (dollars)	
	United States	Mexico
Direct labor.................	$ 35	$ 5
Overhead....................	100	80
Mechanical parts.............	50	50
Tooling......................	20	20
Components.................	795	795
Total manufacturing.........	$1,000	$950
Additional transportation.......	NA	6
Inventory in transit[a]...........	NA	3
Losses on inventory[b]..........	NA	15
Total cost..................	$1,000	$974

[a]Assumes 10 percent cost of funds.
[b]Assumes one week's production per year of finished goods sold at cost.
NA = Not applicable.
SOURCE: Office of Technology Assessment, 1992.

of finished goods (as little as a single day's worth). While these firms may hold larger quantities of parts inventories, to allow rapid assembly of final products and to take advantage of dips in component prices, production in Mexico would require larger stocks of completed products, which, if they must be marked down because of rapid shifts in consumer demand, could erase at least some of the savings achieved through production in Mexico (table 8-12). In mature, high-volume industries, where demand is more stable and predictable, the chances of being left with unsold inventories are greatly reduced.

The cost differential shown in table 8-12 would probably not justify production in Mexico. ADDS Corp., for example, recently decided to move production of computer displays from Taiwan to the United States. The company estimates that production costs will rise from $300 to $320, but will be offset by reductions in overhead costs for managing

production—costs omitted from table 8-12 for simplicity, but not necessarily insignificant even for Mexican production.

Deficiencies in the Mexican supplier base will also limit investments by firms working towards JIT production. Electronic components produced by Mexican firms are high in price and low in quality compared with those available on the world market. MNCs operating in Mexico also note that delivery is unreliable. The local supplier base will probably be slow to develop. Most circuit boards for TVs are already stuffed in Mexico, with components imported from Asia. (Only Philips currently assembles circuit boards for TVs in the United States.) Because most of these components are standardized, made in high volumes in low-cost Asian plants, and inexpensive to ship, there is little incentive for producing them in Mexico. Development of a supplier base for more complex products will be paced by the overall development of the Mexican electronics industry.

Intrafirm Linkages and Investment Costs

Despite the global dispersion of manufacturing in recent years, many MNCs try to maintain close linkages among manufacturing, marketing, and R&D departments. This is true especially for development of goods made in low volume with customized features—as for large computers and telecommunications equipment—and also for high-volume, high-technology products such as laptop computers. Linkages between marketing and manufacturing become especially crucial when products must be customized for each user.

Table 8-13—Distribution of Expenses in the Computer and Television Industries

	Computer			Television
	Mainframe	Minicomputer	Personal	
	(percentage of total expenses)			
Production...........	49%	51%	58%	89%
R&D...............	11	11	6	4
Marketing............	32	31	25	7
Other...............	5	5	4	—
Profit...............	4	2	7	—

SOURCE: Benjamin Gomes-Cassares, "International Trade, Competition, and Alliances in the Computer Industry," paper presented at the World Trade and Global Competition Colloquium, Harvard Business School, Boston, MA, December 1991; and corporate annual reports.

The differences between products like computers and televisions are reflected in corporate expenditures (table 8-13). For minicomputer and mainframe manufacturers, R&D and marketing costs top 40 percent of annual revenues; even for PCs, they can exceed 30 percent. In contrast, TV manufacturers spend only 11 percent of total revenues on R&D and marketing; almost all their revenues go to cover manufacturing costs.

Compaq Computer, for example, recently announced two new portable computers priced for the low-end market. Compaq decided to produce these computers in its Houston plant rather than offshore so that the design engineering staff could work closely with production engineers. These products incorporate new technologies that may need refinement over the first few months as they are tested in the market.[16] In some segments of TV manufacturing, too, market considerations can make it advantageous to keep design and production teams near each other. Several TV firms state they will keep production of projection and large screen TVs in the United States at least until these markets stabilize. U.S. sales of projection TVs are only 200,000 per year, while product features have been in constant flux as companies strive to push costs down and improve performance.

Investment Costs, Worker Skills, and Technological Infrastructure

For many sophisticated products, including telecommunications switches and semiconductors, the capital costs of manufacturing plants continue to increase. State-of-the-art semiconductor fabrication facilities cost between $500 million and $1 billion to construct; for telecommunications switches, investment costs run to hundreds of millions of dollars. At these levels, companies build no more plants than necessary, and examine location decisions very carefully. There is no reason to close existing plants and move them, even if the technologies are not demanding, unless costs can be recovered quickly—which is not the case when front-end capital costs are high.

Mexico is an unlikely choice for new capital-intensive manufacturing because of its relatively poor technological infrastructure. Whereas the production of TVs and electrical equipment is largely a matter of assembling components, the manufacture of products such as semiconductors and picture tubes requires workers and organizations able to cope with complex production equipment that may need constant "tuning" to keep productivity and quality high. For products such as mainframe computers and telephone switching systems, each unit may be built to somewhat different specifications, requiring highly skilled workers. Mexico has little capability in these areas today. For reasons discussed in chapter 5, it would probably be several decades before Mexico could catch up even with NICs like Korea, where production of complex semiconductors began during the 1980s.

With declining direct labor content in many electronics products, the relative importance of indirect labor—engineers, equipment repair techni-

---

[16] Joe Tasker, Compaq Computer Corp., personal communication, February 1992. Hyundai, too, recently announced plans to shift its PC operations from Korea to the United States. Despite the potential cost savings of a Mexican plant, Hyundai opted to build in the United States in order to be nearer new technical developments. Managers noted that assembly would be moved, along with design, development, and marketing, to help the company respond more quickly to shifting market demand. Hyundai has promised the new U.S.-based division substantial autonomy for worldwide PC operations. Jim Carlton, "Hyundai Plants to Move Its Division for Personal Computers to the U.S.," *Wall Street Journal*, Apr. 20, 1992, p. A2. Reportedly, Goldstar and Samsung are considering exiting the PC market because they have been having so much trouble keeping up, yet do not wish to follow Hyundai to the United States.

Table 8-14—Advantages and Disadvantages of Electronics Production in Mexico Compared to the United States

	Labor costs	Suppliers/ JIT	Interfirm linkages	Market size	Investment costs	Workforce skills
Television						
Assembly....................	+	0	0	0	0	0
Picture tubes.................	0	-	0	0	-	-
Computers......................	0	-	-	-	0	-
Peripherals.....................	+	-	0	0	0	-
Semiconductors................	0	0	-	0	-	-
Telecommunications						
Switches....................	0	0	-	-	-	-
Customer premises equipment...	+	0	0	0	0	0
Electrical equipment.............	+	0	0	0	0	0

Key: + = Mexico at an advantage.
    0 = Little or no difference, or not a significant factor.
    - = Mexico at a disadvantage.
SOURCE: Office of Technology Assessment, 1992.

cians, managers, and administrative personnel—has increased. These are precisely the kinds of workers that are in shortest supply in Mexico. As a result, wages for skilled technicians, engineers, and managers are rising. Whereas wages for production workers are perhaps one-tenth those in the United States, pay for skilled technicians and engineers may be one-fifth to one-third of U.S. levels. Some Mexican managers earn as much or more as their U.S. counterparts. Thus, the growing importance of indirect labor reduces Mexico's ability to attract investment and jobs in electronics by requiring skills in short supply in the Mexican labor force and reducing the cost advantages of manufacturing in Mexico.

NAFTA Impacts

By itself, a NAFTA is unlikely to radically alter patterns of investment and development in the Mexican electronics industry. Investment would continue without an agreement in response to Mexico's unilateral policies for attracting FDI, the dismantling of trade restrictions on computers, and the opening of TelMex procurements following privatization. NAFTA may, in some cases, speed the flow of investment dollars to Mexico by reducing uncertainty about the future. Specific NAFTA provisions, for example on rules of origin, will also affect trade and investment patterns in both near and long terms.

Table 8-14 summarizes Mexico's capabilities in electronics manufacturing compared to those of the United States. As the table shows, the relative advantages of each country vary greatly from sector to sector. For products such as TVs, customer premises telecommunications hardware, and electrical equipment, labor costs outweigh other factors, so that Mexico can attract production away from the United States.

While most of the movement in TV production has already occurred, as Mexico's infrastructure of suppliers and its design/development capabilities improve, Mexico will be able to attract more technologically sophisticated production. For example, Hitachi announced in February 1992 that it would move production of projection TVs from Anaheim, California to Mexico; Sony already makes projection TVs in Mexico.

Manufacture of picture tubes will probably remain in the United States, at least in the near term. New picture tube plants cost $100 million to $200 million, while existing plants can be retooled for $10 million to $20 million. Because production is highly automated, labor cost savings would not offset the investment costs associated with a transfer to Mexico, particularly given the narrow profit margins in this business. Newer entrants, such as Korean firms, are more likely to put tube plants in the United States than in Mexico, where skilled workers would have to be trained because no base of picture tube manufacturers exists today. Dependable supplies of water, a critical element in picture tube fabrication, also are a problem in Mexico, particularly in the border region. Perhaps most important, Mexican suppliers cannot at present supply the glass funnels and blanks needed for picture tubes. These would have to be imported from the United States or the Far East.

In the absence of government policies forcing them to do so, computer firms have little reason to manufacture in Mexico. The potential cost savings do not appear adequate to justify branch-plant forms of production. Leaders in the industry such as IBM, Apple, and Compaq differentiate their products through technology rather than pricing. Besides, most U.S. computer manufacturers are consolidating manufacturing operations due to overcapacity. Generally speaking, the Mexican market, by itself, is too small to justify additional investments. However, some new production capacity for PCs may go into Mexico in the medium term to serve domestic and export markets. Rapid growth rates, estimated at 20 percent by the U.S. Department of Commerce, could see sales in Mexico doubling, to $2 billion from the current level of $1 billion, within 4 years. Mexico already has plants assembling micro and minicomputer systems, and companies might choose to expand them or supplement them.

From TV production, moreover, Mexico could probably move into computer displays. Zenith already manufactures color displays in Mexico, and has announced plans to move monochrome display production from Taiwan to Mexico. Development of skills for more advanced peripherals would require significant investments by companies based in the United States, or, more likely, Japan and Singapore, which excel in such products. While some incentive may exist for Japanese printer manufacturers to locate in Mexico to reduce transportation costs, disk drives are easy to ship, and manufacture in Mexico offers no apparent advantage to current producers. On the other hand, a major technological change in mass storage devices could conceivably see Mexico entering on the ground floor.

Mexico is not a contender for advanced semiconductor production. It would be very difficult to build and operate a clean room facility in Mexico today. Chip assembly operations that have not already been automated have long since moved to the Far East. Moreover, there are few fabrication facilities in the United States that could ship parts to Mexico for assembly, and few prospects for new wafer fabrication installations given current levels of overcapacity. Very high costs for building a state-of-the-art semiconductor facility, the economies of scale inherent in semiconductor production, and the very high risks involved, ensure that new capacity will be added in developed countries or in advanced developing countries like Korea.

Economies of scale will also prevent current U.S. manufacturers of telecommunications switches from shifting production to Mexico. In the United States, both AT&T and Northern Telecom produce major CO switches at only one location. The Mexican market, although it is expected to grow rapidly, is still only one-eighth the size of the U.S. market (800,000 lines per year compared with about 6 million here). Mexico would probably need to call on government inducements to attract switch production beyond what it has today. More likely, the output of U.S. plants, which have excess capacity, will be directed toward Mexico. If the Mexican market grows at a faster pace, perhaps at 1 million lines per year, OTA interviews indicate that it could be profitable for a third competitor to manufacture CO switches there—provided it could expect to capture a third of sales. Such an operation would be viable only if foreign manufacturers, with larger economies of scale, were prevented from shipping switches duty-free to Mexico. In effect, new investment in Mexico would only be attractive if competition were limited to existing Mexican manufacturers. Table 8-15 summarizes the results of the preceding discussion, and identifies the primary constraints on production in Mexico.

A NAFTA is likely to affect investment decisions in electronics primarily through rules of origin. These could have considerable impact on picture tube production, for instance. Currently, Asian picture tubes go into many sets assembled in Mexico for sale in the United States. Tubes from the Far East cost less than $65 ($61 to $62 in production costs and less than $3 for shipment to Mexico), and can be incorporated duty-free into sets assembled in *maquiladoras*.[17] When shipped to the United States, tubes face a 5-percent duty—the rate charged on value-added in Mexico for completed TVs (only one-third the 15-percent tariff levied on picture tubes imported separately). At the 5-percent level, Asian picture tubes cost about $68 delivered into the United States—substantially less than U.S.-made tubes, which run $72 to $75. A good deal of new tube capacity has been put in place or announced in Southeast Asia, with much of this directed at the North American market (since there is little new assembly capacity going into Asia). A NAFTA

---

[17] These cost figures come from Duane Welch, Corning Inc., January 1992.

Table 8-15—Likely Effects of a NAFTA on Investment in Mexico's Electronics Industry

Product	Effect of a NAFTA	Comments
Consumer electronics	Continued transfers of production to Mexico.	High-end products such as projection TVs may remain in the United States until the market stabilizes.
Computer peripherals	Some movement of low-end peripherals such as keyboards, power supplies, and monitors from Asia and the United States.	Limited skills and suppliers for higher-end disk drives in Mexico.
Personal computers/minicomputers	Little movement to Mexico. Some new capacity could be added in the medium- to long-term to serve the Mexican market.	Limited Mexican supplier base; additional inventory costs in a rapidly changing market; overcapacity in existing U.S. facilities.
Mainframes/supercomputers	No movement to Mexico.	Lack of skills.
Telecommunications switches and PBXs	No movement without government inducements and protection from third-country imports.	Relatively small market.
Semiconductors	No movement to Mexico likely except for simplest products.	Limited worker and organizational skills; economies of scale.
Customer premises telecommunications equipment	Some movement of production from Asia to Mexico to reduce shipping times and costs.	
Electrical equipment	Continued movement of high-volume production.	

SOURCE: Office of Technology Assessment, 1992.

requiring a sufficiently high level of North American content could keep most or all of these tubes out.

Rules of origin would also have implications for computer manufacturers. U.S. producers currently import many components and subassemblies. Requiring a high degree of local content, while helping U.S. component manufacturers, could place U.S. computer manufacturers at a disadvantage. Some components such as active matrix displays for portable computers are not yet available from U.S. suppliers. Many other components are available more cheaply overseas.

Longer Term Impacts: Paced by Skills Development

Longer term evolutionary patterns will depend to a large extent on organizational and worker skills in both countries. In the United States, manufacturers must pursue high-wage production strategies to fend off low-wage rivals. Mexico must develop managerial and technical skills to move upscale in electronics. For Mexico, this will require three mutually supportive processes:

1. state-led programs to provide basic educational skills and attract foreign investment;

2. investments in worker training and supplier development programs by the government and by companies currently operating in Mexico; and

3. technology transfer from MNCs.

Mexico's government is unlikely to go back to full-blown protectionism and subsidization. But this does not mean that Mexico will not offer incentives to attract foreign multinationals through limited forms of managed trade, investment controls, or tax credits. Nations such as Taiwan, Korea, and Singapore have found these valuable in attracting foreign investors, fostering strategic alliances with domestic firms, and promoting local industries. Mexico has no such policies at present in electronics. Indeed, SECOFI, the Mexican Ministry of Commerce, has only $25 million available for facilitating technology absorption, funding research centers in Mexico's states, and stimulating private sector innovation.[18]

---

[18] Interview with Santiago Levy, SECOFI, May 20, 1992.

Box 8-E—Technology Transfer[1]

While many electronics companies operating in Mexico have failed to locate or develop local sources for key inputs to their production, IBM in Guadalajara has recorded something of a success. IBM purchases planar boards for its PCs from a local company, ADTEC, a joint venture between one of IBM's U.S. suppliers and a Mexican firm. ADTEC produces double-sided boards using surface mount technology on a state-of-the-art production line. Most of the 300-plus components come from the United States. Production yields in Mexico exceed 80 percent, compared to 65 percent in a comparable U.S. plant. ADTEC has now begun to sell to other computer manufacturers in Guadalajara, including Hewlett-Packard.

ADTEC has succeeded in part because its engineers learned from the experience of the U.S. plant that installed a surface-mount line in 1985, 2 years before the Mexican plant opened. Training also played an important role. The first workers hired by ADTEC received a full 6 months of training—very unusual in the Mexican electronics industry—although the company now finds it can get by with 3 weeks of training for new workers. Turnover is low: 1 percent a month compared with 7 or 8 percent in typical electronics *maquiladoras*.

IBM helped start ADTEC because it wanted a local source to aid in JIT production and because the Mexican Government required heavy investments in technology transfer as a condition for a fully-owned affiliate in Mexico. Still, while ADTEC produces quality products at high yields, the company hardly qualifies as "high" technology: three-quarters of the workforce are in direct production jobs, and their tasks resemble those in many TV assembly plants.

As part of its investment agreement with the Mexican Government, IBM also shares in the funding of a $22 million Semiconductor Technical Center for the custom design of semiconductor chips. In addition, the center began offering masters degrees in engineering in February 1991 and hopes to add a doctoral program in the future. Manufacture of chips designed at the center takes place in the United States, however.

---

[1]Based on "NAFTA and the Electronics Industry in Mexico," report prepared for OTA under contract No. H3-7200 by Patricia Wilson, February 1992 and OTA interviews.

CONCLUDING REMARKS

Mexican-owned firms including contract *maquiladoras* will need to improve the skills of their workers if they hope to take on more complex production tasks. Automation—increasingly necessary for meeting quality standards in electronics production—raises skill requirements for workers who maintain equipment and trouble-shoot manufacturing processes. As more customers demand that their suppliers use statistical process control and JIT production methods, training needs will grow. Mexico will also have to develop an adequate supplier base to attract assemblers that wish to implement JIT systems.

Skills development—and concomitant increases in industrial capability—will depend largely on foreign investment. Multinationals control the technology that Mexico must learn to use. Government initiatives to provide training in the electronics industry have so far been weak. Only large corporations are likely to be willing to support supplier development programs or extensive workforce training (box 8-E).

Some upgrading of capabilities in electronics *maquiladoras* has taken place in recent years. *Maquiladoras* have been investing in automated equipment—e.g., for assembling circuit boards, injection molding plastic parts, winding transformer coils, and testing final products—in part to meet the quality standards of their customers in export markets.

Expansion of the Mexican electronics industry into more technologically sophisticated product lines, such as at Hewlett-Packard (H-P), suggest what the future may hold for Mexican electronics. H-P has established an R&D facility in Guadalajara that now designs memory boards for company-wide applications. Guadalajara has also become the primary center for production of impact printers and handles design changes. At present, however, this is the only electronics R&D center in Mexico operated by a multinational. Development of a modern electronics industry will be a long-term undertaking for Mexico.

Chapter 9

Apparel

Contents

Boxes

Figures

Tables

SUMMARY[1]

U.S. imports of clothing, primarily from Asia, have been rising for years, from $2.5 billion in 1974 to more than $26 billion in 1991—roughly 40 percent of U.S. spending on apparel. Meanwhile, U.S. employment in the garment industry has shrunk—from more than 1.3 million workers during the 1970s to about 1 million currently. More than 150 low-wage countries ship apparel to the United States. While some U.S. apparel jobs will move to Mexico in the years ahead, Mexico has so far been a minor supplier of garments to the United States and will have difficulty dislodging established Asian producers. The threat to U.S. apparel jobs is global, not regional.

Apparel production is highly labor-intensive and, as in other manufacturing sectors, it is assembly (sewing) that has been most difficult to automate, and hence most susceptible to low-wage competition. Equipment is inexpensive, easy to buy and to use. The sewing machines found in many apparel factories cost well under $1,000.

Two broad sectors characterize the U.S. industry. Companies in one produce large quantities of basic, standardized commodities such as blue jeans and underwear. The other sector manufactures smaller runs of fashion-sensitive goods, much of it women's wear. Both sectors have been under severe pressure from imports. Women's outerwear—the largest fashion-sensitive category—accounts for about one-third of total U.S. apparel employment. Much of this employment is concentrated in the garment centers of New York and California, reflecting the continuing importance of design in this industry; production takes place near both major retail markets and styling centers.

The Mexican share of U.S. apparel imports has risen from 2 to 6 percent since the early 1980s,

almost all of this from *maquiladora* plants that sew clothing originally cut in the United States. Finished garments shipped to the U.S. markets are charged duty only on the value added in Mexico. Production in the *maquiladora* sector is based on very long runs of standard items; like mass production everywhere, plant operations are designed to minimize skill requirements and to accommodate a high-turnover workforce. While the United States imports large volumes of women's wear, very little comes from Mexico. Asia is the major source, with much of the apparel air freighted to the United States in a global version of "Quick Response."

Production workers account for a greater share of U.S. employment in apparel than in other manufacturing industries—nearly 85 percent, compared to 68 percent for all of U.S. manufacturing. Moreover, the apparel workforce is dominated by sewing machine operators. About two-thirds of all workers in the industry are classified as operators, and another 6 percent are laborers or material handlers; only about 10 percent of the workforce hold technically oriented jobs such as mechanic or precision production worker.[2] Although sewing requires considerable skill, operators with little formal education or training can become proficient in a matter of weeks or months. Thus, U.S. apparel producers have tended to locate in areas with large supplies of low-wage labor: in immigrant communities in the Northeast and California, and in the Southeast.

In early 1992, sewing machine operators in Mexico's *maquiladora* sector earned between $7 and $10 a day, compared to an average of $6.25 per hour in the United States— a difference so large that it may seem inconceivable that U.S. production could survive direct, unprotected competition with Mexico. To date, a complicated set of import quotas has limited apparel imports into the United States

---

[1] This chapter is based on "The North American Free Trade Agreement and the U.S. Apparel Industry," report prepared for OTA under contract No. I3-0615 by Thomas Bailey and Theo Eicher, May 1992. The Bailey and Eicher report is based on interviews in Mexico and the United States, data and information from the Mexican and U.S. Governments, and industry sources including unions and employer associations. It also draws on other studies conducted by the authors over the last 3 years, including site visits to more than 40 U.S. apparel factories. For OTA, the first author visited companies in Mexico City, Aguascalientes, and Tijuana. Some of these plants produce for the Mexican market, others are *maquiladoras* shipping to the United States. He also interviewed representatives of the national and the Aguascalientes apparel chambers, the national textile chamber, and Mexican experts on the textile and apparel industries.

[2] These figures are based on the public use sample of the March 1988 Current Population Survey.

from Mexico, at least on paper. If a North American Free Trade Agreement (NAFTA) ended these restrictions, it might appear that U.S. apparel jobs would quickly melt away. To make matters worse, many U.S. apparel workers have relatively little education, and face limited opportunities in the labor market—particularly those living in rural areas in such States as Georgia and the Carolinas.

In practice, the quotas negotiated by the U.S. and Mexican governments have been only a minor drag on Mexico's shipments of apparel to the United States. Nevertheless, a NAFTA would further stimulate growth of *maquila*-like production. U.S. imports of apparel from Mexico doubled between 1987 and 1991. With a NAFTA, the current *maquila* sector would continue expanding, perhaps at a higher rate (while coming to be identified by its export-oriented character, rather than the special trade rules under which it was established). *Maquiladora* apparel plants currently employ in the neighborhood of 45,000 people, a figure that could grow to as much as 130,000 by the end of the decade. Not all of these jobs would replace U.S. jobs one-for-one. But if they did, that would represent about 8 1/2 percent of current employment in the U.S. industry. Even without a NAFTA, the *maquila* sector would probably continue to expand. The simple fact is that production of basic apparel costs much less in Mexico than here. Because of Asian competition, on the other hand, exports of fashion-oriented apparel from Mexico to the United States, almost nonexistent today, seem unlikely to grow rapidly.

THE U.S. AND MEXICAN INDUSTRIES

Apparel Products and Apparel Jobs

The apparel industry is extremely diverse, producing one-of-a-kind gowns that sell for thousands of dollars as well as millions of identical copies of plain white t-shirts worth only a few dollars. It is possible to make a broad distinction between standardized commodities, sold year round and produced in large runs, and more fashion-sensitive items. The latter, produced in large numbers of styles that change from season to season and year to year, include much women's wear and a good deal of men's and children's clothing. Fashion-sensitive clothes are not necessarily expensive: mass market retailers like Walmart and J.C. Penney have been leaders in popularizing marketing strategies based on ever-changing styles of low-priced clothing. Standardized, commodity-like items include work clothes and white dress shirts.

Table 9-1 breaks down U.S. apparel employment—84 percent of which is in direct production—into three groups: Group 1, women's outerwear; Group 2, men's outerwear; and Group 3, underwear, nightwear, and infant's and children's wear. Women's outerwear, the most fashion-sensitive group, accounts for nearly 44 percent of U.S. employment. The most standardized goods are found in Group 3, which accounts for less than 20 percent of U.S. apparel jobs, with the men's wear group falling in the middle of the standardized to fashion-sensitive range and accounting for nearly 40 percent of employment.[3]

Imports in all three categories have been increasing for years, with women's outerwear above the average, primarily as a result of high import ratios for sweaters and blouses. Group 3, dominated by underwear and nightwear, shows the lowest import penetration.

Table 9-2 shows that imports are highest in fashion-sensitive categories—the categories in which, according to table 9-1, U.S. employment remains highest.[4] Two opposing forces are at work in fashion-sensitive clothing. Because such items are made in small lots with hand labor, offshore plants in low-wage countries can undercut U.S. costs substantially. But frequent design changes and the importance of timely delivery to retailers help U.S. plants overcome cost disadvantages through superior customer service. At the same time, well-managed foreign operations, especially in Asia, have

---

[3] In terms of market share, basic products sold year-round account for about 20 percent of U.S. apparel sales, "seasonal" products, with a 20-week life, roughly 45 percent of sales, and "fashion" products, with a 10-week life, the remaining 35 percent. *The U.S. Textile and Apparel Industry: A Revolution in Progress* (Washington, DC: Office of Technology Assessment, April 1987), p. 16. Thus it appears that about two-fifths of the industry, whether measured by employment or sales, is quite sensitive to fashion, while about one-fifth is accounted for by basic, commodity garments.

[4] The range within the categories in table 9-2 extends from a low of 11 percent for women's swimsuits to a high of 80 percent for women's sweaters. Import penetration for women's blouses, the largest single subcategory in terms of imports ($5.1 billion), stood at 59 percent in 1990. *Apparel*, Current Industrial Reports, MQ23AS1-90 (Washington, DC: Bureau of the Census, 1990), table 7.

Imports grew particularly rapidly over the period 1980-1987, when the trade deficit in apparel increased from $5 billion to $20 billion.

Table 9-1—U.S. Apparel Employment by Product Category, 1991[a]

	Number (thousands)	Percent of total
Group 1, women's outerwear		
WMJ blouses, shifts and dresses (2331, 2335)[b]	102.6	
WMJ suits, skirts, and coats (2337)........................	36.9	
WMJ outerwear, NEC (2339)............................	187.2	
	326.7	43.5%
Group 2, men's outerwear		
MB suits and coats, trousers (231, 2325)...................	132.4	
MB shirts (2321)..	63.8	
MB work clothing (2326)................................	43.3	
MB clothing, NEC (2329)................................	49.5	
	289.0	38.5%
Group 3, underwear, nightwear, and infant's and children's wear		
WMCI underwear and nightwear (2341).....................	50.0	
MB underwear and nightwear (2322).......................	16.8	
GCI outerwear, NEC (2369).............................	34.5	
GCI dresses, blouses and shirts (2361)....................	22.8	
Foundation garments (2342).............................	11.4	
	135.5	18.0%
Total for Groups 1, 2, and 3..............................	751.2	100%

GCI = girl's, children's, and infant's
MB = men's and boy's
NEC = not elsewhere classified
WMCI = women's, misses, children's, and infant's
WMJ = women's, misses, and junior's

[a]Excludes 203,000 workers employed in miscellaneous fabricated textiles (SIC 239, which includes home furnishings and a variety of industrial products), 43,400 in miscellaneous apparel and accessories (SIC 238), and 26,500 in hats, fur goods, and men's neckwear (SICs 2353, 237, and 2323).
[b]Numbers in parentheses are Standard Industrial Classification (SIC) codes.

SOURCE: *Employment and Earnings*, March 1992, except SIC codes 2322 and 2369, for which employment figures have been estimated from 1989 figures reported in *County Business Patterns* based on ratios of 1991 to 1989 employment equal to that for SIC 23 as a whole.

Table 9-2—Import Penetration by Class of Apparel, 1990[a]

	Apparent consumption[b]	Imports	Imports as percent of apparent consumption[c]
	(billions of dollars)		
Group 1, women's outerwear............	$ 29.9	$ 13.8	46%
Group 2, men's outerwear...............	23.0	8.6	37%
Group 3, underwear, nightwear, and infant's and children's wear............	8.2	2.8	34%
Total............................	$ 61.1	$ 25.1	41%

[a]Group definitions differ slightly from those in table 9-1, but are broadly consistent.
[b]U.S. production plus imports minus exports.
[c]Import shares are understated because import figures are based on customs values that exclude U.S. costs included in the apparent consumption column for domestically produced goods.

SOURCE: *Apparel*, Current Industrial Reports, MQ23AS1-90 (Washington, DC: Bureau of the Census, 1990), table 7.

demonstrated over several decades that they can compete quite successfully except at the very top end of the market, where imports tend to come from Europe. Of course, fashion sensitivity varies a great deal within each of the three groups.

U.S. jobs in producing the standardized items found in Group 3—which show lower import penetration in part because low costs have been achieved in the United States through mass production—are vulnerable because such goods can now be made with similar production methods and cheaper labor almost anywhere in the world.[5] Unless U.S. plants can maintain cost advantages through further automation (which itself cuts into job opportunities), production of these price-sensitive goods will continue to move to low-wage countries.

Shorter Product Cycles

Today, even the most basic apparel items, which previously came in only one style and color (denim jeans, sweatshirts) now can be bought in many styles and colors, while shifts in consumer tastes and retail marketing strategies have led to a proliferation of fashion seasons. In earlier decades, there were three fashion seasons; now some designers change their lines six times a year, and retailers seek almost continuous changes in stock. Although design has always been important at the upper end of the market, constantly changing style and fashion have come to dominate much larger segments in the last two decades, as innovative producers and retailers marketed fashion-oriented goods to low- and middle-income consumers.

Segmentation of markets and rapidly changing styles have cut deeply into opportunities for producing long runs of identical items sold on a year-round basis. The result has been to increase the importance of timely response to market shifts, and production flexibility generally.[6] At the same time, product quality has become more important.

Traditional Production: The Bundle System

Most U.S. apparel plants continue to base production on the "bundle" system, in which cut garment parts are delivered to operators tied into bundles of about 30 pieces. The operator performs one, usually very small, task—such as sewing a hem or attaching a pocket—on each item in the bundle. After completing the bundle, she processes a work ticket to keep track of her output, reties the bundle, and begins work on another.

By fragmenting the production process, engineers in bundle-system plants can focus on maximizing productivity at each step. Operators can be paid piece rates, according to their actual output. Work-in-process (WIP) inventories isolate each task from disruptions that might occur elsewhere in the production chain. Because a man's shirt, for example, requires between 40 and 60 operations, and each operator usually has two bundles waiting at her station for processing, at any given time there will be thousands of garment pieces sitting on the factory floor in bundles. Thus typical plants carry 15 to 20 days of WIP inventory for garments requiring no more than 20 standard minutes of labor.[7] As in other production systems with large stocks of in-process inventory, quality suffers because problems can accumulate for long periods of time before they are discovered. Moreover, piece workers who see errors or quality problems have little incentive to report or correct them since their pay is based solely on the number of operations they perform.

Automation and Skills

Complete automation of apparel manufacture is not yet possible because it is so difficult to manipulate limp fabric, particularly partially assembled garments that have taken on three-dimensional shape. Once the design has been completed, "markers" (patterns, one for each size, used for cutting the cloth for each piece of the garment) can be generated and stored in a computer, which then guides an automated cutter. Such operations as making button holes (and sewing on buttons), preparing collars, and

---

[5] Group 3 production in the United States is more capital intensive than the other two categories:

	Capital stock per production worker	Average hourly wages
Group 1, Women's outerwear............	$ 6,640	$ 5.87
Group 2, Men's outerwear..............	7,560	5.87
Group 3, Underwear, nightwear, etc........	8,020	5.72

These figures, for 1987, come from *1987 Census of Manufacturers Industry Series, MC87-I-23A, 23B, 23C, 23D* (Washington, DC: Bureau of the Census, 1987), tables 3a and 3b. More capital per worker suggests higher levels of automation in Group 3, indicating that U.S. apparel plants have been able to compete with low-wage offshore producers when they can take advantage of technologically sophisticated production systems.

[6] With only a single exception, each of more than 40 apparel plants visited since 1988 by OTA's contractors was producing more styles than they had in earlier years. For discussion of changing apparel markets, see *The US Textile and Apparel Industry: A Revolution in Progress,* op. cit., footnote 3, pp. 15-18; *The Coming Revolution in Apparel Manufacturing* (Washington, DC: American Apparel Manufacturers Association, 1988); and Thomas Bailey, "Skills and Education in the Apparel Industry," Technical Report #7, Institute on Education and the Economy, Teachers College, Columbia University, New York, NY, 1989.

[7] *The Coming Revolution in Apparel Manufacturing,* ibid., p. 12.

attaching pockets can be completed before assembly. But eventually, operators must guide the pieces by hand through a sewing machine.

Through the middle 1980s, many in the U.S. garment industry saw straightforward, labor-reducing automation as the key to meeting foreign competition.[8] But predictions of "lights-out" factories, freed from the "labor element," disregarded investment costs, which frequently could not be justified based on the small amounts of labor saved. Highly automated apparel production has so far proved cost effective only for large production runs of standardized goods. In particular, it has not made sense to install specialized material handling equipment in factories that produce many different and constantly changing styles.

If automation could not eliminate workers, many apparel firms hoped it could reduce labor costs by reducing the skills needed to assemble garments. The savings would come, not through lower wages for less-skilled workers—because apparel companies pay low wages already—but through reductions in training costs as automated systems replaced moderately skilled sewing machine operators with machine tenders.[9] Like automation, deskilling has its greatest impacts in production of standardized goods: the division of labor can be taken to its logical extreme, with workers specializing in a single task and no requirement for broad skills.

In standardized apparel, then, plant location decisions turn on the costs of automated production versus traditional methods in low-wage offshore plants, and on whether low-wage countries have the technical infrastructure to efficiently operate plants with high levels of automation. For style-sensitive items, product variety and short production runs work against attempts to routinize, automate, and deskill production. These segments depend on versatile workers who can move from one task to another as needed. Lacking possible advantages through automation and deskilling, U.S. producers have turned to immigrant workers to reduce their labor costs. Lacking employment alternatives, many immigrants have been willing to accept low wages.[10]

Fashion-sensitive production, especially of women's wear, concentrates in New York City and Los Angeles in part for easy access to immigrant labor. In addition, these cities are centers of apparel design and marketing, with a constantly shifting mix of small shops providing a broad range of services.[11] These services—many of them provided internally in large firms producing standardized clothing—include design, cutting, technical support, repair, equipment leasing, credit, warehousing, trucking, and specialized apparel-related educational institutions. These cities are also at the centers of large regional markets, which is particularly important for small producers of fashion-sensitive items, where constantly changing styles and short selling seasons put a premium on close cooperation among designers, producers, and retailers. As figure 9-1 shows, women's wear (Group 1) accounts for more than three-quarters of apparel jobs in California—the only State to enjoy significant growth in apparel employment during the 1980s. And while New York has two-thirds of its jobs in Group 1, Texas has a lower than average percentage, suggesting that apparel workers there may be especially vulnerable if a NAFTA accelerates transfers of standardized production to Mexico.

Quick Response

It can be a year from the time a retailer orders clothes until they arrive.[12] Retailers want to be able to stock new styles in modest amounts that can be

---

[8] A typical example, from the trade press:

Our main hope for a return of production of basic apparel items to the U.S. mainland is automation of the production process. Only with the labor element essentially eliminated through robotic automation can the advantages of the emerging countries be overcome by the U.S. manufacturer.

Sid Riley, "The Industrial Revolution: Our Time Has Arrived," *Bobbin*, April 1987, pp. 67-88 (quote on p. 76).

[9] Plant surveys suggest that training times for attaching collars can be cut by 60 percent, for setting hip pockets in trousers by 40 percent, for making button holes and attaching the buttons by 30 percent, for setting front pockets in jeans by 70 percent, and for decorative embroidery stitching by 90 percent. Kurt Hoffman and Howard Rush, *Micro-Electronics and Clothing: The Impact of Technical Change on a Global Industry* (New York, NY: Praeger, 1988).

[10] Many arrive in the United States with some sewing skill or experience. See Thomas Bailey and Roger Waldinger, "Primary, Secondary, and Enclave Labor Markets: A Training Systems Approach," *American Sociological Review*, vol. 56, 1991, pp. 432-445.

[11] Roger Waldinger, *Through the Eye of the Needle: Immigrants and Enterprise in New York's Garment Trades* (New York, NY: New York University Press, 1986).

[12] William R. Cline, *The Future of World Trade in Textiles and Apparel*, revised edition (Washington, DC: Institute for International Economics, 1990), p. 86.

Figure 9-1—Distribution of Apparel Employment, 1989

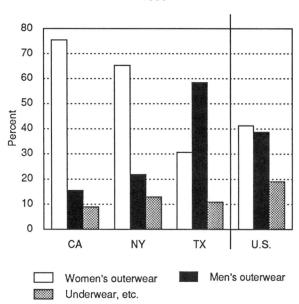

Women's outerwear   ■ Men's outerwear
▨ Underwear, etc.

SOURCE: *County Business Patterns.*

replenished quickly, rather than risk having to mark down goods that do not sell or run out of styles that prove popular. Many U.S. managers assert that quick response (QR, box 9-A) strategies are critical for the continued viability of apparel manufacture in this country.

But implementation of quick response has been slow. Existing practices have become deeply entrenched in apparel firms. For over a hundred years, production has shifted first from the Northeast to the Southeast, and then abroad, as companies sought cheaper labor. U.S. plants also remain attached to the piece-rate system, resisting internal QR reforms based on employee involvement and a workforce with better skills and a broader understanding of the overall production process. Such reforms almost always imply a shift from piece rates at least to hourly rates and often to group incentive schemes. Apparel workers themselves sometimes resist abandonment of piece rates and the added responsibilities

implied by group-based production systems. Thus, a 1988 survey found that fewer than 10 percent of U.S. apparel workers held jobs in plants with such features of internal QR as modular manufacturing or group incentive schemes.[13] Preliminary data from a survey of apparel producers conducted in 1991 and early 1992 show some increase, but only to the 10 to 15 percent range, and mostly in large plants producing standardized apparel—the firms in Groups 2 and 3 in table 9-1, rather than women's wear producers or the more fashion-sensitive men's wear manufacturers.[14] The large majority of U.S. garment factories still use traditional high-inventory production systems and pay workers piece rates.

Why this resistance? Despite a good deal of experience in other industries, and some in apparel, the advantages of internal QR have been hard to pin down. Innovators keep quiet about the details of their successes. Common measures of productivity, such as value added per production worker hour, or standard labor minutes required to produce a particular garment, fail to capture benefits associated with flexibility. Work reorganization may not reduce labor inputs (it may actually increase them) even though it reduces throughput time from days or weeks to a few hours, but apparel producers have no systematic way of evaluating the payoffs. Nor is it clear how much benefit can be achieved through external QR without internal QR. Put another way, how much will retailers pay for shorter delivery times?

A final set of questions relates directly to production in Mexico: Can QR serve to offset high U.S. labor costs, slowing the movement of jobs southward? Conversely, might a NAFTA cause some U.S.-based manufacturers to look to Mexico for cheap labor rather than implement QR here? Will U.S.-based firms implement QR strategies in which Mexican production is an integral component, thus displacing U.S. labor while helping U.S.-based firms meet competition from other developing countries?

---

[13] *Making the Revolution Work: How to Implement Flexible Manufacturing Through People* (Washington, DC: American Apparel Manufacturers Association, 1989).

[14] These preliminary results come from a survey being conducted by Thomas Bailey of a random sample of 1,000 apparel and textile plants. As OTA's report was being completed, responses were available from 240 apparel plants. Even in plants which have instituted some features of internal QR, the approach tends to be piecemeal—best viewed as a series of techniques rather than a fundamental reorganization of production. Thomas Bailey, "Organizational Innovation in the Apparel Industry: Technique or Strategy," *Industrial Relations*, forthcoming.

Box 9-A—Quick Response: Lean Production in the Apparel Industry

During the 1980s, employers, employer associations, consultants, and unions began seeking alternatives to traditional production methods based on the bundle system, with its high inventory levels and division of production into narrowly defined tasks. Emerging Quick Response strategies represent the industry's attempt to create a system yielding better quality, lower throughput times, and greater flexibility—hence quick response to market shifts.

As in "just-in-time" or "lean" production systems in other industries, QR strategies have two basic components. "External" QR (outside the plant) entails better communication and coordination among firms in the vertical production chain—fiber and textile suppliers, apparel manufacturers, and retailers. "Internal" QR (inside the plant) entails changes in the production process itself. By working together more effectively with their suppliers and customers, apparel firms can coordinate their production schedules and deliveries to reduce the time that materials and finished goods spend on loading docks, in warehouses, and in transit. With shorter lead times, retailers can adjust their orders depending on what sells. With lower inventory levels inside the plant, and new forms of work organization, apparel firms can turn out finished garments faster and with higher quality. Moreover, to the extent that QR shortens delivery times and helps U.S. plants produce a greater variety of apparel, it offers advantages relative to foreign plants. Nearby producers are in the best position to work interactively with textile firms and retailers; although many QR techniques can be used with international sourcing of fabric, person-to-person contact remains important.

Despite many expressions of support and enthusiasm for internal QR by industry managers, they have moved to implement external QR much more rapidly. Industry representatives worked out bar coding practices to facilitate electronic data interchange during the mid-1980s, and have devoted much effort to management of in-transit inventories and deliveries and procedures for reordering. The 1992 death of Sam Walton brought to public attention the sophisticated links between his Walmart stores—the nation's largest retail chain—and their hundreds of suppliers. Each supplier gets information in real time about the sales of their products in each Walmart store. Such practices have spread to other retail chains.

In many cases, apparel makers have chosen to meet the accelerated delivery requirements of their customers through the simple expedient of holding larger inventories of finished goods. Such an outcome represents little more than a transfer of inventories from retailers to apparel producers. To reduce their finished goods inventories, apparel firms will have to implement internal QR. This will require a fundamental reshaping of human resource practices and work organization—e.g., production systems based on work groups and employee involvement—steps that only a few U.S. firms have been willing to take.

In one team-based approach, known as modular production, each worker passes her completed work more or less directly to the next worker. By avoiding the bundle system, modular production cuts in-process inventories drastically. Employees must work closely together so that the flow of production is smooth; they must have broader skills so that they can share time consuming tasks and compensate for potential bottlenecks in the flow of production. Through employee involvement, particularly in quality control, and constant improvement of product design and the production process, U.S. plants should be able to compete more effectively.[1] In addition, lower inventories reduce operating costs directly.

---

[1]Many apparel managers claim that work reorganization has led to productivity increases though employee involvement. *Making the Revolution Work: How to Implement Flexible Manufacturing Through People* (Washington, DC: American Apparel Manufacturers Association, 1989).

Mexican Apparel Production

About 650,000 people work in some 11,000 Mexican apparel firms, most of them very small.[15] U.S. apparel output is more than 10 times greater, produced with a workforce larger by only about one half. Most Mexican apparel firms turn out inexpensive, low-quality goods for the domestic market. About 80 percent of exports go to the United States almost all from the *maquiladora* sector. Although

---

[15] Ovidio Botella C., Enrique García C., and José Biral B., "Textiles: Mexican Perspective," *U.S.-Mexican Industrial Integration: The Road to Free Trade*, Sidney Weintraub, Luis Rubio F. and Alan D. Jones, eds. (Boulder, CO: Westview, 1991), pp. 193-220; "Mexican Government Initiative to Revitalize Textile and Apparel Industry," cable from U.S. Embassy, Mexico City, to U.S. Department of State, Washington, DC, Apr. 16, 1992.

Table 9-3—Growth of the *Maquiladora* Apparel Sector

	1986	1987	1988	1989	1990	1991
Employment (thousands)...	25.3	30.3	34.7	42.4	40.9	45.7
Exports to the United States (millions of dollars).......	$360	$410	$468	$565	$657	$844
Value added in Mexico (millions of dollars)......	$ 84	$101	$128	$183	$200	$250

SOURCE: *Instituto Nacional de Estadística, Geografía e Informática,* Mexico City, 1992.

maquila production has been growing rapidly, the 300 plants in this sector employ fewer than 50,000 workers (table 9-3).

Despite their low wages, Mexican apparel firms—burdened with small and inefficient plants, obsolete methods, and poor quality—have had great difficulty competing with Asian imports since the removal of Mexico's trade barriers. As of 1985, production weighted tariffs on Mexican apparel imports averaged nearly 50 percent; 100 percent of domestic production was covered by import licenses. By the end of 1987, import licensing requirements had been eliminated and average tariffs had been reduced to 20 percent. The industry's trade balance went from a $290 million surplus in 1987 to a deficit of about $450 million in 1990.[16] Clandestine imports of apparel also enter Mexico in large volume, so that the actual trade deficit could be substantially higher than official figures indicate; many such imports, which include used clothing, never enter formal economic channels, but are sold by unregistered retailers and sidewalk vendors.[17]

During the last few years Mexican exports have also grown significantly—from $149 million in 1987 to $254 million in 1990. *Maquiladoras*, which have substantial cost advantages over U.S. producers, accounted for almost all the growth.[18] Export-oriented apparel firms are much larger and more efficient than producers oriented toward the Mexican market. But the *maquiladoras* remain committed to classic mass production techniques for assembling standardized commodities. In contrast, Mexican firms that supply the domestic market, with very few exceptions, employ small-scale craft-oriented production processes in which individual workers often produce entire garments.

The owner of a large *maquila* in Tijuana, who had had experience in production for the domestic market as well, offered the following set of contrasts:

Production in Mexico for:

U.S. Market	Mexican Market
Volume	Short runs
Basic commodities	Varied styles
Severe time pressure	Looser deadlines
Growing demand for quality	Quality less important

Other interviews tended to confirm this picture. *Maquiladoras* produce extremely long runs, while domestically oriented plants produce in small lots. One successful pants-maker stated that he sought orders calling, at a minimum, for 10,000 units a week or more for at least a year, and would rarely accept smaller orders; this firm had been supplying 90,000 units a week for one customer.[19] In contrast, a swimwear maker producing for the Mexican market never makes lots of more than 3,000 suits; when visited, this plant (with about 100 employees) had over 100 styles in process. A maker of children's clothes for the domestic market had typical runs of 600, producing about 30 different styles a month.

Large U.S. firms have urged the *maquilas* with which they do business to increase production rates and reduce turnaround time. The typical response has been a traditional mass production approach—

---

[16] "The Textile Industry," *Review of the Economic Situation in Mexico*, Banamex, vol. LXVII, No. 787, June 1991, pp. 249-255. According to official figures, import penetration now runs around 20 percent, much of it originating in Asia but entering Mexico through the United States. Gordon H. Hanson, "U.S.-Mexico Free Trade and the Mexican Garment Industry," report prepared under purchase order No. B9412764 for the U.S. Department of Labor, September 1991, p. 46.

[17] Laura Carlsen, "Coming Apart at the Seams?" *Business Mexico*, December 1990, pp. 50-54.

[18] Labor-intensive sewing (and cutting) costs up to 50 percent less in Mexico than in the United States. *The Likely Impact on the United States of a Free Trade Agreement with Mexico*, USITC Publication 2353 (Washington, DC: U.S. International Trade Commission, February 1991), p. 4-39.

Value added figures compiled by the *Cámara Nacional de la Industria de la Confección* show *maquila* exports doubling from $101 to $200 million between 1987 and 1990, while non-*maquila* exports only grew from $47 to $52 million. According to the U.S. Commerce Department, imports from Mexico in square meter equivalents grew by 59 percent between 1985 and 1990.

[19] A much smaller *maquiladora*, with about 120 workers, usually ran only one style of one color at a time. When visited, this plant had been working on the same style for three weeks. A third plant that produces a variety of men's and women's clothes for U.S. firms placed their typical run size at about 100,000.

[20] One manager interviewed explained that in order to keep his turnaround time down, he tried "never to change anything."

longer runs, more time-and-motion study.[20] Indeed, *maquiladoras* fight for fewer styles and larger orders. In contrast, domestically-oriented firms lament their fate as producers of small lots, feeling that they cannot justify investments in new technology or more sophisticated work organization practices without much longer runs.

While many of the *maquilas* are U.S.-owned, and others have longstanding contractual ties with U.S. manufacturers, distributors, and retailers, interviews conducted for OTA indicate that QR techniques hardly exist in the country. For instance, modular production evidently has not been tried in Mexico. Interviews revealed only limited awareness of this and other teamwork-based, low-inventory approaches, although consultants have begun advising Mexican firms and industry associations about these and other QR techniques.[21] Early in 1992, the government announced plans to encourage QR as part of a program to revive the import-battered industry.[22] The intent would be to take advantage of QR for exporting to the United States, capitalizing on delivery times that should be shorter than for Asian producers shipping by sea. The slow spread of QR in the United States suggests that it may be equally difficult for Mexico to move in this direction.

Trade Management

Quotas and Tariffs

The primary effect of a NAFTA would be to reduce or eliminate U.S. tariffs on Mexican exports and weaken or do away with import quotas. The United States has protected its apparel and textile industries for many decades.[23] For the last 30 years, the Multi-Fiber Arrangement (MFA), in place since 1974, and its predecessors, the 1961 Short-Term Agreement and the 1962 Long-Term Agreement, have provided a structure for controlling the rate of growth of imports of apparel and textiles. The early agreements covered cotton textiles and clothing; the MFA extended coverage to wool and manmade fibers. In 1986, the agreement was further extended to "new-MFA" fibers such as linen, ramie, and silk blends.

MFA signatories negotiate bilateral agreements concerning quotas on covered textile and apparel items. The United States restricts imports from about 40 countries, nearly all of them developing economies. Despite tariffs averaging 17 to 18 percent—one of the highest duty levels imposed by the United States—and MFA-sanctioned quota restrictions, which have the effect of an additional tariff averaging an estimated 28 percent, U.S. apparel imports have increased steadily.[24] Multilateral negotiations as part of the Uruguay Round, in progress under the auspices of the General Agreement on Tariff and Trade (GATT), seek an agreement on phasing out the MFA, which limits the ability of Third World countries to export in a sector in which many have significant competitive advantages.[25] While the developing world sees the agreement as egregiously protectionist, the industrial countries see it as a necessary means of cushioning adjustment in sectors employing large numbers of relatively low-skilled workers who have limited prospects for alternative employment. Proponents also argue that by creating a multilateral framework, the MFA has forestalled

[21] For example, "promoters" at a training center started by the Mexican labor ministry (see ch. 5) in the state of Tlaxcala, visited by OTA staff in May 1992, have arranged for small local apparel shops to learn the rudiments of production management and the benefits of reducing in-process inventories.

[22] "Mexican Government Initiative to Revitalize Textile and Apparel Industry," op. cit., footnote 15.

With a good deal of pent-up demand to be satisfied, economic growth in Mexico will stimulate domestic clothing sales. A revived and restructured Mexican industry should be able to take back some of the market share recently lost to imports from the Far East. But growing Mexican demand will not stimulate U.S. exports; the United States sends little except partially assembled garments south today, and will not be able to compete on price in the future.

[23] The U.S. Tariff Act of 1922 placed high duties on imported cotton and woolen goods. Quotas on textile and apparel imports from Japan date to 1936 (and are still in force, although imports from Japan have been small in recent years). *Trade Restraints and the Competitive Status of the Textile, Apparel, and Nonrubber-Footwear Industries*, (Washington, DC: Congressional Budget Office, December 1991).

[24] The estimated tariff equivalent of U.S. quotas comes from *Trade Restraints and the Competitive Status of the Textile, Apparel, and Nonrubber-Footwear Industries*, ibid., p. xv. When added to the actual tariffs, the net impact of the two forms of trade restraint is to increase prices for garments delivered into the U.S. market by almost half (46 percent), on average.

Textiles and apparel account for almost one-quarter of all tariffs collected by the United States, according to the American Apparel Manufacturers Association.

[25] Irene Trela and John Whalley, "Do Developing Countries Lose from the MFA?" Working Paper No. 2618, National Bureau of Economic Research, Cambridge, MA, June 1988. For an extensive discussion of U.S. trade policy in textiles and apparel, see Cline, *The Future of World Trade in Textiles and Apparel*, op. cit., footnote 12.

Box 9-B—*Quotas on Apparel From Mexico*

Since 1963, the U.S. tariff code has included provisions under which goods assembled abroad from U.S.-made parts or components are charged duties only on foreign value added. Originally Item 807, these provisions are now found under Item 9802 of the Harmonized Trade Schedule, which took effect in 1989. It is Item 807/9802 that has permitted the export of textiles or cut fabric to Mexico or (elsewhere), with duties charged when assembled clothing is reimported only on the value added in the *maquiladora* plant. The 807/9802 share of total U.S. apparel imports (from all countries) rose to 10 percent in the late 1970s, and remains at roughly that level. Essentially all imports of clothing from Mexico enter under 807/9802. Table 9-4 illustrates typical cost advantages of 807/9802 production.

Table 9-4—Costs for U.S. and Offshore Production of Men's Shorts

	Unit cost (dollars)	
	U.S.	Offshore (807/9802)
Fabric and cutting............	$ 1.91	$ 1.91
Assembly labor and overhead..	1.66	.58
Freight and duty.............	NA	.59
	$ 3.57	$ 3.07

NA = Not applicable.

SOURCE: "The US Textile Industry: Challenges and Opportunities," *The Working Papers of the MIT Commission on Industrial Productivity*, vol. 2 (Cambridge, MA: MIT Press, 1989), p. 20.

Until 1986, and the establishment of the Caribbean Basin Initiative (CBI), apparel items entering under Item 807/9802 were charged against the relevant quotas (i.e., as negotiated with the country of origin under the MFA). The CBI contained a special access program for apparel known as Item 807A. Under 807A, apparel imported from CBI countries (including Mexico) assembled from "U.S. cut and formed" fabric was subject to "generous" quotas referred to as "Guaranteed Access Levels" (GALs). These quotas are in practice unlimited. According to the U.S. Department of Commerce, "the GALs may be increased on request by the exporting government and barring unusual circumstances of market disruption, increases are virtually automatic and unlimited."[1]

Apparel assembled from components cut and prepared in the United States but made of fabric produced elsewhere is subject to separate quotas referred to as Designated Consultation Levels (DCLs) and Specific Limits (SLs) which are set lower than the GALs. Apparel assembled from foreign-made but U.S.-cut fabric remains eligible for Item 9802 tariff treatment, however.

The 1989 "Special Regime" agreement between the United States and Mexico included another set of provisions. Articles assembled from U.S.-formed fabric or from other fabric were all subject to DCLs and SLs. Because U.S.-formed and cut fabric was no longer eligible for GALs, there was no longer a presumption, as there was under Item 807A, that quotas would be raised more or less on request. But in many cases, a large share of the quota (as high as 80 percent) has been reserved for Special Regime garments. The remaining quota could be used for 807/9802 items made from non-U.S.-formed fabric (cut in the United States for Mexican assembly) or items not eligible for 807/9802. If Special Regime items exceeded their share of the quota, any remaining quota for the relevant category of apparel could be used. But non-Special Regime items are limited to their share of the quota even if the Special Regime share is not fully utilized. Thus the Special Regime not only encouraged the use of U.S.-formed fabric, it also restricted the available quota for non-807/9802 items—for example, Mexican-assembled garments made from Mexican, Asian, or European fabric that was not cut in the United States.

Mexico accounted for about one-fifth of all 807/9802 apparel imports in 1990, and 70 percent of Mexico's 807/9802 apparel imports came in under the Special Regime. But there is little evidence that the Special Regime either promoted Mexican imports or boosted the 807 share.[2] Despite the complexities of this system of quotas, it rarely if ever appears to limit Mexico's shipments to the United States.

Quotas set in annual bilateral negotiations apply to about 75 categories of apparel imports from Mexico. During the year, Mexico's government allocates shares of the quota for each item to exporters. In interviews, both apparel manufacturers and Mexican experts on the subject noted that until the late 1980s the quota allocation system was cumbersome and often corrupt. Managers spent a great deal of time traveling to Mexico City to negotiate quota

---

[1]This quotation is from an unpublished 1987 Commerce Department summary of the program.

[2]The sharp rise in 807/9802 shipments after the Special Regime took effect in 1989 was paralleled by growth in non-807/9802 imports. Furthermore, the 807/9802 share dropped in 1990, and, indeed, was at that time below its 1985 share. The fall in overall apparel imports in 1990 was probably due to the U.S. recession, which hit this industry in that year and may have had a differential impact on 807/9802 operations. Many *maquiladoras* operate as contractors and are particularly vulnerable to recessions, as manufacturers are likely to cut contract production before laying off their own workers.

allocations with government officials. In many cases, quota allocations had to be "purchased." Since 1987, the system has been reformed and decentralized to Mexico's major garment centers.

Midyear changes in the quotas to which the two governments have agreed are common.[3] For example, the quota for underwear was doubled during such an adjustment in 1987, and was still more than 95 percent filled by the end of the year. At the end of 1988, 10 quotas had been filled to the 80 percent level or higher; 9 of these had been raised during the year. The need for mid-year adjustments dropped off in 1989 and 1990; only 7 quotas were more than 80 percent full during those years, and most of those received adjustments. The categories that tend to fill are those in which Mexican suppliers specialize. Trousers is the largest export category and it also has had the highest utilization rates and the most adjustments.

Thus the quotas have not been irrelevant. But neither have they been holding back a potential flood of imports. Indeed, the frequency of mid-year adjustments and year-to-year quota increases suggests that quotas follow rather than restrict exports. With one exception, every apparel maker interviewed (in early 1992) claimed that they could get all of the quota they needed. One very large *maquiladora* plant noted that the trouser quota was sometimes a problem.

---

[3]"Monthly Performance Reports," U.S. Department of Commerce. As these reports show, U.S. and Mexican officials are in frequent communication concerning quotas and adjustments. But it is not clear whether Mexico has in all cases been granted the increases it has sought.

---

even more restrictive bilateral or unilateral barriers. In addition, by limiting shipments from nations with the lowest costs, countries such as Mexico that otherwise might not have been competitive can export textile and apparel products.[26]

The MFA is an exception to GATT principles for two primary reasons. First, the MFA permits discriminatory treatment among supplier nations. Second, GATT has always sought markets available to all nations within existing tariff structures, with tariffs preferred to quotas. The agreement does provide for steady expansion of international trade; the 6 percent annual increase in quotas (by quantity, measured in square meters or yards, not value) exceeds the growth rate of U.S. apparel consumption.

Under the MFA, the U.S. Government negotiates quotas on specific items with each trading partner—in practice, the rate at which imports from the country may rise. Imports from Mexico face barriers that are much lower than average. Almost all come from *maquila* plants that assemble garments from cloth shipped in from the United States. Under Item 807/9802 of the U.S. tariff code, shippers pay duties only on foreign value added (box 9-B). Because the nominal duty of 15 to 20 percent applies to a value-added share from assembly that runs at about

35 percent, the effective duty for 807/9802 garments rarely exceeds 10 percent. Moreover, as discussed in the box, quotas on many if not most categories of Mexican exports to the United States either go unfilled or are increased when they are filled, following negotiations between the two governments. Because few quotas are binding, they add little to the "effective" tariff, which has been only about 6 percent.[27]

Quotas that are adjustable on demand may still inhibit exports by creating additional costs and complications, by injecting a level of uncertainty, and perhaps deterring new investments. But at least since 1987, quotas seem to have been at most a minor drag on Mexico's exports. Moreover, this drag is confined to a small number of standardized commodities.

The Structure of U.S. Imports From Mexico

During the first four months of 1992, Mexico supplied about 6 percent of U.S. apparel imports (by value), almost three times its share in 1983 (table 9-5). Figure 9-2 shows that imports from many of the other countries covered by the Caribbean Basin Initiative (CBI), which was established in 1986 to provide easier access to U.S. markets, have increased even faster (at least as measured by area).

---

[26] With few exceptions, industrialized countries have not established MFA quotas against each other. Hanson, "U.S.-Mexico Free Trade and the Mexican Garment Industry," op. cit., footnote 16, argues that Mexican apparel exports to the United States benefit from U.S. quotas on imports from China and other Asian countries.

[27] *The Likely Impact on the United States of a Free Trade Agreement with Mexico*, op. cit., footnote 18, p. 4-38.

Table 9-5—U.S. Apparel Imports by Country of Origin

	1991		First 4 months (January-April) (billions of dollars)	
	Value of imports (billions of dollars)	Share of all imports (percent)	1991	1992
Hong Kong.........	$3.52	13.7%	$1.01	$1.12
China..............	3.46	13.5	0.96	1.37
Taiwan.............	2.60	10.1	0.76	0.76
South Korea........	2.59	10.1	0.69	0.76
Mexico.............	$1.49	5.8%	$0.40	$0.58
Philippines..........	1.01	3.9	0.36	0.39
Dominican Republic...	0.94	3.7	0.25	0.33
Italy...............	0.77	3.0	0.27	0.26
India..............	0.69	2.7	0.25	0.35
Others.............	8.63	33.6	2.68	3.44
Total[a]............	$25.70	100.0%	$7.63	$9.36

NOTE: Many apparel exports from Hong Kong and Taiwan originate elsewhere in Asia, including China. Transhipment, in part to evade MFA quotas, has been common in this industry.

[a]Totals may not add due to rounding.

SOURCE: Office of Technology Assessment, 1992, based on official statistics of the U.S. Department of Commerce.

Figure 9-2—U.S. Apparel Imports from Caribbean Basin Initiative (CBI) Countries

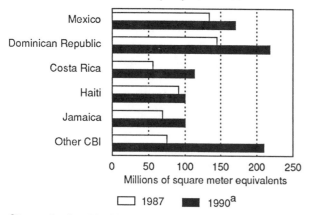

[a]Year ending June 30, 1990.

SOURCE: *Textile Highlights*, American Textile Manufacturers Institute, September 1991, Table 5.

Imports of clothing from Mexico have been concentrated in a few standardized items; imports of more expensive and fashion-sensitive items—women's dresses, skirts, and blouses; men's suits, jackets, and shirts—have come from other countries. As table 9-6 suggests, Mexican suppliers have specialized in inexpensive men's wear (trousers and coats), and in similar items for women. Mexican imports have grown most rapidly in underwear and nightwear; imports of "other" apparel grew at lower than average rates. By 1990, pants, underwear, and nightwear accounted for about 60 percent of all apparel entering from Mexico.

IMPACTS OF A NAFTA

Any trade agreement is likely to provide a lengthy transition period and perhaps substantial residual protection for the U.S. apparel industry. Even so, there could be some acceleration in the growth of *maquila* production of standardized commodities in expectation of a more predictable future. Most Mexican suppliers would probably continue to operate as contractors to U.S. companies. The current 807/9802 structure creates incentives for *maquilas* to limit their production to assembly of material supplied from the United States. Because U.S. textiles are generally cost-competitive, there will be no great incentive in the near term to switch to materials from third countries.[28] Still, U.S. producers offer rather limited ranges of textiles compared to many foreign suppliers (Japan, Taiwan, Germany), while fabrics from low-cost producers like China might suffice for many of the standardized goods produced by *maquiladoras*. American textile manufacturers sought "yarn forward" North American content requirements as part of a NAFTA to

---

[28] The better U.S. textile mills are among the world's low-cost producers. By contrast, Mexican mills have costs that can be more than twice those here. *The Likely Impact on the United States of a Free Trade Agreement with Mexico*, op. cit., footnote 18, p. 4-39. Also see *Trade Restraints and the Competitive Status of the Textile, Apparel, and Nonrubber-Footwear Industries*, op. cit., footnote 23.

Table 9-6—U.S. Imports of Apparel From Mexico

	Millions of square meter equivalents and proportion of total imports from Mexico				1985-1990 Increase
	1985		1990		
Men's and boy's trousers.............	18.9	(17%)	31.6	(20%)	67%
Underwear........................	6.1	(6%)	27.3	(16%)	344%
Women's, girl's, and infants' trousers...	14.5	(13%)	22.5	(14%)	55%
Nightwear........................	2.8	(3%)	14.1	(9%)	406%
Brassieres........................	6.0	(5%)	7.0	(5%)	18%
Other............................	62.3	(57%)	71.6	(41%)	15%
Total......................	109.6	(100%)	174.1	(100%)	59%

SOURCE: "Major Shippers Reports," U.S. Department of Commerce, various.

Table 9-7—Workforce Characteristics in *Maquiladoras*, 1990

	Tijuana (border)	Monterrey (interior)	Apparel	Electronics	Auto parts
Percent of workers with prior industrial experience.........	57%	33%	68%	60%	49%
Average monthly turnover.......	12.7%	3.7%	15.8%	19.5%	9.7%
Average daily wage (pesos).....	33,760	21,840	26,540	34,720	33,700

NOTE: Sector averages include sampled *maquiladoras* in the border city of Ciudad Juarez, as well as Tijuana and Monterrey.

SOURCE: Jorge Carillo, *"Mercados de Trabajo en la Industria Maquiladora de Exportación* [Labor Markets in the Assembly Plant Exporting Industry], *El Colegio de la Frontera Norte*, Tijuana, 1991, pp. 31, 34, 49.

preserve the market positions they have had under 807/9802.

With the possible exception of trousers and a few other basic commodity categories, U.S. quotas have not limited imports from Mexico. There is little reason to expect removal of restrictions to result in accelerated imports in categories where quotas have not been binding, but eliminating formal quotas could lead to greater imports of other items.

Because current 807/9802 regulations require cutting to be done in the United States, more of this work might move south of the border. On the other hand, the rapid growth of computerized cutting in the United States would tend to keep these operations here; Mexican firms have little or no computerized cutting equipment today. There is little likelihood of substantial shipments of finished garments from the United States to Mexico; almost all current U.S. exports consist of cut fabric for assembly in *maquiladoras*. Mexico will continue to import finished apparel items from the Far East.

The Maquilas

The *maquiladora* sector is much better positioned to take advantage of a NAFTA than Mexico's domestic suppliers. The latter face three significant barriers to participation in the U.S. market: financing, distribution, and textile quality. None of these are of great concern for *maquiladoras*, many of which have ready access to U.S. financial markets and distribution channels even if they are Mexican owned, and which rely on imported textiles already.

How rapidly might the *maquila* sector expand? Possibly rising wages, high turnover, skill deficiencies, and poor communications and transportation infrastructure will set the primary limits, as in other sectors OTA has examined:

1. *Wages and turnover*. If wages rise without commensurate increases in productivity, Mexican apparel firms will lose their primary source of advantage. Apparel firms in the border cities must compete for workers with other *maquila* plants (e.g., in electronics). Some have been seeking locations in the

interior, where both wages and turnover have been substantially lower (table 9-7). Indeed, between 1981 and 1988, plants in the interior increased their share of all *maquila* apparel employment from 20 to 40 percent.[29]

Border firms have so far lived with their turnover problems: a mass production system with highly structured tasks is well suited to absorbing new workers with little or no training. Given this approach, *maquila* apparel firms should be able to continue tapping rural reserves through busing or moves to the interior, thus maintaining downward pressure on wages.

2. *Workforce skills. Maquiladora* apparel firms provide entry into the industrial labor force for surplus rural labor, and stepping stones for migrants moving north.[30] Mexico's rural reserve is large and likely to grow as workers in the agricultural sector are forced off the land. Given current production methods, lack of skills is not a serious problem in *maquila* apparel plants. But skill deficiencies will make it difficult for these firms to implement new competitive strategies, including computerized cutting and QR.

Skill pools differ considerably between the border region and the interior. Although the border cities have large transient populations, there are many workers with industrial experience of one sort or another. Expansion in interior cities and rural areas more often means beginning with a nonindustrial workforce.- Skilled workers, particularly those able to maintain and repair electronic equipment, pose the greatest difficulties. But there is still very little of this equipment; managers stated that sophisticated electronics were not expected to play a significant role in currently planned expansions. Skill deficiencies, then, do not appear to be a fundamental barrier to more

widespread hiring of workers in rural areas except as they limit the ability of Mexican suppliers to adopt more flexible, QR-related strategies.

3. *Infrastructure.* Mexico's deteriorated infrastructure presents a problem particularly for the smaller apparel firms. Nonetheless, while better roads might take a day off of the 2-day trip from Aguascalientes to the border, this is only a small decrease in the typical 3-week turnaround time for *maquila* operations in interior cities.

Note that turnaround time and inventory levels also depend on the size of production runs. Given transportation problems, producers ship full truckloads. Very small firms may take several days to fill a truck, while high volume apparel firms can fill several per day. Again, small firms suffer more than large.

In the years ahead, and given their advantages over other Mexican apparel makers—notably greater access to capital and to U.S. markets—*maquiladora* apparel firms will continue to expand. A NAFTA would probably accelerate this expansion. But the emphasis on mass production of standard items seems likely to continue. The highest volume products account for about 150,000 U.S. jobs (Group 3—table 9-1)—less than 20 percent of the total. Some of these jobs will be lost to Mexico in the years ahead, but others will remain in the United States because costs can be lowered through capital-intensive automated production—which will also cut into jobs and job opportunities.

Nonbasics Production in Mexico

It would be very difficult for Mexico to ship substantial volumes of tailored or other fashion-sensitive clothing to the United States in the near term. Mexico has never been an important source for such items. Export growth since 1985 has not taken

---

[29] Hanson, ''U.S.-Mexico Free Trade and the Mexican Garment Industry,'' op. cit., footnote 16, table 6, p. 71.

In interviews conducted for OTA, managers in border plants worried that freer trade would hurt them because it would lead to higher wages. According to a company in El Paso, there is already little advantage in assembling apparel across the border in Ciudad Juarez because wages are rising and much higher turnover offsets existing labor cost advantages.

Interior cities have also felt the pressures of a tightening labor market. For example, all of the employers interviewed in Aguascalientes claimed that wages had risen sharply in the last 2 years. They anticipated more pressure after the opening of a Nissan assembly plant that would employ several thousand workers. One apparel firm with several hundred workers sent buses up to 25 miles from the city to tap the still substantial rural labor reserve.

[30] California apparel firms also seem to benefit. California is the only State with a large apparel industry in which employment has grown in recent years. Almost all the workers are Mexicans or Mexican-Americans, and many are recent immigrants. Some have training and experience acquired in *maquilas*. ''The Economic Effects of a North American Free Trade Agreement (NAFTA) on the U.S. Apparel Industry: Statement on Behalf of the International Ladies' Garment Workers' Union, AFL-CIO by Dr. Herman Starobin, Research Director,'' before the Trade Policy Staff Committee, Atlanta, Aug. 29, 1991, p. 4.

Table 9-8—Employment, Wages, and Productivity in Apparel[a]

	Total employment	Production worker employment	Production worker share of employment	Real hourly wages	Labor productivity index	Union members as share of production workers	Estimated hourly wages: Mexican apparel and textile *maquilas*	U.S.-Mexico wage ratio
	(thousands)		(percent)	(1991 dollars)			(1991 dollars)	
1978......	1,332	1,145	85.9%	$7.91	100	NA	NA	NA
1979......	1,304	1,117	85.6	7.80	96.3	NA	NA	NA
1980......	1,264	1,079	85.4	7.62	95.8	NA	NA	NA
1981......	1,244	1,060	85.1	7.62	100.0	NA	$1.36	5.6
1982......	1,161	981	84.5	7.55	109.8	NA	0.95	7.9
1983......	1,163	984	84.6	7.45	111.7	32.1%	0.77	9.7
1984......	1,185	1,003	84.6	7.39	118.5	26.8	0.78	9.5
1985......	1,121	945	84.3	7.34	126.8	27.3	0.70	10.4
1986......	1,101	927	84.2	7.26	131.4	24.0	0.56	13.1
1987......	1,099	923	84.0	7.09	137.5	22.8	0.52	13.7
1988......	1,088	915	84.1	7.01	138.3	22.4	0.63	11.1
1989......	1,074	906	84.3	6.94	133.6	21.0	0.69	10.0
1990......	1,028	862	83.8	6.85	NA	19.3	0.70	9.8
1991......	1,024	856	83.6	6.75	NA	18.1	NA	NA

NA = Not available.

[a]SIC (Standard Industrial Classification) 23.

SOURCES: **U.S. employment and wage data**—*Employment and Earnings*, March 1992. **Union membership**—Barry T. Hirsch and David A. Macpherson, "Union Membership and Contract Coverage Data from the Current Population Survey," Department of Economics, Florida State University, May 1992. **Mexican wages**—*Maquiladora Industry Analysis*, CIEMEX-WEFA, September 1991. **Labor productivity**—Wayne Gray, Clark University, and the National Bureau of Economic Research.

place in these categories. While Mexican firms make women's wear for domestic consumption, they do so using traditional production processes that are neither technologically advanced nor suited to fast turnaround. Quality is poor by U.S. standards. The firms in this part of the industry have no existing distribution in the United States, little access to financing and to imported fabrics, and little or no experience in what is a highly competitive business internationally.

In addition, most of the obstacles to *maquiladora* expansion also apply to this sector; indeed, workforce skill problems are more serious. High quality, rapid turnaround, and QR-related techniques require greater workforce skills and management sophistication than needed in either the *maquiladoras* making standard items for export or in domestically oriented Mexican firms. In interviews, large U.S. manufacturers that currently supply many of their commodity needs from *maquilas* report that they expect to implement QR through their U.S. plants.

If Mexico could move into nonbasics, it would be the California and Texas industries that would suffer first and more than New York's (because of logistics). But the California industry, centered in the Los Angeles area, is growing today, with an emphasis on women's outerwear. In most categories of women's wear—which accounts for over 60 percent of California apparel employment—less than half the Mexican import quota has been used. Large wage differentials have not been enough to drive this production across the border.

Effects on U.S. Jobs

During the past 15 years, U.S. apparel employment has declined by more than 300,000 jobs (table 9-8). Some cities with large apparel sectors, such as New York, have experienced particularly severe job loss. Despite the low average wages in the industry, about 30 percent of displaced apparel workers who found new jobs in the 1979-1989 period suffered earnings declines of 25 percent or more (ch. 4, table 4-3). Moreover, displaced apparel workers left the labor force during the 1980s at rates about 30 percent higher than for manufacturing as a whole, while more than a quarter of those who lost jobs had not found new work by the time they were surveyed. Many apparel workers have poor basic skills (e.g., reading, arithmetic). They have been poorly served by existing training and retraining programs. Global competition and the threat of relocation to low-wage sites will place continuing downward pressure on wages for production workers in apparel; real wages will probably continue to decline.

Job Loss in Standardized Production

From an overall perspective, the pattern of Mexican imports contrasts sharply with the pattern of U.S. apparel employment. Underwear (including brassieres) accounts for about 30 percent of U.S. imports from Mexico, but provides jobs for only about 8 percent of U.S. apparel workers; underwear plus men's and women's trousers accounts for almost two-thirds of imports from Mexico but about 30 percent of U.S. employment.

Thousands of U.S. jobs remain in basics, and these jobs are at risk (along with the job opportunities associated with growth in demand). In interviews, two very large firms that produce basics, both with extensive manufacturing in Mexico already, reported that, while they do not expect to cut U.S. employment significantly, they do expect future growth to take place in Mexico or in other CBI countries (which have expressed the fear that they will lose jobs to Mexico in the event of a NAFTA). Indeed, the fastest growing garment industry in the Americas lies just south of Mexico, dispersed through the capital city and remote rural areas of Guatemala (box 9-C).

How many jobs or job opportunities might be lost? From 1986 through 1991, *maquila* employment grew at an annual rate of about 12 1/2 percent (despite the U.S. recession that began in 1989). As table 9-3 showed, *maquiladora* apparel employment stood at almost 46,000 in 1991. Continued growth at 12 1/2 percent per year through the end of the decade, with one-for-one loss of U.S. jobs, would mean a decline in U.S. apparel employment of about 86,000 (with *maquila* employment rising to 132,000). This is about 8 1/2 percent of current U.S. production employment in the industry. Much of this job loss might take place even without a NAFTA, given the history of accommodating quota negotiations. If cutting, which has remained in the United States because of 807/9802 requirements, also moved to Mexico, job losses would be higher. But a NAFTA would require that textiles originate in North America if the assembled garments are to enter the United States with minimal restrictions. Given that Mexico's textile industry is uncompetitive, such a provision would help to keep some cutting jobs here.

More than the 86,000 jobs estimated above could move to Mexico if a NAFTA led U.S. apparel managers to view Mexican production as easier or safer, so that they accelerate transfers of production.

Interviews suggest that many larger U.S. apparel firms are taking a new look at Mexico in light of a possible NAFTA. On the other hand, the 86,000 estimate assumes a constant 12 1/2 percent increase in *maquila* employment; because *maquila* employment has been growing from a relatively low base, it might be more realistic to assume some decline in the rate of increase as employment reaches higher levels.

Losses in jobs and job opportunities will be geographically concentrated. Texas seems particularly vulnerable. Figure 9-1 shows that the distribution of apparel employment in Texas is similar to that of Mexican imports (in contrast to California and New York). Texas is a major supplier of men's pants and jeans, along with women's pants. During the last few years, a number of large manufacturers have moved across the border, including, for example, Farrah, which closed a plant in El Paso in favor of a *maquila*. Levi Strauss also has shut down operations in Texas and expanded in Mexico. Other vulnerable sectors include men's pants production in Georgia, Tennessee, and Mississippi, women's underwear in Pennsylvania and New York, and men's underwear in Georgia and Pennsylvania.

Job Loss in Fashion-Oriented Segments

A NAFTA will not make a large enough difference for Mexico to challenge Asian producers of fashion-sensitive clothing. Apparel firms in centers like Hong Kong and Taiwan have the skilled workers and managerial expertise needed to succeed despite their distance from major markets. The apparel industries in these countries consist of dense networks of small firms, often connected by family ties. In Hong Kong, both companies and the government provide training for sewing machine operators to step up to jobs as sample makers and design makers. These highly skilled workers help create advantages when competing for apparel work in a global marketplace. Many companies have the ability to offer a comprehensive package of services to buyers; they can quickly translate orders from U.S. retailers into finished goods, arranging for fabric sourcing, production, delivery, and credit— making use of their own facilities or contract suppliers in many countries.

While U.S. firms tend to specialize in particular lines of clothing, so that retailers may have to deal with different manufacturers for each type of cloth-

Box 9-C—Apparel Production in Guatemala[1]

From around 2,000 workers in 1984, Guatemala's export-oriented apparel assembly industry has mushroomed to 70,000 workers, mostly women between the ages of 14 and 25—more than in Mexico's *maquiladora* apparel sector. Between 1986 and 1991, Guatemala's garment exports to the U.S. rose from $22 million to $350 million, putting Guatemala behind only Costa Rica and the Dominican Republic among CBI countries. The growth of the Guatemalan industry illustrates both the potential for rapid expansion of the Mexican apparel industry in remote rural areas and the intense competition that these areas will face from even lower wage regions.

While Guatemala passed regulations designed to encourage export assembly production in the 1960s, these had little impact until the election of a civilian government in 1986. The new government implemented a stabilization program similar to Mexico's. As in Mexico, this led to depreciation of the national currency and rapid inflation. Guatemala's wages dropped to around 20 cents per hour—perhaps 1/30th of U.S. levels and one-quarter of wages in Mexican *maquiladora* apparel plants. To help investors take advantage of these very low wages, Guatemala's government established a "One Stop to Export" licensing center for new plants, while the U.S. Agency for International Development provided financial, technical, and marketing support for local entrepreneurs.

By comparison with apparel industries in other parts of the Caribbean, Guatemala has a much higher concentration of Asian, primarily Korean, investment. Since 1988, the number of Korean-owned plants has jumped from 6 to 50, accounting for about half of apparel exports. Korean multinationals own a dozen of these plants (Samsung alone has five), most of them large; small and medium-sized firms account for the rest. For Korean apparel manufacturers, Guatemala provided a way around U.S. quotas and a means to contain costs following Korean currency appreciation and wage increases in the second half of the 1980s. An estimated 300 to 500 Koreans work as managers and supervisors in Guatemala, with others in the United States handling marketing and distribution. Korea's Embassy acts as an intermediary for investors.

Alongside the Korean operations stand over 200 locally-owned firms, typically employing less than 100 workers each. U.S. firms account for only 10 percent of total investment in the Guatemalan industry. Van Heusen, the biggest U.S. player, employs over 1,000 workers assembling 20,000 men's shirts per month. Since 1989, Van Heusen has been helping San Pedro, an indigenous village 20 miles outside Guatemala City, move into production for export. San Pedro is a traditional center of production for the domestic market, with over 3,000 sewing machines distributed through homes or shacks each containing 6 to 20 machines.

While the export apparel industry has brought badly needed employment to Guatemala, the new jobs have been accompanied by low wages, very long hours, poor health and safety standards, child labor (particularly in rural areas), and weak protection of worker rights to organize. Attempts to form unions have been met with bribery, discharge, threats of plant relocations, actual relocations, and death threats. Many workers move from job to job to escape bad treatment or in search of slightly better pay, leading to turnover of 15 to 30 percent per month—and 25 to 40 percent in Korean plants, known for intense pace and harsh discipline. Guatemala's need for investment has discouraged government action to improve labor standards.

Guatemalan plants do not assemble high-fashion goods, but they do produce a range of apparel that goes well beyond the most standardized items. Recent capital-intensive investments promise to increase the industry's ability to meet the needs of large U.S. distributors, showing that, with good management—in this case from Korea—low-wage countries can rapidly increase production and move into wider ranges of apparel products. Finally, experience in Guatemala demonstrates that, in this industry at least, the issue of labor standards may have to be addressed in a broader venue than just North America—perhaps the Organization of American States or GATT. If garment trade with CBI countries is liberalized following a NAFTA, or if the MFA is phased out, the United States and its trading partners might consider basing liberalization (or growth in quotas during a transition period) on respect for worker rights, perhaps including the enforcement of a minimum wage scaled to a country's average wage or per capita income. Lacking such provisions, trade expansion would come at the expense of Mexican and Guatemalan as well as U.S. workers.

---

[1]This box is based on Kurt Peterson, *The Maquiladora Revolution in Guatemala* (New Haven, CT: Orville H. Schell Jr. Center for International Human Rights, Yale Law School), July 1992). Also see Shelley Emling, "U.S. May Probe Alleged Labor Abuses in Guatemala," *Washington Post*, August 1, 1992, p. A18.

ing, many Asian firms are broad-line suppliers. Some U.S. firms, such as M.A.S.T. Industries, have been successful with a comprehensive approach to order packaging, but U.S. apparel makers generally appear to be well behind in developing a complete packaging strategy. There have been no signs so far of movement of fashion-sensititve production from garment centers in cities such as New York or Los Angeles to Mexico. A NAFTA, by itself, seems unlikely to make such transfers attractive. Moreover, given that Mexico would bring little in the way of the skills needed for competing with the strategies of Asian firms, a NAFTA would not directly strengthen the North American apparel complex as whole in segments less sensitive to labor costs. Rather than U.S. producers in these segments moving to Mexico, a NAFTA seems more likely to attract Asian firms seeking to transfer their commercial skills and take advantage of guaranteed access to the U.S. market.

NAFTA and Quick Response in the United States

Would a NAFTA encourage or discourage movement toward QR in the United States and/or in Mexico? Thus far, much of the implementation of QR has involved planning and coordination among firms (external QR), with relatively few changes in actual production processes (internal QR). A NAFTA would not slow the movement toward greater interfirm coordination in the United States, and could accelerate it. *Maquiladoras* that supply U.S. firms could be incorporated into external QR without much difficulty, since some are U.S.-owned and many others are contractors that already work closely with large U.S. firms. An extra day or two in transit will not be a barrier. This implies that successful implementation of external QR in the United States would not necessarily prevent shifts of production to Mexico.

The effects on production processes and internal QR are more problematic. Despite the demonstrated success of workplace reorganizations based on employee involvement and work groups in other industries, U.S. apparel firms have shown little enthusiasm. But some of the firms that have made the most progress in internal QR are basics producers— the same group of companies that have transferred production to Mexican *maquiladoras*. These firms may be tempted to move even more production to Mexico, opting for cheap and pliable labor rather than implemention of internal QR in the United States.

At the same time, because Mexico is not a significant force in fashion-sensitive markets, it seems unlikely that a NAFTA would have much impact on the spread of internal QR among producers of such apparel. Nor is it likely that producers in Mexico would move quickly towards technologically and organizationally sophisticated systems of flexible production; so long as they see the solution to their problems in terms of long runs and ''not changing anything,'' they will resist QR even more than U.S. firms. Thus, Mexican production using either traditional or more modern methods does not seem a very attractive option for U.S. firms seeking to compete more effectively in fashion-sensitive goods. Instead, the primary strategic alternatives to Asian imports appear to lie in continued reliance on low-cost immigrant labor, combined with the agglomeration economies in existing U.S. apparel centers, with or without internal QR techniques. Only if tighter limits on Asian imports accompany a NAFTA will it have a major effect on the choices facing makers of fashion-sensitive goods.

The Uruguay Round and the MFA

Among the forces at work in the world apparel and textile industries today, some of which might push the Mexican industry and U.S.-Mexican trade in unforeseen directions, the most significant is the ongoing Uruguay Round GATT negotiations. An end to the MFA would create opportunities for growth in many countries that have labor costs well under those in Mexico. On a smaller scale, a NAFTA that liberalized U.S. imports of apparel from Mexico would probably mean eventual liberalization for other CBI countries. These countries will seek to keep their playing field level with Mexico's, and the U.S. Government will find it difficult to say no.

On the other hand, should the Uruguay Round come to nothing, while a NAFTA took effect, the United States might well seek tighter restrictions on Asian apparel imports in government-to-government negotiations. NAFTA provisions would probably limit transhipments from Asia into the United States via Mexico. But it is not so clear that a NAFTA would discourage Asian investments in Mexico. If it did not, sophisticated producers based in Hong Kong and elsewhere would have strong incentives to set up close to the lucrative U.S. market.

CONCLUDING REMARKS

In the United States and the rest of the world, apparel employment has grown during early stages of national economic development. The industry is typically one of the first large manufacturing sectors in developing countries and often provides the first industrial jobs for agricultural workers. As development proceeds and wages rise, apparel jobs migrate to lower wage regions. Thus, during the 1960s, Japan accounted for about one-third of all U.S. apparel imports, but by the 1980s Japan's share had dropped below 5 percent.

In the United States, apparel jobs migrated from the Northeast to the Southeast during the decades after World War II. During the 1970s and 1980s, the Southeast lost jobs to Asia and the Caribbean. A NAFTA, if it generated rapid economic growth in Mexico with wage increases, would accelerate the process through which Mexican producers would lose advantages based on low wages alone. Within Mexico, this process has already started. Apparel *maquilas* in the border cities must now compete with other manufacturers, at least some of which can afford to pay higher wages. But continuing competition for Mexican producers in both labor markets and product markets provides little consolation for U.S. workers who have lost, or will lose, jobs to Mexico.

Chapter 10

Agriculture

Contents

Boxes

Figures

Tables

SUMMARY

The agricultural and food processing sectors of the United States and Mexico complement and compete, depending in part on static factors such as climate, rainfall, and arable land, and in part on dynamic factors including technology, labor costs, capacity utilization, transportation costs, and government policies (subsidies, trade restrictions). Agricultural imports from Mexico compete primarily with products from warm-weather States, and Florida more than California or Texas.

Today, many of Mexico's agribusiness establishments, some of which are foreign-owned, have relatively low costs and high yields and productivity levels. But their yields—if much higher than in Mexico's small-scale, traditional farming sector—lag well behind those routinely achieved in the United States, depending on the crop and location. This lag reflects a broadbased deficit in agricultural technology—including cultivation practices, mechanization, and seed varieties and agricultural chemicals (fertilizers, herbicides, pesticides) suited to Mexican conditions. With a few exceptions where Mexico's climate creates large advantages, Mexican farmers and food processors, like their counterparts in manufacturing, rely on low labor costs to compete.

Fruits and vegetables—particularly those that require picking, trimming, and packing by hand rather than machine—are much more labor intensive than other agricultural products. These are the products—tomatoes, cucumbers, broccoli, radishes, green onions—in which Mexican growers and packers have been able to undercut U.S. costs. But even here, the seasonal nature of production means that Mexican products may compete with those from some parts of the United States, while complementing production elsewhere. For instance, Florida cucumber shipments reach their highest levels during November-December and April-May, while California ships at relatively constant levels from May through November. Imports of cucumbers from Mexico reach their peak during the December-March gap.

OTA's analysis of U.S.-Mexico trade and competition in agriculture leads to the following conclusions:

- Despite lower labor costs for most agricultural products, Mexico could not expect to achieve across-the-board advantages in agriculture even if all trade restrictions were removed. The United States would retain large advantages rooted in agricultural research (including biotechnology). These advantages include superior plant and livestock varieties and cultivation practices creating yield and productivity margins sufficient to offset Mexico's low labor costs. Indeed, costs increased more rapidly in Mexico than in the United States during the 1980s, in part because Mexico's government has been reducing subsidies (e.g., for fertilizers, fuel, and electricity).

- Mexico's primary agricultural exports—fresh winter fruits and vegetables—compete most directly with production in Florida, which has a similar growing season. Florida is as far or farther from many major U.S. markets (e.g., the West Coast) as the regions in Mexico with which it competes; as Mexico's transportation system improves, the advantages Florida has historically gained from rapid, reliable, low-cost shipping will diminish. Florida farmers would probably experience a greater share of adjustment costs following a North American Free Trade Agreement (NAFTA) than farmers in other States.

- Growing seasons in California less frequently overlap those in Mexico. While substantial production and processing capacity—notably for broccoli—has moved to Mexico, California growers have had little trouble in switching to other crops. Generally speaking, farmers in States other than Florida and California are less likely to face direct competition with Mexico.

- U.S. farmers produce grains at much lower cost than Mexican farmers, much of it for animal feed. Transportation costs for feedgrains would probably preclude the widespread relocation of cattle feeding to Mexico, even if Mexico could achieve comparable efficiencies. Because it is more costly to ship cattle than feed, beef packing will remain concentrated in the U.S. grainbelt. While some meatpacking jobs may be lost to Mexico, U.S. packers have been aggressive in driving down domestic wages and working conditions, reducing the attractions of Mexican labor. Because transportation is less of a barrier for poultry than for beef, Mexico's low labor costs could attract production and processing of chicken and turkey.

- Cow-calf imports from Mexico to supply U.S. feedlots would probably grow following a NAFTA, at the expense of competing operations in Texas and other border States. But limits on Mexican range land, water, and feed, along with transportation costs, would probably limit the market share of imported feeder calves to about 5 percent (compared to past shares in the range of 3 percent).

- Mexico itself faces fundamental limits on production of food, for domestic consumption as well as for export, beginning with limited amounts of arable land and water for irrigation. Competition for water is increasing as the economy industrializes and urbanizes. These factors limit Mexico's ability to expand production for export, reducing the potential threat posed to U.S. agriculture as a whole. Because the population is rising rapidly, and because of U.S. advantages in grain production, Mexico will continue buying wheat, corn, and feedgrains from the United States. Mexico also has the potential to become an important market for grain-based products such as beef as income levels rise.

- A NAFTA would probably increase the rate at which *ejido* farmers are displaced, exerting additional downward pressure on wages for unskilled workers in both Mexico and the United States.

Although the two agricultural sectors have been integrating, the pace has been slow. Three factors account for this: Mexican Government policies; U.S. policies, especially trade restrictions; and the technological advantages of the United States, which for products such as Florida tomatoes have enabled farmers in potentially vulnerable regions to maintain or even increase cost- and quality-based advantages.

For 75 years, Mexico's government has supported small-scale, traditional agriculture through distribution of *ejido* lands and a wide variety of subsidies. The results included farms and food processing plants below minimum efficient size, discouragement of a modern agricultural sector, and rising imports of food. These policies began to change during the 1980s, with restrictions on land ownership lifted in January 1992. While some *ejidos* will be consolidated, much of the land is too poor to produce at competitive cost levels regardless of money spent on improvements.

Where Mexico has achieved competitive costs, it has been in cases where low wages offset low efficiency. Despite high labor costs compared to Mexico, U.S. growers benefit from a broad range of government policies. Some enjoy low cost water for irrigation. Tariffs have helped preserve market share and profits, as have better distribution, superior quality, and longer in-store shelf lives for perishable commodities. Moreover, many U.S. growers faced with low-cost imports in their traditional products have successfully switched to crops more suited to the changing competitive environment.

In the United States, both the private and public sectors are eager to develop and introduce new agricultural and food processing technologies. Government has helped diffuse best practices through the agricultural extension program. In contrast, Mexico has neither the seed companies and agrochemical firms to develop and supply new products, nor the agricultural research organizations to support the underlying technology base. Mexican farmers must usually be content with seed and fertilizers developed for U.S. conditions.

MEXICAN AGRICULTURE: TRADE AND STRUCTURE[1]

Only Japan and the former Soviet Union buy more U.S. agricultural products than Mexico. And only

---

[1] This discussion is based in part on ''Agricultural Issues in U.S.-Mexico Economic Integration,'' report prepared for OTA under contract No. I3-0310 by B. Kris Schulthies and Gary W. Williams, April 1992. Information otherwise uncited comes from this report, which relies heavily on Mexican Government statistics.

For summary information on Mexican agriculture, see *Foreign Agriculture 1990-91* (Washington, DC: U.S. Department of Agriculture, Foreign Agricultural Service, August 1991), pp. 82-83. Also ''U.S., Mexico Seek Economic Boost from Free-Trade Pact,'' *Farmline*, February 1991, pp. 2-6; and *The Likely Impact on the United States of a Free Trade Agreement with Mexico*, USITC Publication 2353 (Washington, DC: U.S. International Trade Commission, February 1991), pp. 4-3 to 4-17.

Table 10-1—U.S.-Mexico Agricultural Trade, 1991

	U.S. exports to Mexico	U.S. imports from Mexico	Balance[a]
	(millions of dollars)		
Total.................................	$2,998	$2,527	$471
Livestock and livestock products (all)...	1,128	392	736
Fats and offals....................	207	1	206
Hides and skins..................	137	4	133
Dairy products..................	121	3	118
Beef............................	185	—	185
Cattle..........................	133	361	(228)
Poultry.........................	131	0	131
Pork............................	68	0	68
Other...........................	146	24	122
Grains and feeds (all)...............	739	64	675
Wheat and wheat flour............	48	—	48
Corn............................	148	—	148
Sorghum.........................	372	—	372
Other...........................	171	64	107
Fruits and vegetables (all)[b]...........	183	1,233	(1,050)
Tomatoes			
Fresh......................	4	250	(246)
Processed..................	—	18	(18)
Broccoli and cauliflower, fresh			
and frozen[c]..................	—	102	(102)
Peppers.........................	—	111	(111)
Onions..........................	5	90	(85)
Cucumbers.......................	—	73	(73)
Squash..........................	—	50	(50)
Strawberries....................	—	37	(37)
Grapes..........................	—	54	(54)
Mangoes.........................	—	54	(54)
Melons..........................	—	98	(98)
Citrus, fresh and processed........	—	78	(78)
Other...........................	174	320	(146)
Coffee............................	2	333	(331)
Seeds............................	87	6	81
Sugar and related products...........	114	33	81
Oilseeds and related products.........	524	43	481

[a]Parentheses denote negative balance (U.S. imports from Mexico greater than U.S. exports to Mexico).
[b]Total includes fresh and processed fruits and vegetables; subheadings refer to fresh produce unless otherwise noted.
[c]The U.S. Department of Agriculture provides only the combined total for imports of fresh and frozen broccoli and cauliflower.

SOURCES: *Foreign Agricultural Trade of the United States: January/February 1992* (Washington, DC: Department of Agriculture, Economic Research Service, 1992), table B-3, pp. B4-B42; *Foreign Agricultural Trade of the United States, Calendar Year 1991 Supplement* (Washington, DC: Department of Agriculture, Commodity Economics Division, Economic Research Service, July 1992), table 23, p. 399.

Canada ships more agricultural goods to the United States. But the relationship between the United States and Mexico is hardly symmetrical (table 10-1): Mexico needs inexpensive U.S. grain and milk products far more than the United States needs Mexican feeder cattle or tomatoes. Mexico sends more than three-quarters of its agricultural exports to the United States, but the United States buys only about 12 percent of its agricultural imports from Mexico.

Crop production accounts for 58 percent of the value of Mexico's agricultural output, livestock for 33 percent, and forestry, fishing, and hunting for the remaining 9 percent. As noted in chapter 3, agriculture accounts for about 9 percent of Mexico's gross domestic product (GDP). The majority of the country's 4 1/2 million farms are small and inefficient. Many still use traditional practices, producing corn and beans for subsistence and local consumption. Corn grows on about a third of Mexico's arable land (figure 10-1). Over half of the agricultural labor

Figure 10-1—Cultivated Acreage by Crop in Mexico

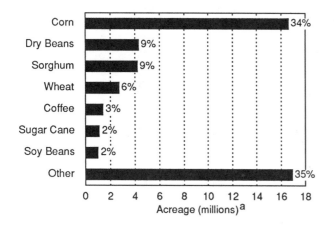

aAverage, 1985-1989.

SOURCE: "Agricultural Issues in U.S.-Mexico Economic Integration," report prepared for OTA under contract No. I3-0310 by B. Kris Schulthies and Gary W. Williams, April 1992, table 4, p. A3.

force works in the traditional sector, many on a casual or seasonal basis; the modern sector, which accounts for only a small minority of farms, produces perhaps three-quarters of total output.[2]

Land and water set fundamental limits for Mexican agriculture. Only 12 percent of the country's land is arable—some 57 million acres—compared with 464 million arable acres in the United States (a little over 20 percent of all U.S. land). Although the United States has eight times more arable land, it has only half as many farms. About half of the arable land in Mexico could be irrigated, but 60 percent of this land remains rainfed.[3] Mexican agriculture suffers from salinity in much of its limited supply of water and from widespread erosion. Irrigated as well

as rainfed lands in Mexico are subject to the vagaries of weather, since most irrigation water comes from reservoirs rather than underground aquifers (many of which are being rapidly depleted in any case).

After Mexico's revolution, foreigners were barred from owning land. Thus, foreign direct investment (FDI) in agriculture has been very low, with officially recognized investment totaling only a cumulative $30 million in 1990 compared with $18 billion for industry. Food processing plants operated by a dozen or so U.S.-based multinational corporations (MNCs) account for about half a billion dollars of Mexico's FDI ($470 million in 1989, included in the industry total), and a substantial share (perhaps one-third) of Mexico's total food processing capacity.[4]

Subsistence Farming: The Traditional Sector

In January 1992, the Salinas government's land reform program went into effect.[5] The intent is to modernize traditional farming, beginning with changes in laws governing land ownership and use that date to 1917. The *ejido* system was intended to reduce the power of prerevolutionary landowning families by redistributing their huge holdings to the peasantry, while ensuring that peasants retained their land. The state held title to *ejido* plots—in principle 10 hectares (about 25 acres), but in practice averaging less than half that—and granted peasants usage rights. *Ejidos* could not be legally sold, rented, or used as collateral. Over the years, slightly over half of those eligible received land.[6] The Mexican Government also maintained highly restrictive ownership policies on land outside the *ejido* sector. For example, individuals cannot own more than 100

---

[2] Alejandro Portes and Lauren Benton, "Industrial Development and Labor Absorption: A Reinterpretation," *The Informal Economy: Studies in Advanced and Less Developed Countries*, Alejandro Portes, Manuel Castells, and Lauren A. Benton, eds. (Baltimore: Johns Hopkins University Press, 1989), pp. 589-611. Many *ejidatarios* must seek employment on larger, more prosperous farms in the modern sector to supplement their income. Martine Vanackere, "Conditions of Agricultural Day-Labourers in Mexico," *International Labour Review*, vol. 127, 1988, pp. 91-110.

[3] Lloyd E. Slater, "Food: U.S. Perspective," *U.S.-Mexican Industrial Integration: The Road to Free Trade*, Sidney Weintraub, Luis Rubio F., and Alan D. Jones, eds. (Boulder, CO: Westview, 1991), p. 276.

[4] Libby established a food processing facility, currently owned and operated by Heinz, in 1929. Other examples of U.S. MNCs with processing facilities in Mexico include: Green Giant, Kellogg, Gerber, Del Monte, and Ralston Purina. Slater, "Food: U.S. Perspective," ibid., pp. 280-281, and industry interviews. In addition, a number of U.S.-owned *agro-maquilas*, like their counterparts in manufacturing, import everything from tractors to corn to cardboard packaging, perform labor-intensive processing (e.g., of tortilla chips) in Mexico, then send the finished products back to the United States. But these operations are not very representative. While the *agro-maquila* sector has been expanding rapidly, in 1990 there were fewer than 50 such firms, producing goods valued at around $100 million. Joel Millman, "'There's Your Solution'," *Forbes*, Jan. 7, 1991, pp. 72, 76.

[5] This discussion is based on an interview with Guillermo Ramos, Agricultural Counselor, Embassy of Mexico, Washington, DC, July 14, 1992.

[6] Some 2 1/2 million Mexicans still have outstanding claims, while 3 million have received land. "The Legal Proposal for Mexico's Agricultural Reform: Background Information," Embassy of Mexico, Washington, DC, November 1991, p. 5.

hectares of irrigated farmland.[7] Corporations could not own land at all.

Today, modern agriculture is concentrated on irrigated land in northwestern Mexico, with the bulk of the *ejidos* in the central part of the country. Crops are raised on a little over 20 percent of *ejido* acreage; the rest is wooded or used for grazing. *Ejidatarios* had little incentive to leave their land, which they could not sell, nor to invest in improvements; only 17 percent of *ejido* croplands are irrigated.

The burden of these policies finally proved unsustainable. As noted in chapter 3, Mexico was left with a great many people in agriculture in proportion to output, while the government continued pumping money into price supports and subsidies for fertilizer, water, electricity, and diesel fuel.[8] Both price supports and subsidies have been heading downward since the middle 1980s, a consequence of crisis and *apertura*.

The 1992 reforms substantially changed the rules for land ownership and use. *Ejidatarios* will get title to their lands. While individuals are still limited to 100 hectares, foreigners can purchase land on much the same basis as Mexican citizens. Corporations, domestic and foreign, may own up to 2,500 hectares (about 6,200 acres).

Steady reduction in subsidies, coupled with the changes to the *ejido* system, promises to displace many small farmers from marginal land, which will no longer be worth cultivating. Meanwhile, the modern sector will expand as more prosperous farmers assemble larger plots and purchase higher quality *ejido* acreage. More *ejidatarios* will be able to join the modern sector; others will be displaced and seek work in market-oriented agriculture or move to cities. Management of this transition by Mexico will have consequences for the United States, most likely in higher levels of immigration, as well as for the future of the Mexican economy.

Industrialized Agriculture and Food Processing: The Modern Sector

While the traditional sector came close to collapse, the modern sector increased in scale and scope, becoming substantially integrated into the North American regional market. The modern sector has drawn to considerable extent on U.S. know-how, buys U.S. farm machinery, and relies to some extent on U.S. capital. Even so, it remains on average significantly less advanced than commercial farming as practiced in the United States. The development of large commercial farming and food processing operations in Mexico has been driven, not only by exporting, but by the need to feed a rapidly growing urban population.

Mexican farmers devote only 2 to 4 percent of their land to fruits and vegetables, but horticultural products account for 9 percent of total output value and for more than half of Mexico's total agricultural exports.[9] Mexico supplies more than 80 percent of all fresh vegetables imported by the United States—not surprising given that fresh vegetables do not travel well.[10] Tomatoes account for nearly half of

---

[7] Limits vary by use: up to 400 hectares (967 acres) of grazing land and 200 hectares of nonirrigated farming land, but for certain crops (e.g., cotton, coffee, bananas, fruit trees), 150 hectares of irrigated land or 300 hectares of nonirrigated land. These restrictions, like those on *ejido* holdings, have been circumvented in various ways. For example, a large farm might be put together with title to the land distributed among family members. Many *ejido* lands are leased and many are part of Mexico's modern farming sector.

[8] The agricultural labor force continued to rise at least through the 1980 census, growing from an estimated 4.8 million in 1950 to 5.6 million in 1980, despite the industrialization and urbanization taking place over this period. Francisco Alba, "Migrant Labor Supply and Demand in Mexico and the United States: A Global Perspective," *U.S.-Mexico Relations: Labor Market Interdependence*, Jorge A. Bustamante, Clark W. Reynolds, and Raúl A. Hinojosa Ojeda, eds. (Stanford, CA: Stanford University Press, 1992), pp. 243-256.

With CONASUPO (*Compañía Nacional de Subsistencias Populares*, the government's agricultural distribution and marketing organization) purchasing corn and many other farm products at guaranteed prices, subsidy and support levels in some years exceeded 60 percent of the value of agricultural output. "Mexico After the Oil Boom: Refashioning a Development Strategy," World Bank Report No. 6659-ME, Washington, DC, June 23, 1987, p. 38; Myles J. Mielke, "Government Intervention in the Mexican Crop Sector," Staff Report No. AGES89-40, U.S. Department of Agriculture, Economic Research Service, Washington, DC, September 1989. As recently as the mid-1980s, the government subsidized purchases of diesel fuel by 30 percent and fertilizer by about 60 percent. *NAFTA: Effects On Agriculture; vol. IV, Fruit and Vegetable Issues* (Park Ridge, IL: American Farm Bureau Research Foundation, 1991), p. 104. The government also used negative subsidies to discourage some types of production.

[9] *NAFTA: Effects on Agriculture; vol. IV, Fruit and Vegetable Issues*, ibid., pp. 4, 6.

Reportedly, 2 percent of Mexican agribusinesses account for three-quarters of value-added. Steven E. Sanderson, *The Transformation of Mexican Agriculture: International Structure and the Politics of Rural Change* (Princeton, NJ: Princeton University Press, 1986), p. 100.

[10] Of Mexico's total shipments of vegetables to the United States, 85 percent is shipped fresh, 10 percent frozen, and 5 percent canned. *NAFTA: Effects on Agriculture: vol. IV, Fruit and Vegetable Issues*, op. cit., footnote 8, pp. 19, 20. The percentages quoted here and below fluctuate depending on price levels, which in turn reflect output as influenced by the vagaries of the weather in the growing regions of both countries.

Mexico's fresh vegetable shipments to the United States, although Mexico also exports cucumbers (taking about 40 percent of the U.S. market), peppers, broccoli, strawberries, melons, and much else besides.

Some of the products of the export-oriented modern sector compete directly with those from growers in California, Florida, Texas, and other warm-weather States. Others complement U.S. production, supplying U.S. supermarkets during winter months. Many of the imports are controlled by a few large distributors, typically located in Arizona, who have longstanding ties with Mexican growers and U.S. buyers.

Legal restrictions on land ownership hindered but did not foreclose commercial agriculture. Contract growing evolved to meet the needs of U.S. distributors and processors, who agree to purchase the farmer's output at a stipulated price (which may depend on the market price at the time of sale), and frequently provide seeds and technical advice as well. Contract production reduces risks for both parties; it also transfers know-how from the United States to Mexico.[11] Agribusiness operations benefited from many of the same subsidies as small farmers, especially cheap water from government irrigation projects and subsidized electricity. With the elimination of these subsidies, their costs have risen substantially.

U.S.-based processors and distributors have moved into Mexico for three major reasons:

1. low costs;
2. rising U.S. demand for fresh fruits and vegetables in season and out; and
3. Mexico's expanding domestic market for processed food, and for off-season fresh produce that can be supplied from the United States.

Investments will continue, but—given that, for instance, a canning plant for tomato products costs $35 million to $40 million—only where significant, long-term cost advantages seem assured. At present, Mexico has considerable excess capacity for processing frozen vegetables. This promises to discour-age additional investment for export until the market expands, unless new plants can achieve absolute cost advantages against competitors pricing at variable cost.

As U.S.-based companies began to penetrate Mexico's processed food sector, the government put in place policies to support and protect domestic firms, several of which were able to develop nationwide distribution and widely recognized brand names like Bimbo Bread.[12] These large firms use much the same processing and packaging technologies as their U.S.-based counterparts. But the policies of Mexico's government also ensured the survival of a large number of smaller firms with a local or regional focus that operate plants resembling those found in the United States before World War II. A NAFTA would expand the market opportunities for larger Mexico-based as well as U.S.-based food processors as the two industries integrate on a regional basis. It would also accelerate the consolidation and rationalization of the Mexican food processing industry, with new competition leading to the exit or merger of smaller firms without a defendable market niche or other source of advantage.

COMPETITION AND COMPLEMENTARITY: VEGETABLES AND BEEF

Farmers in northwest Mexico, particularly in the state of Sinaloa, have marketed winter vegetables in the United States for years. During the "tomato wars" of the 1960s and 1970s, Florida growers sought protection under U.S. trade law from Mexican producers and U.S. distributors, accusing them of dumping and other "unfair" practices. In fact, with their warm winter weather, farmers in northwest Mexico can often produce tomatoes and other fruits and vegetables more cheaply than U.S. growers. Because of variations in soil and climate, yields (output per acre per year) vary greatly from place to place and year to year in both countries, but in most cases are higher in the United States. While Mexican

---

[11] One U.S. processor interviewed by OTA reported a contract price for jalapeno peppers from Mexico of about 35 cents per pound (including duty), compared with spot prices that fluctuated wildly above and below this figure (peaking above 60 cents per pound). Production costs are about the same in the Mexico and the United States, at 15 to 18 cents per pound, with transportation costs, in refrigerated trucks from Mexico to Texas, adding about 4 cents. This processor contracted for peppers in Mexico to ensure supplies during times of the year when U.S. peppers might not be available at an acceptable price.

[12] Slater, "Food: U.S. Perspectives," op. cit., footnote 3, pp. 281ff.

farmers have lower per-acre production costs, lower yields coupled with transportation, marketing, and other distribution expenses can offset this, depending on the product and its final destination (and on U.S. tariff levels).[13] Hence, landed unit costs at the U.S. border are frequently similar to U.S. costs.

Mexico sends not only tomatoes and other horticultural products northwards, but coffee and cattle as well. At the same time, with population growth outstripping the country's ability to feed its population, Mexico purchases corn, soybeans, and, in recent years particularly, milk products and wheat from the United States. Indeed, Mexico imports more dairy products than any other country in the world—nearly all in the form of surplus dried milk from the U.S. Commodity Credit Corp. Government agencies purchase about 40 percent of Mexico's imports of agricultural products.

Mexican farmers ship fresh fruits and vegetables to the United States primarily in the winter months (box 10-A). This puts them in direct competition with Florida, but Mexican crops come in before those in California.[14] Given normal weather, winter fruits and vegetables from Mexico supply west coast U.S. markets, those from Florida the east coast. In the center of the country, produce from Mexico and Florida competes on the basis of delivered costs. With this primary exception, then, Mexican agriculture complements more than it competes with U.S. agriculture. In most years, depending on tomato

prices, coffee is Mexico's biggest agricultural export to the United States, which grows coffee only in Hawaii.

Where the two countries compete, both governments have called on a broad range of direct and indirect policies—including tariffs, import licenses (Mexico), and agricultural marketing orders (the United States)—to manage trade and protect domestic farmers. Many U.S. tariffs on fresh fruits and vegetables are seasonal; that is, they apply or increase during domestic harvesting periods.[15] Although Mexico has reduced many of its trade barriers since joining the General Agreement on Tariffs and Trade (GATT) in 1986, import licenses were still required for corn, wheat, and a number of other commodities as the NAFTA negotiations concluded. Typically, the government would not issue licenses until the domestic crop had been bought up.[16] In some cases, Mexico's government has raised tariffs after removing licensing requirements.

On the U.S. side, the Agricultural Marketing Agreement Act of 1937 permits fruit and vegetable growers to enforce standards for grade, size and other characteristics through marketing orders that apply to imports as well as domestic produce. Foreign growers often claim that marketing orders have been artificially manipulated to keep out their products (e.g., by imposing minimum size require-

---

[13] Stephen Fuller and Charles Hall, "The U.S.-Mexico Free Trade Agreement: Issues and Implications for the U.S. and Texas Fresh Vegetable/Melon Industry," TAMRC International Market Research Report No. IM-2-91, Texas A&M University, College Station, TX, April 1991. Production costs in Sinaloa (which currently accounts for 40 percent of Mexico's horticultural exports to the United States) are significantly lower (40 to 80 percent) than in Texas, but are often similar to those in California and Florida. Transportation (usually by truck because of perishability) and marketing costs can exceed production costs; delivered costs of Mexican vegetables in the United States break down approximately as follows: production and handling, 50 percent; transportation and marketing within Mexico, plus border crossing costs, 30 percent; and, transportation and handling within the United States, 20 percent.

[14] Because northern Mexico is on the same latitude as Florida, growing seasons are similar. Florida farmers compete with Mexico primarily in tomatoes, cucumbers, peppers, and squash. *NAFTA: Effects On Agriculture; vol. IV, Fruit and Vegetable Issues,* op. cit., footnote 8; Nicholas G. Kalaitzandonakes, and Timothy Taylor, "Competitive Pressure and Productivity Growth: The Case of the Florida Vegetable Industry" *Southern Journal of Agricultural Economics,* December 1990, pp. 13-21.

[15] *U.S.-Mexico Trade: Trends and Impediments in Agricultural Trade,* GAO/NSIAD-90-85BR (Washington, DC: U.S. General Accounting Office, January 1990). The United States tends to use tariffs to restrict imports of products for which Mexico has a delivered cost advantage. Also see *U.S.-Mexico Trade: Extent to Which Mexican Horticultural Exports Complement U.S. Production,* GAO/NSIAD-91-94BR (Washington, DC: U.S. General Accounting Office, March 1991); and *U.S. Mexico Trade: Impact of Liberalization in the Agricultural Sector,* GAO/NSIAD-91-155 (Washington, DC: U.S. General Accounting Office, March 1991).

[16] For corn, the quotas imposed through licensing have had the effect, on an annual average basis, of a tariff of about 55 percent. Sherman Robinson, "Agricultural Policies and Migration in a U.S.-Mexico Free Trade Area: A Computable General Equilibrium Analysis," presentation at the Symposium on Economy-Wide Modeling of the Economic Implications of a FTA with Mexico and a NAFTA with Canada and Mexico, U.S. International Trade Commission, Washington, DC, Feb. 24-25, 1992.

Mexico also imposes export tariffs, charging, until early 1990, $60 per head for feeder cattle shipped to the United States. This tax has since been reduced in stages to $5 per head, and is scheduled to be eliminated completely. *NAFTA: Effects on Agriculture; vol. II, Livestock and Dairy Issues* (Park Ridge, IL: American Farm Bureau Research Foundation, 1991), p. 58.

Box 10-A—Seasonality in Fruit and Vegetable Production

Growers in Florida and Mexico ship fresh tomatoes from November through May, with California, and to a lesser extent the Baja area of Mexico, the primary suppliers during the summer (figure 10-2). It is only from January through March, when Florida weather is somewhat colder (and more variable) than that in Sinaloa, that Mexican production has been fully competitive. Only in Dade Country, the southernmost growing region in Florida, does production peak during these months. Over the last 10 years, Florida's share of the U.S. winter tomato market has ranged from 56 to 68 percent. Prices fluctuate wildly when weather disrupts production in either Florida or Mexico.

Fresh strawberry imports exhibit a similar seasonal pattern, with shipments from Mexico rising from November through March, before ending in April. The California harvest peaks in May and declines steadily until December, when it begins to rise again. Florida's growing season, in contrast, is limited to the period November-April, with peak harvests when California production is relatively low. Mexico's Bajío region (not far from the Federal District) has a growing season similar to Florida's, but obsolete technology and inferior product quality have led to a steady decline in share of the U.S. strawberry market.

Figure 10-2—Monthly Fresh Tomato Production by Growing Region, 1990

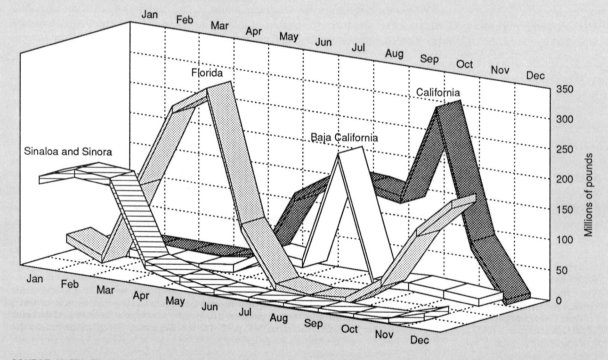

SOURCE: *NAFTA: Effects on Agriculture; Vol. IV, Fruit and Vegetable Issues* (Park Ridge, IL: American Farm Bureau Research Foundation, 1991), table X-3, p. 287.

ments that imported fruits and vegetables do not meet).[17] Claims are also heard that sanitary and phytosanitary regulations serve as nontariff barriers, while concerns have been raised that a NAFTA would increase imports of food products from Mexico with excessively high levels of pesticide residues.[18] As explained in box 10-B, there is little evidence suggesting that pesticide residues on fresh produce imported from Mexico constitute a significant danger to consumer health.

---

[17] U.S. marketing orders covered 14 percent by value of agricultural imports from Mexico in 1989. *U.S.-Mexico Trade: Extent to Which Mexican Horticultural Exports Complement U.S. Production*, op. cit., footnote 15.

[18] In OTA interviews, for example, Florida growers have questioned the adequacy and timeliness of monitoring at the border and whether current procedures are capable of detecting deliberate violations.

Box 10-B—Pesticides In Food: Cause For Concern?[1]

Do pesticide residues in foods imported from Mexico, particularly fresh fruits and vegetables, exceed U.S. standards (e.g., because of excessive or inappropriate application) and therefore constitute a potential hazard to consumers? In theory, produce with residual levels of pesticides exceeding U.S. tolerances, or for which no tolerances exist (because the pesticide is not registered for use in the United States), will be detected and stopped at the border. In practice, excessive levels might not be detected.

Both exporters and the Mexican Government take steps to ensure that fresh Mexican produce will not be barred from the United States because of pesticide violations. Mexican pesticide regulations increasingly resemble those here. As in the United States, pesticides must be registered before they can be sold or used. The number of pesticides registered in Mexico that have no U.S. tolerances has been reduced from 35 in 1988 to 19 in 1991. If they intend to ship to the United States, Mexican growers must register with export associations that provide information on the types of pesticides permitted and appropriate application practices. U.S. and international agencies provide information, training, and technical assistance on pesticide use to Mexican growers, and multinationals assist their contract growers.

The U.S. Environmental Protection Agency sets standards for pesticide residues, with the Food and Drug Administration (FDA) responsible for sampling shipments at border crossings. Although less than 10 percent of all U.S. food imports enter from Mexico, and less than one-quarter of horticultural imports, one-third of all samples analyzed by the FDA originate in Mexico. Intensive sampling dates to 1979, when the U.S. Government undertook to improve Mexican compliance with U.S. regulations.

In recent years, violation rates have been relatively low. In 1991, 3.8 percent of food shipments from Mexico failed to meet the standards. About three-fourths of these were "no-tolerance violations"; most were cases in which the pesticide had not been approved for that product, although the levels detected were below those allowed for that pesticide on other foods.[2]

---

[1] This box draws on: *NAFTA: Effects on Agriculture; vol. I, General Issues* (Park Ridge, IL: American Farm Bureau Research Foundation, 1991); Teofilo Ozuna and Ramon Guajardo-Quiroja, "The U.S.-Mexico Free Trade Agreement: Natural Resource and Environmental Issues," TAMRC International Market Research Report No. IM-8-91, Texas A&M University, College State, TX, April 1991; *Food Safety and Quality: Neurotoxicity: Identifying and Controlling Poisons of the Nervous System* (Washington, DC: Office of Technology Assessment, April 1990); *Five Countries' Efforts to Meet U.S. Requirements on Imported Produce*, GAO/RCED-90-55 (Washington, DC: U.S. General Accounting Office, March 1990); *Pesticide Residues in Food: Technologies for Detection* (Washington, DC: Office of Technology Assessment, October 1988); and *Pesticides: Comparison of U.S. and Mexican Pesticide Standards and Enforcements*, GAO/RCED-92-140 (Washington, DC: U.S. General Accounting Office, June 1992).

[2] No tolerance violations do not necessarily mean that the pesticide in question constitutes a health hazard, but that the level above which it can be a hazard has not been established for a particular food, perhaps because the manufacturer chose not to incur the costs of registration for the crop in question.

According to the American Farm Bureau Research Foundation, the "results of surveillance indicate that the levels and types of pesticide residues on current imports of agricultural products from Mexico are similar to residues on domestic products and imports from other countries .... These findings do not indicate the use of banned pesticides that give Mexican producers a competitive advantage at the expense of the health of the U.S. consumer." *NAFTA: Effects on Agriculture; Vol. I, General Issues*, ibid., p. 48. The U.S. Department of Agriculture concurs that produce exported to the United States from Mexico is generally free of dangerous pesticide residues. See *U.S.-Mexico Trade: Trends and Impediments in Agricultural Trade*, GAO/NSIAD-90-85BR (Washington, DC: General Accounting Office, January 1990), p. 17.

Frozen Broccoli and Strawberries: Cheap Labor Is Not Enough[19]

Broccoli, along with cauliflower, is perhaps the most labor intensive of all vegetables to freeze, and was the first for which processing moved to Mexico. Indeed, almost all of Mexico's frozen vegetable exports consist of these two products, and almost all of these exports go to the United States. California grows most of the U.S. broccoli and as Mexico's production and exports expanded, California farmers switched from frozen broccoli to fresh, or planted their fields with more profitable crops. Thus, output is down, and there is excess processing capacity in

---

[19] This section draws upon *NAFTA: Effects on Agriculture; vol. IV, Fruit and Vegetable Issues*, op. cit., footnote 8, pp. 97-138, 171-204; David Runsten and Sandra O. Archibald, "Technology and Labor-Intensive Agriculture: Competition Between Mexico and the United States," *U.S.-Mexico Relations: Labor Market Interdependence*, Jorge A. Bustamente, Clark W. Reynolds, and Raúl A. Hinojosa Ojeda (Stanford, CA: Stanford University Press, 1992), pp. 449-476; and industry interviews.

both countries. Shipping costs are significant, and California processors increasingly supply frozen broccoli to West Coast markets only. (There is little demand for frozen food in Mexico currently, in part because many households do not have freezers.)

Processing, not cultivation, gives Mexico its advantages in broccoli (table 10-2). Growing broccoli is not particularly labor intensive compared to other horticultural products: cultivating strawberries takes 25 to 30 times as much labor as broccoli, which in turn requires 25 to 30 times as much labor as wheat.[20] Removing the current tariffs of 17.5 percent on frozen broccoli and 25 percent on fresh would permit Mexican farmers to undercut prices for California production by even larger margins.

A very different picture emerges for frozen strawberries. Packers in Mexico have been sending strawberries north since about 1950, but California farmers have maintained huge yield margins. They can produce an average of 23 to 24 tons per acre, compared with about 8 tons per acre in Mexico, and have better quality.[21] These advantages have been more than enough to counter Mexico's lower costs for labor and other inputs, even for this very labor intensive crop. (Tariffs on frozen strawberries are too small to have much effect.)

The most important reason that Mexico has been cost-competitive in broccoli but not strawberries appears to be that U.S. agribusiness firms invested not only money but know-how in Mexican broccoli production. By contrast, U.S. investors financed strawberry cultivation in Mexico, but left production to local growers. Technologically based productivity increases were rapid in California, while Mexico fell behind in strawberry yields and quality. U.S. success came with painstakingly developed high-yield plants having a longer growing season, thus permitting more crops per year. Mexico uses the same plant varieties, but they are not designed for Mexican growing conditions. California farmers

Table 10-2—Cost Comparison for Frozen Broccoli, 1990

	Mexico	California
	(cents per pound)	
Harvested product............	12.0¢	18.5¢*
Freezing and packaging........	23.0	39.0
Transportation to border........	2.5	NA
Customs fees and border crossing costs.....................	1.0	NA
U.S. import duty (17.5 percent)..	4.6	NA
Total....................	43.1¢	57.5¢*

NA = Not applicable.

SOURCE: *NAFTA: Effects on Agriculture; vol. IV, Fruit and Vegetable Issues* (Park Ridge, IL: American Farm Bureau Research Foundation, 1991), pp. 123, 126.

also rely on such practices as fumigation, which, at costs of $1,000 per acre, far exceed the budgets of Mexican farmers.

Tomatoes[22]

About three-quarters of Mexico's tomatoes are sold fresh, many of them in the United States. The rest are processed as tomato paste, ketchup, salsa, and the like. Tomatoes grow in many parts of the country, with the fresh export industry concentrated in Sinaloa, Sonora, and Baja California, and the processing tomato industry in Sinaloa and Sonora. Farms in Baja—many of them under U.S. ownership—match or nearly match southern California yields for fresh tomatoes, but yields of processing tomatoes are nearly twice as high in California.

Sinaloa is Mexico's tomato processing center, producing about 85 percent of its tomato paste. Lower yields, together with shipping costs and a tariff of 13.6 percent, have prevented Mexican farmers from achieving a sustainable cost advantage. But if the tariff goes to zero under a NAFTA, the price of tomato paste from Mexico would probably fall below prices for imports from Europe

---

[20] In U.S. agriculture, labor, on average, accounts for about 15 percent of direct production costs, but about 50 percent for vegetables and fruits. H.L. Goodwin, Jr. "The U.S.-Mexico Free Trade Agreement: Agricultural Labor Issues," TAMRC International Market Research Report No. IM-11-91, Texas A&M University, College Station, TX, April 1991.

[21] Both California and Florida growers have maintained a significant advantage in quality over their competitors in Mexico. Differences in quality are particularly important for fresh strawberries. It is not uncommon for fresh strawberries grown in these two States to command prices that are as much as a third higher than those from Mexico.

[22] This section draws on *NAFTA: Effects on Agriculture; vol. IV, Fruit and Vegetable Issues* , op. cit. footnote, 8, pp. 1-23 and pp. 234-237; Barney H. MacClure, "Growing Importance for Mexican Imports," *Supermarket Business*, March 1991, pp. 23ff; and presentations at the Conference on the Impact of the Free Trade Agreement with Mexico on the California Fruit and Vegetable Industry, Santa Clara University, Nov. 4, 1991.

Table 10-3—Costs for Fresh Tomatoes, 1990-91

	Sinaloa	Florida
	(Dollars per box)[a]	
Preharvest cost (including seed, chemicals, land, labor, machinery).......	$ 2.75	$ 3.41
Harvest cost, including transport to packing point.....	.36	.84
Grading and packing...........	.28	1.77
Boxes......................	.88	.67
Marketing and miscellaneous....	.91	.15
Transport to border............	.67	NA
Customs fees and border crossing costs........	.30	NA
U.S. import duty...............	.38	NA
Total.....................	$ 6.53	$ 6.84

[a]A box of tomatoes holds 25 pounds.

NA = Not applicable.

SOURCE: *NAFTA: Effects on Agriculture; vol. IV, Fruit and Vegetable Issues* (Park Ridge, IL: American Farm Bureau Research Foundation, 1991), p. 281, table X-1.

Photo credit: John Colwell, Grant Heilman Photography

Transplanting tomatoes.

(which are heavily subsidized) and Chile, the apparent low-cost producer.[23]

For fresh tomatoes—a much more important crop for both U.S. and Mexican farmers—the situation is very different. California and Florida produce three-quarters of U.S. tomatoes, but west coast winters are too cold for tomatoes. Only Florida can compete with Mexico from December until May or June, although freezes in some years harm the Florida crop, driving up prices (as in the winter of 1989-90). Growing, harvesting, and packing costs are all substantially lower in Sinaloa than in Florida. Even so, Florida growers have managed to compete successfully because of higher yields. Tomato plants suited to staked cultivation, plastic mulch, and mechanized harvesting have offset higher labor costs. Nonetheless, costs in Sinaloa and Florida have tended to converge, with U.S. import duties—38 cents to 52 cents per box (25 pounds), depending on time of year—keeping delivered costs similar (table 10-3). There is little question that with comparable technologies, and even comparable wages, farmers in Sinaloa—with their superior climate—could produce tomatoes considerably more cheaply than Florida growers.

Beef

Mexican ranchers buy semen and breeding stock from the United States to support both beef and dairy herds. While selling almost all their beef and dairy products domestically, Mexico does ship feeder cattle to U.S. producers for fattening and slaughter, more than a million of them in 1990, about one-third of all cattle fed in the Texas panhandle.[24]

Mexico cannot grow enough grain to feed many more cattle. Transportation costs for imported grain approximately offset Mexico's labor cost advantages for feeding and slaughtering cattle. The cost estimates in Box 10-C indicate that, even after improvements in Mexico's transportation system, costs in the northern part of the country would drop only slightly below those in the United States. Because there is substantial U.S. overcapacity, and per capita beef consumption is decreasing, neither feeders nor packers have much reason to contemplate investments in Mexico.

Trade data also indicate that Mexico does not have significant cost advantages in the production, slaughter, and packing of beef. Mexico is currently the third largest export market for U.S. red meats, taking $472 million, or 11 percent of exports, and

---

[23] At present, Mexico supplies about 17 percent of U.S. imports of tomato paste. A Uruguay Round GATT agreement that drastically reduced subsidies and duties on tomato paste would enable both Chile and Mexico to displace higher-cost U.S. producers and most imports from Europe. Everything else the same, Mexico would appear to be able to gain a cost advantage of 3 to 5 cents per pound in the U.S. market.

[24] Mexico's imports of bull semen in 1990 were valued at $3.4 million, imports of dairy cattle at $36 million (for 30,000 head), and imports of beef cattle at $18 million (for about 35,000 head). *NAFTA: Effects on Agriculture; vol. II, Livestock and Dairy Issues,* op. cit., footnote 16, pp. 80, 85, 117, 146. In recent years, the total number of beef and dairy cattle in U.S. herds has averaged a bit under 100 million.

Box 10-C—Boxing Beef: Will It Go To Mexico?[1]

Years ago, beef was a growth industry in the United States. Cattle were fattened on the range, then shipped by rail to Chicago and other Midwestern cities for slaughter by unionized workers in packing plants designed around gravity-driven disassembly lines. Boxed beef made these plants obsolete by simultaneously reducing labor, inventory, transportation, and feeding costs, while improving quality.[2] Meat packers built new plants in low-wage regions closer to feedlots. To minimize transportation costs of grain and cattle, most production takes place in such States as Texas, Kansas, and Nebraska, where feed is abundant. After butchering, boxed beef is shipped to the customer, reducing costs for supermarkets which could avoid many of the meat cutting operations once performed in the store by butchers.

Meat products cannot enter the United States unless they originate in packing plants approved by the U.S. Department of Agriculture (USDA). Mexican packers lost their approvals in 1984, after USDA found that the inspection procedures in use in Mexican plants could not detect chemical residues at the required levels. Only in 1989 were five Mexican packing plants again approved, all in the border region.[3] But given that wages are so much lower in Mexico, isn't it possible that meat packing will migrate there? The answer to this question turns on transportation costs for cattle and feed and the ability of Mexico to increase the size of its herd.

The Mexican cattle herd averages about 20 million. Each year, Mexico exports about 1.2 million feeder cattle to the United States for finishing—essentially all the steers that meet U.S. quality and type specifications. Mexico does not have enough rangeland, water, or croplands suitable for feedgrains to increase cattle production. As table 10-4 shows, even with improvements in the country's transportation system that reduced shipping costs to U.S. levels, costs for importing feed and shipping beef back to the United States would add more than $30 per animal for feedlots in northern Mexico, and about $60 for feedlots near Mexico City. Labor costs per animal (including benefits) in the United States, for both feeding and packing, are in the neighborhood of $40 to $50.

Actual costs in Mexico would in most cases be higher than shown in table 10-4.[4] These estimates assume that cattle are held in feedlots in both countries for 180 days, which is at least 30 days longer than currently required by the most efficient U.S. feeding operations. Today, even the best Mexican feedlots and packing plants are relatively small and inefficient, using practices characteristic of the 1960s in the United States (in part, because the low cost of labor has discouraged mechanization).

Both feedlots and packing plants exhibit large economies of scale in purchasing, production, sales, and distribution, which reduces the vulnerability of large, efficient U.S. plants to competition from Mexico.[5] At present, the United States has considerable excess capacity in both sectors, much of it below efficient size and thus likely to be closed at some point in the future. In 1990, for example, 205 U.S. feedlots with capacities of 16,000 head or more accounted for more than half of production (52 percent); 44,000 smaller feedlots supplied the remainder. Ninety-one plants accounted for more than 90 percent of all U.S. beef packing (again in 1990) in an industry with more than 1,000 packing plants. One of the largest packers, IBP, has recently been operating at around 75 percent of capacity.

---

[1] This box is based on industry interviews; annual reports and 10-K filings; *NAFTA: Effects on Agriculture; vol. II, Livestock and Dairy Issues* (Park Ridge, IL: American Farm Bureau Research Foundation, 1991); *1991 Meat Facts* (Washington, DC: American Meat Institute, August 1991); *Livestock & Poultry: Situation and Outlook Report* (Washington, DC: Department of Agriculture, Economic Research Service, January 1992); and *U.S. Industrial Outlook '92* (Washington, DC: Department of Commerce, January 1992), pp. 32-3 to 32-7 and 40-11.

[2] Kathleen Stanley, "The Role of Immigrant and Refugee Labor in the Restructuring of the Midwestern Meatpacking Industry," contract report prepared for the U.S. Department of Labor, October 1988, pp. 10-18.

[3] *U.S.-Mexico Trade: Trends and Impediments in Agricultural Trade*, GAO/NSIAD-90-85BR (Washington, DC: U.S. General Accounting Office, January 1990), p. 16. Six more *maquila* packing plants had been certified by early 1992, although not all were producing beef for export to the United States. Mexico sends some exports to Japan from these plants.

[4] Today, shipping costs for grain evidently render feedlots in northern Mexico unprofitable, on average. Some have gone out of business. *NAFTA: Effects On Agriculture; vol. II, Livestock and Dairy Issues*, op. cit., footnote 1, p. 28.

[5] Clement E. Ward, *Meatpacking Competition and Pricing* (Blacksburg, VA: The Research Institute On Livestock Pricing, July 1988), pp. 21-33.

Unless U.S. red meat consumption rises more rapidly than expected—unlikely given consumer trends—there will be little incentive to move production operations to Mexico. Depressed wages in the U.S. industry also reduce the attractiveness of relocation, as does competition for water with other industrial and agricultural sectors in northern Mexico.

Table 10-4—Estimated Costs of Cattle Feeding and Meat Packing[a]

	Cost (dollars per steer)		
	Texas	Northern Mexico	Mexico City
Feedlot costs			
Feeder steer purchase[b]	$ 552.48	$ 550.50	$ 550.50
Purchase price of feed[c]	250.79	250.79	250.79
Additional transportation costs for feed[d]	NA	22.32	41.16
Management fee and labor[e]	21.00	12.00	12.00
Veterinary medicine	3.00	3.00	3.00
Interest[f]	35.44	37.72	36.21
Attrition[g]	8.18	8.18	8.18
Packing costs			
Wages, salaries, and benefits[h]	33.93	11.31	11.31
Supplies	13.41	13.41	13.41
Overhead	22.66	22.66	22.66
Additional transportation costs to U.S. market[i]	NA	8.93	17.85
Total	$ 940.89	$ 940.82	$ 967.07

[a]Assumes a NAFTA is in place and that Mexico's transportation system has improved so that rail costs are the same in both countries. Based on industry interviews, along with *Livestock & Poultry: Situation and Outlook Report* (Washington, DC: Department of Agriculture, Economic Research Service, January 1992), table 36, p. 26; and *1991 Meat Facts* (Washington, DC: American Meat Institute, August 1991), p. 33.

[b]Assumes feeder cattle purchase price and commission the same in Mexican and the United States, with transport to U.S. feedlots at $3.96 per steer, and half as much for transport to Mexican feedlots. Each steer is assumed to yield 714 pounds of beef.

[c]Assumes 4,200 pounds of feed per animal, over 180 days (to achieve a weight gain of 500 pounds). OTA's estimates assume the same feed mix and purchase price for both countries. Mexico prohibits the use of corn as a feedgrain, although it can be imported as part of prepared cattle feed; sorghum is the primary feedgrain in Mexico. Alfalfa is seldom fed to cattle in Mexico, but it is assumed that substitutes cost the same. The assumed feed mix: 1,500 pounds of corn (U.S. cost of $104.50 per ton); 1,500 pounds of grain sorghum ($94.46 per ton); 800 pounds of alfalfa ($134.75 per ton); and 400 pounds of cottonseed meal ($240.00 per ton).

[d]Assumes 3,400 pounds of feed must be imported into Mexico, with the other 800 pounds purchased locally. The northern Mexico estimate assumes grain is shipped by rail from Kansas to the border region ($13.13 per ton, including elevator costs), then trucked to the feedlot. The Mexico City case assumes shipping by rail to New Orleans ($10.57 per ton), by sea to Mexican ports ($8.18 per ton, including unloading, fumigation, and customs clearance at $4.54 per ton), then by rail to the feedlot ($5.45 per ton).

[e]Assumes $10.50 management fee in both countries, including overhead. U.S. labor, $10.50; Mexican labor, $1.50.

[f]Based on an annual interest rate of 10.54 percent on the purchase price of the steer, minus commission and transportation to the feedlot, for 180 days, plus half the cost of feedgrain and feedgrain transportation charges. (In fact, interest rates are significantly higher in Mexico.)

[g]At 1.5 percent of the purchase price of the steer.

[h]Mexican plants are assumed to have less automation, hence require more labor.

[i]Based on 1,000 miles of incremental transportation from Mexico City, 500 miles from northern Mexico. Transportation by truck, 44,000 pound capacity, at $1.10 per mile.

NA = Not applicable.

SOURCE: Office of Technology Assessment, 1992.

also imports beef from South America and Australia. (It is also a net importer of chicken and pork, both of which require significantly less feed to produce a pound of meat.) Most of the U.S. beef goes to supply the tourist trade and wealthy consumers who can afford it, although Mexico also buys some cheap cuts and products that have little appeal here. Thus, the pattern by which Mexico sends feeder cattle to the United States and imports beef in return seems unlikely to change.

Mexican cow-calf operators can compete successfully with their U.S. counterparts because both labor

Box 10-D—Increasing Irrigated Fruit and Vegetable Acreage[1]

Figure 10-3 shows that irrigated land produces higher yields per acre. Of Mexico's 12.1 million acres of irrigated land, about 2.5 million acres, or 20 percent, is planted in horticultural products. Corn grows on 19 percent of the remaining irrigated land. Past subsidies for irrigation water led to inefficient use, while subsidies for corn encouraged planting on irrigated land.

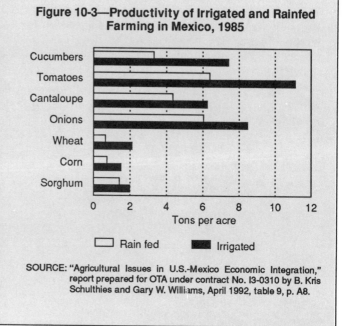

Figure 10-3—Productivity of Irrigated and Rainfed Farming in Mexico, 1985

SOURCE: "Agricultural Issues in U.S.-Mexico Economic Integration," report prepared for OTA under contract No. I3-0310 by B. Kris Schulthies and Gary W. Williams, April 1992, table 9, p. A8.

[1] The discussion of irrigation in this box is based on interviews, plus Santiago Levy and Sweder van Wijnbergen, "Transition Problems in Economic Reform: Agriculture in the Mexico-US Free Trade Agreement," *Economy-Wide Modeling of the Economic Implications of a FTA with Mexico and a NAFTA with Canada and Mexico*, Addendum to the Report on Investigation No. 332-317 Under Section 332 of the Tariff Act of 1930, USITC Publication 2508 (Washington, DC: U.S. International Trade Commission, May 1992), pp. 299-357; *NAFTA: Effects On Agriculture; vol. IV, Fruit and Vegetable Issues* (Park Ridge, IL: American Farm Bureau Research Foundation, 1991); and "Agricultural Issues in U.S.-Mexico Economic Integration," report prepared for OTA under contract No. I3-0310 by B. Kris Schulthies and Gary W. Williams, April 1992.

and land costs are important in breeding and raising calves for sale to feedlots. But Mexico's cattle raising capacity is fundamentally limited.[25] Feedgrain production in Mexico will likewise continue to be severely restricted by shortages of water and suitable land; in the end, Mexico needs to grow food for feeding people, not animals.

Currently, no more than half of Mexico's population can afford beef, even at CONASUPO's subsidized prices. Rather than investing in *maquila*-like operations in Mexico, U.S. feedlot operators and packers—facing a saturated market in the United States—will probably seek to expand into Mexico through acquisitions, joint ventures, and wholly-owned subsidiaries with the aim of serving the Mexican market as it expands. The terms of a NAFTA, and government policies within Mexico, will shape these strategies and their outcomes.

THE FUTURE

Output Growth in Mexico

Mexican farmers can compete effectively in some crops already, notably fruits and vegetables grown on irrigated land. If Mexico could increase its production of these crops, it might pose more serious threats to U.S. growers. Mexico could increase production by bringing more land under irrigation, shifting irrigated land now planted in other crops to horticultural products, or by increasing yields from existing acreage. For reasons explored below, increased yields through better technology offers the best prospects for Mexican farmers to increase their output.

Irrigated Horticultural Production

If Mexico irrigated all its suitable land, and shifted all irrigated land now planted in corn to export-oriented horticultural crops, farmers might be able to devote another 2 million acres to horticultural production (box 10-D). This would be a large increase for Mexico, but not so impressive relative to the 9 million acres currently under irrigation in California. Still, Mexico might in principle be able to increase its production for export by a factor of about 4. In fact, such an outcome is unlikely for reasons discussed in the box. Moreover, growing Mexican demand would absorb much of any in-

[25] Grazing lands are relatively poor in quality, and already stretched to capacity; Mexico's cattle herd has declined substantially over the last 4 years because of drought. Examination of these limits leads to estimates that Mexico could not send more than 2 or 2 1/2 million feeder cattle per year northwards—roughly 10 percent of the number of cattle on feed at any one time in the United States. Most of the impacts of these shipments will continue to be felt in Texas. Ibid., pp. 27, 70-72.

In principle, land now planted in corn could be switched to horticultural products, while more land could be irrigated for growing fruits and vegetables. Horticultural exports have come from the 12 Mexican states listed in table 10-5.[2] A total of 1.2 million acres in these states is currently irrigated but planted in corn. An estimated 0.77 million acres not now under irrigation has potential for irrigation. Mexico might thus be able to add as much as 2 million acres of horticultural production, an increase of 78 percent, by switching from corn and irrigating land that is now rainfed. This suggests that Mexico might in theory be able to increase its production of fruits and vegetables for export by up to four times, assuming that all the new horticultural acreage produces for export. But such an outcome is unlikely. With rapid economic development in northern Mexico, the prime growing region for fruits and vegetables, demand for water for industrial uses and growing cities has cut into the water available for irrigation. Even today, most irrigation projects provide only enough water for one crop per year. The Mexican Government's high priority for industrialization suggests that investments in new, large-scale irrigation projects will proceed at modest rates. And to the extent that agriculture might prove unable to compete for water with industrial and urban consumption, horticultural acreage could even decline.

Table 10-5—Potential for Increased Horticultural Production in Mexico's Primary Exporting Regions

	Land under irrigation	Irrigated corn	Potential new irrigated land	Possible increase
	(thousands of acres)			
Sinaloa......................	2,280	245	455	670
Tamaulipas..................	968	310	32	342
Michoacán...................	677	169	101	270
Sonora......................	1,655	166	7	173
Jalisco......................	388	78	32	110
Guanajuato..................	981	97	7	104
Guerrero....................	106	54	47	101
Nayarit.....................	232	15	54	69
Colima......................	104	20	27	47
Morelos.....................	96	30	12	42
Baja California..............	541	12	—	12
Total.....................	8,028	1,196	774	1,970

SOURCE: Santiago Levy and Sweder van Wijnbergen, "Transition Problems in Economic Reform: Agriculture in the Mexico-US Free Trade Agreement," *Economy-Wide Modeling of the Economic Implications of a FTA with Mexico and a NAFTA with Canada and Mexico*, Addendum to the Report on Investigation No. 332-317 Under Section 332 of the Tariff Act of 1930, USITC Publication 2508 (Washington, DC: U.S. International Trade Commission, May 1992), pp. 299-357.

[2] Sinoloa (47 percent of exports in 1989-90), Sonora (14 percent), and Baja California (11 percent) account for the bulk of exports. For 1989-90 production in the other exporting regions, see *NAFTA: Effects On Agriculture; Fruits And Vegetable Issues, vol. IV*, ibid., table IV-1, p. 49; and Levy and van Wijnbergen, *Mexican Agriculture in The Free Trade Agreement*, ibid., p. 48.

crease. Currently, Mexico exports no more than 18 percent of its horticultural production.[26]

Technological Improvements

Increasing yields on existing horticultural acreage to levels comparable to those achieved in the United States has greater potential for increasing horticul-

ture output at reasonable cost than bringing more land into production. Here the hurdles begin with lack of the agricultural research necessary for developing technologies optimized for local conditions, including the varied microclimates in this arid and mountainous country.[27] Mexican farmers growing winter vegetables for export buy almost all their

[26] Roberta Cook, "Mexican Free Trade Agreement: Who Will Be The Winners And Losers?" *American Vegetable Grower*, February 1992, p. 30.

[27] Runsten and Archibald, "Technology and Labor-Intensive Agriculture," op. cit., footnote 19.

seed from the United States because Mexican-produced seed is inferior.[28] But most of this seed is adapted for U.S. growing conditions, not those in Mexico. Viruses plague farmers particularly in the central and southern part of the country; Mexico lacks resistant varieties or other means of control. Without investments in research, in diffusion of best practices, and in training of agricultural research workers, farmers, and agribusiness managers, Mexico will remain dependent on seeds and agrochemicals developed for conditions in the United States and elsewhere, on farming practices improved through slow-paced trial-and-error, and on animals bred for conditions in other countries.[29]

Plainly, there is a great deal of room for improvement. Yet in many respects, the country's agricultural sector declined during the 1980s—a consequence of withdrawals of government support, as well as the troubled economy. Seed production fell, along with fertilizer consumption and Mexico's stock of tractors and other farm machinery (prices for imported equipment increased rapidly with peso devaluation during the 1980s).[30] With government investments low, multinationals have been the major channel for inflows of agricultural know-how. Their interests focus on the fertile northwest, where the modern sector and FDI have concentrated, providing little or no help in meeting the needs of small farmers in other parts of the country.

Applications of biotechnology will diffuse relatively slowly into the agricultural sectors of both Mexico and the United States. Because most potential applications involve manipulations of multiple genes, research is difficult and expensive. Mexico's expenditures on both traditional agricultural research and on biotechnology are tiny fractions of those in the United States, ensuring that Mexico will be a follower rather than a leader.

Because there are few apparent limits to improvements in agricultural productivity through technol-ogy in the United States, growers who have been able to maintain advantages in delivered costs through yield and productivity improvements in the past have good prospects for continuing to do so in the future. Mexico will have to achieve substantial increases in productivity to maintain its competitive position over time, and may be hard pressed to do so.

NAFTA Impacts

Agriculture is heavily regulated and subsidized around the world, primarily for domestic political reasons. The United States and Mexico are no exceptions. Government policies affect prices and output levels, and hence trade patterns. The current Uruguay Round of GATT negotiations seeks to moderate subsidies in agriculture. If it succeeds, trade between the United States and Mexico would be affected. Regardless of the outcome of the GATT negotiations, a NAFTA would contain provisions affecting trade and therefore employment in the agricultural sectors of both countries, no doubt including transition periods and ''snapback'' provisions (triggering increases in tariffs if imports rise beyond specified levels) to protect vulnerable sectors. The U.S.-Canada Free Trade Agreement, for instance, provides for staged tariff reductions over a 20-year period for some agricultural products.

California produces more fruits and vegetables than any other State. Despite their apparent vulnerability to competition from Mexico, California growers expect a NAFTA to have only limited adverse consequences. The common view: impacts would limited, and felt over relatively long time periods.[31] There will be some losers, but winners will predominate. These views reflect confidence in California's advantages, which are both broad and deep. Those advantages include, for example, the workforce skills needed to keep expensive farm machinery operating continuously during critical planting and harvesting periods. They also include the capabilities of research organizations, universities, and the

---

[28] David R. Mares, *Penetrating the International Market: Theoretical Considerations and a Mexican Case Study* (New York, NY: Columbia University Press, 1987), p. 32.

Although two-thirds of *ejido* farms make use of fertilizers and/or herbicides, only about 40 percent grow crops from improved seed varieties. *NAFTA: Effects on Agriculture; vol. IV, Fruit and Vegetable Issues,* op. cit., footnote 8, p. 8.

[29] The process of developing hybrid seeds in Mexico, particularly by agencies of the government, has been criticized for paying insufficient attention to local conditions. John Heath, ''An Overview of the Mexican Agricultural Crisis,'' *The Mexican Economy,* George Philip, ed. (London and New York: Routledge, 1988), pp. 129-163.

[30] *NAFTA: Effects on Agriculture; vol. IV, Fruit and Vegetable Issues,* op. cit., footnote 8, pp. 23, 24.

[31] Industry interviews; and Conference on the Impact of the Free Trade Agreement with Mexico on the California Fruit and Vegetable Industry, Santa Clara University, Nov. 4, 1991.

agricultural extension system. The views of California growers also reflect three other factors:

1. The complementary nature of production in California and Mexico.

2. Superior management skills, marketing, and distribution.

3. Confidence that vulnerable sectors will get protection, or at least transition periods long enough for growers to shift to other crops.

Florida competes more directly with Mexico. Many growers are worried that transition periods will be too short and that they will have trouble identifying new crops and mastering new techniques. Overall, Florida's agribusiness industry exhibits little of the dynamism, innovation, and confidence evident in California. Even so, growers in the various parts of Florida can be expected to specialize on the basis of comparative production, transportation, and marketing costs, and to succeed in carving out new markets.

Impacts of a NAFTA on U.S. jobs in agriculture would be localized, with farm workers in Florida most likely to be displaced. Mexico's advantages in growing and freezing broccoli also threaten jobs in California. By and large, these are not good jobs, although for those who hold them now, a bad job may be better than no job.

Hired (nonfamily) agricultural workers are paid less than workers in any other U.S. industry.[32] In 1990, seasonal agricultural workers earned median hourly wages of $4.85. Fewer than half are covered by unemployment insurance; fewer than a fourth have health insurance. Seventy percent of seasonal agricultural workers are Hispanic, 62 percent are foreign born, and perhaps 20 percent are undocumented. Because demand for hired farm workers has been declining in the United States (from about 4.7 million at the end of the 1950s to a little over 2 million currently), those displaced—most of whom are poorly educated and few of whom have other skills—will experience substantial difficulty in finding new jobs.

The 600,000 or so jobs in food processing pay better than farm work. The range in 1991: from an average of $7.07 per hour for poultry workers (about one-third of all food processing workers) to $9.39 per hour in fruit and vegetable processing (two-fifths of food processing workers). Wages for meatpacking workers, the other major group of food processing workers (about one quarter of the total), have been under great pressure during the last 15 years as the industry restructured (see box 10-C, earlier in the chapter). In 1978, meatpacking workers earned 80 percent more than poultry workers; in 1991, they averaged $8.91 per hour, only 26 percent more than poultry workers. This relative decline is the result of radically lower union coverage and the breakdown of pattern bargaining as packers decentralized and built new plants in rural areas near feedlots. Many of these plants depend heavily on immigrant workers. Injury rates increased as wages fell; the combination of machine pacing and a vulnerable, sometimes illegal immigrant workforce brought work conditions not seen in decades in this industry. But because fresh rather than processed food accounts for most U.S. agricultural imports from Mexico, and because there seems little likelihood of meat packing moving to Mexico, a NAFTA itself would probably make little difference for most U.S. food processing workers, with the possible exception of those in the poultry sector.

In the longer term, new entrants in Central and South America may pose greater threats to U.S. production of both fresh and frozen horticultural products than exports from Mexico. Countries including Chile, Peru, and Guatemala have been expanding production for export in regions with extended growing seasons. Their agribusiness sectors promise continuing competition for both Mexican and U.S. farmers.[33] On balance, U.S. producers of grain and beef should benefit from increased exports to Mexico, although some small feedlots and packing plants near the border could close.

Mexican agriculture faces a more troubled future than U.S. agriculture, particularly in the traditional sector. Rapid population growth, urbanization, and rising per capita income suggest that demand for

---

[32] *Findings From the National Agricultural Workers Survey (NASW) 1990*, Office of Program Economics Research Report No. 1 (Washington, DC: Department of Labor, July 1991). Also see Victor J. Oliveira, *Trends in the Hired Farm Work Force, 1945-87*, Agriculture Information Bulletin 561 (Washington, DC: Department of Agriculture, Economic Research Service, April 1989); and Runsten and Archibald. ''Technology and Labor-Intensive Agriculture,'' op. cit., footnote 19, pp. 449-486.

[33] Taiwan and China, as well as Chile and Peru, for example, send canned asparagus to the United States, while Canada, Chile, and Peru ship frozen asparagus. *NAFTA Effects On Agriculture: vol. IV, Fruit and Vegetable Issues*, op. cit., footnote 8, pp. 78-79.

food could increase at 5 to 6 percent per year, with Mexico likely to become more dependent on imported food. The agricultural sector must overcome a decade of declining investment, adjust to lower government supports and subsidies, and contain rapidly rising costs per unit of output—all the while depending on outsiders for technology.

CONCLUDING REMARKS

A NAFTA would accelerate the integration of North American agribusiness. Mexico must buy food abroad, and the United States will be the preferred source for many products. In return, Mexico will send larger quantities of fruits and vegetables northwards. These shipments will not overwhelm U.S. farmers, who have amply demonstrated their flexibility and resilience in the face of manmade as well as natural obstacles. Still, gains and losses from a NAFTA will be concentrated geographically and by product, and for growers who have trouble switching to new crops there will be little solace in a NAFTA that benefits U.S. agriculture as a whole.

The seasonal nature of fruit and vegetable production means that Florida competes most directly with Mexico. But restricted supplies of land and water will limit Mexico's capacity to expand production, and, together with rising domestic demand, limit the volume of fresh fruits and vegetables shipped to the United States. OTA's analysis, finally, suggests that Mexico poses little threat in cattle feeding and meat packing. Limited grazing lands and rising beef consumption will preclude a dramatic increase in exports of feeder cattle. Transportation costs for grain counterbalance Mexico's low labor costs in feeding and packing. Indeed, Mexico will probably import greater quantities of U.S. beef in the years ahead.

Movement of people, rather than movement of goods, may have the greatest implications for the United States. Mexico's agricultural reforms will drive large numbers of people off the land. Many of these people will move to urban areas where they will put downward pressure on wages for low-skilled jobs, with spillover effects here. Some will emigrate to the United States.

Glossary

Apertura: opening, referring to the opening of the Mexican economy beginning in the mid-1980s (see ISI, below).

Big Three: the three major U.S.-owned automobile manufacturers—General Motors, Ford, and Chrysler.

CANACINTRA, *Cámara Nacional de Industrias de Transformación*: Mexico's association of small manufacturers, with which industry-specific chambers and individual manufacturers are affiliated.

CBI, Caribbean Basin Initiative: a package of trade and investment incentives extended by the United States to Mexico and other nations in the Caribbean, intended to permit those countries to increase their "nontraditional" exports to the United States. Nontraditional exports include, for example, apparel and winter vegetables (as opposed to bananas, sugar, and coffee).

CETS, *Centros de Enseñanza Terminal*: Mexican vocational-technical schools.

CIMO, *Capacitación Industrial de la Mano de Obra*: a Mexican Government program that provides business advice and training to smaller companies.

CO switch, central office switch: a large telephone exchange, typically computerized.

CONALEP, *Colegio Nacional de Educación Profesional Técnica*: Mexican program for vocational-technical education and worker training.

CONASUPO, *Companía Nacional de Subsistencias Populares*: the Mexican Government's agricultural distribution and marketing organization.

Contracto leyes: literally, law contracts—sectoral labor contracts established under Mexican labor law.

CTM, *Confederación de Trabajadores Mexicanos*: Confederation of Mexican Workers, the dominant labor union federation in Mexico.

EC: European Community.

EDWAA, Economic Dislocation and Worker Adjustment Assistance: U.S. Government program providing training and job-placement assistance to displaced workers.

Ejidos: plots of land owned by the Mexican Government with usage rights extended to farmers known as *ejidatarios*. Land reform policies now being implemented include privatization of *ejidos*.

FDI, foreign direct investment: assets within a country—e.g., equity holdings in a corporation—wholly or partially owned by foreign residents, individual or corporate.

GATT, General Agreement on Tariffs and Trade: an organization and set of rules under which more than 100 nations negotiate trade agreements and seek to resolve trade-related disputes.

GDP, gross domestic product: the value of goods and services generated *within* a national economy, generally on a yearly basis.

GNP, gross national product: GDP adjusted for revenues that enter and leave an economy as a result of financial flows associated with foreign investments.

Greenfield plant: a new plant built on a new site (as opposed to a remodeled "brownfield" plant).

Inexistente: illegal, referring to labor strikes ruled not to exist for a variety of procedural or substantive reasons by Mexican arbitration boards.

IRCA, Immigration Reform and Control Act of 1986: among its provisions, IRCA provides amnesty for qualifying undocumented aliens already in the United States, while penalizing employers who knowingly hire undocumented workers.

ISI, import substitution industrialization: Mexico's industrial development strategy up until the middle 1980s, which relied on trade barriers to protect Mexican firms and investment controls to attract foreign manufacturers.

JIT, just-in-time: a production system that minimizes inventories, generally requiring close working relationships between labor and management and suppliers and customers.

Keiretsu: groups of Japanese companies linked by partial equity holdings.

Knock-down kits: parts and components shipped ready for assembly, typically in a foreign plant.

Lean production: a form of production organization, especially in the auto industry, that relies on just-in-time manufacturing and rapid product development.

Mainframe computer: a large and powerful computer, normally intended for general-purpose data processing.

Maquiladora, maquila: a Mexican plant that imports components duty-free from the United States and exports finished goods to the United States, paying duty only on the value added in Mexico.

Mestizo: a Mexican of mixed Spanish and Native American ancestry.

MFA, Multi-Fiber Arrangement: an international framework for negotiating bilateral agreements on quotas for textiles and apparel items.

Microcomputer: small computer designed around a single-chip processing unit.

Minicomputer: intermediate in cost, size, and processing power between a microcomputer and a mainframe.

MNC, multinational corporation: a company with substantial foreign direct investments that seeks to operate on a more or less integrated basis in the countries in which it does business.

NAFTA, North American Free Trade Agreement: proposed agreement negotiated by representatives of the United States, Mexico, and Canada that would remove many existing barriers to the free movement of goods, services, and capital in North America. Implementation would require ratification by the legislative branches of the three countries.

NIC, newly industrializing country: examples include Singapore, Taiwan, South Korea, and Hong Kong.

NIE, newly industrializing economy: term used to distinguish Asian countries such as Indonesia, Thailand, and Malaysia from the NICs. The NIEs are less developed than the NICs, but industrializing rapidly.

NLRA, National Labor Relations Act of 1935 (Wagner Act): protects the right of U.S. workers to organize and bargain collectively.

NLRB, National Labor Relations Board: established under the NLRA to adjudicate disputes.

NTB, nontariff barrier: any trade restriction other than a tariff or duty on imports—e.g., a numerical quota or requirement for licensing.

OSHA, Occupational Safety and Health Administration: a part of the U.S. Department of Labor with responsibility for issuing and enforcing workplace health and safety standards.

Pacto, Pacto de Solidaridad Económica: wage and price control policy to bring down inflation, established by the Mexican government in consultation with business and labor in 1987. Subsequently renamed the *Pacto de Estabilidad y Crecimiento Económica*.

Pattern bargaining: collective bargaining that limits variation of wages and benefits within an industry by establishing similar union contracts at competing companies.

PBX, private branch exchange: a small telephone exchange typically installed in offices.

PC, personal computer: a general-purpose microcomputer.

PEMEX, *Petróleos Mexicanos*: Mexico's state-owned oil company.

PRI, *Partido Revolucionario Institucional*: the dominant political party in Mexico, with roots tracing back to 1929.

PRONALF, *Programa Nacional de Alfabetización*: Mexican literacy program.

Scientific management: see Taylorism.

SECOFI, *Secretaría de Comercio y Fomento Industrial*: Mexico's Secretariat (or Ministry) of Commerce and Industrial Promotion.

SEDUE, *Secretaría de Desarrollo Urbano y Ecologia*: Mexico's former Secretariat of Urban Development and Ecology, with responsibilities paralleling those of the U.S. Environmental Protection Agency. SEDUE was merged with the large social welfare agency, PRONASOL, in 1992 to form the Secretariat for Social Development (SEDESOL).

SEP, *Secretaría de Educación Pública*: Mexico's Secretariat of Public Education.

SIC, Standard Industrial Classification: U.S. Government classification system for industries and industrial groupings.

SMEs: small- and medium-sized enterprises (typically those with less than 500 employees).

SPC, statistical process control: method for ensuring product quality based on statistical distributions of measurements.

STPS, *Secretaría del Trabajo y Previsión Social*: Mexico's Secretariat (or Ministry) of Labor and Social Welfare.

Strategic alliance: corporate relationships intended to further the interests of both partners such as joint ventures and cooperative marketing agreements.

Surface mount technology: method for assembling printed circuit boards using an adhesive solder (rather than pins inserted into holes on the board).

TAA, Trade Adjustment Assistance: U.S. Government program that provides income support and training to workers displaced because of international trade.

Taylorism: workplace organization, especially common in assembly line production, based on simplifying individual tasks and setting effort levels through such methods as time-and-motion study.

TelMex, *Teléfonos de México*: Mexico's monopoly provider of telephone service, state-owned until privatized in 1990.

Transplant: a plant built in the United States by a foreign manufacturer to serve the U.S. market, often to substitute for exports that had previously been shipped to the United States.

QR, Quick Response: organization of production and distribution in the apparel industry intended to de-crease the time between ordering by retailers and delivery of new stock to them.

UAW: United Auto Workers.

UI, unemployment insurance: U.S. system for providing income support to unemployed workers, typically for periods of up to 26 weeks.

Wagner Act: see NLRA.

Index

U.S. GOVERNMENT PRINTING OFFICE : 1992 O – 331–019 : QL 3

Order Processing Code:

* 6360

☐ **YES**, please send me the following:

_____ copies of *US-Mexico Trade: Pulling Together or Pulling Apart? (232 pages)*
S/N 052-003-01306-1 at $12.00 each.

The total cost of my order is $ _____. International customers please add 25%. Prices include regular domestic postage and handling and are subject to change.

_____
(Company or Personal Name)   (Please type or print)

_____
(Additional address/attention line)

_____
(Street address)

_____
(City, State, ZIP Code)

_____
(Daytime phone including area code)

_____
(Purchase Order No.)

May we make your name/address available to other mailers?   **YES NO**
☐ ☐

Superintendent of Documents **Publications** Order Form

Charge your order.
It's Easy!

To fax your orders (202) 512–2250

P3

Please Choose Method of Payment:

☐ Check Payable to the Superintendent of Documents

☐ GPO Deposit Account ☐☐☐☐☐☐–☐

☐ VISA or MasterCard Account

☐☐☐☐☐☐☐☐☐☐☐☐☐☐☐☐☐☐☐☐☐

☐☐☐☐ (Credit card expiration date)   *Thank you for*
your order!

_____
(Authorizing Signature)   10/92

Mail To: New Orders, Superintendent of Documents
          P.O. Box 371954, Pittsburgh, PA 15250–7954

ISBN 0-16-038096-0

9 780160 380969

90000